A STUDY OF THE PLAYS OF THOMAS D'URF STANLEY FORSYTHE AND THOMAS D'URFE .

Publisher's Note

The book descriptions we ask book-sellers to display prominently warn that this is an historic book with numerous typos or missing text; it is not indexed or illustrated.

The book was created using optical character recognition software. The software is 99 percent accurate if the book is in good condition. However, we do understand that even one percent can be an annoying number of typos! And sometimes all or part of a page may be missing from our copy of the book. Or the paper may be so discolored from age that it is difficult to read. We apologize and gratefully acknowledge Google's assistance.

After we re-typeset and design a book, the page numbers change so the old index and table of contents no longer work. Therefore, we often re-move them; otherwise, please ignore them.

Our books sell so few copies that you would have to pay hundreds of dollars to cover the cost of our proof reading and fixing the typos, missing text and index. Instead we let most customers download a free copy of the original typo-free scanned book. Simply enter the barcode number from the back cover of the paperback in the Free Book form at www.RareBooksClub.com. You may also qualify for a free trial membership in our book club to download up to four books for free. Simply enter the barcode number from the back cover onto the membership form on our home page. The book club entitles you to select from more than a million books at no additional charge. Simply enter the title or subject onto the search form to find the books.

If you have any questions, could you please be so kind as to consult our Frequently Asked Questions page at www. RareBooksClub.com/faqs.cfm? You are also welcome to contact us there.

General Books LLC™, Memphis, USA, 2012.

⛟ ⛟ ⛟ ⛟ ⛟ ⛟ ⛟ ⛟

WESTERN RESERVE UNIVERSITY BULLETINS
New Series
   Vol. XIX. MAY. 1916 No. 5
LITERARY SECTION SUPPLEMENT
   Western Reserve Studies, Vol. 1, No. 2.

   A STUDY OF THE PLAYS
OF
   Thomas D'urfey
WITH A REPRINT
OF
A FOOL'S PREFERMENT
   Part I
BY
ROBERT STANLEY FORSYTHE, Ph. D.
Instructor in English.
   Western Reserve University Press
Cleveland, Ohio

CONTENTS

PAGE
   D'urfey's Life 1
   D'urfey's Plays 4
77? SiVe *of Memphis* 8
A Fond Husband 10
Madam Fickle"
The Fool Turn'd Critick 18
Trick for Trick J! 21
Squire Oldsapp 27
The Virtuous Wife 31
Sir Barnaby Whigg 37
The Royalist 41
The Injured Princess 4'
A Commonwealth of Women 55
The Banditti 61
A Fool's Preferment to appear in *Part II*
Love for Money 67
Bussy D'Ambois 75
The Marriage Hater Match'd 82
The Richmond Heiress 91
Don Quixote, Part I 97
Don Quixote, Part II 103
Don Quixote, Part III 108
Cinthia and Bndimion 113
The Intrigues at Versailles 117
The Campaigners 123
Massaniello, Part I 130
Massaniello, Part II 135
The Bath 138
The Old Mode and the New I44
Wonders in the Sun 150
The Modern Prophets 156
The Two Queens of Brentford 164
The Grecian Heroine 169
Ariadne 13
The English Stage Italianiz'd 175

PREFACE

I have aimed in the following pages to give an account of the numerous but now forgotten dramatic works of the Restoration writer, Thomas D'Urfey. So far as I am aware, there has been no adequate previous treatment of D'Urfey as a playwright. This deficiency I am attempting to remedy. I am under no illusions as to the worth of D'Urfey's dramas. He was distinctly a third-rate *I* writer—one to be classed with Raven-scroft and Tate. However, in spite of his general mediocrity, D'Urfey has some claims on our consideration: as a hither-to neglected early writer of sentimental comedy, and as a member of that group of Restoration dramatists who looked frequently back to the Elizabethans for their inspiration.

My reprint of D'Urfey's farce, *A Fool's Preferment/which* will appear in the second part of this study (to be published in *97)/* is due to the fact that D'Urfey's plays are inaccessible to the general reader, since they exist only in early editions. The last reprint of any of them was that of the *Don Quixote* comedies in 1729. I _) am aware that my choice of a play for reproduction is open to criticism. Leaving out of the question the special point in its favor — that of accessibility,—I believe, however, that *A Fool's Preferment* illustrates D'Urfey's general methods of work as well as does any other of his plays, and that, furthermore, it should acquire additional interest as being an alteration of an Elizabethan farce, and thus an exemplification of the differences in taste between the audiences of 1688 and of

1625.

On account of considerations of space, the discussion of D'Urfey's plays will appear as *Part I* of the entire study; *Part II* being devoted to the reprint of *A Fool's Preferment*. As my chief interests are critical rather than biographical, and dramatic rather than poetical I have given but a very brief sketch of D'Urfey's life, and have barely mentioned his more important non-dramatic works.

In all parts of the study—in the quotations given in the introduction, as well as in the text of the reprinted comedy—I have endeavored to reproduce exactly the spelling, punctuation, and capitalization of the originals. In some few cases I have called attention to peculiarly atrocious misprints, but usually I have not noticed them. For all matter quoted, its author, then, is entirely responsible as regards the points abovementioned. I desire, also, here to call attention to the fact that even in copies of the same edition, there is sometimes a considerable difference in punctuation and other matters.

Because of the rareness of the old editions (and only editions) I have thought it advisable to append short summaries of each to the discussions of the respective plays. For the benefit of the student of stage history, I have given the *dramatis persona* of each play and the actors' names, as nearly as possible in the form in which they occur in the printed plays.

From many sources I have received invaluable assistance in my investigations and in the preparation of this study. I wish first to acknowledge the kindness of Librarian W. H. Brett, who permitted the use of the Cleveland Public Library's copy of *A Fool's Preferment* for the making of the reprint which will appear in *Part II*. To Mr. C. P. P. Vitz and other members of the staff of the Cleveland Public Library my thanks are due for many favors. Mr. George F. Strong, Librarian of Adelbert College, has most courteously assisted me in many ways; and his constant aid has been invaluable. To the libraries of Columbia, Harvard, and Yale Universi-

ties I am indebted for the use of the early editions of many of D'Urfey's plays and poems. During the progress of my work, I have been many times a debtor to Professor W. H. Hulme of Western Reserve University for advice regarding the form and contents of the volume. Professor Hulme has also been so kind as to read the proofs. Lastly, I wish to emphasize my dependence through the whole course of my research upon the rich results of the investigations of that careful and indefatigable student of Restoration and eighteenth century drama, the Reverend John Genest.

R. S. F.

Cleveland, Ohio, June, 1916.

THE PLAYS OF THOMAS D'URFEY
D'urfey's Life.

Thomas D'Urfey, or Durfey, was born in Exeter in 1653. His grandfather, a French Protestant who had fled to England from La Rochelle in 1628, was probably a brother1 of Honore D'Urfe, author of *L'Astree*. On his mother's side D'Urfey was related to the family of Shackerley Marmion, the comic dramatist.

Thomas D'Urfey, it is said, was intended for the law, but early he turned his attention to letters, appearing in 1676 as the author of a heroic tragedy, *The Siege of Memphis*. From that time forward he occupied himself with literature and music.

D'Urfey's songs and his ability as an entertainer seem soon to have won him the place in London society which he retained until his death nearly fifty years later. His favor with Charles II was such that he and the king sang together from the same paper.2 Although a violent opponent of the Whigs and Shaftesbury in con edy and satirical verse in 1679-82, D'Urfey so modified his views at the Revolution as to be *persona grata* at the court of William and Mary, and to have entertained them as he had their predecessors. *Cinthia and Endimion*, D'Urfey tells us, was to have been performed before Queen Mary.3 He appeared also before King William, as his "ode" *The King's Health. ...;Perform'd before His Majesty King William at Montague-house* testifies. From the

dedication of *Don Quixote, Part III*, Charles Montague and his wife, it seems, were responsible for the Queen's "gracious smiles" on D'Urfey. Under succeeding sovereigns D'Urfey was fortunate in favor at court, so that in 1719 he was able to boast that during his career he had performed some of his "Things" before Charles II, James II, William and Mary, Anne and George Prince of Wales "with happy 1 All biographers of D'Urfey seem to unite in calling Honors D'Urfe a brother of Thomas's father. That this was the case seems hardly possible, since the French romancer was born in 1568 and died in 1625. Indeed, the writer has been unable to find any trace of a relative of Honore D'Urfe' who emigrated to England *(La Grande Encyclope'die, XXXI, 606-07)*. *Pills to Purge Melancholy, I, 246 ff.; The Guardian, Number 67 (May 28, 1713)*. See the extract from D'Urfey's dedication of *The Old Mode and the New* to the Duke of Richmond and Lennox, son to Charles II, p. 144, following. Titlepage and dedication. *Pills to Purge Melancholy, II, 92 ff.* and commendable Approbation."5 It is rather interesting to note that the entertainer of the perfectly upright Queens Mary and Anne, with Congreve and Vanbrugh, was proceeded against by the Middlesex Grand Jury in 1698 for the immorality of his *Don Quixote*. Among D'Urfey's other patrons and patronesses were the Dukes of Richmond, Argyll, Albemarle, Ormond, Bedford, and Wharton, the Duchess of Chandos, the Earls of Dorset, Leicester, Romney, Berkeley, and Carlisle, Lords Lansdown, Morpeth, Leigh and Cowper, and Speaker Bromley.

In his later days D'Urfey seemingly fell into poverty. Various theatrical benefits were given for him, one of which Addison and Steele advertise in the *Guardian* as necessary to pay the old dramatist's debts and so prevent his imprisonment.6 Several times, too, we find D'Urfey delivering poetical "orations" in the theatre.7

The Duke of Wharton, the Earl of Dorset, and William Bromley seem to have given more or less help to D'Urfey in his lean years. He had been a guest at Winchendon, Wharton's countryseat,8 as well as at Knoll, Dorset's residence,9 Speaker Bromley presented D'Urfey with a lodge, and Mrs. Bromley gave him the less substantial compliment of her husband's portrait.10 D'Urfey, it should be noted, was in the country when his volume, *New Operas*, was published and hence was unable to correct the proofs.11 Doubtless it was during earlier visits to the country, if not in his boyhood in Devonshire, that D'Urfey acquired the proficiency in angling for which Addison praised him.12

It is not impossible but is improbable that in his last days D'Urfey was a resident at Windsor as a pensioner. In the affidavit appended to *The English Stage Italianiz'd* he is spoken of as a "poor knight of Windsor." That D'Urfey visited at Windsor in Queen Anne's time is evidenced by his *New Windsor Ballad. The Muse complaining and making Satyrical Remarks upon Sir Jan Brazen, a Man in Office there.13* In 1718 Arbuthnot, writing to Swift, suggested that Pope be appointed Poet Laureate to succeed Rowe, and 5 Dedication of *Pills to Purge Melancholy.* a Numbers 67 and 82, respectively. The play presented was *Madam Fickle, or the Plotting Sisters.* Elwin and Courthope conjecture that it was for this performance that Pope wrote his *Prologue Designed for Mr. D'Urfey's Last Play* (Pope's *Works,* IV, 416-17).

7*Pills to Purge Melancholy,* I, 337 ff.; II, 313, 317 ff., 339 ff. 8 *New Operas,* pp. 369-70. *"Ibid,* pp. 371-72. *"Ibid,* pp. 345, 348, respectively. 11 *Ibid,* preface. 12 *Guardian,* Number 67. u Printed in *Pills to Purge Melancholy.* that he have the power of appointing D'Urfey his deputy to perform the duties of the office.14 The Duke of Buckinghamshire in his *Election of a Poet Laureate. M. DCC.XIX,* mentions him as among the candidates for the place.

D'Urfey's death occurred at the age of seventy on February 26, 1723, according to the inscription on his tomb in St. James's Churchyard, Piccadilly. Various authorities differ, however, as to the date of his death. Genest gives March

11, 1724, as that of D'Urfey's funeral, and cites as his source of information what is probably a newspaper in the British Museum.15 Mr. Temple Scott says that D'Urfey's death took place in February, 1722-23.16 In the preface to *The English Stage Italianiz'd* and in the accompanying bookseller's deposition D'Urfey is asserted to have been alive in 1726. This claim is disposed of in the discussion later of the authenticity of *The English Stage Italianiz'd."* The truth seems to be that the discrepancy in dates is due to a failure to consider the difference between New and Old Style. The year of D'Urfey's death was probably 1723 Old Style or 1724 New Style.

Letters of administration of the old writer's will were taken out in the Archdeacon of Middlesex's court on March 15, 1723.18 Some time after his death the Earl of Dorset erected a monument over his grave.19 His burial itself, it is said, was at Steele's expense.20

D'Urfey's most striking personal trait, to the modern student, is his colossal vanity. Few writers have had more faith in themselves than this now nearly forgotten Restoration song writer and dramatist. This characteristic appears in the prefaces and dedications to most of the plays, as, to cite instances at random, in the dedications to *The Banditti, The Intrigues at Versailles,* and *The Old Mode and the New.* His boast of his appearances at the courts of all the English sovereigns from Charles II to George I has been noticed above. Gildon in D'Urfey's own time rather reproves D'Urfey for repeating in his dedication of *Cinthia and Endimion* the statement of the titlepage that the opera had been intended for performance at court before Queen Mary.21 As a further proof of the

"Swift's *Correspondence,* edited by Ball, III, 22.
» *Stage,* II, 517.
16 Edition of Swift's *Works,* I, 37, note.
"P. 176 ff.
"Aitkin, *Life of Steele,* II, 290.
19 The writer wishes to acknowledge his general indebtedness in his sketch of D'Urfey's life to the *Biographia Dramatica* and to Mr. J. W. Ebbsworth's ar-

ticle on D'Urfey in *The Dictionary of National Biography.* 20 Aitkin, *op. cit.* 21 Gildon's Langbaine's *English Dramatic Poets,* p. 49. dramatist's self-esteem, one may mention Addison's facetious quotation of D'Urfey's comparison of himself to Horace and Terence. 22 That D'Urfey like most professional men of letters of his day was an arrant tuft-hunter may be easily seen from the dedications to his various plays. An amusing story is told in regard to D'Urfey's desire to ingratiate himself with the influential by Steele in the *Tatler.23* He says:

"That ancient Lyric M. D'Urfey, some years ago writ a dedication to a certain lord,.in which he celebrated him for the greatest poet and critic of that age, upon a misinformation in Dyer's Letter, that his noble patron was made lord chamberlain." Ward mentions "persistent amiability" as a trait of D'Urfey, and asserts that Jeremy Collier "could hardly disturb" it.24 It seems to the writer, however, that D'Urfey was really much perturbed by Collier's assaults and wrote his defense of himself which he printed with *The Campaigners* in an extremely bad fit of temper. Too, the writer is of the opinion that D'Urfey, as a vain man, was very susceptible to criticism and that the prefaces and dedications to his unsuccessful plays show this fact plainly.

Certainly, however, D'Urfey must have been an amiable man in general, when his pride was unruffled. The friend of Addison and Steele, whom, although they do not take him at his own valuation, ,, they write of with affection and good-humor, must have possessed an attractive personality. And there must have been something besides impudence or the ability to flatter which introduced D'Urfey into, and kept him in, the best of English society for forty and more years. We may perhaps take him to have been what Addison calls him, a diverting companion and a cheerful, honest, and goodnatured man.26

D'Urfey's dramatic pieces are thirty-two in number. Of these twenty are comedies; five, tragedies; three, tragi-comedies; and four are operas. In addition a farce, *The English Stage Italianiz'd,* has been ascribed to D'Urfey, but is probably not his. Of these a 22 *The Guardian,* Number 67.

25 Number 214. What the dedication accompanied and who the "certain lord" was, the writer does not know. 24 *History of English Dramatic Literature,* III, 454. Ebbsworth in his notice of D'Urfey in the *Dictionary of National Biography* belittles D'Urfey's anger at Collier's attack. 25 The *Tatler,* Number 68. According to Aitkin, *Life of Steele,* II, 290, D'Urfey bequeathed his watch to Steele. For the terms on which D'Urfey, and Addison and Steele were, see, for example, the *Tatler,* Number 214, the *Guardian,* Numbers 29, 67, and 82. D'URFEY'S PLAYS.

and two operas were never acted.

In his own day, D'Urfey, while not occupying a distinguished position as a dramatist, still was considered a writer of rather more than average ability in some directions. Gildon, for instance, commends D'Urfey as a "master of farce."26 In our own times, however, D'Urfey has received little mercy at the hands of the critics. Ward calls him the "literary nadir of Restoration comedy— and indeed of the Restoration drama in general."27 Nettleton terms him an "example of prolix mediocrity."28 Gosse alludes to D'Urfey as "a scurrilous and witless buffoon... needless to discuss in any grave examination of British'dramatic literature."29 Whibley calls D'Urfey "a man of very slender talent."30 Since Gildon's day perhaps the only favorable mention of D'Urfey's dramatic productions has been that in the *Biographia Dramatica,* which is not uncomplimentary.31

D'Urfey's comedies are, for the most part, as Gildon and the *Biographia* have noticed, in the main, really farces. Their humour is usually that of situation, or of plot. In his later comedies particularly, D'Urfey tried more and more to introduce studies of character, and turned his attention toward finding new types in life to bring into his plays. Certain of these he has done very amusingly indeed and with a truth that one may recognize to-day, as in Madam La Pupsey,

the lap-dog loving lady of *The Marriage Hater Match'd,* or Delia, the wheedling, whining wife, in *The Bath.*

D'Urfey's contribution to Restoration comedy is, however, an important one. He is one of the forerunners of eighteenth century sentimentalism. As the writer attempts to demonstrate later, D'Urfey introduced a genuinely sentimental vein into his *Love for Money* in the plot dealing with Mirtilla and Young Merriton. Likewise, the relations of Fulvia and Quickwit in *The Richmond Heiress,* of Angellica and Dorange in *The Campaigners,* of Sophronia and Transport in *The Bath,* of Gatty and Frederick in *The Old Mode and the New,* and of Betty and Ned in *The Modern Prophets* partake more or less of the same quality of sentimentality. No claim is made here that D'Urfey originated sentimental comedy, but that he was in the field several years before Cibber entered it with *Love's Last Shift.* 2e In his edition of Langbaine's *English Dramatic Poets,* p. 48.

27 *History of English Dramatic Literature,* III, 454. 28 *English Drama of the Restoration,* p. 116. 28 *Life of Congreve,* p. 110. 30 *Cambridge History of English Literature,* VIII, 199-200. "I, 212.

Disguise is a feature of D'Urfey's earlier comedies, being used on any and all occasions, in certain of them. Eavesdropping is another convenient device which is employed with unfailing regularity.

Generally D'Urfey's comedies have at least two plots. These may both be comic, or one may have a romantic cast, as in *Love for Money.* There are all sorts of complications, misunderstandings, lost letters, overheard conversations. Hence, one of the chief structural defects of the comedies is that their plots are overcomplicated. Not infrequently, as in *The Marriage Hater Match'd* or in *The Old Mode and the New,* the transactions upon which the play rests are even more intricate and confusing than those in the drama itself. A fault which is noticeable in many of the comedies is that, the dramatist introduces one or more characters whose share in the ac-

tual plot is small but who take up much time in the revelation in conversation of their own folly. This is illustrated in *Sir Barnaby Whigg,* as well as in any of the plays. D'Urfey seems, too, to have much difficulty in providing endings for his plays. Indeed, in several of the earlier plays there is no real conclusion, but a mere stopping of the action at the end of five acts.

While the language of the comedies is not especially witty or lively, still generally, save-where one of D'Urfey's "humorous" characters has the stage, the comedies are vivacious. They are bustling and moving, and, to the student of Restoration comedy, entertaining.

In morality and decency D'Urfey is no worse or no better than his contemporaries. In some plays, he stops short of portraying actual wifely infidelity, in others Ije does not hesitate to depict vice very frankly. On the whole, however, his plays are in this respect superior to Mrs. Behn's or Wycherley's. In such matters D'Urfey-was of his age. However, as the years passed D'Urfey grew more decent. After 1700 his plays are scrupulously clean.32

The tragicomedies, or, more properly, romances, are all three.of them based on earlier plays to a greater or less extent. Their chief interest lies in this fact, indeed, not only because of the nature of the originals but because they show a tendency in a typical Restoration writer towards the romantic plots of the older drama.

D'Urfey's tragedies are greatly inferior to the comedies. Only two of them were certainly acted, and of these one is an alteration of an old play. D'Urfey's blank verse is bad. His attempts at eleva 82 Never, however, could he reconcile himself to treating the London citizen with respect. He could not, it seems, forget his satires against the citizen adherents of Shafteshury in Charles II's time.

tion of style to express an emotion or passion are rant. His plots are sensational and bloody to the highest degree and are interspersed with songs and dances. The characters are mere puppets. In short, there is no doubt but that the tragedies of D'Urfey deserve the oblivion in which they have rested for two hundred years.

The operas are generally mediocre. In *Cinthia and Endimion* we have a clever combination of plot, and in *Wonders in the Sun* an original conception or two. The songs are, in general, not notable for their poetical qualities.

D'Urfey was addicted to using certain characters over and *pver* again. Chief among these is the old-fashioned knight who will believe nothing modern to be good. Such figures as Sir Roger Petulant in *A Fond Husband;* Sir Arthur Oldlove in *Madam Fickle;* Sir Lawrence Limber in *The Marriage Hater Match'd;* Sir Carolus Codshead in *The Bath;* and Sir Fumbler Oldmode in *The Old Mode and the New* belong in this class. Hoydenish young girls are to be found in a number of the later comedies. Among these are Jenny and Molly in *Love for Money;* Mary the Buxsom in the *Don Quixote* group; Gillian in *The Bath;* and Gatty in *The Old Mode and the New.* Various dialect parts also occur, such as those of La Mure in *The Commonwealth of Women;* Le Prat in *Love for Money;* Mrs. Stockjobb in *The Richmond Heiress;* Bertran in *The Campaigners;* Pistole in *The Old Mode and the New;* Tokay in *The Two Queens of Brentford* (French). Certain of the hoydens mentioned above speak a Western dialect; in addition to these we find using the same speech, Flaile in *Madam Fickle;* the Tenants in *The Royalist;* Numps in *The Richmond Heiress;* Jaques and Teresa in the *Don Quixote* plays; the Sergeant and the Page in *The Bath;* Copyhold in *The Modern Prophets,* besides Roger in *A Fool's Preferment.*

Other favorite characters of D'Urfey's are the doltish young countrymen, such as are met with in *Madam Fickle, Love for Money,* and *The Bath*; the villainous dissenter and Whig, as in *Sir Barn'aby Whigg;* the unfaithful wife, such as in *A Fool's Preferment;* the witty young lady, as in *The Richmond Heiress;* and the amorous, intriguing young man, as in *Love for Money.*

Perhaps, in concluding this brief and incomplete discussion of D'Urfey's dramatic works, the charge of plagiarism so frequently brought against him should be mentioned. This rests not so much upon a comparison of D'Urfey's plays with others of Elizabethan and Restoration times, as upon a misunderstanding of Langbaine's idea of literary robbery. That critic who attacked D'Urfey most vigorously for "plagiarism" was of the opinion that every author who dramatized a novel, or utilized even a particle of material from any source other than his own invention was an arrant thief. In truth, D'Urfey while not hesitating to borrow from other writers, dramatic and non-dramatic, or to alter earlier plays, was no more dishonest than any of his contemporaries. All dramatists of the time borrowed from all sources, including each other. D'Urfey did as he was done by. In one respect, however, he is nearly unique in respect to his use of other authors' plays: he never borrowed from Moliere.

A list (which does not aim at completeness) of D'Urfey's nondramatic poetical works includes *Archerie Revived* (a heroic poem with Richard Shotterel); *Hudibras,* the *Fourth Part,* 1682; *New Collections of Songs and Poems,* 1683; *Wit and Mirth, or Pills to Purge Melancholy,* 1684, 1699, 1700, and on, to a definitive edition in six volumes, 1719-20; *Tales Tragical and Comical,* 1704; *Tales Tragical and Moral,* 1706; *Songs Compleat,* 1706, 1710, and so on; *New Operas,* 1721.33

The shorter poems by D'Urfey contained in the above volumes need no particular notice here. They are popular songs of the Restoration and Augustan periods for the most part. *Hudibras* and the various tales in verse by D'Urfey have no literary merit. The only point of interest connected with them is that one narrative poem, *The Plague of Impertinence: or a Barber a Fury,* which is printed in the *New Operas* volume, is from the *Story Told by the Tailor* in *The Arabian Nights' Entertainments.3* This poem which is interesting as an example of the early utilization of Galland's version of the tales is not noticed by Miss

Conant in her *Oriental Tale in England.* DRAMATIC WORKS.

D'Urfey's first attempt in dramatic writing35 was a tragedy, *The Siege of Memphis,TM or the Ambitious Queen.* This play was acted at the Theatre Royal in 1676 and was published in the same year with the following titlepage:

''the SIEGE Oe MEMPHIS, Or The Ambitious Queen, A Tragedy, Acted at the Theatre-royal. Written by *Tho. Durfey,* Gent. *Non sit sine Periculo facinus magnum & memorabile,* Terent. *LONDON,* Printed for *W. Cademan* at the Popes Head at the entrance in of the *New Exchange* in the *Strand,* 1676."

M Based partly on Ebbsworth's incomplete list in *D. N. B.,* XVI, 251 ff. *u* See Lane, *Arabian Nights,* I, p. 368 ff. 85 D'Urfey in his dedication calls the play "the first fruits of an Infant Muse." M Misprinted as *The Siege of Menphis* at the opening of I, 1.

The tragedy was not successful. In his dedication of the play to Henry Chevers, the author says of it, " *The Siege* has got little credit with the World," because of "the meaness of the stile, the want of good design, and the ill representation at the Theatre, being Play'd to the worst advantage." The drama is written in rhyme, and is an excellent example of a bad heroic play. The language is bombastic to absurdity; witness Zelmura's introduction of herself to Moaron, I, 2 (p. 7):

"I am Zelmura... By me the Trees and Plants do spring and grow, My breath can check or *Nilus,* ebb or flow;" and the example given by Genest37 from the same act (p. 11), from a speech by Moaron:

"I'll rip my breast, and drown thee with my blood."

It is stated by the early dramatic historians that *The Siege of Memphis* has a historical basis.38 This seems to be true only insofar that the Egyptian city of Memphis underwent several sieges during its existence and that in the course of many centuries we find the names of Amasis (as a king), Ptolemy, Philopater, and Selabdin (Saladin?) occurring in Egyptian history.

The action of *The Siege* is hasty and

confused. The motivation for certain incidents is not clearly shown. The characters are not well drawn, and the amount of unnecessary bloodshed in the drama is appalling. Genest/9 with his characteristic charity, while admitting the badness of the tragedy, says that it is "not dull" and that "Zelmura... is a spirited character." This, however, is the most that can be said for it.

The *dramatis persona*, which does not give the performers' names, runs thus: *"Persons Represented*
Melechadel, King of *Egypt.*
Ptollemy, his Son
Phillopater, Caliph and General
Achmades) TM „
Halem Tw0 Peers
_.,. (Brother to *Halem*, and a V,. *Zxchmi* commander under *Phillopater* Egyptians
Zelmura, Queen of *Egypt*
Amasis, Sister to *Zelmura*
Saphrena, Amasis Confident
Messengers, Souldiers, Guards, and Attendants, Men and Women.
Stage, I, 183".
n *Biographia Dramatica*, III, 272. «
Stage, I, 183. *Selabdin*, Sultan of *Syria Moaron*, his Son *Psamnis*, friend to *Moaron Aldabar*, Captain in *Selabdin's* Army
Souldiers, Guards, and Attendants.

The Scene, *Memphis* besieged." The plot of *The Siege of Memphis* may be thus summarized: The Egyptians are besieged in the city of Memphis by a Syrian army under Moaron. By the efforts of Zelmura, Queen of Egypt, the Syrians are driven off and Moaron captured. Zelmura protects Moaron from the vengeance of her husband, King Melechadel.

Moaron falls in love with Amasis, sister to Zelmura. He sends secretly to Syria for an army to come against the Egyptians, but his design is discovered and he is arrested. By strategy, Zelmura makes her husband swear an irrevocable oath to do as she desires. The Queen then asks sole control over Egypt for three days, and obtains her wish. She proceeds to free Moaron and imprisons Melechadel and his son Ptollemy.

The Queen who has fallen in love

with Moaron prevents his departure for Syria. On discovering the mutual love of him and Amasis, Zelmura imprisons him again. The Queen now sets Ptollemy free but condemns Melechadel to death.

Zelmura offers Amasis her life if she will renounce Moaron and this she does. The Queen tenders her love to Moaron but is spurned by him. As she is about to kill him to revenge the insult, Ptollemy announces the approach of an army led by the Sultan of Syria. Zelmura frees Moaron, so that he may lead the Syrian army against her own. Zichmi, an Egyptian general whose brother has been slain by Zelmura's orders, for revenge designs to ravish Amasis and then betray Memphis to the Syrians.

Zelmura rescues Amasis from the attack of Zichmi and kills him. The Queen then tricks Amasis into admitting that she still loves Moaron, and in a rage kills her. As the victorious Syrians enter, Zelmura stabs herself. Ptollemy succeeds to the Egyptian throne.

A Fond Husband; or, the Plotting Sisters, would seem to have been D'Urfey's second play and first comedy. Although in James Magnes and Richard Bentley's list of *Books Printed* accompanying *A Fond Husband*, we find the following: *"Madam Fickle*, or *the Witty False One A Fond Husband*, or *the Plotting Sisters The Fool Turned Critic.* In the Press;" nevertheless, the priority of presentation of *A Fond Husband* may be considered as practically established, since it was licensed for printing on June 15, 1676, while the license of *Madam Fickle* is dated November 20, 1676. It is reasonable to suppose that *A Fond Husband* was first published very shortly after the granting of the *imprimatur*, and not six months or more later. Probably the date of 1677 on the titlepage of the Harvard University Library copy_o_l *A Fond Husband* merely means that the play was reissued with a new date, early in 1677. There seem to have been copies extant with the date 1676.40

The titlepage of *A Fond Husband* reads thus: "A Fond Husband: OR, *XLbC* Plotting SlSterS. A COM-' EDY: As it is Act-

ed at His *Royal Highness* The DUKE'S Theatre *Hac, dum incipias, gravia sunt, dumque ignores, ubi cogndris, facilia,* Terent. Written by *THO. DURFEY* Gent. Licensed *June* 15, 1676. Roger L'estrange. *LONDON:* Printed by *T. N.* for *James Magnes* and *Rich. Bentley,* in *Russel-street* in *Covent-Garden,* near the Piazza's. 1677." The comedy, as was *Madam Fickle,* the dramatist's next play, was dedicated to the Duke of Ormond by whose family D'Urfey appears long to have been patronized—in 1692 he dedicated his *Marriage Hater Match'd* to the second duke, grandson of him who is mentioned above.

A Fond Husband was well received on its first presentation. The author says in his dedication, "it has indifferently past in the Opinion of the Town." Steele in *The Guardian,1* reminding his readers of a performance of the play that night for D'Urfey's benefit, says, "This comedy was honoured with the presence of king Charles the Second three of its first five nights." A certain degree of more or less lasting popularity of the comedy is shown by other recorded performances of it in 1707 (at the Haymarket); in 1710 (at Greenwich); in 1715, 1726, 1732 (at Lincoln's Inn Fields); in 1740 (at Drury Lane).42 Otway in his *Soldier's Fortune*, III, 2, has seem 40 The *Biographia Dramotica* gives the date of the first edition as 1676 (II, 242). 41 Number 82, June 15, 1713. See also Addison in the *Guardian,* Number 67, May 28, 1713.

«Genest, *Stage,* II, 373, 374, 468, 581; III, 183, 189, 351, 626: the 1713 performance is mentioned, II, 516-17. The play was reprinted in 1685 and 1711 *(Biographia Dramatica,* II, 242).

ingly drawn upon Emillia's pretense of having been attacked by Ranger in IV. In Otway's comedy Lady Dunce is caught with Beaugard by her husband, Beaugard flees, and Lady Dunce recounts a tale of how Beaugard had attempted to ravish her, thus diverting her husband's anger and suspicion from her.

In the *Guardian,* as quoted above, Steele praises the ingenuity shown by D'Urfey in the management of this comedy, but perhaps not altogether seriously. He particularly commends the "excellent use of a table with a carpet, and the key of a closet," as well as the employment of the trapdoor. Of *A Fond Husband*, Genest says, "... On the whole a good play, but there is too much of Ranger and Maria."43

Among the weak points of the comedy is the too frequent employment of eavesdropping. By this means every secret is learned by those from whom it is to be kept. Too, the deception after deception of husband by wife become monotonous. The end of the play is flat and unsatisfactory—which, it may be mentioned, is a frequent fault of D'Urfey's dramas. The device used by Emilia and Rashley to get out of their scrape when Bubble surprises them (V) is clever, but Bubble's credulity is too great to be convincing.

"*Drammatis Personal Rashley*, a Gentleman, Friend to *Emillia*. Mr. *Smith*.
Ranger, his Rival.. Mr. *Harris*.
Perrgrine Bubble, A credulous fond Cuckold, Husband to *Emillia*. Mr. *James Nokes. Old Fumble*, a superannuated Alderman, Mr. *Anth. Leigh*. that dotes on Black Women: He's very deaf and almost blind; and seeking to cover his imperfection of not hearing what is said to him, answers quite contrarily. Sir *Roger Petulant*, a jolly old Knight Mr. *Sandford*. of the last Age.
Sneak, Nephew to Sir *Roger*, a young Mr. *Jevan*.
raw Student.
Spatterdash, Servant to *Fumble. 1 Jeremy*, Servant to *Rashley*.)

Apothecary. Mr. *Percival. Emillia*, Wife to *Bubble*. Mrs. *Barrer. "Ibid*, I, 192.

X "Incomplete as omitting Mrs. Snare, formerly mistress to Sneak.

Mr. *Richards. Maria*, Sister to *Bubble*. Mrs. *Marshal. Cordelia*, Niece to *Bubble*. Mrs. *Hughes. Betty*, Woman to *Emillia*. Mrs. *Napper. Governess*. Mrs. *Norrice*.

Servants and Attendants." A summary of the plot of *A Fond Husband* follows: Emillia, wife to Bubble, loves, and is loved by Rashley. Pretending he has a mistress living near Bubble's house, Rashley tells Bubble of all that passes between himself and Emillia, as having taken place between himself and the imaginary lady. Ranger, who also loves Emillia, is jealous of Rashley, and after they have made game of him, plots against Emillia with Bubble's sister Maria, who loves Rashley. To blind the jealous Maria, Emillia and Rashley feign to quarrel.

Bubble tries to "reconcile" them, and is successful. The two sisters-in-law quarrel over Rashley, and each vows revenge on the other.

A conversation in which an assignation is made by Rashley with Emillia is overheard by Ranger, who determines to prevent its occurring. Maria, aided by Ranger, tries to convince Bubble of his wife's guilt. At last, Bubble, believing them, resolves on revenge. Learning of the assignation, Bubble intends to surprise his wife. She finds that she has been betrayed and plots against Bubble. Sneak, who has been an unsuccessful suitor to Bubble's niece Cordelia, is caught by Bubble with a woman, in place of Rashley and Emillia. Consequently Bubble's suspicions are allayed.

At the wedding feast of Fumble and Cordelia, Bubble receives an anonymous letter accusing his wife and Rashley. Maria posts Bubble at his wife's chamber-door. By the treachery of the Governess, Ranger gets into Emillia's chamber while she is there with Rashley. Bubble tries to enter. Ranger prevents Rashley's flight. Emillia hides Rashley under the table, takes the door-key, which she puts in Ranger's pocket, and cries "Rape!" She pretends that Ranger has attacked her. Rashley is discovered, but claims to have been concealed to prevent Ranger's assault upon Emillia. Ranger and Maria are again in disgrace, and Rashley and Emillia in favor.

Again Maria surprises Rashley and Emillia together. By a trick Emillia puts out Maria's light, and then she and Rashley escape through a trap-door. Hence, when he enters, Bubble finds no one save Maria. Later, Bubble again attempts to surprise the lovers, but they slip away, leaving a pair of servants making love in their place. This device succeeds. Finally, however, Bubble catches the two together, and is at last made certain of Emillia's infidelity.

An underplot deals with Sneak's courtship of Cordelia. As he is a booby, she is averse to the match. Sneak is followed up from Cambridge by Mrs. Snare, who, claiming he has seduced her, blackmails him. Cordelia is designed finally to be given to Fumble, an old dotard, as wife. Wishing to escape this match, she substitutes her governess for herself, an easy matter since Fumble is nearly blind and very deaf. She is taken by Sneak's uncle, Sir Roger Petulant, to visit Sneak, who is reported as sick of love for her. Arriving unexpectedly, she learns Sneak's sickness to be the result of his dissipation and therefore refuses him absolutely.

Madam Fickle: or the Witty False One, according to Genest,45 was produced in 1676. It was printed46 with the following titlepage: "MADAM FICKLE: Or The Witty False One. A COMEDY. As it is Acted at his Royal Highness the DUKE'S THEATRE. Written by *Tho. Durfey* Gent. Horat. *Non cuivis homini contingit adire Corinthum*. Licensed November 20, 1676. Roger L'estrange *LONDON1* Printed by *T. N.* for *James Magnes* and *Rich. Bentley* in *Russel Street* in *CoventGarden* near the *Piazza's*. M.DC.LXXVII" The comedy would seem to have been not unfavorably received. If we may trust D'Urfey in his dedication (like that of *A Fond Husband*, addressed to the Duke of Ormond) King Charles gave it "a particular Applause,. which was seconded by your Grace the Duke." It was reprinted or reissued in 1682. *Madam Fickle* was revived later in 1704 (as the benefit of Short and Mrs. Willis) and in 1711.47 According to Whibley,48 D'Urfey's play afforded some hints for Farquhar's *Constant Couple*. There is indeed some resemblance between Madam Fickle's determination to revenge upon mankind her husband's conduct towards her, and Lady Lyrewell's similar resolution because of her seduction as a girl *(The Constant Couple*, III).

According to the *Biographia Dramatical* D'Urfey's play is 15 *Stage*, I, 195. 46 The Harvard University Library copy of *Madam Fickle,* which was used for this study, was once the property of Genest and contains his autograph. « Genest, *Stage*, II, 310, 487. 48 *Cambridge History of English Literature*, VI-II, 199. « II, 4. "wholly made up from other comedies. " In proof of this assertion the statement is made that Sir Arthur Oldlove is copied from Veterano in Marmion's *Antiquary,"0* and that Zechiel's creeping into the Tavern Bush while Tilbury ("Tilburn" in the *Biographia)* is drunk under it is from a scene between Sir Reverence Lamard and Pimpwell in *The Walks of Islington and Hogsden.* It is said further that there is in D'Urfey's play a use of several hints from Marston's *Faivn.* In addition to these alleged plagiarisms, Miles suggests that D'Urfey drew upon Jasper Mayne.51

The founding of D'Urfey's Oldlove upon Veterano in *The Antiquary* is extremely doubtful. For an original there is no need of turning back to Marmion's play,52 since in the same year as *Madam Fickle* was acted, Shadwell's *Virtuoso* appeared. That *The Virtuoso* was acted before D'Urfey's comedy is probable, since Shadwell's dedication of his play to the Duke of Newcastle is dated June 26, 1676. Genest53 gives the date of licensing of *The Virtuoso* for publication as May 31, 1676. Hence, we may conclude, since in Restoration times plays were printed very shortly after their production, that November 20, the date of licensing of *Madam Fickle,* was-not far from the time of its first presentation. *The Virtuoso* also, it should be noted, was played at the Theatre Royal, *Madam Fickle* at the Duke's Theatre. What more natural than that a popular play at one theatre should engender an imitation at another? The characters of the two plays correspond roughly thus: *Madam Fickle The Virtuoso*

Sir Arthur Oldlove Sir Nicholas Gimcrack
 Captain Tilbury Snarl
Madam Fickle Lady Gimcrack54

Oldlove's exhibition of his curiosities (III, I) recalls Gimcrack's explanation of various of his scientific discoveries, *The Virtuoso,* V. Veterano, however, in *The Antiquary,* II, III, IV, lists over some of his prizes in a way not unlike Oldlove's.

The writer, since he has been unable to secure *The Walks of Islington and Hogsden,* cannot judge as to the influence of that play upon D'Urfey's. *The Fawn* seems to contribute very little, if anything, to *Madam K* It should be remembered that through his mother D'Urfey was related to Shackerley Marmion. 81 *The Influence of Moliere Upon Restoration Comedy,* p. 108. *"Stage*, I, 188.

"Cartwright's *Ordinary* contains an antiquary (Moth) also. They are alike in wit and resourcefulness. *Fickle.* Their only resemblance is that both plays contain jealous husbands who are disciplined by their wives. In Marston's *What You Will* occurs a husband who has been long separated from his wife, but there seems to have been no borrowing by D'Urfey.

The part of *Madam Fickle* concerned with the supposed widow's being courted by several suitors is based upon Rowley's *Match at Midnight,* a fact hitherto unnoticed. In this comedy the Widow is courted by Old Bloodhound for his silly son Tim, who has a roistering brother Alexander. She also is beset by Randal, Ancient Young, and Old Bloodhound himself, as suitors. It is finally made known that Jarvis, her supposed servant, is in reality her husband, who, having become jealous of her, had left her, and returning in disguise had been hired as a servant by his apparent Widow.55 It should be remarked that in Shadwell's *Humorists,* Sir Richard Loveyouth, who has deserted his wife because of her "Foolishness and Vanity" and her contentiousness, returns after three years, and gives out a report of his own death. He then enters his wife's service as gentleman-usher. After his wife's marriage to Crazy, Sir Richard discloses his identity. There is little likeness of character, however.

To the modern reader, *Madam Fickle* is a mediocre comedy with the conventional rich widow (who, however, turns out not to be a widow), the antiquary, the merry old men, the doltish country boys, the men about town, and the pretty, witty, intriguing ladies of a host of late Elizabethan and Restoration comedies.

The characters and their performers follow:

"DRAMATIS PERSONAE56
Lord *Bellamour* Mr. *Betterton* Manley, Friend to *Bellam.* Mr. *Smith.* Sir *Arthur Oldlove,* an Antiquary Mr. *Sandford.*

Captain *Tilbury,* an old fashion'd) ,,,,, ,, blunt Fellow Mr" *Medboum Zechiel 1* ,, Mr. *Anthony Leigh .Toby* Sons to TM&«ry Mr. *James Nokes Old Jollyman* Mr. *Underhilt Harry,* Son to *Jollyman* Mr. *Jevon Flaile,* Servant to *Tilbury* Mr. *Richards Dorrel,* alias *Friendlove* Mr. *Norrice*

M The second title of *Madam Fickle—The Witty False One*—recalls Shirley's *WittyFair One.* 56 Incomplete, as lacking the Nurse to Madam Fickle. WOMEN . *Madam Fickle Constantia,* Daughter to *Sir Arthur Arbella Silvia,* Attendant to *Fickle* THREE WENCHES *Constable, Watch, Footmen, Maskers, Musitioners and Attendants* SCENE Covent-Garden"

A summary of the plot follows:
Tilbury comes up from Salisbury with his son Toby in order to marry him and Tilbury's other son Zechiel — a student in the Temple, — respectively, to a rich widow, Madam Fickle, who lodges at the antiquary, Sir Arthur Oldlove's, and Sir Arthur's daughter Constantia. Zechiel takes his country-bred brother in hand to make a beau out of him.

They accost Constantia and her friend Arbella in the Mall. The ladies are rescued from them by Manley. Madam Fickle has been deceived in love and so she vows revenge on the male sex by playing with them. She leads on Lord Bellamour, Manley, Harry Jollyman, and many others. Tilbury, his sons, and Old Jollyman visit Sir Arthur.

Toby breaks a curiosity — a vial containing the tears of St. Jerome — and falls into a disgrace which extends to his brother Zechiel. Constantia jeers then at the brothers until they leave. Manley and Harry Jollyman discover that they are rivals. Manley sets out to confront Madam Fickle with her duplicity, but, as he tells Bellamour of the state of affairs, he is overheard by her. Manley surprises her with Bellamour. She convinces Bellamour that Manley who begins to denounce her is mad. While Bellamour runs for a doctor, she tells Manley that Bellamour has been forced upon her as a suitor by her uncle.

After the dismissal of Tilbury and his sons by Sir Arthur, Jollyman becomes a candidate for Constantia's hand. Constantia places Manley where he can overhear Madam Fickle with other suitors, but Madam's Nurse betrays the plot. The Nurse plays her mistress in the dark, and Harry Jollyman caresses her, while Manley and Constantia eavesdrop. Madam Fickle then discovers herself

Mrs. *Mary Lee*
Mrs. *Barrer*
Mrs. *Gibbs*
Mrs. *Napper*

to Manley elsewhere, pretending that Constantia has deliberately tricked him, and thus deceives him again. Bellamour enters and attacks Harry who is with the Nurse. The mistake is now discovered. Madam Fickle assures each separately that the other is the husband designed for her by her uncle. Manley enters as mad and deceives the others. Madam Fickle now invites the various suitors to visit her in the morning. Each thinks he will marry her then.

In the meantime, she runs away in man's clothing. On meeting at Sir Arthur's in the morning, the suitors discover how they have been tricked. Madam Fickle returns in her disguise and threatens them. They discover her identity and upbraid her. She then tells of her marriage, her subsequent desertion by her husband, and her resulting vow. A servant, Dorrel, now discovers himself to be Friendlove, Madam Fickle's husband. Bellamour transfers his affections to Arbella, and Manley his to

Constantia. The Tilburies who have gotten drunk with Old Jollyman and have rioted in the street and have been arrested forsake London for their country home.

The Fool Tum'd Critick was probably first acted in 1678." The titlepage of the play runs thus:

"the FOOL Tum'd Critick: A COMEDY: As it was Acted at the Theatre-Royall. *By His Majesties Servants.* By *T. D.* Gent. *LONDON,* Printed for *James Magues* and *Richard Bentley,* at the *Post-Office* in *Russel-Street* in *Covent-Garden,* 1678."

In its printed form this comedy lacks a *dramatis persona,TM* and appears not to have been dedicated to any one, as no epistle dedicatory accompanies it. In this latter respect *The Fool Tum'd Critick* is nearly unique among D'Urfey's dramas.

According to the *Biographia Dramatical,* the characters of Old Winelove, Tim,60 and Smallwit were copied by D'Urfey from Simo, Asotus, and Ballio in Randolph's *Jealous Lovers.* It is not unlikely that this borrowing occurred, as the plays correspond closely in certain places. For example, we find in *The Jealous Lovers,* I, 1, the father (Simo) giving his son (Asotus) into the tutor's (Ballio's) hands; to this the parallel is *The Fool Tum'd Crit* "Genest, *Stage,* I, 229.
58 *Ibid.*
M II, 243.
« Called "Trim" in the *Biographia.* ick, I, 2. In *The Jealous Lovers,* III, 4, the son engages in a drinking-bout in his father's presence; the same occurs in II, 2, of D'Urfey's comedy. The *Biographia* asserts further that D'Urfey stole the prologue to the Earl of Orrery's *Master Anthony* and used it as prologue to the present comedy. As to the truth of this the writer cannot judge, not having met with Orrery's comedy. Whoever the real author of the prologue may be, it seems nearly certain that for a part of the plot of the play D'Urfey resorted to a comedy in part by a noble author—*The Country Captain1* of the Duke of Newcastle and Shirley. This borrowing is to be met with in the con-

spiracy of Frank Amorous and Betty against Tim, which results in their making the last believe Betty, a serving girl, is an heiress. The title of D'Urfey's comedy brings to mind Carlell's *Fool Would Be a Favorite.* Tim's setting out to learn politeness seems borrowed from D'Urfey's own Toby in *Madam Fickle.* Similar characters are not rare in late Elizabethan drama. They occur, besides in *The Jealous Lovers,* as indicated above, in *The Sparagus Garden* of Brome, *The Noble Stranger* of Sharpe, *The Constant Maid* of Shirley, and *The Fool Would Be a Favorite* of Carlell. D'Urfey repeats this again, as in *The Banditti* where Don Ariell tries to make Diego his boobyish supposed son a wit and employs a number of masters to facilitate the process.

D'Urfey employs again in *The Virtuous Wife,* IV, the passing off of a lover as a brother of a female character as used in *The Fool Turn'd Critick,* II. In the later play, a lady introduces her lover to her husband as her brother, whereas in the present comedy the maid assumes the pretended relationship. In *Squire Oldsapp,* IV, Christina introduces Welford as her cousin.

In *The Country Wake* by Dogget and in *Vice Reclaimed* by Wilkinson, similar tricks are employed.

The Fool Turn'd Critick is styled by Genest62 "an indifferent comedy." He considers it to have been written as a satire upon "playhouse criticks, and pretended town wits." The play is written partly in bad blank verse and partly in prose. In spite of the unfavorable criticism given above, *The Fool Turn'd Critick* seems to the present writer to be a rather clever play in some ways. It contains the usual amount of eavesdropping — a favorite device of D'Urfey. The use of disguise is carried to an unnatural extent, 61 Also published (from MS.) under the title, *Captain Underwit,* by A. H. Bullen. 82 *Stage,* I, 229. even suggesting the typical disguise comedy of seventy or eighty years earlier. There seems to be no adequate reason for breaking off the marriages at the end of the play. An interesting commentary upon stage conditions at the time is furnished by these lines of the epilogue, "He the nonconformist melts in durance half his grease away, To get, like us the players, poor thirteen Pounds a day." The *dramatis persona* may be supplied thus:

Frank Amorous.
Bernard, his friend.
Old Winelove.
Tim, a fool, his son.
Smallwit, an oratorical pedant.
Sir Formal Ancient.
Ralph, Bernard's servant.
Penelope, daughter to Sir Formal.
Lucretia, (or Lucia) her friend.63
Lady Ancient, her mother.

Betty, her maid.

A summary of the plot follows:

Old Winelove, to make a man of fashion of his heir Tim, hires Smallwit to act as his son's tutor in fashionable diversions and good manners. Tim is accepted by Sir Formal Ancient as a suitor for his daughter Penelope. Sir Formal forbids the house to Bernard who loves Penelope. Frank Amorous, Bernard's friend, visits Penelope as an emissary from Bernard. Frank there falls in love with Lucia, Penelope's friend. Penelope herself is attracted by Frank.

She sends a letter to Bernard by Frank which makes Bernard suspect them. Frank is introduced into her bedchamber, and discovers her passion for him. They are surprised by Sir Formal, but Frank pretends to be the brother of Penelope's maid Betty, just returned from abroad, and tells of the wonders of Rome of which he really knows nothing, thus successfully deceiving Sir Formal.

Bernard challenges Frank to a duel. Their meeting is witnessed by Old Winelove. Bernard, who is disarmed, gives up Penel 63 The names of Lucia and Lucretia are both applied to this character in the course of the play.

ope. Pleased by Frank's prowess, Old Winelove engages him as a companion for Tim, to second Smallwit.

Old Winelove takes Frank to Sir Formal's house where he meets Penelope again. Smallwit enters, his head broken by Bernard for ogling Lucia, Bernard's new mistress. Frank plans in a soliloquy

to steal this mistress from Bernard, but is overheard by Betty who informs Penelope. Penelope writes to Bernard, desiring his return to her. Betty, who is thought by Tim to be Frank's sister and rich is courted by him. Lucia, as she entertains Bernard, is visited by Frank. Bernard, hiding, hears Frank offer himself to Penelope. He discovers himself and quarrels with Frank who has slandered his character.

Bernard returns to Penelope and arranges a secret marriage with her. Smallwit who overhears them informs Sir Formal, who has just come to blows with Old Winelove over the marriage settlements of Penelope and Tim. Smallwit announces the marriage of Tim and Betty, the latter as Frank's sister and an heiress. Frank and Lucia are together, when she drops a letter from Bernard concerning their plot on Frank. Frank finding it, reads it, and discovers the trick. Smallwit meets Frank and gives him the disguise in which Bernard is to steal away Penelope. Penelope enters and, thinking the disguised Frank is Bernard, elopes with him. Smallwit arranges to substitute Lucia for Penelope, and, after disguising himself as her, is married to Bernard by Ralph, Bernard's servant, who is disguised as a parson. Frank and Penelope are supposedly married, but their parson turns out to be Sir Formal in disguise. At the end of the play the only valid marriage is that of Tim and Betty, who is now discovered to be no heiress but only a servant.

The first of D'Urfey's adaptations of older plays appeared early in 1678 (New Style). This was his *Trick for Trick: or The Debauch'd Hypocrite*, an alteration of Fletcher's *Monsieur Thomas*. It was printed with the following titlepage:

"Trick for Trick: Or xтbe DebaUCb'fc t)VOCVit, A COMEDY, as it is Acted at the Theatre-Royal, By His Majestie's Servants. Written by *Tho. D'Urfey*, Gent. Licensed, April 30th, 1678. *Roger L'Bstrange. LONDON,*. Printed for *Langley Curtiss*, in *Goat-Court* upon *LudgateHill*, 1678."

According to the early writers on the

stage, *Trick for Trick* was. "little more than a revival.... of *Monsieur Thomas.* "9 Genest, however, is much nearer the truth when he says, "D'Urfey has reduced the blank verse to prose, and made very considerable alterations."66 The appended table will show scene by scene the dependence of *Trick for Trick* upon *Monsieur Thomas: Monsieur Thomas06 Trick for Trick*

I, 1 I, 1 (very slightly) 2 II, 1 3 II, 1 II, 2 II, 1 3-. II, 1 4' III, 1
5
III, 1 III, 1 2.2 3 IV, 1, 2 3 IV, 1 2 IV, 1

Thus it will be seen that D'Urfey has utilized only one scene (IV, 2) from the nineteen composing the last two acts of *Monsieur Thomas*. The following table shows verbal borrowings from Fletcher listed as to the number of lines and fractional lines taken over by D'Urfey and as to the scenes from which they were drawn and those to which they were transferred:

Here we see that D'Urfey took only 575 lines either wholly or in part from eight scenes of *Monsieur Thomas* and utilized them in five scenes of his own play. The fact that he inverts the relationship of the borrowings in IV, 3 and IV, 1, from respectively

M *Biographia Dramatica,* III, 3S0.
"*Stage,* I, 236.
68 Darley's edition of Beaumont and Fletcher has been used for this and all other tables of like nature dealing with D'Urfey's indebtedness to them.

Fletcher's III, 3, and IV, 2, is perhaps worth calling to the reader's attention.

D'Urfey's changes of one sort and another in the *dramatis persona* may be gathered from the following: *Monsieur Thomas Trick for Trick*

Valentine Valentine (and Hylas)
Monsieur Thomas Monsieur Thomas
Sebastian-Sir Wilding Frollick
Hylas Hylas
Launcelot Launcelot
Three Physicians Three Physicians
Francisco Franck
An Apothecary An Apothecary
Cellida Cellide (and Mary)
Dorothea Dorothy Alice Sabina
D'Urfey as shown above, has combined certain of Fletcher's characters. Others,

as may be seen by a glance at the *dramatis persona* of the two plays, have been omitted, while still others have been added.

To sum up briefly the relations between the two plays: D'Urfey uses only 575 of Fletcher's lines or parts of lines. He does not adhere to Fletcher's plot. The story of Francisco and Cellide is entirely absent from *Trick for Trick*. D'Urfey calls Fletcher's Mary — the mistress of Monsieur Thomas — by the name of Cellide. D'Urfey's last act is entirely original. In it the marriage of Hylas and Dorothy does not take place, as in *Monsieur Thomas*. Thomas's disguise as a woman is left out. Finally, in D'Urfey's comedy, Thomas does not win Cellide, as Fletcher's Thomas wins Mary. Fletcher does not introduce Mary's father as D'Urfey does Cellide's. Of course, *Trick for Trick* has no convent scenes.

In fact, D'Urfey has showed more originality in his remodelling of this play than was usual with him in making over old dramas. His changes, with one exception, are, however, for the worse. The elimination of the story of Francisco, Valentine, and Cellide makes for the unity of the play; and, furthermore, removes a rather tiresome portion of the plot. On the other hand, D'Urfey's recharacterization of Thomas is distinctly inferior to Fletcher's conception of him. The Thomas of *Trick for Trick* is no longer an amusingly mischievous rattlepate, but a filthy "debauch'd hypocrite." Cellide is, also, altered for the worse; while Dorothy's delightfully amusing adventures are entirely omitted. In short, D'Urfey has vulgarized Fletcher's rather *risque* but amusing comedy.

As an example of what D'Urfey has done to Fletcher's verse the following lines may be quoted from *Trick for Trick* together with the original Fletcherian passage: *"Launce.* More, ay, and the best too, Sir—for at last we quit the Ladies house on composition—and to the silent Street turn'd all our furies. A sleeping Watchman here we stole the shooes from: there make a noise, at which he wakes and followes—then

cryes out Theeves, and throwes his bilboe at us— and Wades the Kennel in no footed stockings.
Sir Wild. Oons—this is the rarest Boy, ha ha—
Launce. Windows and Signs we sent to *Erebus*—a cry of
Butchers Curs we entertain'd last, and having let the Pigs loose in out-Parishes, made every Street look like a Bear-Garden."
Trick for Trick, IV, 1. *"Laun.* Nor here, sir,
Give we the frolic over, though at length
We quit the lady's sconce on composition;
But to the silent streets we turn'd our furies:
A sleeping watchman here we stole the shoes from,
There-made a noise, at which he wakes and follows;
The streets are dirty, takes a Queenhithe cold,
Hard cheese, and that, chokes him o' Monday next;
Windows and signs we sent to Erebus:
A crew of bawling curs we entertained last,
When having let the pigs loose in out-parishes,
Oh, the brave cry we made as high as Aldgate!
Down comes a constable and the sow his sister
Most traitorously tramples upon authority."
Monsieur Thomas, IV, 2.
Among the points of interest in the play are these: Haines (who played Launce) spoke the prologue "in a Red Coat like a Common Souldier," and in it he mentions the "French Campaigne" to which he designs to go. Launce, it should be noted, is the first of a long succession of characters in D'Urfey's plays to speak more or less broken English. In V, 2 (p. 58), a mention is made of sending "all the Lobsters in the *Levant* to Massaniello the Fisherman." Some twenty years later appeared the two parts of D'Urfey's *Tragedy of Massaniello.* Another pointing to a later play occurs in the same act and scene (p. 59) where mention is

made of *"Heere Hander van Dander Scopen."* Van Scopen is a character in D'Urfey's *Campaigners.*

In D'Urfey's *Virtuous Wife,* IV, the entrance of Launce and his upsetting his master's plans by his injudiciously blurting out certain damaging statements, *Trick for Trick,* III, 1, is utilized. The borrowing is rather a close one.

The characters and their performers are thus given:

The plot of *Trick for Trick* may be summarized thus: Monsieur Thomas and Hylas return from a continental tour together. On his arrival, Thomas pretends to Cellide, with whom he has been in love, that he has left off his previous debauched courses. However, she and her friend Sabina, Valentine's sister, with whom she is staying, are hidden by Valentine and Franck, so as to overhear Thomas's account of a wild adventure of his in Paris. He then tells of a pretended meeting of his with Cellide, but is confronted by her, and forced to retract his story, after which she leaves him in anger.

Thomas's servant Launce reports to his master's father Sir Wilding Frollick his son's wildness abroad, thereby greatly delighting Sir Wilding, who has encouraged Thomas in all his debauchery. Thomas, however, on meeting his father, professes to have reformed, thus angering Sir Wilding immeasurably. Thomas persuades his sister Dorothy now to plead his conversion to Cellide. Dorothy gives Cellide a letter from Thomas at his request, but it shows signs of anything but reformation.

Franck, Thomas's friend, falls ill. Three physicians treat him, but Thomas drives them away at Franck's desire. Cellide and Sabina then visit Franck. Thomas, Valentine, and Hylas eavesdrop. At the proper moment Thomas enters as insane with remorse for his evil life. Cellide is relenting towards Thomas, when Launce enters and blurts out that he has arranged a merry evening for his master as he had been ordered. Undeceived and angry, Cellide leaves Thomas. In the meantime, with the intention of securing another heir than Thomas, Sir Wilding prepares to marry a prostitute he had met with, but, at Dorothy's entreaty, he postpones this deed until he may give Thomas one more trial as to his conversion. He accordingly sends a servant to report upon Thomas's whereabouts.

The servant returns to Sir Wilding with the news that Thomas is making merry at Valentine's house. Launce then tells of Thomas's pranks on the preceding night. These stories overjoy Sir Wilding, but he is again cast down by the appearance of his son who delivers a sermon to him. Sir Wilding gives Thomas two hundred pounds (which he immediately takes back), and bids him shift for himself. Alarmed at the prospect of being disinherited, Thomas gives his father some hints of his unregeneration, and is taken back into favor, while Sir Wilding renounces his scheme of marriage. With his friends and a fiddler, Thomas now serenades Cellide. She encourages Thomas to mount a rope-ladder, and then, while he is ascending, throws a scuttle upon his head. As he climbs again, Lucilla, Cellide's maid, frightens him with a deviF's vizard so that he falls from the ladder. He promptly cries out that his leg is broken. In great alarm Cellide comes out of the house to care for him. Thomas seizes her, intending to take her to his lodgings, but by a stratagem she escapes indoors.

Cellide's father, Sir Peregreen, comes to London to prevent a match between his daughter and Thomas. Thomas, who has entered Valentine's house where Cellide is staying, is hidden in a clothespress in order to avoid Sir Peregreen, by Cellide's maid Lucilla whom he has corrupted. Being introduced to Hylas, Sir Peregreen is attracted by him and considers giving Cellide to him as a wife. In order to punish Thomas for his treatment of her, Cellide, knowing that he can hear her, pretends to encourage the match with Hylas. Launce, who is caught prowling about the house, is brought before Sir Peregreen. Thomas then appears from the press and claims that he had been shut in it by Cellide's contrivance. In his anger, Sir Peregreen resolves to dis-

inherit Cellide. To prevent this, Cellide invites Thomas to her room, having previously arranged that Sir Wilding be placed where he can hear them. She hides Sir Peregreen in disguise nearby. Thomas and Launce are now seized by the servants and bound. The two fathers discover themselves. Assisted by Lucilla, Cellide mocks Thomas and beats him. Launce, however, loosens his bonds, and releases Thomas. They then set upon Cellide and Lucilla, intending to ravish them. The women are rescued in the nick of time, and depart in great anger, whereupon Thomas rejoices at the idea of being no longer in danger of marriage, while Sir Peregreen vows revenge upon him.

Squire Oldsapp: or, the Night-Adventurers," seems to have been first acted in 1678,[68] probably in the early part of the year. It was printed in 1679 with this titlepage:

"Squire Oldsapp; Or, The Night-Adventurers, A COMEDY: As it is Acted at His *Royal Highness* The DUKE'S Theatre. *Incidit in Scyllam qui vult vitare Charybdin,* Juven. Written by THO. DURFEY Gent. Licensed *June* 28, 1678. ROGER L'ESTRANGE. LONDON: Printed for *James Magnes* and *Richard Bentley* in *Russel-street* in *Covent-Garden,* near the Piazza. 1679."

Genest's verdict upon *Squire Oldsapp* is that it "is on the whole a good comedy... there is so much stage business in the 3d and 4th acts of this play, that it must appear to more advantage in representation than perusal."[69] With this judgment the modern reader can agree, but with certain reservations. While the somewhat farcical plot is intricate and well-managed for the most part, yet the end of the play, as often is the case with D'Urfey's dramas, is flat and feeble. Too, the conclusion seems due rather to the arbitrariness of the author than to any natural process of readjustment of relationships by the characters.

"So the titlepage, but the running title through the play is *The Night-Adventures.* "Genest, *Stage,* I, 240. "*Ibid.'*

As the *Biographia Dramatica*[70] says, D'Urfey was "greatly obliged to

several novels and dramas" for the plot and characters of the play. The conjurations of Oldsapp in the hope of his rejuvenation[71] and Pimpo as a devil tying him to a tree with Welford's subsequent meeting with Tricklove in I, 2, are, as the *Biographia* states, from the *Histoire Comique de Francion,* Tome I. There, in the hope of renewing his youth, Valentin performs incantations. Francion comes upon him and ties him to a tree,.being mistaken the while for a devil by Valentin. Francion then goes to meet Laurette, the bride of Valentin. Tricklove's device of the bell with the attached string hanging from the balcony for Henry to announce his arrival by, and Oldsapp's discovery of it, together with Pimpo's substitution of himself for Henry and Oldsapp's discomfiture threat (IV, 3), are, as the *Biographia* states, from Boccaccio, the *Decameron,* Day VII, Novel 8. Iolante's substitution of Calypso for herself in Massinger's *Guardian,* III, 6, ought also to be compared, as well as *Women Pleased,* III, 4.[72] The *Biographia* points out another borrowing from Boccaccio (the *Decameron,* Day VII, Novel 7) in the same scene (IV, 3) of Squire *Oldsapp.* This occurs where Tricklove sends Oldsapp, dressed in her clothes, to be beaten by Welford who pretends to spurn the advances of the supposed woman. A similar incident is found in Ravenscroft's *London Cuckolds* (V).

Certain points have not been noticed in the *Biographia.* Sir Frederick Banter's telling Pimpo of the whale that came from the moon suggests *The Fair Maid of the Inn,* IV, 2.[73] Sir Frederick further indulges in banter in IV, 2. D'Urfey again gives us an example of bantering in *The Richmond Heiress,* III, 2, between Cunnington and Sir Quibble. Sir Frederick's gibberish, I, 1 (p. 5), V, 3 (p. 59),brings to mind the soldiers in *All's Well that Ends Well,* IV, 1. Like passages occur in *Love for Money,* II, 1 (p. 14), and *Don Quixote, Part II,* III, 2 (p. 31). Christina's supplying her own place in bed with a Moor (V, 2) is certainly based upon Mary's like trick upon Monsieur Thomas, *Monsieur Thomas,* V, 2.[7i] It will be remembered that this amusing scene was not utilized by D'Urfey in his *Trick for Trick.* TM III, 297.

71 For the belief of old men in their rejuvenation, see Forsythe, *The Relations of Shirley's Plays to the Elizabethan Drama,* pp. 122-23. 73 The *Biographia Dramatica* errs in giving a reference to *Women Pleased* in connection with Tricklove's device for having Oldsapp beaten. 73 For similar passages, see Forsythe, *The Relations of Shirley's Plays to the Elizabethan Drama,* pp. 362-63. 74 More or less similar cases of substitution of one woman for another at meetings with lovers are listed in Forsythe, *ibid,* pp. 330-31.

The characters and their performers are thus given:

"Drammatis Persona
Welford, a. wild debauch'd Town-Spark Mr. *Betterton.*
Henry, his Friend and Companion Mr. *Smith.*
Lovell, Friend to *Henry* Mr. *Crossby.*
Squire *Oldsapp,* a credulous, merry, old, Mr. *Nokes.* debauch'd Fool, very infirm, yet keeps a Miss for the credit on't. Sir *Fredrick Banter,* a Foolish Knight, whose Mr. *Leigh.* humour is to banter every body. Colonel *Buff,* a blunt old Souldier of the Mr. *Sandford.* last Age.
Pimpo, a sneaking Pimp, (Servant to Mr. *Underhill. Tricklove)* cunningly religious if not well rewarded, but else very vitious and mercinary. Madam *Tricklove,* Mistress to *Oldsapp,* de-Mrs. *Currer.* ceitful, mercinary, and cunning.
Christina, Wife to *Henry.* Mrs. *Price.*
Sophia, Neice to *Christina.* Mrs. *Barrer.*
Cornet, Woman to *Tricklove.* Mrs. *Norrice. Lucinda,* Woman to *Christina.* Mrs. *Seymour.* Constable, Watchmen, Chairmen, Masquers,
Servants, and Attendants."

The plot of *Squire Oldsapp* follows:
Squire Oldsapp, an old dotard whose mistress is Madam Tricklove, seeks by conjurations to renew his youth. He is tricked by Pimpo, his mistress's servant, who pretends that he has grown young. Pimpo in the guise of a devil ties Oldsapp to a tree.

While Oldsapp is out of the way,

Welford is entertained by Tricklove. Lovell releases Oldsapp and betrays to him the trick that has been played. Henry who has lately been married to Christina, brings her to town and attempts to keep her hidden from Welford, of whom he is a trifle jealous. In the meantime, Colonel Buff and Sir Frederick Banter nearly surprise Welford with Tricklove. Welford escapes, and is attacked in the street by the indignant Oldsapp. He is rescued by Henry and Lovell, the former of whom enters in a sedan. Seeing the sedan vacant, Welford pops into it. The chairmen, thinking him to be Henry, bear him away. Henry returns and is mistaken for Welford by Tricklove who has come out to separate Welford and Oldsapp.

Welford is carried in the sedan to Henry's house, where he meets Christina. She persuades him to leave before her husband returns, promising him a meeting the next night. Oldsapp prevails on Lovell to go to Tricklove in the dark and woo her as Welford, learn thereby her feelings toward Welford, and then return and report to him. Missing Lovell in the dark, Oldsapp meets Welford as he returns from Henry's. Oldsapp mistakes Welford for Lovell and sends him to Tricklove. Oldsapp and Welford surprise Henry with Tricklove. In the dark Oldsapp takes Henry for Welford as Lovell and then loses him. Blundering about in the darkened house, Henry collides with Welford and the two are equally frightened. Tricklove enters and leads Henry away to the garden where Lovell meeting him mistakes him for Oldsapp, who had not met Lovell earlier. Lovell and Henry quarrel. On the entrance of Oldsapp and his servants they, together with Welford, escape in the confusion.

Christina is visited the next night by Welford whom she passes off on her niece Sophia as a cousin. Sophia quizzes him and discovers him to be an impostor. On Henry's return home, Welford leaves. Christina's suspicions are aroused by Henry, and so, on his announcing that he will be out late that night, she sets her maid Lucinda to spy

on him. In the meantime, Oldsapp has engaged the Constable and watch to guard Tricklove's house. Henry escorts Tricklove home, but does not go in. Thinking he has entered, Lucinda knocks at the door. The Constable arrests her and Oldsapp also. Tricklove comes out and accuses Oldsapp of an intrigue with Lucinda. The Constable finally frees both of them and leaves. Henry returns and awaits a signal from Tricklove. Welford enters and collides with Henry in the dark. After scuffling a moment, they both leave. Tricklove has arranged a. bell with a string tied to it whereby Henry can announce his arrival. Welford finds the string and pulls it, but, since Oldsapp has discovered the device, he is warned away by Tricklove, who mistakes him for Henry. When Henry does appear, Oldsapp plays the part of Tricklove and admits him, thereby capturing him. Pimpo rescues Henry by substituting himself for him in Oldsapp's momentary absence. Tricklove tells Oldsapp of an appointment of hers in the garden with Welford and sends him there to meet Welford. She tells Welford of it and despatches him to beat Oldsapp under the pretense that he thinks the old man her. In the meantime, she and Henry make merry. Welford meets Oldsapp and carries out his and Tricklove's plot.

i

Welford goes to an assignation with Christina, and is introduced into her bed-chamber. He discovers that the bed is occupied by an old Moor who had been placed there by Christina to make him ridiculous. Welford then enters the room where Christina is and attempts to ravish her. Henry comes in. As he and Welford are about to quarrel, Sophia announces that Welford is to marry her. On learning that she has six thousand pounds, Welford agrees to pose as her betrothed, and thus the quarrel is adjusted. Henry visits Tricklove again and is found there by Welford who, hitherto, has not known his rival. As they are speaking of their adventures of the night before, Oldsapp enters and overhears them, but they, observing him, pretend to speak of some one else and his state of ignorance continues. Then Christina and Sophia enter, and upbraid Henry and his companion. Pimpo now appears and exposes Sir Frederick Banter, Colonel Buff, and Lovell whom he has promised to introduce to Tricklove, but whom instead he has frightened and concealed. Oldsapp then iterates his faith in Tricklove's constancy, and so the play ends.

The Virtuous Wife; or, Good Luck at Last, was probably first acted in 1680. 75 The comedy was printed in that year with this titlepage:

The VIRTUOUS WIFE;76.or, Good Luck at last, A COMEDY. As it is Acted at the Dukes Theatre, By His ROYAL HIGHNESS His Servants, Written By THOMAS DUR-FEY, Gent. In the SAVOY: Printed by *T. N.* for *R. Bentley,* and *M. Magnes,* in Russel-Street, near the *Piazza,* at the *Posthouse. Anno Dom.* 1680."

As sources for *The Virtuous Wife* Marston's *Fawn* and Dryden's *Marriage a la Mode* have been mentioned. 77 The only possible borrowing from the first-mentioned play is in II, 1 (p. 15). There Isabella on being begged for an interview by Beauford refuses him one but tells him of her visits in the morning to a chapel, which he takes as a hint for him to meet her there—and rightly. In *The Fawn,* IV, 1, Dulcimel pretends to reveal a plot of Tiberio against her and relates the means by which he expected to enter her chamber. He takes the hint and reaches her apartment in the way suggested to him by her story. Maria uses a like device toward Geraldine in 71 Genest, *Stage,* I, 286.
76 The running title in the book is *A Virtuous Wife.* 77 *Biographia Dramatica,* III, 385. *The Family of Love,* I, 2.
78 D'Urfey uses a similar incident again in *The Campaigners,* I, 1 (p. 5), in the Marquise's letter to Dorange. Shadwell uses the hint in a like manner in *The Amorous Bigot,* III, 1; and Mrs. Centlivre employs the same device in *The Busy Body,* III, 5. It should be noted, however, that this stratagem, as it occurs in *The Virtuous Wife,* may be based upon Doralice's telling Palamede of her design to pray for him, *Marriage a la Mode,* II, 1 (he follows up her hint in III,

2). Debts to Dryden's comedy are found in several other parts of *The Virtuous Wife.* In I, 1 (p. 5), Beverly quarrels with his wife Olivia, alleging that he is tired of her; and in II, 2, she swears revenge upon him for his inconstancy. These incidents seem based upon *Marriage a la Mode,* III, 1, where Rhodophil and Doralice quarrel and the latter vows she will procure herself another husband. The source for Beauford's constantly telling his love affairs to the husbands of the ladies concerned (I, 1, pp. 6-7; II, 1; V. p. 55 ff.) is perhaps Palamede's telling Rhodophil of his love for Doralice, wife of the latter, *Marriage a la Mode,* II, 1. His constantly spoiling his plans by injudicious talk is, in general, not unlike the similar misadventures of Sir Martin in *Sir Martin Mar-all.* However, Beauford's story of his intrigue with the Judge's wife and the manner in which the Judge learned of it would seem to come from Chaucer's *Reeve's Tale.* In this connection, also, a similar incident in *The Plain Dealer,* V, 2, should be kept in mind. There Manly not knowing Vernish to be really Olivia's husband tells him of an intrigue with her. The various blunders of Beauford in this sort have been utilized by D'Urfey in later plays, as in *Love for Money,* III, 2 (p. 31), where Le Prat tells Amorous of his assignation with the latter's mistress, Jiltall; and in *The Campaigners,* IV, 1 (pp. 41-2), where Dorange tells Bertran of an engagement with the Marquise de Bertran, but does not betray her identity.

In II, 2 (p. 23), Olivia catches her husband Beverly in the company of Jenny Wheadle in the same way as Rhodophil surprisesDoralice, his wife, with Palamede in *Marriage a la Mode,* III, 2. When she is challenged to a duel in IV, 3 (p. 47), Olivia, who is masquerading as a man, says, "My name's Dangerfeild." In *Marriage a la Mode,* V, 1, Palamede says to Rhodophil when the latter challenges him, "I shall answer you by the way of Dangerfield." Beauford's intrigue with Olivia, and the pursuit of Jenny Wheadle by Beverly, Olivia's husband, is, perhaps, indeed only a variation 78 See Forsythe, *The*

Relations of Shirley's Plays to the Elizabethan Drama, pp. 89,. 250, for further analogues.
upon the situation in *Marriage a la Mode* (see II, 1, of that play) where Rhodophil loves Melantha whom Palamede is to marry although he himself is enamored of Rhodophil's wife Doralice.

It has not been noticed by writers on this play that I (p. 11) owes to *The Comedy of Errors.* The confusing of Beauford and Beverly as Beauford by the Jeweller and his man, together with the Jeweller's assertion of his having delivered a ring to Beverly (which he had really given to the true Beauford), as related in II, 2 (p. *22),* seem based on the confusing of the two Antipholuses by Angelo, *The Comedy of Errors,* III, 2, IV, 1. Sir Lubberly Widgeon's reciting some lines to Lady Beardly as his Boy prompts him is an appearance of a familiar Elizabethan comic device used by Shakespeare in TheMerry Wives of Windsor, I, I.79 In *The Virtuous Wife,* III (p. 35), Beverly tells Beauford that Olivia's husband who is Beverly himself is out of Beauford's way. This with its subsequent ill-results for Beauford and Brainworm brings to mind Ford and Falstaff, *The Merry Wives of Windsor,* II, 2, III, 5, V, 1. The stripping of Beauford and Brainworm and their entrance in blankets and pretending to be Irishmen (IV, 1, p. 37) is drawn on again for Toby's attire, *A Fool's Preferment,* V, 1. The passage suggests an indebtedness to *The. Night Walker,* V, 1. Brainworm's innocent betrayal of his masquerading master, IV, is borrowed from Launce's similar blunder, *Trick for Trick,* III. Beauford's servant Brainworm derives his name from *Every Man in his Humor,* but the borrowing does not extend to the characterization. Sir Lubberly Widgeon recalls the foolish Widgeon of Brome's *Northern Lass,* while sir Frolick Whimsey brings to mind Sir Wilding Frollick in D'Urfey's own *Trick for Trick. The Virtuous Wife* is given the credit by the *Biographia Dramatica* of being "as entertaining a comedy as any its author wrote."80 It is indeed a lively and amusing farce, but full of improbabilities and incredible coincidences. The close of the play is better managed than is usual with D'Urfey. The action does not stop because of its having filled the time allowed for the presentation of the comedy, but because of the final disentanglement of the various threads of the plot. The play contains two songs which are worth noting. The"! first, *"Let Casar Live Long,"* I (pp. 8-9), is one of D'Urfey's best as regards swing and vigor of metre. This is perhaps the *Joy to*

"For other cases, see Forsythe, *The Relations of Shirley's Ploys to the Elizabethan Drama,* p. 345. M III, 385. *Great Casar* which, according to Addison,81 "gave the whigs such a blow as they were not able to recover that whole reign Charles II'sJ." The *Scotch Song* ("Yet Sawney will ne'ere be my Love agen") in III (pp. 30-31) was also celebrated in its day.82

A proof of the popularity of *The Virtuous Wife* lies in the fact that it was revived at the Haymarket, June 18, 1705, and repeated three times.83 According to Genest,84 Mrs. Cowley utilized Jenny Wheadle's return of Beverly's jewels to his wife Olivia who is disguised as a man and with whom Jenny has fallen in love (IV) in her *Bold Stroke for a Husband.* Whibley in *The Cambridge History of English Literature* says, "The well-de'served misfortunes of Beau Clincher and Old Smuggler owe something to the disaster which overtakes Beauford and Brainworm in *The Virtuous Wife.*" A careful comparison of *The Constant Couple* and D'Urfey's play, however, leads one to believe that, although a slight resemblance between the misadventures of the two pairs of characters exists, yet there is no actual borrowing on Farquhar's part.

The *dramatis persona* is thus given:
"Drammatis Personae80 *Beverly.* A wild extravagant Gentleman, Husband to *Olivia*
Beauford. A young wild unfortunate fellow, always engaging himself in *Intrigues,* but never prospering in any. J *Sir Frol. Whim.* A humorous old Knight, vext that now he is old, he can-

not follow the vices and debauchery off youth. J *Sir hub. Widg.* His Nephew and Ward,"!
an incorrigible Fool, suitor to my Lady *Beardly.* J
Brainworm. A clownish fellow servant to
Beauford
Amble. Servant to *Beverley.*
Crochett. A Singing-Master.
81 The *Guardian,* Number 67. 82 C. W. Previte-Orton, *The Cambridge History of English Literature,* VIII, 110. 83 Genest, *Stage,* II, 333. 84 *Ibid.*
"VIII, 199.
96 Incomplete. Isabella, wife of Sir Frolick Whimsey is omitted. Jenny Wheadle is; called Matilda in the play up to p. 3 and goes by that name again in IV, 3 (p. 46), and: V (p. 56). Probably D'Urfey renamed her. Genest suggests that, since Amble's part is a "very trifling" one, Underhill played Brainworm instead *(Stage,* I, 286).
Mr. *Harris.*
  Mr. *Smith.*
  Mr. *Jevan.*
  Mr. *Lee.*
  Mr. *Underhil.*
Mr. *Bowman.*
  Women.
Olivia. The Virtuous Wife, a witty high A spirited Woman, Wife to *Beverly.* J Mrs-*BarrerLa Beardly.* An amorous impertinent old
Woman one that has buried three Husbands, yet still very desirous to be courted.
Jenny Wheadle. A Town Tilt, kept bv),, ,, *Beverly.* Mrs-*Currer*
Mrs. *Nokes.*
Mrs. *Seymour. Lidia.* Sister to Beverly, in love with
Beauford.
Tissick. Woman to Lady *Beardly.* Mrs. *Norris.*
Goldsmith, Servants, and Attendants. Scene Cheslsey." The story of the play may be given as follows: Beverly, by passing himself off as Beauford, who has fled the country, wins Olivia, who had been destined to marry Beauford, but had seen him only once before his flight. After the marriage Beverly confesses the imposture. As a result, he and

Olivia fall out. Beverly then takes a mistress, Jenny Wheadle. Beauford returns and discovers from Sir Frolick Whimsey that he is supposed to be-married and resident in Chelsey. Peter, a jeweller's man, enters to Beauford with a ring, tells him of an order left by the spurious Beauford (Beverly), and gives him the ring. Brainworm, Beauford's servant, in the name of Amble, Beverly's servant, receives a-watch from the jeweller. A letter from Olivia now informs Beauford of Beverly's marriage to her under Beauford's name. She arranges an assignation with Beauford.

Beauford goes to the house of his aunt, Lady Beardly. There "he meets Isabella, to whom he makes love. She informs him of her visits to chapel in the morning. He takes the hint and resolves to-waylay her there. Beauford is to be supplied with money by Lady Beardly, but on learning of his design against Olivia she refuses it to him. Beauford attempts to borrow from Sir Frolick, but fails,.when Beauford tells him he intends to seduce Isabella, Sir Frolick's-wife. Beauford also reveals the assignation in the chapel to Sir Frolick. The knight challenges him, but Beauford flees to meet 'Olivia. Jenny Wheadle visits Beverly. Olivia surprises them together, and in spite of her husband's efforts at concealing his mistress discovers her and threatens her. Beverly protects Jenny. Olivia for revenge before him courts his servant Amble, whom Beverly then drives away. Olivia vows a further revenge.

Beauford meets Olivia at the place appointed. She proposes Beauford shall help her to reform Beverly by making him jealous through Beauford's making love to her. To this Beauford agrees. Beverly in disguise meets Beauford whom he overhears apostrophizing Olivia. Beverly pretends to bear a message from Olivia to Beauford. He tells Beauford that Beverly is out of the'way and that the coast is clear. Beverly then sets his trap for his wife's lover, with such success that both Beauford and his servant Brainworm are beaten and tossed in blankets. They are then stripped and turned out of the house.

Beauford and his servant meet Sir Frolick Whimsey, and in order to escape recognition pretend to be Irishmen. Isabella enters and recognizes them, just as Sir Frolick, whom they anger, orders their arrest. They secure Isabella's sympathy by a story of their having been robbed, and she lends them clothes. Then Sir Lubberly Widgeon surprises Isabella and Beauford in a compromising situation. By threats they secure his promise not to tell Sir Frolick. Sir Frolick now comes home and Beauford is passed off on him as Isabella's brother newly arrived from abroad. Brainworm entering does not see Sir Frolick and addresses the bogus brother by his real name. Beauford with his servant is then beaten out, while Isabella pleads ignorance of his identity. Beverly and Wheadle quarrel. Olivia in male dress enters and takes Wheadle's part, courts her, and by a promise of marriage wins her. Beverly offers to fight with Olivia, but Beauford appears and, on Olivia's revealing her identity to him, rescues her.

Olivia as a man persuades Wheadle to give her the key to the box of jewels Beverly has given his mistress, in order that they may be presented by Olivia to Beauford. As Beauford awaits the jewels, Beverly comes in disguised, and is confided in by Beauford concerning his designs on the jewels and on Olivia and Wheadle as well. Beauford gives Beverly the key to Wheadle's casket of jewels to keep for him when the key is brought to him by Wheadle. Olivia learns from Beauford what he has done with the key. In her anger she tells Beauford that she is really virtuous, and orders him to cease his addresses to her. Beauford and Brainworm are then arrested for a fraud on the jeweller's man. Beauford appeals to his aunt Lady Beardly who frees the two on her nephew's promise to live quietly in the future. Beverly drags Wheadle in, tells of his previous kindness to her and how she, in spite of it, has fallen in love with Olivia in disguise, and then casts her off. Olivia now reveals her identity. Beverly is so taken with his wife's wit that he is reconciled with her. Beauford in despair vows to

marry the most ugly woman he can find. -Lidia, Beverly's sister, is shown in a veil. He promises her marriage. She discloses herself, and in spite of Beverly's opposition the match is agreed to.

An underplot deals with Sir Frolick Whimsey's marrying his foolish nephew Sir Lubberly Widgeon to Lady Beardly, an old widow. They are married, but almost immediately start to quarrelling violently.

Sir Barnaby Whigg: or, No Wit like a Woman's, appeared in 1681,[87] as is evidenced by D'Urfey's allusion in the dedication to George Earl of Berkeley to the victory of the "St. Georges of Eighty-one" over the "old hissing Dragon of Forty-two." The titlepage runs as follows:

"Sir Barnaby Whigg: Or, *No Wit like a Woman's,* A COMEDY, As It is Acted by their Majesties Servants At The Theatre-Royal. Written by Thomas Durfey, *Gent, Quidquid agunt homines, votum, timor, Ira voluptas, Gaudia, discursis nostri farrago libelli est.* Juven. LONDON, Printed by *A. G.* and /. *P.* for *Joseph Hindmarsh,* at *the Black Bull* in *Cornhil.* 1681." *Sir Barnaby Whigg* is said to be based upon a novel of "Mons. S. Bremond called *The Double Cuckold."* The *Biographia Dramatica* also asserts that "part of the humor of Captain Porpuss" is from Marmion's *Fine Companion.* In regard to this last-named source, the only resemblance between Marmion's Captain Whibble and D'Urfey's Porpuss is to be found in III, 4, *A Fine Companion.* There Whibble blusters and uses many sea phrases. As a matter of fact, the likeness between the two sailors exists only in their calling. Davenant's three sea-captains in *News from Plymouth* might as well be given as sources.

Sir Barnaby Whigg was written distinctly as a party play, as [8] As Genest says, "In the 4th act Sir Barnaby Whig is called Rabbi Achitophel—the play therefore could not have come out till about December" *(Stage,* I, 300). Dryden's poem had appeared in November.[88] *Biographia Dramatica,* III, 274. *The Double Cuckold* was a novel published by D'Urfey's booksellers, R. Bentley

and M. Magnes, and is given in their list of new novels prefixed to *The Virtuous Wife.* the prologue with its references to Catholic and Protestant "plots'" evidences and as the play itself testifies in no uncertain manner. To this fact doubtless it owes such success as it had. D'Urfey says in his dedication, that the play had the honor of pleasing one party, jalthough the Whigs made an effort to cry it down. To the political rancor of the time we owe the *Song* in III, 2 (p. 28), which is directed against the Whig poet Shadwell.[89] It is worth quoting:

"SONG

L_ Farewell my Lov'd Science, my former delight,
    Moliere is quite rifled, then how should I write?
My fancy's grown sleepy, my quibling is done;
And design or invention, alas! I have none
But still let the Town never doubt my condition;
Though I fall a damn'd Poet, I'll mount a Musician.
II
    I got Fame by filching from Poems and Plays,
    But my Fidling and Drinking has lost me the Bays;
    Like a Fury I rail'd, like a Satyr I writ,
    Thersites my humor, and Fleckno my Wit.
    But to make some amends for my snarling and lashing,
    I divert all the Town with my Thrumming and Thrashing."

An interesting paraphrase of a well-known passage in *Julius Casar* (I, 2, 1. 192 ff.) occurs in *Sir Barnaby Whigg,* I, 1 (p. 11). There Sir Barnaby says,

"Ha—what the loud Tray tor to a man of my kidney? a Portly, Jolly, Fat man; a man of Faith and Belly: Away fool, 'tis you lean, you scraggy fellows that Plot mischief; if the Pope himself had been a fat fellow, he had been honest. " Caesar's speech concerning Cassius is immediately suggested: "Let me have men about me that are fat, Sleek-headed men and such as sleep o' nights. Yond Cassius has a lean and hungry look, He thinks too much; such men are dangerous.

Would he were fatter!" In IV, 1 (p. 38), Winnifrid borrows from an exclamation of Evadne, w By 1692, after D'Urfey had become a much more moderate Tory, his opinion of Shadwell had so changed that he it was who supplied the prologue to the laureate's posthumous *Volunteers. The Maid's Tragedy*, II, 1, in her "Oh heavens! what Ravish hur— at these years?"90 The same character later uses a line found in *Romeo and Juliet*, III, 2, and in *Henry IV, Part I*, II, 4, in her "Is there no Honours nor Faith in men?" (p. 39).91 D'Urfey again employs similar speeches in V, 2 (p. 56), of the present play (Gratiana says, ".There is no faith in man; none, none, I swear"); in *The Injured Princess*, II, 2 (p. 16), where Eugenia exclaims, "Then is there nothing in Mankind but Vice? No Faith, No Honour"; and in *The Marriage Hater Match'd*, III, 3 (Phœbe says, "Is there no truth nor no honour in the Sex?"). In *The Richmond Heiress*, V, 5, (p. 64), occur the lines, "The Race of Men are all Deceivers." Gratiana's description of Wilding which she gives him in IV, 2 (pp. 45-46), are reminiscent of the similar Elizabethan passages of abuse, such as may be found in Shirley's *Hyde Park*, III, 2.02 Sir Walter's diverting his wife's attention from his courtship of Livia by setting Townly to pay his addresses to her is used by Burnaby in his comedy, *The Modish Husband.* Livia's device for securing Townly's escape, III, may have been borrowed from *Sir Patient Fancy.* D'Urfey uses it again in *The Intrigues at Versailles.* The new actress spoken of in the heading to the epilogue was the celebrated Mrs. Verbruggen, then Mrs. Percival, who during her stage career of nearly twenty-five years was very highly esteemed as a performer of low comic parts.93 Winnifrid, the "Welsh Jilt," whose part Mrs. Percival played, is a member of a group of Welsh prostitutes who make their first appearance in Middleton's plays, as in *A Chaste Maid in Cheapside.* The second title of *Sir Barnaby Whigg*, it may be noted here, *No Wit like a Wo-*

man's, is very close to that of Middleton's *No Wit, No Help like a Woman's.* In fact, it is conceded that the last-mentioned play was performed at Dublin as *No Wit to a Woman's.*9 Genest refers to *Sir Barnaby Whigg* as "a pretty good comedy... the merit of it consists chiefly in the characters of Townley and Livia. "95 It is a farce with a rather clever plot, but the action, as is frequently the case in D'Urfey's plays, is hampered by the characters who have nothing to do with the main plot, but merely reveal in dialogue their own folly. The end of the play is unsatisfactory: the action does not come to an end, but simply stops.
80 See Forsythe, *The Relations of Shirley's Plays to the Elizabethan Drama*, p. 413. 81 *Ibid*, pp. 368-69. See also Genest, *Stage*, I, 337. 82 *Ibid*, p. 354, and pp. 80-82. 03 Genest, *Stage*, II, 277-80.
M Bullen's Middleton's *Works,* I, xl. 85 *Stage,* I, 300.

The characters and actors follow:
"Dramatis Personam
Wilding.—*A Loyal and Witty Gentleman) ortly addicted to rail against Women.)* Townly.—*A Modish inconstant young fel- low, in Love with, and beloved by all Women, and courts all alike J*
Sir Wal. Wiseacre.—*An Opinionated Foot)*
and Cuckold: A Lancashire *Knight, and . in Love with* Livia. J
Capt. Porpuss.—*A blunt Tarpawlin, Captain*
and one that uses his Sea-phrases and terms upon all occasions.
Sir Barn Whigg.—*A Phanatical Rascal, one*
of Oliver's *Knights; one that always pretends to fear a change of Government yet does his best to cause one*
Benedick.—*An Intriguer, and Friend to* Wilding.
Swift.—*Servant to* Wilding.
WOMEN
Gratiana.—*Witty and proud, and one that*
values her self by railing against men.)
Livia.—*Wife to* Porpuss, *cunning and wan-*
ton, and in love with Townly

Millicent.—*Wife to* Sir Walter, *in Love also*
with Townley. £
Winnifrid.—*A young* Welsh *Jilt.*

Waiters, Men and Women, Musicians,
Officers and Attendants.
SCENE LONDON."
The plot of *Sir Barnaby Whigg* runs as follows:
Sir Walter Wiseacre sets Townly to courting Sir Walter's wife Millicent so as to direct her attention from her husband's pursuit of Livia. Millicent recommends to Townley to court Livia who, she says, loves him. Millicent's purpose is to make Townly a rival to Sir Walter.

Millicent gets Livia and Townly together and goes away to find Sir Walter in order to show him the two in company. Sir Walter surprises them, but Townly pacifies him by saying he was asking Livia to intercede for him with Millicent. Millicent over
Mr. Clark. Mr. Goodman.
Mr. Jermaine. Mr. Griffin. Mr. Powell.
Mr. Perin.
Mr. Cosh.
Mrs. Corbet. Mrs. Cook. Mrs. Moyle.
Mrs. Percival. hears Sir Walter urging Townly to push his suit with her and stating his own weariness of her. She then resolves to be revenged on Sir Walter.
Townly goes to meet Livia, but Sir Walter finds him in her closet. Captain Porpuss, Livia's husband, returns and discovers Sir Walter, but not Townly who has shut himself up in the closet. Sir Walter informs the Captain that he has caught Townly with Livia and has locked him in the closet. Livia holds the attention of the two men with a letter, while her maid goes to release Townly. By mistake Benedick who has wandered into the closet is let go, while Townly remains. The Captain and Sir Walter enter the room to find that Townly has escaped by leaping out the window.

Townly disguises himself as a woman and passes himself off on Porpuss as Livia's sister. By means of a false message Porpuss is gotten out of the way, but Sir Walter appears and overhears Townly and Livia rejoicing over the success of their trick. Porpuss returns and is told by Sir Walter of the latter's discovery. Porpuss laughs at Sir Walter's story, since he has not penetrated Townly's disguise. Porpuss then hustles Sir Walter off the stage.

Porpuss follows the disguised Townly to a tavern, where he changes to his own clothes, and then the Captain discovers the true identity of the supposed lady. He blurts out his discovery and betrays to Millicent who is in the tavern room that Townly's disguise has been assumed on Livia's account, not hers. Sir Walter enters and, finding Millicent with Townly, sets on him, seconded by Porpuss. Townly is saved, however, by a mock arrest for debt devised by Livia. Porpuss and Sir Walter pursue Townly and their wives to Gratiana's house, where the truth comes out, and every one is exposed. Sir Walter resolves to go back to Lancashire (having been made a "double cuckold—in wife and mistress" by Townly) and Porpuss decides to go to sea.

A subplot concerns the pursuit of Winnifrid, a Welsh girl, by Benedick and her final tricking of him, and the wooing of the witty and sharp-tongued Gratiana by Wilding. The villainy of Sir Barnaby Whigg who changes from Whig Dissenter to Catholic and then to Mahometan in hopes of bettering his fortunes is showed in the play.

As Genest points out,96 The Royalist was first presented before the return of the Duke of York from Scotland in 1682 (see the epi "Stage, I, 356.

logue). Whether this comedy preceded The Injured Princess, apparently produced first also in 1682 but at the Theatre Royal, the present writer cannot say. The Royalist was printed with the following titlepage:

"the ROYALIST, A COMEDY;-As it was Acted at

The Duke's Theatre. By Thomas Durfey, Gent. LONDON.

Printed for Jos. Hindmarsh at the Sign of the Black-Bull near the Royal-Exchange in Cornhill, Anno Dom. 1682. "

The comedy is dedicated in the preface to the "few that feelingly remember the fatal Scene of Boscabell." As might be expected from the title and the dedication, The Royalist is a violent attack upon the Whigs, their authors, and the supporters of the Exclusion Bill. These are struck at in the preface where the Earl of Shaftesbury and Oates are singled out for rough handling. It would seem from D'Urfey's own statements in his preface that the comedy was not received with particular favor. However, Genest says, "It was well received on the stage, as being expressly written against the republicans and whigs."97 The Biographia Dramatica (the statements of which should never be taken on faith) corroborates Genest.98 The fact is, probably, that the play was applauded by the extreme Tories and hissed by the Whigs. The tone of the preface certainly does not indicate any general success on the part of the drama.

Like Mrs. Behn's Roundheads (acted in 1682 at the Duke's Theatre)99 The Royalist is to some degree historical. 100 The action dates back to the summer of 1658 shortly before Cromwell's death. Alexander Brome, the Cavalier song-writer, is a figure in the action. It may be well to mention here that Brome is mentioned as "Sawney Broome" in A Fond Husband, I (p. 9); while in Sir Barnaby Whigg, I, 1 (p. 15), Captain Porpuss says, "We have not had a good bold well-season'd Song, as Gad save me, since Old Broom dy'd." Brome's chief part in The Royalist is to sing D'Urfey's songs. D'Urfey seems to have invited comparison of his own works with those of the popular lyricist. The plot of Captain Jonas and the disaffected tenants to charge Kinglove with having attempted to burn London (II), and the equally false charge of Phillipa's having committed a rape are doubtless satires upon the wild stories of preposterous con 87 Stage, I, 355. 08 III, 231.

"Summer's Behn's Works, I, 335. 100 Much less, however, than is The Roundheads. spiracies, and the accompanying volumes of false testimony

which were so frequent in the years following 1678. There is a possibility that Captain Jonas, the "seditious rascal" and informer, may be meant for Sir William Jones, the Attorney-General, "... bull-fac'd Jonas, who could statutes draw, To mean rebellion, and make treason law."101 This theory acquires weight, when the Captain's connection with false testimony is considered. A reference to Lord Howard's sacrilege, as celebrated in Absalom and Achitophel, Part I, 11. 575-76, may exist in the First Committeeman's speech, V, 1 (p. 59), "Nor you never gave 'em the Sacrament in Lambswool and Plumb-Cake to be secret did you?" In Dryden's poem, as above cited, are these lines: "And canting Nadab let oblivion damn, Who made new porridge for the paschal lamb." In Phillipa, who, as a boy, follows Kinglove with whom she is infatuated, we have a figure familiar in the drama from the days of Shakespeare and Fletcher. It should be noted that Eugenia in D'Urfey's Injured Princess, acted at about the same time as The Royalist, assumes a similar disguise. Kinglove as a name for an eminently loyal character is employed by D'Urfey later in his Campaigners, and Queenlove is found in The Old Mode and the New.

As early writers102 on the drama have pointed out, D'Urfey has borrowed in The Royalist from the Decameron. In III, 3, Sir Charles Kinglove asks Camilla to contrive for him as a proof of her love three things: that she pull out two of her husband's (Sir Oliver's) soundest teeth and present them to Sir Charles; that Sir Charles shall kiss and embrace her before her husband's eyes; that Sir Charles shall give her husband three fillips on the nose, Sir Oliver knowing it, yet bearing it patiently. We find in the Decameron, Day VII, Novel 9, the original of these demands. As a proof of Lydia's affection for him, Pyrrhus causes her to kill her husband's favorite hawk before his face; to send Pyrrhus a lock of her husband Nicostratus's beard; and finally to present her lover with one of her husband's soundest teeth. These things Lydia accom-

plishes by stratagem, the tooth-drawing being managed, as in D'Urfey, by the assistance of the servants who pretend that their master's breath is offensive. 103 The idea of the proofs and the tooth-drawing episode 101 *Absalom and Achitophel, Part I,* 11. 581-82.
102 *Biographia Dramatica,* III, 231.
103 For the carrying out of the stipulations, see IV, 1, V, 1, 2. D'Urfey's tootbdrawing episode differs from Boccaccio's in certain details, as does the pear-tree incident. The face-slapping is D'Urfey's variation upon the beard-pulling of Boccaccio. are from the same part of the story, but Boccaccio makes the peartree episode a final proof of the ladyrs love for Pyrrhus, whereas D'Urfey uses it as one of the three demands of Kinglove. Dash, a servant, first climbs the tree in *The Royalist* (V, 1), and not the lover as in the novel. Chaucer's *Merchant's Tale* furnishes an analogue.
J The title of the song in IV, 2 (pp. 49-50), is incorrectly given by the *Biographia DramaticaWi* (it is said there to have been stolen by D'Urfey from *The Shepherd's Oracle,* 1644).105 The refrain, which is used for a title as given in the play, is *Hey then up go We* and not *Hey Boys up go we,* as stated in the *Biographia. The New English Dictionary* quotes from W. Roger's *Voyages* an interesting criticism of this song: "Our Musick play'd, Hey Boys up go we! and all manner of noisy paltry Tunes."106 *The Royalist* is written in a mixture of verse and prose, the former being used for the more solemn passages, such as Sir Charles's various expressions of fidelity to the Royal cause. Genest107 points out in one of these (V) a fine example of what he properly enough calls "sad nonsense."
The characters and actors are thus listed:
Sir *Charles Kinglove,*
"Actors Names.108
The Royalist, one of the King's Colonels at *Worcester-Fight,* a
Lover of Monarchy and Pre-f Mr. *Smith.*
rogative
Heartall, His Friend, a Moderator, Mr.

Williams. Broom, His Lieutenant, Mr. *Bowman.*
Chairman to the Committee of)
-Sequestration, a busie Factious-Mr. *Lee.*
fellow J
A Justice of Peace, and Orator)
that takes Bribes on both sides) Mr. *Jevan.*
A Seditious Rascal that dis-"
_ turbs the People with News and I
'Lyes to Promote his own In-Mr. *Percival.*
terest
l« III, 231.
lm The song is printed in *Pills to Purge Melancholy,* II, 286 ft., as *The Whigs Exaltation, To an Old Tune of Forty One. 1»N. E. D.,* art. "Hey." *m Stage,* I, 356.
J in The Yale University Library copy of the play has not the names of the Commit'teemen, but includes "Dash, Clark to Oldcut."
Sir *Oliver Oldcut,*
Sir *Paul Eitherside,*
Captain Jonas,
Copyhold, fTwo of Sir Charles's Tenants,"! Mr. *Underbill.*
Slouch,-afterwards made Evidences & against him J Mr. *Bright.*
Sir *John Zounds,* Sir *Peter Codshead,* Alderman *Thrum* Committee Men.
Captain, Soldiers, Tenants and Servants,
Men and Women.
Camilla, (Wife to *Oldcut,* Vertuous, and)
(secretly Loyal *)* Mrs. *Betterton. Aurelia,* Her Niece, Mrs. *Twyford.* fA young-Lady that follows *KingA Phillipa,* love in Mens Clothes through all Mrs. *Petty.* his troubles J *Crape,* Woman to *Camilla,*
Footmen and Attendants. Scenes, Boscabell and London." The story of the play may thus be given:
Disguised as a boy, Phillipa saves the life of her lover Sir Charles Kinglove whom she follows to the battle of Worcester. Sir Charles then takes her under his protection. He has had nothing to do with her under her own guise, as she is the daughter of a Puritan and Sir Charles is a rabid Royalist. Sir

Charles's estate is sequestered and his property seized by Sir Oliver Oldcut, a Puritan official. Sir Charles resists arrest, but is captured and imprisoned, together with the disguised Phillipa. He is visited by Camilla, wife to Sir Oliver but a secret loyalist. Upon learning her identity, Sir Charles courts her for revenge, but is interrupted by Sir Oliver's approach. Sir Oliver locks the door to Phillipa's room, so that she must stay with Sir Charles (who suspects neither her sex nor her identity) and share his bed, which she does without exciting any suspicion on his part.
Captain Jonas, an informer and spy, the next morning tries to get Sir Charles to assassinate Sir Oliver, so that Jonas may secure Sir Oliver's places, but Sir Charles refuses and chases him away. Camilla obtains Sir Charles's liberty from her husband, on condition that Sir Charles's assistance shall be forthcoming when she requires it. He is given an assignation by Camilla; they agree that Camilla shall help Sir Charles to his revenge upon Sir Oliver. Camilla's assistance is to prove to Sir Charles that she loves him. She is required by Sir Charles to pull out two of Sir Oliver's teeth and send them to Sir Charles; to kiss and embrace Sir Charles before her husband's face; and to arrange that Sir Charles may fillip Sir Oliver three times on the nose. Sir Charles is now forced to flee, for Jonas for revenge upon Sir Charles has concocted with two of the knight's former tenants a plot against him. They allege that Sir Charles had attempted to fire London. It is announced that Phillipa has been arrested for rape and been taken before a justice.
Upon going before the justice, Phillipa denies that she has committed a rape, but is given no hearing and is bound over on perjured testimony furnished by Jonas and his tools. Camilla now begins to carry out the terms of her engagement with Sir Charles. Aided by her servants she convinces Sir Oliver that he needs dental attention, on account of his bad breath. The Surgeon pulls two sound teeth, the fact is discovered, and he is driven out. Sir Charles and Phillipa, still in disguise, must sleep together again at

Sir Oliver's. Sir Charles discovers that she is a woman, learns her identity, and, touched with her affection and fidelity, vows his love to her.

Phillipa must maintain her disguise a little longer to allow Sir Charles to expose Jonas's perjury. She subscribes twenty thousand pounds to the royal cause. Camilla appears with Sir Oliver. Dash, her servant, climbs a tree after pears. As Sir Oliver and Camilla talk, Dash shouts shame to them from the tree. He descends and claims that he has seen them in a delicate relationship. The hypothesis that the tree is enchanted is offered. Sir Oliver climbs the tree to verify this suspicion. When he is up in it, Sir Charles enters and fondles Camilla. Sir Oliver descends to find only Dash with Camilla, Sir Charles having fled.

Aurelia, niece to Camilla, has been seduced by Sir Charles's friend Heartall. Heartall marries her to Sir Paul Eitherside, at present a Puritan justice. She refuses to share her apartment with Sir Paul the night of their marriage. He slips to her room and sees Heartwell there. Sir Paul steals Heartwell's breeches as a proof of his wife's infidelity. Camilla takes Sir Charles to Sir Oliver in order to carry out the third clause of her agreement. Sir Charles strikes Sir Oliver thrice. Sir Oliver who has now become suspicious takes off his belt and binds Sir Charles and Camilla together as they embrace before Sir Charles leaves. Sir Paul enters with Heartwell's breeches on a staff. It is shown that Aurelia is not an heiress, as Sir Paul had thought, but is in debt to her uncle Sir Oliver. Sir Charles is rearrested, but is freed on orders from Cromwell himself, who recognizes his worth and returns his sequestered estate. Sir Charles then announces Phillipa's true sex and his approaching marriage to her. Lieutenant Broom enters with the news of Cromwell's sickness, and reports a rumor that the "times will change."

Captain Jonas and his accomplices earjier have been exposed and punished for their plotting and perjury regarding Sir Charles.

The Injured Princess, 10 or the Fatal *Wager,* was first acted, it would seem, in 1682.110 It was published in the same year with the following titlepage: "The Injured Princess, Or The jfatal *XDD&Qet:* As it was Acted at the Theatre-Royal, By his Majesties Servants. By *Tho. Durfey,* Gent. Printer's device. LONDON: Printed for *R. Bentley* and *M. Magnes* in *Russel-street* in *CoventGarden,* near the *Piazza.* 1682."

This tragicomedy111 is based upon Shakespeare's *Cymbeline,* "being in fact a rewriting of that play. According to D'Urfey's epilogue, the comedy, as he calls it, had been written nine years before its presentation. If this were the case, some of its absurdities might be excused as having been the work of a twenty year old boy.

In the following table the dependence of the corresponding scenes in *The Injured Princess* and *Cymbeline* is shown: 1M So-called on the titlepage, but the running title in the book is *The Unequal Match; tor the Fatal Wager.*
""Genest, *Stage,* I, 331-34.
111 D'Urfey calls the play a comedy, but it is much nearer tragedy than is *Cymbeline.*
It will be seen that D'Urfey has re-arranged his material to a considerable degree and has failed at all to use some eight of Shakespeare's scenes except insofar as here and there he has borrowed a few phrases from the dialogue.

In the next table is shown the indebtedness verbally of one play to the other:

Thus it is shown by the above table that *The Injured Princess* utilizes 765 lines drawn from nineteen scenes of *Cymbeline.*

D'Urfey's alteration of Shakespeare's characters may be seen from the following:112 *The Injured Princess*
Cymbeline
Ursaces
  Pisanio
  Cloten
  Jacimo
  Silvio
  Shattillion
Beaupre 112 D'Urfey omits the Doctor from his *dramatis persona;* peare's Cornelius.

Cymbeline
Cymbeline Posthumus
(Second Lord
(Pisanio
  Cloten
  First Lord
  Second Lord
  Iacimo
  Philario he corresponds to Shakes*The Injured Princess Cymbeline*
  Don Michael
  Bellarius
  Palladour
  Arviragus
  Lucius
  Queen
  Eugenia
  Clarina
  Sophronia
  Aurelia
  A Frenchman
  Bellarius
  Arviragus
  Guiderius
  Lucius
  Queen
  Imogen
  Helen
The various changes of name and shifting about of parts as shown above are most of them absolutely unnecessary, except D'Urfey's purpose had been to make his play outwardly as much unlike *Cymbeline* as possible. One of the most important alterations affecting the characters is the making Pisanio a lord and confidant to Ursaces, and possessing a daughter Clarina, herself confidante to Eugenia. Again D'Urfey's Jachimo is apparently an Englishman who, like Shakespeare's Iachimo, is a villain, but unlike him an extremely crude one. The Guiderius of *Cymbeline* has, in *The Injured Princess,* the name of Arviragus while in place of the second prince we have, in D'Urfey, Palladour. The other changes of name do not involve any material alterations of character.

Certain of D'Urfey's revisions of the plot should be called here to the reader's notice. For example, D'Urfey in I, 1 (p. 3), makes the Queen an open enemy to Eugenia (cf. *Cymbeline,* I, 1). In I, 1 (p. 2), Ursaces goes to France instead of to Italy, as in *Cymbeline,* I, 1 (1. 96). Ursaces makes his wager upon his wife's virtue (I, 2, p. 8 ff.), with Shattillion, a Frenchman, before Beaupre, a Frenchman, corresponding to Philario, and Don Michael who takes the part in the scene that "A Frenchman" does *(Cymbeline,* I, 4). In *The Injured Princess,* II, 2 (p. 19), Pisanio is suspicious of the Queen's intentions in giving him the cordial, unlike the honest but credulous servant in *Cymbeline,* I, 5. In III, 3, D'Urfey introduces Eugenia in men's clothes; in *Cymbeline,* III, 3, Imogen disguises herself after the corresponding scene. Too, D'Urfey's Pisanio is at first convinced of Eugenia's infidelity to Ursaces and is not certain of her innocence even at the end of the scene. He is not an ardent partisan of her, as Shakespeare's Pisanio is of Imogen. "Cloten in Ursaces Cloaths" is brought in by D'Urfey in IV, 3, 4, but no use is made of the garments, as in *Cymbeiine,* IV, 2. When Eugenia arouses from her swoon, IV, 4, she does not seem even to see the body of Cloten. The last act of *The Injured Princess* is comparatively not close to the conclusion of *Cymbeline.* It is much shortened in D'Urfey's pla'y. There is no vision or prophecy. Shattillion, it should be noted, is slain by Ursaces, a more equitable method of disposing of him than Shakespeare employed.

The prologue to *The Injured Princess* is a result of a raid by. the author upon his own works, as it had served some four years before as epilogue to *The Fool Turn'd Critick.* An interesting bit of carelessness on the part of the printer or proof-reader occurs in a stage-direction, II 1. It runs, *'Enter behind* Cymbeline, Queen, *a Purse,* Pisanio, Doctor *and* Guards, *a Viol,* Mrs. Holten, Sue. " These last two-mentioned were probably the actresses who performed the *roles* of Aurelia and Sophronia. Genest113 suggests that "Mrs. Holten" was Mrs. Holden, a veteran actress of the day. A ludicrous error by the printer occurs in IV, 2 (p. 36). In *Cymbeline,* III, 6, occur the following lines: *"Bel.* Stay; come not in But that it eats our victuals, I should think Here were a fairy."

D'Urfey in *The Injured Princess,* IV, 2 (p. 36), has *"Bellar.* Stand back a little: But that he eats our Victuals, I shou'd think He were a Fury," "Fury" being an obvious misprint for "fairy." A similar blunder occurs in *A Commonwealth of Women,* IV, 2 (p. 38), where we have, "Sure they are furies." In *The Sea Voyage,* III, 1 (first folio edition), the line runs, "Sure they are Fairies." One incident introduced by D'Urfey, the blinding of Pisanio by Cloten on the stage, seems to be derived from the putting out of Gloucester's eyes, *King Lear,* III, 7. Genest quotes114 a passage from a misogynistic soliloquy V, 1 (p. 45), by Ursaces, which for the sake of the anachronism116 may well be given here:

"The full fed City-Dame would sin in fear;
The Divine's Daughter slight the amorous Cringe
Of her tall Lover; the close salacious Puritan
Forget th' Appointment with her canting Brother."
"'Stage, I, 336.
»1 *Ibid,* I, 333.
115 *Ibid,* I, 334, for as delightful an anachronism.

The Injured Princess is, as Genest aptly says,116 "a vile alteration" of *Cymbeline.* Many of D'Urfey's changes are for the worse decidedly, with the exception of his rewriting of the last act. As V stands in *Cymbeline* it is extremely long and cumbersome. These defects at least D'Urfey has avoided, although unfortunately he has replaced Shakespeare's verse with his own which at best is better than mediocre. In spite of its great inferiority to the Shakespearian play, *The Injured Princess* was revived at times for nearly sixty years. Genest records a performance of the play at Lincoln's Inn Fields, January 7, 1720,117 and at Covent Garden, March 20, 1738. On the latter occasion the drama was produced as *"Cymbeline,* written by Shakespeare, and revised (by D'Urfey) with alterations."118 As an example of D'Urfey's alteration of the lines of *Cymbeline* the following passages may be compared: *"Eugen.*

My Life indeed—But Good old Sir,
Tell me (for there's a Theam of Truth log'd in that Face)
What was the last kind word he spoke of me?
Pisan. His Queen, his Wife, and then remov'd from shore.
Just as I left him,
I saw him clasp his hands, and kiss your Ring.
Eugen. Senseless Jewel, happier far than I!
But could'st thou leave him so?—had I been there,
I would ha' broke my Eye-strings, crack'd 'um,
And look'd after him till the diminution of space
Had pointed him, sharp as my Needle;
And when the envious distance barr'd my sight
Of that bless'd Object, turn'd my eyes and wept."
The Injured Princess, I, 1 (p. 5). "Imo
What was the last
That he spake to thee?
Pis. It was his queen, his queen! *Imo.*
Then wav'd his handkerchief? *Pis.* And kiss'd it, madam. *Imo.* Senseless linen! happier therein than I!
And that was all?
Pis. No, madam; for so long
As he could make me with this eye or ear
'"*Ibid,* I, 333.
»7 *Ibid,* III, 35.
Ibid, 557..;
Distinguish him from others, he did keep
The deck, with glove, or hat, or handkerchief,
Still waving, as the fits and stirs of's mind
Could best express how slow his soul sail'd on,
How swift his ship.
Into. Thou shouldst have made him
As little as a crow, or less, ere left
To after-eye him.
Pis. Madam, so I did.
Into. I would have broke mine eye-strings;
crack'd them, but
To look upon him, till the diminution
Of space had pointed him sharp as my

needle;
Nay, follow'd him, till he had melted from
The smallness of a gnat to air, and then
Have turn'd mine eye and wept...."
Cymbeline, I, 3, 11. 4-22.
The *dramatis persona* of the play unfortunately does not include the actors' names. It follows, as printed:

"Dramatis, 110 SCENE Lwcfo-Town, alias *London.*
Cymbeline, King of *Britain.*
Ursaces, A noble Gentleman married to the Princess
Eugenia.
Pisanio, Confident and Friend to *Ursaces.*
Cloten, A Fool, Son to the Queen by a former Husband.
Jachimo, A roaring drunken Lord, his Companion.
Silvio, Another Companion.
Shattillion, An opinionated *Frenchman.*
Beaupre, Don Michael, His F"ends.
Bellarius, An old Courtier, banish'd by *Cymbeline. Palladour,* 1 Two young Princes, Sons to *Cymbeline,* bred
Arviragus,) up by *Bellarius* in a Cave as his own.
Lucius, General to *Augustus Casar.* 118
The above list is imperfect as wanting the Doctor's name. *Women The Queen, Eugenia, Clarina,*
The Princess. Her Confident.
Sophronia, ? Women, one to the Queen, the other to the
Aurelia,) Princess."
The plot of *The Injured Princess* may be sumarized as follows: The Princess Eugenia, daughter to Cymbeline King of Britain, is privately married to Ursaces, a mere gentleman. Enraged at the *mesalliance,* Cymbeline banishes Ursaces, and is urged into greater anger by his Queen whose foolish son (by an earlier marriage) Cloten has been designed as a husband for Eugenia. As she hates Pisanio, Ursaces's friend, the Queen resolves to poison him and bargains with a doctor for the proper drugs. Arriving in France at his friend Beaupre's, Ursaces falls into an argument with Shattillion, a Frenchman, concerning Eugenia's virtue. Shattillion wagers ten thousand ducats against Ursaces's diamond

that he can seduce "Eugenia. With letters of introduction from Ursaces, Shattillion accordingly sails for England.

The Queen-obtains from the doctor what she supposes is a poison but which really is only a sleeping potion, since the physician suspects her of murderous intentions and desires to prevent any crime on her part. Shattillion appears in Britain with Ursaces's letter and is welcomed by Eugenia. Shattillion pretends that Ursaces has been disloyal to Eugenia, and attempts to move her to his will. She withstands him, whereupon he makes his peace with her by pretending to have been testing her fidelity to Ursaces. Then he obtains permission from her to leave a chest of plate overnight with her for safekeeping. The Queen gives the medicine which she has had from the doctor to Pisanio, recommending it to him as a sovereign cordial. Pisanio takes the drug, but is suspicious of the Queen's sudden kindness to him. In the meantime, Shattillion has been conveyed in the chest or trunk into Eugenia's apartment. After she is asleep he comes out and notes the decorations of the room, certain marks on Eugenia's body, and finally steals a bracelet given her by Ursaces. Then he returns into the trunk and is carried out in it in the morning. Eugenia is awakened by a serenade by Cloten. On appearing, she receives from him a proposal of marriage which she scorns, saying she values Ursaces's meanest garment more than she does him. This contempt angers Cloten so that he sets off to tell Cymbeline of his reception.

Shattillion returns to France where by producing the stolen bracelet he convinces Ursaces of Eugenia's infidelity, and is paid the wager. Ursaces writes his friend Pisanio, asking him to put Eugenia to death as a punishment for her apparent disloyalty. In men's clothing Eugenia leaves the court and starts to France to join her husband. Pisanio accompanies her, intending to kill her in pursuance of Ursaces's wish. Pisanio gives Eugenia Ursaces's letter to read, and then prepares to slay her. She offers herself to the sword. Her actions and words weaken Pisanio's purpose. He

therefore resolves to leave her in the wilderness and send Ursaces a bloody cloth, as directed by him, to evidence Eugenia's death. Pisanio, however, is not wholly convinced of her innocence. He gives her the supposed cordial received by him from the Queen as he leaves.

Eugenia's flight is discovered at court and causes great anger in Cymbeline and the Queen, who punish Clarina for her complicity in it by giving her to Cloten and Jachimo to use as they will. News of the landing of a Roman army under Caius Lucius brings new matters before them. In the meantime, Eugenia has wandered in the wilderness to a cave inhabited by Bellarius with his supposed sons Palladour and Arviragus. In their absence, Eugenia helps herself to food, is surprised by them and befriended by the woodsmen who accept her as Fidele, a boy. Pisanio has returned to court in time to rescue his daughter Clarina from Cloten and Jachimo who were about to ravish her. Pisanio kills Jachimo, but is wounded by him, a fact taken advantage of by Cloten who puts out Pisanio's eyes as he lies nearly helpless. Cloten then goes in search of Clarina who has fled. He loses her and wanders to the cave of Bellarius where he meets Arviragus. They quarrel and Arviragus kills Cloten. Cloten's head is thrown into the sea, in order to prevent the slain man's identity being discovered. Palladour now finds that Eugenia who had taken some of Pisanio's "cordial" is apparently dead. The foresters mourn over her, and lay her in their tomb. The Roman army under Lucius enters. Eugenia who is just recovering from the effects of the potion is discovered and taken with them as a page to the General.

In disguise Ursaces returns to Britain in the invading army, intending actually to fight for his native country. The Britons and Romans meet in battle. Through the bravery of Bellarius, Palladour, and Arviragus, who are volunteers, the Britons win, capturing Lucius, the disguised Eugenia, and others. Ursaces meets Shattillion who discloses the fact of Eugenia's real innocence.

They fight and Shattillion is slain. In great remorse for his part in the supposed death of Eugenia at Pisanio's hands, Ursaces tries to commit suicide, but is prevented and arrested as the murderer of Eugenia, his lamentations over her supposed death having been overheard. Ursaces is brought before Cymbeline, and confesses his responsibility for the murder of Eugenia. Eugenia reveals herself. Pisanio and Clarina who had been captured by the Romans and who are now free are brought in. Pisanio reveals the Queen's having given him the box which he had presented to Eugenia. The death of Cloten at the hands of Arviragus is brought out and to save the young man's life Bellarius discloses that Arviragus and Palladour are Cymbeline's own sons whom he had stolen in their infancy for revenge. The play then ends in general rejoicing.

D'Urfey would seem to have ceased dramatic writing for several years, as his next play, *A Commonwealth of Women,* was licensed September 11, 1685. The titlepage reads:

"a Commonwealth Of WOMEN, A PLAY: As it is Acted at the Theatre Royal, By their Majesties Servants. By Mr. *DURFBY. Anguillam Cauda tenes.* Eras. Licensed Sept. 11, 1685. *ROGER L'ESTRANGE. LONDON.* Printed for *R. Bentley* in *Russel-street* in *Covent-Garden;* and *I. Hindmarsh* at the *Golden Ball* in *Comwell,* over against the *Royal Exchange,* 1686."

The play is dedicated to the second Duke of Albemarle. In his epistle dedicatory D'Urfey mentions the Duke's services against the rebels in Monmouth's rebellion which occurred in the summer of 1685. In the prologue, spoken by Haines with a scythe in his hands, are several loyalistic references to the collapse of the insurrection.

A Commonwealth of Women, TM as the author admits in the prologue, was taken from Fletcher, *The Sea Voyage* being the source. The alterations, as Genest says,121 are considerable. D'Urfey has condensed the action of Fletcher's five acts into four and has added an act, the first of *A Commonwealth of Women,* in which the 120 The original name was

later substituted, Genest, *Stage,* I, 446. 121 *Ibid.* play opens in London, and which transfers various of the characters thence to the islands in which the earlier play is laid. From the beginning of the second act up to the last D'Urfey has followed Fletcher rather closely. In IV, however, Aminta's wooing Albert for Glarinda is not used, and certain other parts of the act are omitted from the later play. Also in Fletcher's play the Amazons were cast ashore with Rosellia; in D'Urfey she is marooned among them. In the fifth act he has substituted his own lines for most of Fletcher's, and has altered the action so as to make the conclusion approach more rapidly.

Nicusa in *The Sea Voyage* is Sebastian's nephew, while in *A Commonwealth,* he is Sebastian's son. Fletcher does not make Aminta and Clarinda daughters of Sebastian, whereas D'Urfey does: in *The Sea Voyage* Aminta is no relation to Sebastian.

D'Urfey's revision of the old play of *The Sea Voyage* is by Genest characterized as decidedly for the worse, but still a good play.122 The *Biographia Dramatica123* calls it "very indifferently executed." Both are perhaps correct. Enough of Fletcher's dialogue remains to redeem the comedy from verbal dullness, and D'Urfey has considerably shortened the fifth act. Certain absurdities occur in *The Commonwealth of Women* that are of D'Urfey's invention, as, for example, La Mure's speaking broken English while the Portuguese speak the language perfectly, correctly and fluently.124 This fault is to be found, however, in later plays of D'Urfey's, and occurs in the plays of greater dramatists than he. In spite of its shortcomings, *The Commonwealth of Women* held the stage, being revived at intervals for sixty years. Genest records performances of the play under its original name at Lincoln's Inn Fields, April 6, 1715 (Cory's benefit); and the title of *The Sea Voyage* at Drury Lane, June 26, 1708; Lincoln's Inn Fields, March 19, 1716; Drury Lane, June 20, 1721; Drury Lane, April 21, 1746.125 In the last mentioned performance Macklin acted Du Pier; Mrs. Clive, Clarinda; and

Mrs. Woffington, Aminta.

In his part of the comedy D'Urfey has borrowed, it would seem, from *The Merchant of Venice,* II, 6. The flight of Aminta with Marine after she has appeared above and dropped a casket to her 122 *Stage,* I, 446. 128 II, 116.

121 Noticed by Genest, *Stage,* I, 446. *TMIbid,* II, 568, 404; 585-86; III, 51; IV, 184. lover (I, 3) is apparently founded upon Lorenzo's elopement with Jessica. The following table shows the derivation respectively of D'Urfey's scenes, as regards *The Sea Voyage:*

Certain of Fletcher's scenes, as V, 1, 2, are not used by D'Urfey at all, or only in the most general way.

The distribution of D'Urfey's verbal borrowings is shown by

Eleven scenes of *The Sea Voyage* supply 810 lines and parts of lines, therefore, to *A Commonwealth of Women.*

D'Urfey's alterations of Fletcher's characters may thus be shown: *The Sea Voyage A Commonwealth of Women*

It will be seen that while D'Urfey has rechristened some characters, and combined others, for the most part he has adhered unusually closely to the original *dramatis persona.*

The following passages from the two plays will illustrate D'Urfey's verbal alterations: "*Mar.* What Heavenly place is this?

Where Beings more than humane keep their Residence?

Sure I have past the baleful stygian Gulf?

And now touch on the blessed Shore: 'Tis so,

This is Elizium: And these the happy Spirits:

That here enjoy all pleasures.

Clita. He comes towards us! O Lord! won't it eat me?

Hip. Stand, or Fle shoot. *Clar.* Hold.— he makes no resistance." *A Commonwealth of Women,* III, 2, (p. 26).

"*Alb.* Do I yet live?

Sure it is air I breathe! What place is this?

Sure something more than human keeps residence here.

For I have past the Stygian gulph,

And touch upon the blessed shore: 'Tis so;
This is the Elysian shade: these happy spirits.
That here enjoy all pleasures!
Hip. He makes towards us.
Jul. Stand, or I'll shoot! *Croc.* Hold! he makes no resistance." *The Sea Voyage,* II, 2,
The characters and actors of *A Commonwealth* are thus listed in the only edition of the play:
"Dramatis Personam
Captain *Marine.*
Du Pier, his Lieutenant.
Boldsprite, The Ships Master.
   Mr. *Williams.*
   Mr. *Griffin.* Mr. *Percival. Franvil*
Three Wild Fellows of the Town, Mr. *Jevan. Don Sebastian Frugal.* that Ramble to Sea, and
Hazard.) desert their Wives.
Surgeon of the Ship.
Governor of several
Portuguize Islands, but chasd from thence by
French Pyrates.
Nicusa. His Son.
La Mure. A Vilainous *French Pyrate.*
Bourcher, His Companion and Friend.
Boatswain.
Chaplain,
Women. *I Roselia,* Protectress of the Amazonian Countrey.
Clarinda. Her Eldest Daughter.
Her youngest Daughter, ravish'd from her by *La Mure,* in her Infancy, and bred up with him. j
Menalippe. 1 Mrs. *Twiford.*
Julietta. Mrs. *Percival. Hippolita.* I.
Amazonians Mrs. *Price. Ariadne.* f
Mrs. *Osborn. Aglaura.* Mrs. *Knight.*
Clita. J Miss *Nanny. Sailers, Dancers, Guards,* and *Attendants.*
SCENE, *Covent-Garden."*
   Mr. *Leigh.* Mr. *Hains.* Mr. *Sanders.*
   Mr. *Gillow.*
   Mi;. *Bowman*
Mr. *Norris.*
Mr. *Harris.*
Mr. *Low.*
Mr. *Farr.*
Mrs. *Cory.*
Lady *Slingsby.*
Mrs. *Cook.*

A Commonwealth of Women may thus be summarized:

Aminta, younger daughter to Don Sebastian, Portuguese governor of certain of the Happy Islands, is captured, when an infant, by La Mure, a French pirate, who maroons her mother and little sister upon a desert island. La Mure brings Aminta to London and there rears her. Although he makes love to her, she loves, and is loved by, Marine, a sea-captain. Aminta and Marine arrange to flee in Marine's ship. Du Pier and Boldsprite, officers of the vessel, agree to aid the escape. Marine, Du Pier and Boldsprite go to La Mure's house for Aminta. In leaving, she arouses La Mure. She and Marine flee, but La Mure and his servants set upon Marine's companions. La Mure summons the watch, but Du Pier turns them upon La Mure, declaring that the old pirate is a disguised Turk who has attempted a rape upon a lady whom he and Boldsprite have rescued. In the diversion thus created, Du Pier and his friend escape.

In a storm Marine's ship is abandoned by crew and passengers, among the latter of whom are Franvile, Frugal, and Hazard, who have taken an oath to travel away from their wives, of whom they have tired, for three years. They land upon a desert island. Here they meet Sebastian and Nicusa, respectively father and brother to Aminta, who have been dwelling on the island since they had been wrecked there in their flight from pirates under the leadership of La Mure. They show their store of treasure to Marine and his company, and, while the new-comers are scrambling for the gold, seize the ship which has not been wrecked after all, and make off in it, leaving the others prisoners on the island.

As Marine and Aminta wander apart in the island they hear hunters' horns (which had been mentioned to them previously by Sebastian). Marine leaves Aminta and swims across a river or strait to the island whence the sounds had come. The island on which he lands is inhabited solely by women. Their governess is Roselia, the lost wife of Sebastian, and mother to Aminta and

Nicusa; with her is her elder daughter Clarinda. On arriving Marine is discovered by the Amazons, who are growing tired ol living without male companionship and who therefore protect him from the wrath of Roselia. They even obtain from her a promise that she will allow Marine and his companions to come to their island. The Amazons obtain further permission each to choose a husband for a month from among the marooned party. Marine mentions Aminta as being his sister. Clarinda falls in love with him. Marine returns with food for his companions and finds Franvile, Frugal, Hazard, and the Ship's Surgeon in the act of killing Aminta, whom they intend to devour. He rescues her and gives the food to his party. They then depart for the land of the Amazons.

Their passage across the strait is observed by La Mure who has come in search of Aminta and who has taken up Sebastian and Nicusa. The pirates land on the Amazons' island, La Mure searching for Aminta, and Sebastian seeking a favorable opportunity for revenging himself on La Mure. Marine and his party arrive. The Amazons quarrel over the men, until Du Pier assigns the men to the various women. Du Pier then produces the treasure obtained from Sebastian. Roselia recognizes the jewels as hers, and orders the death of the party. Clarinda obtains a respite for them, alleging that a greater cruelty than death would be to keep the strangers alive and make them perform menial tasks. She herself proposes to take charge of Marine whom Du Pier has allotted her and with whom she is in love.

Clarinda tells Aminta of her parentage, but Aminta, while suspecting their relationship, says nothing of it. Clarinda confesses to Aminta her love for Marine and requests her to inform him of it. Hazard, Franvile, Frugal, and the Surgeon, who, having been set by the women at the lowest sorts of task, have been mocked by Du Pier, for revenge inform Clarinda of the true relations of Marine and Aminta. In anger she sets out with her guards to find them. Aminta, who, in the meantime, has gone to look for Marine on Clarinda's errand, is captured by La Mure. Immediately La Mure is himself taken prisoner, since Nicusa has slipped away and warned Roselia of La Mure's presence. Then the respective identities and relationships of Sebastian, Roselia, Aminta, Clarinda, and Nicusa are disclosed. All are now reconciled and Du Pier is given Clarinda as a wife while La Mure and Bourcher, his companion and fellow-pirate art imprisoned to await sentence.

The Banditti, or, A Ladies Distress, was probably first acted late in 1685 or early in the next year (New Style). Its titlepage is as follows:

"the BANDITTI, Or A Ladies Distress, A Play, Acted at the Theatre-Royall. Written by Mr. *DURFEY. Non omnes arbusta juvant humilesque myrica.* Virg. Licensed, *March* 1, 1685-6 *R.L.S. London,* Printed by /. *B.* for *R. Bentley* at the Post-House in *Russel Street* in *Covent-Garden,* and /. *Hindmarsh* at the *Golden-Ball* in *Cornhill,* over against the *Roy all-Ex change,* 1686."

The plot of *The Banditti* is partially from a novel called *Don Fenise* (printed 1651 as from the Spanish).126

In the preface D'Urfey says:

"The distress of the Story was hinted to me by the Late Blessed King of ever-glorious Memory,127 from a Spanish Translation, and tho' I was advis'd to call the Play the Banditti, or Sbanditti, because of the Newness of the Title, and lay the Scene in Spain instead of the Kingdom of Naples, yet the more proper Title wou'd ha' been the Spanish Out-laws, tho in such a Case as this in Dramatick-Poetry, I think any Poet may do as he pleases, Especially since Naples is substitute to the King of Spain as well as Madrid."

The portion of the play, which deals with Don Antonio, Elvira, Lawra, and Don Fernand, is related to Mrs. Behn's *Dutch Lover* which is based upon *Don Fenise.1TM* There is a possibility that D'Urfey's comedy is founded upon *The Dutch Lover* (produced in February, 1673)129 rather than upon the novel, but as the writer has not had an opportunity of comparing the plays with the story, he can form no judgment as to this point. Gildon180 suggests a nov-

el called the *History of Don Antonio* as contributing to the play and cites Book IV, p. 250, as a portion of the story used by D'Urfey. This volume also has been inaccessible.

It has been suggested131 that D'Urfey for his low comedy— the tribulations of Diego—drew upon Shirley's *Sisters.* This would seem to be a fact; and it, furthermore, is not unlikely that another of Shirley's dramas, *The Gentleman of Venice,* was levied upon. In III, 1, of *The Banditti,* for example, Diego joins the robbers and suggests the robbery of his supposed father. This may be based upon Piperollo's similar action in *The Sisters,* I, 1. There Piperollo is captured by robbers instead of going to join them, but he enters the band readily enough upon being asked. In *The Gentleman of Venice,* III, 4, Thomazo, supposed son of the Duke 126 *Biographia Dramatica,* II, 46. 127 So Charles I is said to have suggested the plot of *The Gamester* to Shirley. 128 Summers, Mrs. Behn's *Works,* I, 219. 129 *Ibid.* 130 Gildon's Langbaine's *English Dramatic Poets,* p. 49. 131 *Biographia Dramatica,* II, 46. of Venice, exhibits to his companions a cabinet of crown jewels which he has stolen from the Duke, and threatens further depredations. Megaera's affection for Diego (really her own son) as exhibited in *The Banditti,* III, 1, is paralleled by that of Ursula for Thomazo (thought the Duke's son but actually hers) in *The Gentleman of Venice,* II, 1. In *The, Banditti,* IV, 1, Diego and Frisco rob Don Ariell, supposedly the father of Diego. Piperollo in *The Sisters,* II, 1, leads the thieves to plunder Fabio and Morulla, his father and mother. In Shirley's play, however, Piperollo's treachery so disgusts the outlaws that they bind him after the deed is done and leave him to his parents' mercy. The discovery by Leon to Fernand of Fernand's true parentage and Megaera's like disclosure of Diego's real origin, *The Banditti,* V, 1, 2, while suggesting an indebtedness to Morulla's confession of the substitution of her own child Paulina for the dead Paulina whose nurse Morulla was *(The Sisters,* V, 2), is really closer to *The*

Gentleman of Venice, V, 4. Here Ursula confesses that she has changed her doltish profligate son Thomazo for Giovanni, who, after having grown up as her son, has won fame as a soldier, as has Fernand in *The Banditti.* The leniency of the Corregidore towards Leon, Diego, and the other outlaws, *The Banditti,* V, 2, is reminiscent of the pardoning of Frapolo, his band, and Morulla, in *The Sisters,* V, 2. Thomazo, his companions, and Ursula are also' pardoned in *The Gentleman of Venice,* V, 4, after full disclosures have been made.132 Among the interesting points connected with *The Banditti* is the repetition of the attempt to make a wit of a dull son, such as Don Ariell's supplying Diego with many masters of one sort and another (see I, 1). This had been employed by D'Urfey in his *Fool Turn'd Critick.* Don Fernand's stabbing Don Antonio in the dark, having mistaken him for a bravo, is reminiscent of *The Duke's. Mistress* of Shirley V, 1." Lawra's seeking refuge among the outlaws in III, 1, is not unlike Silvia's action in *The Two Gentlemen of Verona,* V, 3, 4. The same Shakespearian comedy is recalled hy Leon's attempted rape on Lawra and Fernand's rescue of her, *The Banditti,* IV, 1. There is a close resemblance between this incident and Proteus's attack upon Silvia and Valentine's rescue of her, *The Two Gentlemen,* V, 4. In V, 2 (p. 61), of D'Urfey's play is an allu 182 For cases of lost and substituted children in pre-Restoration drama, see Forsythe, *The Relations of Shirley's Plays to the Elizabethan Drama,* p. 240. 18» For other instances of the same, see *ibid,* pp. 204-05. sion to the swearing and forswearing of Oates and Bedloe which was soon to be looked into and punished by the authorities.

Although Genest134 calls *The Banditti* "on the whole a good play," it was damned at its appearance. As a consequence of this unfavorable reception, the drama is prefaced by an epistle to "The Extreme Witty and Judicious Gentleman, Sir Critick Cat-call." In this the dramatist vents his spleen against those who had condemned his play which he calls, *"a poor Out-cast Or-*

phan, ... *Stifl'd in its very Birth, by* Malevolent Influence, *and Suffered under the Weight of your* Sir Critick's *particular* Condemnation, *and* Dreadfull Sentences, *almost as soon as it was so unhappy to have 0 Being."*

Further quotation from the preface may be of interest:135

"I was so unlucky to hope, that tho' my Play might be too long, which is a general fault amongst us, and not to be remedy'd 'till the first day is over, and tho' some Scenes might seem Tedious 'till it was shorten'd, which is always the Second Days Work, yet I had the confidence to think, that the Variety of a pretty Tale, a good Plot, not very ungratefull Characters, and I am sure very good Musick, both Vocal and Instrumental, with Vaulting, Dancing, and all that I cou'd think of to please, might have oblig'd 'em to a Civil Sufferance, tho not a liking; but in the Contrary your Sir Critick's prejudice took vent, even before the Play began; the Actors were Disturb'd, and cou'd not perform, particularly in the Second Act: After which the Scenes were all promiscuously decry'd both good and bad, the Songs and Musick hoop'd and whistl'd at, tho they have since been Sung in several other plays with generall Applause, which I think sufficiently discovers the ungenerous Malice, and poor partiality that was us'd; yet only to show the Itch of Vitiated Affections, one Mock-Song that hit the Farsical Humour, because there was nothing in't took extreamly, (Viz.) From drinking of Sack by the Pottle, Thrum, Thrum, Thrum, Thrum, Thrum, Thrum,"136" 1M *Stage,* I, 453. 188 In this quotation as well as one elsewhere in the discussion of *The Banditti,* the author has not seen fit to follow D'Urfeys rather eccentric italization of words; with this exception the quotations are *verbatim et litteratim.* 186 D'Urfey's reference elsewhere in the dedication to the popularity of "Jobson's. Wife" is a hit at the reception of *The Devil of a Wife* by Jevon, an actor in *The Banditti.*
As a matter of fact, D'Urfey's anger at the reception accorded *The Banditti* seems justified, for although not an ex-

cellent play, it is no worse than some of his which were applauded. Its principal defect is the crowding of so much action into the play as to make it confusing. This is best observed by a comparison of its plot with the comparatively simple, yet much more amusing and interesting stories of either *The Gentleman of Venice* or *The Sisters.* The *dramatis persona* of *The Banditti* reads thus: "dramatis Persons187 Don Garcia, *Captain of the King's Guards. Mr.* Gillow. Don Antonio, *His Son. Mr.* Kinaston.

Don Fernand, *Son to* Eugenia, *Suppos'd Murder'd, Mr.* Williams.

Don Ariell, *Brother to* Eugenia, *Mr.* Leigh.

Don Diego, *Suppos'd Son to* Don Ariell, *Mr.* Underhill.
Signior Frisco, *An Affected Spanish Taylor, Mr.* Jevan.
Leon, *Captain of the* Banditti, *Mr.* Griffin.

Corrigidore, *Mr.* Harris

Domingo, *A Soldier attending on* Don

Garcia *Mr.* Low.

Grillon, Servant to Don Antonio

Lopez, A Mathematician. *Mr.* Percival.

WOMEN

Eugenia, *An Old Lady Sister to* Don Ariell, Mrs. *Cory.*

Lawra, *Daughter to* Eugenia, *Mrs.* Barrer.

Dona Elvira, *A Rich Heiress. Mrs.* Cooke.

Lucia, *Confident to* Laura, *Mrs.* Percival.

Christina, *Woman to* Dona Elvira *Mrs.* Twiford.

Megaera, *Wife to* Leon, *Mr.* Ja. Nokes.

Banditti, Dancers, Musicians,
Officers and Attendants.
The Scene Madrid."

The plot of *The Banditti* runs as follows: Don Antonio, who loves, and is loved by, Lawra, is designed by his father Don Garcia to marry Dona Elvira, an heiress. As he is about to meet Lawra, his father joins him and frustrates the meeting. Antonio writes Lawra, making an assignation with her for eleven that night at her apartment.

Imperfect, as lacking "Signior Semibreif the Singing-man," who is introduced II, 1 (p. 15), but does not speak.
A poor young soldier, Don Fernand, has been befriended and promoted by Don Garcia, who is captain of the King's Guard. Don Fernand returns half-intoxicated from a merry meeting with friends. As he passes under Lawra's window, she, mistaking him for Antonio who has already arrived but who has retired again at the supposed approach of Dona Eugenia, Lawra's mother, throws out the door-key to him and invites him to enter the house. After Fernand's entry, Antonio returns and follows him into the house which he is able to do since Fernand has left the door open. Fernand and Antonio meet in the dark. Thinking the other a bravo, Don Fernando stabs him and then flees from what he considers a house of ill-repute. Don Antonio believes himself to have been attacked at Lawra's instigation and so reports to Dona Eugenia, her mother, who finds him. Eugenia goes in search of Lawra but discovers that she, fancying her mother the author of Antonio's wound, and fearing the results of Eugenia's learning of their intrigue, has run away. Fernand ventures back to see what has become of his adversary, but, hearing of Lawra's flight and Antonio's condition, he does not disclose his part in the affair.

Tired of his supposed father Don ArielPs severity, Don Diego runs away to join the banditti who are headed by Leon, and with whom he already has had some connection. Leon and his companions propose to Diego the robbery of Don Ariell. As the robbers are at breakfast, Lawra still in flight from her mother's, enters and asks from Leon and his wife Megaera shelter and aid to continue her journey to Toledo to the house of her uncle Don Ariell, who is, however (unknown to her), at Madrid. In the meantime, Don Antonio recovering from his wound puts by thoughts of Lawra and goes to court Elvira, the heiress intended for him by Don Garcia. They meet and, although previously both opposed to their marriage, they now begin to incline towards each other.

In Megaera's company Lawra sets out for Toledo. By previous arrangement, Leon sets on Lawra to rob her, and Megasra having fled, he attempts to ravish her. Don Fernand who is journeying to Toledo now enters, wounds Leon, and rescues Lawra. He learns her name and story and acquaints her that he is going to Toledo himself in Don Ariell's company. They avoid Don Ariell, who now enters and go in search of Megsera. Don Ariell and Lopez, his companion, are set upon by Diego and Frisco, who has posed as a tailor but who is really a robber. The identity of Diego is discovered by Ariell but the robbery proceeds. The thieves bind and gag the two travellers. As they rejoice over their booty, Fernand and Lawra surprise the highwaymen, and Diego is captured by Fernand. Leon who has been lying helpless is now umasked and is recognized by Fernand as his own supposed father whom he had left on account of Leon's dishonest practices. Lawra and Fernand now return to Madrid to halt the contemplated wedding of Antonio and Elvira. As Antonio is about to serenade Elvira, Frisco enters and is brought to join in the serenade. Lopez enters with some officers and recognizes Frisco, who is then arrested for his part in the robbery. Dona Elvira now enters. She learns of Lawra's relations with Antonio, and as a result breaks off her match with him, but at his earnest entreaty yields and receives him back again.

The wounded Leon confesses to Don Fernand that Fernand is really not his son but that his parent was the father of Lawra and brother of Don Ariell. Diego is brought to trial, whereupon Megaera testifies that he is her son and not Don Ariell's, having been substituted by her for an infant son of Don Ariell's carelessly smothered by her while she was acting as its nurse. Don Fernand accompanies Lawra to the wedding of Antonio and Elvira. He calls Antonio aside and forbids the marriage. The two then fight, but are separated by the guests. Fernand then announces his true identity and is recognized by his mother Eu-

genia. Leon is then brought in. He tells of how he had come into possession of the infant Fernand and shows trinkets which the child had worn and which Eugenia identifies. The misadventure of Antonio in the dark at Eugenia's is now explained. Elvira gives up Antonio who returns to Lawra. The banditti's sentences are commuted and they are whipt from the stage at the close of the play.

Whether *Love for Money* or *Bussy D'Ambois* was the next of D'Urfey's plays188 is uncertain. They would seem both to have been acted in 1691.139 Since, however, in a "Catalogue of Plays lately Printed" to be found at the back of the 1691 edition of *Bussy,*

" To follow *A Fool's Preferment,* the discussion of which immediately precedes the reprinted text in the second part of this study.
338 Genest, *Stage,* II, 9-10; 13-14.
Amorous fixes the date *oi-Love for Money* in the following speech: "This Charming Angel of yours has been my Whore these seven years; I settled an Estate upon her in 87, carried her to *Flanders* in 88, and spent two thousand pounds upon her in 89, brought her over with me in 90, and now this present year find myself jilted." Evidently their relations had begun in 1684, if we are to understand "seven years" literally, which is to be doubted. *Love for Money* is listed, it appears probable at least that the priority of publication denotes the order of performance of the two dramas. Hence, *Love for Money* will be taken up first here. The titlepage of the edition used by the present writer reads as follows: "LOVE For MONEY, Or, The Boarding School, A COMEDY. As it is Acted at The Theatre Royal. Written by Mr. *DURFBY. LONDON:* Printed for *A. Roper* and *B. Wilkinson,* at the *Black-Boy* in *Fleetstreet;* and */. Hindmarsh,* at the *Golden-Ball* against the *Royal Exchange,* 1696." According to Gildon,140 D'Urfey's friend, *Love for Money* met with a by no means wholly favorable reception on its first day. In his preface to the play D'Urfey asserts that an opposition to the comedy had been organized by the dancing-masters. The efforts of this faction, however,

were overcome, as the author shows by his reference to the well-known success of the comedy. In the dedication (to Charles Viscount Lansdown) D'Urfey says that his friends have vindicated his comedy against the ridiculous malice of a prejudiced party and that *Love for Money* had received the applause of the "Impartial, and Judicious." D'Urfey disavows the report of his having spent a summer in a boarding-school collecting material for his play. Furthermore, he denies having intended to reflect in it upon a certain noble family or to direct some words of Lady Addlepate's at "a certain noble person in distress" (James II?).

It seems likely to the present writer that, as a matter of fact, any attempt at condemning the play was the result, not of a combination of indignant dancing-masters and boarding-school keepers, but of members of the Jacobite party. For *Love for Money* is as indecently and rampantly Williamite in its politics, as *Sir Barnaby Whigg* or *The Royalist* was ultra-Tory. This play indeed would seem to mark the change in D'Urfey's politics which enabled him: to be called nowadays the amuser of four successive sovereigns.

There is a possibility that no underlying motive was responsible for the mixture of approval and unfavorable criticism which saluted the comedy, since concerning its merits critics differ widely. The *Biographia Dramatical* calls it "far from a good play on the whole," and "very poor." Gildon142 considers *Love for Money,* on the other hand, to have "something more than ordinary" in it; while Genest14 140 Gildon's Langbaine's *English Dramatic Poets,* p. 51.
141II, pp. 386, 51.
142 Gildon's Langbaine's *English Dramatic Poets,* p. 51.
143 Genest, *Stage,* II, 14. says it is "on the whole a good comedy," but thinks that the scenes between Young Merriton and Mirtilla are dull and that the political part would have been better omitted. There were two editions of the play, in 1691 and 1696, respectively. It was revived as Bickerstaffe's benefit, May 21, 1708, at Drury Lane, Bickerstaffe

taking the part of Will Merriton,1" and again at the same theatre, July 11, 1718, being acted four times during the summer.145 A "ballad farce" in two acts, called *The Boarding School Romps, or the Sham Captain,* by Charles Coffey, and based on *Love for Money,* was presented at Drury Lane, January 29, 1733, but seems to have been a failure.146

In some respects *Love for Money* is notable. The part of the plot which deals with the love of Young Merriton and Mirtilla is distinctly romantic with various features of modern melodrama or eighteenth century sentimental comedy. We find the lost heiress, the villainous guardian, the good young man with a good old father. At the end of the play the villain is discomfited and virtue triumphs. The various scenes between Mirtilla and her lover are obviously intended to appeal to the sentimentally sympathetic side of the hearers. They bid for the sympathy of the audience through the tender emotions. In these passages are no attempts at wit or intrigue (in the Restoration sense). In V, 3 (p. 49), Merriton shows quite serious scruples about marrying the now-rich Mirtilla. No hero of genuine Restoration comedy would have ever thought of making any bones about such a deed.

Bernbaum in his volume on *The Drama of Sensibility* says:

"The drama of sensibility, which includes sentimental comedy and domestic tragedy, was from its birth a protest against the orthodox view of life, and against those literary conventions which had served that view. It implied that human nature, when not, as in some cases, already perfect, was perfectible by an appeal to the emotions. It refused to assume that virtuous persons must be sought in a romantic realm apart from the everyday world. It wished to show that beings who were good at heart were found in the ordinary walks of life. It so represented their conduct as to arouse admiration for their virtues and pity for their sufferings. In sentimental comedy, it showed them contending against distresses but finally rewarded *Ibid,* II, 402. 1 *Ibid,* II, 621-22.

Ibid, III, 368; *Biographia Dramatica,* II,

63.

by morally deserved happiness. In domestic tragedy it showed them overwhelmed by catastrophes for which they were morally not responsible. A new ethics had arisen and new forms of literature were thereby demanded."147

If the foregoing definition of sentimental drama be applied to *Love for Money,* it will be seen that D'Urfey's play fulfils all the requirements of sentimental comedy. Bernbaum, however, has made the mistake, a fundamental one indeed, of following tradition—the poorest of guides in literary classification—and has considered Cibber's *Love's Last Shift* (acted 1696) as the first comedy of the sentimental sort. This traditional idea of Cibber's priority in sentimental drama the writer wishes to go on record as believing absolutely unfounded. On the other hand, he does not consider D'Urfey its originator, but as merely an early exponent of the type.

To the present writer, *Love for Money* is another evidence of the fact that no one can put his finger upon a piece of literature and say, "This was the first poem to show the revival of romanticism," or "This was the first realistic novel," or "This was the first—" of any literary type. In offering *Love for Money* as a specimen of sentimental comedy, he does not, he repeats, wish to be considered as terming it the first; for there are evidences of sentimentality all through the Restoration period. On the other hand, he wishes to submit the play as preceding *Love's Last Shift* and *The Lying Lover* in their own *genre.*

The plot of *Love for Money* is "in general" D'Urfey's, according to Gildon.148 This is true, unless one construe "in general" too rigidly. In II, 2, (p. 20 ff.), in which Young Merriton, disguised as a dancing-master, enters the boarding-school to visit Mirtilla, we have what would seem to be a borrowing from Wycherley's *Gentleman Dancing Master,* II, 2, in which Gerrard in a similar guise gains access to Hippolita. Merriton's courting Mirtella in this shape in III, 1 (p. 22 ff), recalls Gerrard's paying his addresses to Hippolita, *The Gentleman Dancing Master,*

II, 2, III, 1, IV, 1. However, as to these scenes of D'Urfey's one must not forget the device of Lucentio and Hortensio for courting Bianca, *The Taming of the Shrew,* II, 1, III, 1.149 There is possibly a use by D'Urfey in the story of Young Brag's heroism at the siege of Buda in IV, 1 147 P. 10, Bernbaum apparently had read only one of D'Urfey's comedies—*Madam Fickle,*—and he seems confused as to the plot of it (see *The Drama of Sensibility,* p. 87, note).

148 Gildon's Langbaine's *English Dramatic Poets,* p. 51. 149 Coupee's courting song also recalls *The Taming of the Shrew.* (p. 34), of Bobadill's exploits as related by himself in *Every Man in his Humor,* III, 1. Le Prat's telling Amorous of his success with Jiltall (itself a reminiscence of Beauford in *The Virtuous Wife*) is duplicated in Mountfort's *Greenwich Park,* produced in the same year as *Love for Money* and at the same theatre. There Young Reveller tells Worthy of the satisfactory ending of his courtship of Dorinda, Worthy's mistress. In Burnaby's comedy of *The Reformed Wife,* performed at Drury Lane in 1700, Freeman shows a letter to him from Astrea to her husband, Sir Solomon. A speech of Jiltall's, V, 3 (p. 50), seems based upon Celestina's remarks concerning her coach, *The Lady of Pleasure,* I, 2. Jiltall's speech runs thus:

"Methinks *Oyley,* the Coach is not easie enough, I'll have the Cushions alter'd, and the Velvet finer; I'll have Six Horses too, I find every tawdry Gentlewoman has a couple.

No, they have too much of the dull City Air; I'll make Sir

Rowland change 'em. I'll have my Page's coat cover'd with

Gold Lace, and lin'd with Tissue." The name of Semibrief, the singing-master, had previously been applied to a member of the same calling (who does not appear in the *dramatis persona*) in "Signior Semibreif" in *The Banditti.*

The characters and their performers are thus listed:

"dramatis Persons

Sir *Rowland Rakehell,* A covetous mercenary vicious swearing atheisticall

Old Fellow, Uncle to *Amorous,* who by cheating an Infant Orphan to whom he was Guardian, possessed an Estate of 3000 1. a Year. By Mr. *Underhill. Jack Amorous,* a witty Extravagant of the Town, generous and well-natur'd, but so extreamly given to Women, that he keeps a Jilt, and has spent his Estate upon her,

Mr. *Mountfort. Will. Merriton, A* witty modest well-bred Gentleman, tho' of small fortune, a great lover of Learning, and skill'd in

Philosophy, Poetry and Musick, Mr. *Hodson.*

Old Merriton, his Father, an honest Religious, conscientious

Gentleman, that privately plac'd *Mirtilla* in a Boarding-

School, and maintains her unknown to Sir Rowland.

Mr. *Freeman. Nedd Bragg,* alias Captain *Bouncer,* an impudent lying Town

Sharper of infamous Birth and no Merit, yet being kept by

Lady *Addleplot,* wears rich Cloaths, keeps high Company, and passes for a Captain. Mr. *Powell.* Old *Zachary Bragg,* Father to *Ned,* an ignorant Old blant peevish Granadeer of King *William's Army,* that by his stupid bluntness always shames his Son in Company, and hectors him into an allowance, Mr. *Bright.* Deputy *Nicompoop,* Deputy of a Ward, a softly sneaking uxorious Citizen, 'Husband to Lady Addleplot, and ridiculously fond of her and the Romp his Daughter.

Mr. *Dogget. Monsieur Le Prat, An* impertinent, noisie, singing, dancing, prating French Fop, perpetually gabling in Company, and crying up the Actions of the French King. Mr. *Bower.*

A Singing Master, Mr. *Kirkham.*

A Dancing Master, Mr. *Bowman.*

A Presbyterian Parson. Mr. *Peire.* WOMEN, *Lady Addleplot,* A Lusty flaunting imperious Lady, a highflown Stickler against the Government, and always raling at it, in talking of Politics. — Mrs. *Anthony Leigh. Lady Stroddle,* her Companion, a Papist and Grumbler.

Mrs. *Richardson. Mirtilla,* The Orphan, witty, modest, and virtuous, kept privately at a Boarding School by *0. Merriton,* and true Heiress of 3000 /. a year. Mrs. *Bracegirdle. Miss Jenny,* Daughter to *Lady Addleplot. Miss Molly,* Daughter to *Nicompoop*—two tawdry hoyden overgrown Rompes of the Boarding-School. Mrs. *Knight.*

Mrs. *Davis. Betty Jiltall,* A cunning, singing, weeping, wheedling, toying, chattering Mercenary Town Jilt, kept by *Amorous,* that imposes upon him, and preaches foundness meerly for interest. Mrs. *Butler. Crowstich,* Teacher to the Boarding-School. Mrs. *Cory. Tearshift,* Woman to Lady *Addleplot.* Mrs. *Osborn. Oyley,* Woman to *Jiltall.* Mrs. *Leigh.*

Constable, Musitians, Guards, Mob, Footmen, and Attendants.

The Scene. *CHELSEY,* by the River. The time 36. hours."

The plot of *Love for Money* may be given as follows:

Sir Rowland Rakehell embezzles the estate of his ward Mirtilla and is thought to have made way with her. His nephew Amorous plots at the suggestion of Old Merriton to introduce his mistress Betty Jilta.ll as the heiress Mirtilla returned from the Indies India whence she had been conveyed by Sir Rowland's treachery. Betty is placed by Amorous at a boarding-school where his friend Young Merriton's beloved, the true Mirtilla, is. Young Bragg under the name of Captain Bouncer is the lover of Lady Addleplot, Nicompoop's wife, and is intended for a husband to Nicompoop's daughter Molly. Old Bragg blackmails his son, threatening to expose him, as Young Bragg pretends to be an officer and a gentleman.

Amorous introduces himself to Sir Rowland as just arrived from the "Indies" with Mirtilla, whom he had found there. Sir Rowland begins to plot how to prevent an exposure of his fraud. Young Merriton in the guise of a dancing master is admitted to the boarding-school and there courts the real Mirtilla.

At an exhibition held at the school Jiltall dances and is made love to by Le Prat, a Frenchman, who has previously aspired to her favors. She yields to Le Prat's solicitations and his offer of a "hundred guineas. As Young Bragg is boasting of his ancestry, his father enters and reveals their relationship. Young Bragg announces to his parent that he is about to marry an heiress, Molly, and so is able to pacify the old man, whom he introduces as a retired officer, Colonel Bragg. Amorous and Jiltall under the name of Mirtilla confront Sir Rowland. She pretends not to know Sir Rowland and curses and threatens him until he is badly frightened. Amorous proposes to compromise with him for Mirtilla's estate. In his fear, Sir Rowland agrees. After Sir Rowland has left and after Amorous and Betty Jiltall have rejoiced over the success of their plan, Le Prat enters to Amorous who is now alone. He lets slip that he lias a letter from Jiltall, arranging a meeting with him. Le Prat and Amorous fight, and the Frenchman is disarmed. Amorous now resolves revenge upon Jiltall.

Old Bragg as a colonel and Young Bragg meet Young Merriton and Amorous at a tavern and accidentally disclose their true ranks in life. At the boarding-school, Jenny, Lady Addleplot's daughter, is discovered to have a weakness for Coupee, the regular dancing-master, and Molly is found to be in love with the singingmaster, Semibrief. Old Merriton finds his son and Mirtilla together. They confess to him their mutual love, of which he has already learned from his son. To revenge himself on Jiltall, Amorous hides Le Prat, whom he has convinced of her falseness, in a closet off Jiltall's chamber. Under the pretence of increasing his settlement upon her, Amorous gets from Jiltall the papers for the settlement already made, and destroys them. He then gives her her letter to Le Prat and calls in the Frenchman. After the men leave, Sir Rowland enters. Jiltall tells him that Amorous has abused her. To revenge herself upon Amorous, she offers to marry Sir Rowland, who, seeing a chance thereby of keeping his supposed fortune, agrees.

After some difficulty Semibrief and Coupee steal Molly and Jenny from the boarding-school. Young Bragg, who sees them, goes to inform their parents. He finds Lady Addleplot (who is a rabid Jacobite) with her husband and others on the eve of a revolt. The parents forsake the idea of an insurrection and go in search of the elopers. They find the two pairs of fugitives too late to prevent the respective marriages. Amorous, who has been gloating over his ruining Jiltall is surprised to meet her richly dressed. On learning of her marriage to Sir Rowland, he throttles her. Sir Rowland who rescues her breaks his earlier promise to Amorous of a thousand pounds a year to him as long as he would keep the supposed Mirtilla quiet concerning her guardian's treatment of her. Sir Rowland attempts to enter his house in company with his bride, but is prevented by Old Merriton. The true state of affairs is revealed to Sir Rowland who is finally convinced of Jiltall's perfidy. Then Sir Rowland is arrested for his machinations against his ward in her childhood. It is now shown that Old Merriton, thought to have been an accomplice of Sir Rowland's, has maintained Mirtilla in the boarding-school on the money allowed him by Sir Rowland for his part in the plot. Mirtilla now offers her hand to Young Merriton who has been backward in lovemaking recently because of their inequality of fortune. He accepts her. The angry parents of the elopers now enter and meet their children who have accepted shelter in Young Merriton's house. Old Bragg, dressed as a friar, is now chased in by a mob, headed by his son, who has so disguised his father, and then set the mob upon him, as a revenge for the old man's blackmail and exposure of the younger.

Bussy D'Ambois, or the Husbands Revenge, was printed in the year of its production with the following titlepage:

"BUSSY D'AMBOIS, Or The DUSbaitDS HCVCXXQC A

Tragedy. As it is Acted at the Theatre Royal Newly Revised by Mr. ID'THrfe. *Audere est operae pretium, procedere recte Qui machis non vultis, ut omni parte laborent, Utque illis multo corrupta dolore voluptas, Atque hac rara, cadat dura inter Sape pericla. Hor. Sat.*

2. lib. 1. xOnftOtl, printed for *R. Bentley* in *Covent Garden, Jo. Hindmarsh* over against the *Royal Exchange,* and *Abel Roper* at the *Mitre* near *Temple Bar.* 1691."

The play is an alteration of Chapman's *Bussy D'Ambois.* Of his revision of the old tragedy D'Urfey says, in his epistle dedicatory to "Edward Earl of Carlisle, Viscount Howard of Morpeth &c.":160 "About Sixteen Years since i. e., 1675, when first my good or ill Stars ordained me a Knight Errant in this Fairy Land of Poetry, I saw the *Bussy 'D'Ambois* of Mr. *Chapman* Acted by Mr. *Hart,* which in spight of the obsolete Phrases and intolerable Fustian, with which a great Part of it was cramm'd, and which I have altered in these new Sheets) had some extraordinary Beauties, which sensibly charmed me; which being improved by the graceful Action of that eternally Renowned, and Best of Actors, so attracted not only me, but the Town in general, that they were obliged to pass by and excuse the gross Errors in the Writing, and allow it amongst the Rank of the Topping Tragedies of that Time.

"For a long time after it lay buried in Mr. *Harts* Grave, who indeed only could do that noble Character Justice, till not willing to have it quite lost I presumed to revise it, and writ the Plot new, mending the Character of *Tamira,* whom Mr. *Chapman* had drawn quite otherwise, he making her lewd, onely for the sake of lewdness; which I have altered, and in the first Act mentioned a former Contract between her and *D'Ambois,* which gives some Excuse for her Love afterwards, and renders the Distress in the last Act to be much more lyable to Pity.

"Amongst the rest of your Lordships extraordinary Favours, for which I can never enough express my Gratitude, you did me the Honour at my reading this Play to you particularly to commend that Alteration, which, I confess, encouraged me to get it Acted, though without Success, till Mr. *Mountfort* did me the Favour; who, though he was modestly very diffident of *1K A Fool's Preferment* is dedicated to Charles Lord

Morpeth.

his own Action, coming after so great a Man as Mr. *Hart,* yet had that Applause from the Audience, which declared their Satisfaction, and with which I am sure he ought to be very-well contented."151 D'Urfey's alterations are not quite so great in the case of *Bussy D'Ambois* as in his other revisions. The relationship of the scenes in the two plays is shown below:

All but two of D'Urfey's scenes, as the table shows, are from corresponding scenes in Chapman's tragedy.

The verbal indebtednesses of D'Urfey to Chapman are given in the table following together with the scenes in the respective plays in which they occur: 1MIn the dedication D'Urfey quotes, "as immortal *Shakespear* says, the Toe of the Peasant treads so near the Heel of the Courtier, that it galls his Kibe" *Hamlet,* V, I, 11. 151-52.

D'Urfey, as is shown above, employs 977 lines, wholly or in part, out of eleven scenes in Chapman's *Bussy D'Ambois.*

D'Urfey's changes in the *dramatis persona* are so few as not to warrant a listing opposite Chapman's characters. Anapelle, Charlot, and Pero in the earlier *Bussy* are, respectively, the maids of the Duchess of Guise, Beaupre and of Tamira. In D'Urfey's *Bussy* they are assigned to Beaupre, Tamira, and the Duchess, respectively. D'Urfey's Magician and his Teresia, Tamira's governess, play the part of Chapman's Friar. Laffoil, the fencing-master, is the only other new character.

The most important variations in plot are the representation of Bussey's duel (II, 2) intsead of reporting it as in II, 1, of Chapman's *Bussy;* the omission of the vision of Monsieur, Guise, and Montsurry which appears to Bussy in the old play, IV, 2; and the putting to death of Tamira. D'Urfey further introduces a comic scene, centering around Maffc, the steward of Monsieur (IV, 2).

Much of Chapman's language has been modernized, thereby often totally removing the poetic flavor and flattening the diction. Some of the best passages D'Urfey has retained; others he has cut out. As an example of his rewriting of Chapman's lines, the following passage may be quoted: *"Mont.* Hereafter! 'tis a suppos'd Infinite,

That from this Point will rise Eternally,

When a feign'd Vertue is discover'd Vice.

Excuses, Damn her! they, like Fires in Cities,

Enrage with those Winds that less Lights extinguish.

Sing, *Syren,* Sing, and dash against my Rock, *Pulls her by the hair.*

Thy Ruffian Gally burnt with flaming Lust.

Sing, I mean write, and then take from my Eyes,

The Mists that hide the most instructable Pander

That ever lap'd up an Adulterous Vomit,

That I may see the Devil and Survive,

That I may hang him, and then cut him down,

Then Rip him up, and with true Cunning search

The Cells and Cabins of his Brain and Study,

Like him the Wilderness of a Womans Heart

Where half the World that venture in are lost.

Oh! wretched Man, that still will haunt the Coast

Of Fatal Marriage, and hunt the dear-bought Game,

Till he does find within his Wives two Breasts,

All *Pelion* and *Cytharon* with their Beasts.

Will ye write yet"

D'Urfey's *Bussy D'Ambois,* V, 1 (p. 42)

Chapman's version of the same passage runs thus:

"Mont. Hereafter? 'Tis a supposed infinite,

That from this point will rise eternally:

Fame grows in going; in the 'scapes of virtue

Excuses damn her: they be fires in cities

Enraged with those winds that less lights extinguish.

Come, syren, sing, and dash against my rocks

Thy ruffian galley, rigg'd with quench for lust;

Sing, and put all the nets into thy voice

With which thou drew'st into thy strumpet's lap

The spawn of Venus; and in which ye danced;

That in thy lap's stead, I may dig his tomb,

And quit his manhood with a woman's sleight,

Who never is deceived in her deceit.

Sing (that is, write), and then take from mine eyes

The mists that hide the most inscrutable pander

That ever lapp'd up an adulterous vomit;

That I may see the devil and survive

To be a devil, and then learn to wive:

That I may hang him and then cut him down,

Then cut him up, and with my soul's beams search

The cranks and caverns of his brain, and study

The errant wildness of a woman's face;

Where men cannot get out, for all the comets

That have been lighted at it; though they know

That adders lie a-sunning in their smiles,

That basilisks drink their poison from their eyes,

And no way there to coast out to their hearts;

Yet still they wander there, and are not stay'd

Till they be fetter'd, nor secure before

All cares devour them; nor in human consort

Till they embrace within their wife's two breasts

All Pelion and Cythaeron with their beasts.

Why write you not?"

Chapman's *Bussy D'Ambois,* V, 1

Genest132 doubts whether D'Urfey's making Tamira precontracted to Bussy before her marriage to Montsurry is an improvement. The altering of the Friar into an old woman, Teresia, he thinks

"very properly" done. The representation of the duel on the stage ("which Chapman had related very badly") by implication he considers a betterment of the play. The introduction of the fencingmaster is a "botch." Genest sums up his criticism by saying, "On the whole D'Urfey has made this play quite as good as the generality of tragedies at this time." Gildon153 says of D'Urfey's conception of Tamira, "He'll hardly persuade that pity is due to a woman that quits her honor and virtue on any account."

D'Urfey ostensibly, it seems, presented the tragedy as a sermon. He closes the prologue with this couplet:

"For in this Glass ye all without mistaking, May see the dangerous Crime of Cuckold-making." Such a lesson comes with a poor grace, however, from the author of *Sir Barnaby Whigg* and *The Campaigners.*

The persons of the play and the performers are given as follows: "Dramatis Persona?154

King Henry III *of* France

Monsieur, his Brother

Duke of Guise

D'Ambois *Favorite to* Henry

Montsurry

Monsieur Masse *Steward to* Monsieur

Monsieur Laffoil *A Fencing Master*

Bariser *Captain of the Guards* Mr. Lanoo

Mr. *Freeman.*

Mr. *Hodson.* Mr. *Kynaston.* Mr. *Mountfort.* Mr. *Powell.* Mr. *Bright.* Mr. *Bowen. Verbruggen.* Mr. *Harris.* Mr. *Barnes.* Mr. *Sibber.* Mr. *Kirkham.* WOMEN.

Dutchess of Guise

Tamira *Wife to Montsurry*

Teresia her Governess

Charlot her Women

Beaupre a Court Lady

Scene. PARIS." TM» *Stage,* II, 10.

153 Gildon's Langbaine's *English Dramatic Poets,* p. 49. 154 Imperfect as lacking a Magician; Anaple, woman to the Dutchess of Guise; Pero, woman to Beaupre.

Mrs. *Lasselles.* Mrs. *Bracegirdle.*

Mrs. *Corey.* Mrs. *Richardson.* Mrs.

Perin.

The plot of D'Urfey's tragedy may thus be summarized:

Tamira is forced to marry the rich Montsurry, whereas she loves the poor Bussy D'Ambois to whom she had once been betrothed. Hearing that Bussy is melancholy, Tamira desires Teresia, her governess, to seek him out and give him a purse; she arranges also that Bussy may visit her in her apartment by means of a secret passage and trap-door if he so wishes. In the meantime, Monsieur, brother to the King, who is ambitious to succeed to the crown, goes in search of Bussy with the purpose of attaching him to Monsieur's faction. After his talk with Bussy, Monsieur sends him a thousand crowns by Masse,156 his steward. Masse tries to embezzle nine hundred crowns, but is detected by Bussy, who secures all the gold and beats Masse.

Bussy is taken to court by Monsieur. There, by his persistent courting of the Duchess of Guise, Bussy rouses the jealousy and hatred of the Duke, her husband. After the Duke's departure, Bussy quarrels with Bariser, Lanoo, and Pyrrot. A duel results in which Bussy's two seconds and their three adversaries fall, Bussy being the sole survivor. In the meantime, Monsieur courts Tamira but is repulsed by her. She tells her husband Montsurry of the Prince's suit, but he does not resent Monsieur's actions. Soon Montsurry leaves to be gone all night. Teresia then introduces Bussy into Tamira's chamber through the secret passage. Tamira is coy at first, but Bussy overcomes her scruples.

After D'Ambois leaves Tamira, Montsurry returns. She pretends to have spent the night in waiting for him. He assures her that he will never be away from her another night. Montsurry now informs Tamira that the King has taken. D'Ambois into favor on account of his having hinted to the monarch that Monsieur had designs against him. For this reason, Monsieur now hates Bussy. Guise and Bussy meet and quarrel in the King's presence, but at Henry's request are apparently reconciled and vow amity. After the King's departure to a banquet in company with Bussy, Guise,

Monsieur, and Montsurry plot against Bussy. They call in Charlot, Pero, and Anaple, the waiting-women, respectively, of Tamira, the Duchess of Guise, and the Lady Beaupre, niece to the Duke of Guise. Each questions one of the servants. None reports any relations between her mistress and Bussy, save Charlot who, having peeped through a hole in the wall, had seen Tamira and Bussy together in 135 This name (Maffe in Chapman and in the text of D'Urfey's play) is used here asgiven in the *dramatis persona,* and so with certain other names.

her mistress's chamber the night before. This Charlot tells Monsieur while Montsurry is questioning Anaple; therefore Montsurry does not hear the story. Monsieur remains, after the others have left, meditating over a way of removing Bussy. Bussy enters, forcing his way in. He and Monsieur describe each the other's character in unflattering terms. The two then leave together for the banquet as bitter, but silent, enemies.

At the conclusion of the banquet, Tamira and Bussy feign not to be acquainted. Monsieur hints to Bussy that he will expose to Montsurry Bussy's relations with Tamira. Bussy threatens Monsieur with immediate and condign punishment in that event, and frightens him badly. Monsieur "makes horns" at Montsurry, nevertheless, when they and the Duke of Guise are alone together. Monsieur promises to explain in writing his gesture and leaves as Tamira enters. Montsurry accuses Tamira of infidelity but she claims innocence and alleges that Monsieur has been revenging himself for her refusal of his desires. A scene of comic relief now interposes. Masse, Monsieur's steward, whom Bussy has beaten, in order to defend himself in the future, decides to take fencing-lessons. Laffoil, Montsurry's groom, being introduced as a fencing-master, relates some previous exploits of his, including a fight at a play, and illustrates upon Masse how he had handled his opponents. He then fences with Masse, the two using bed staves, and beats the steward severely. Masse hears Laffoil mention Bussy's name. Imagin-

ing he hears Bussy approaching, Masse flees in terror, while Laffoil takes off his disguise and with the other servants prepares for a debauch. Masse's fright had been planned by them as a means of removing him so that he would not interfere with their sport. In the meantime, Bussy and Tamira are together with Teresia. Montsurry returns with Monsieur and Guise. Bussy escapes through the trap door and so they do not find him. After Tamira's exit, Charlot brings in a letter stolen from Tamira's cabinet, being a copy of her last missive to Bussy. The letter is sufficient evidence of Tamira's guilt. Montsurry resolves to force Tamira to confess the name of the go-between of her and Bussy; this done he intends to cause his wife to write a letter to be sent to Bussy by this messenger, appointing a meeting. Bussy then would be surprised in Tamira's chamber by concealed armed men and slain.

Montsurry drags Tamira in by the hair, and tortures her. She refuses to reveal the messenger or to write the letter to Bussy. Finally, Teresia, who is in the secret passage, to save her mistress, appears and confesses that she has carried the letters between the lovers. Montsurry kills Teresia and hides her body in the vault. Meanwhile Tamira has written in her own blood the required letter to Bussy appointing a meeting. Bussy has a Magician raise a spirit, Behemoth, who shows Bussy in a dream the manner of his death. Bussy is then warned by the Magician against his next meeting with Tamira, but when Charlot brings him his mistress's letter he resolves to visit her. On ascending from the passage with Charlot, Bussy is warned of his danger by Tamira. He kills Charlot, but is set upon by Monsieur, Guise, and the Murderers. Bussy beats out the Murderers, killing some. He then attacks Monsieur and Guise, disarming the former and getting the better of the latter, but is attacked from behind by three or four Murderers. While he engages them, Monsieur and Guise escape. As Bussy embraces Tamira, Montsurry enters and fights with him, but Bussy gets him down. As

Bussy grants Montsurry his life, Monsieur and Guise enter and shoot Bussy in the back with pistols, wounding him mortally. Bussy dies. At the desire of Monsieur and Guise, Montsurry forgives Tamira, but, rejecting a reconciliation, she kills herself.

The Marriage-Hater Match'd was printed with the following titlepage: "the Marriage-hater Match'd: A COMEDY. Acted at the Theatre Royal By Their Majesties Servants. Written by Tho. D'urfey, Gent. *LONDON,* Printed for *Richard Bentley,* at the Post-House in *Russel-Street* in *Covent-Garden.* 1692. 156"

There is a possibility that this comedy was D'Urfey's next dramatic production after *A Fool's Preferment.* In IV, 2 (p. 40),an indenture is dated August 15, 1690, in the third year of the reign of William and Mary. This date, however, may have been chosen merely at random by the author, and so not have any connection with the actual time of composition or of presentation of the play. Genest157 includes it among the plays performed in 1692. Since Motteux is quoted in the *Biographia Dramaticd1TM* as writing of the play in the *Gentleman's Journal* for February, 1691-92, the date of 106 So the copy in the Harvard University Library. The Yale University Library copy was "Printed for *Richard Parker,* at the *Unicorn* under the *Royal Exchange;* and *Sam. Briscoe,* over against *Will's Coffee House* in *Covent-Garden,* 1692." *m Stage,* II, 19-20.

lss III, 21-22. the first performance of the comedy may be safely set as the first months of the year 1692 (New Style). Whincop who dates it in 1693 in his *List* is probably in error.159 D'Urfey dedicated *The Marriage-Hater Match'd* to the second Duke of Ormond. In his epistle dedicatory the author mentions the.encouragement which he had as a youth from the Duke's grandfather, the famous Viceroy of Ireland.

According to Gildon,160 *The Marriage-Hater Match'd* was very well received. It was acted six nights successively.161 D'Urfey in his dedication says that the play at last acquitted itself well on the stage, "tho' the thronging, imperfect Action, and worse than all, the faulty length, which I will never be guilty of again, render'd it little Diversion the first day."

Suffixed to the play is an interesting letter by Charles Gildon, a summary of which, together with some quotations, may not be unprofitable:

Some critics, Gildon says, plead that a bundle of dialogues is all that is necessary to a good play and that Terence's only excellence was neatness of phrase. To disprove this and to show Terence's excellence in plot, Gildon gives a synopsis of the *Andria* and remarks upon Terence's other comedies. He then states that a comedy should have a plot satisfactory in conclusion, and surprising and diverting in presentation. Going on to comment on D'Urfey's excellence in plot-making Gildon says, "By what has been said i. e., concerning the necessity of a plot for a comedy, will appear that you, Sir, keep up to the noble Standard of the Antients, and tho' it be one of the greatest and most difficult parts of the hard task of a Comick Poet, yet you have always been very fortunate in it, especially in this last Comedy of yours, called the *Marriage-Hater Match'd.* I must needs say I think it is your best, and far beyond that of the *Boarding School;* the turns are so surprizing, and so natural, that I may say without flattery, 'tis not in the power of any Person to out-do them. The wit of Sir *Philip* and the Widow, like sprightly Blood in youthful Veins, runs through the whole Play, giving it a Noble and vigorous Life; you have further observ'd that *decorum* of Poetick Justice, in making Sir *Philip* — P. 226.

180 Gildon's Langbaine's *English Dramatic Poets,* pp. 51-52. *191* Motteux's *Gentleman's Journal,* February, 1691-92. (Quoted, *Biographia Dramatica* III, 21-22. See also Gildon's epistle to the author as quotea later). be caught in his own Plot, to deceive another, and marry her, who had so well merited him, as *Phoebe,* alias *Lovewell,* who made a very pretty Figure on the Stage. Such a variety of Humours and Characters I have seldom seen in one Play; and those so truly drawn, that they all look like principal Parts; and that, which is more, they are all *New,* and so worthy observation, that indeed I admire the humour of Madam *La Pupsey* has been so long neglected, since grown to so general a custom, that the Lap-Dog takes up all the thoughts of the fair Sex, whilst the faithful Lover sighs in vain, and at a distance unregarded; This was an usurpation on our Prerogative,-and had been born too long.162 The humour of *Van Grin* is new, and not so unpleasant, but that it deserves to be more taken notice of, being very material to set off the rest. "Then the skittishness of Miss *Margery,* and the freakishness of *Berenice,* are faults too general not to be exposed; besides, who is there so, wedded to Melancholy, like the Son of the Emperor *Philip* the First, but must give way to Laughter, to see the pleasant Humour of *Bias,* and the extraordinary diversion of *Solon.*

"I am sensible that *Callow* was so like the Life, that the *Rot me* Sparks openly declar'd their dissatisfaction at the Satyr:16S but 'tis a sign it hit them, when they complain of the wound. 'Tis a base and ill-natur'd, as well as ignorant Age of Chriticism, when the Vertues of a *Play* shall be Arraigned as Defects; for if these Gentlemen understood either the Original, or end of Comedy, they wou'd never quarrel with the Satyr of it, since from the beginning 'twas design'd to correct Vice, and Folly, by exposing them."

Gildon then discourses on the origin of comedy and quotes the lines from Horace, *Satires,* Bk. I, Sat. 4, that D'Urfey had placed on the titlepage of *A Fool's Preferment.* The critic proceeds, "... So that to eccept against your Play, for the Satyr of it only, shows your Enemies are wretchedly put to't to find a real fault in't, when they condemn that which is an Excellence, without which, the Poet gains but half his point, losing the Utile, which is an essential part of his Design and Duty.

lra *A Song, Pills to Purge Melancholy,* I, 280, is directed at the fondness of ladies for lapdogs. 1M Probably not on account of the satire upon profanity, but because of the attempt at making a Jacobite ridiculous.

"But if you cou'd meet with generous Enemies, they would/ forgive those Errors their quicker sight might discover, for the Beauties and delightful Entertainment of the Lyric part, the Songs I mean, in which I think there is none will (I am sure none ought to) dispute your Title to the Preheminence. J

"If there be any fault in this Play, 'tis that which few are guilty of; that is, there are too many good Characters, too full of Humour, a very pardonable failing, which only proceeds from Variety, the life of Pleasure and Wit, tho' the Stage's being throng'd with Spectators, did not a little contribute to the imperfect Acting of it, which accidental Misfortunes concurring with the Endeavours of an opposite Faction, must needs have damn'd it, had it not by the Force and Vigour of its own Worth rais'd itself the second day with the general Applause of all that saw it. *Horace* thinks it a sufficient proof of a good Poem, if it will bear a second view; *Hac placuit semel, hac bis repetita placebit.* But the *Marriage-Hater* went further, and in spight of all the disadvantages it labour'd under of Action and Audience, pleas'd on, after several times Repetition, and will as long as *Wit, Humour,* and *Plot* shall be esteem'd as necessary Materials to compose a good Play."

The high praise Gildon accords *The Marriage-Hater Match'd* in the foregoing letter is somewhat qualified several years later in his edition of Langbaine's *English Dramatic Poets.* There164 he says that the play is the best of D'Urfey's comedies, but that the epistle to the author printed with it goes too far in eulogy of it. The *Biographia Dramatical* "cannot subscribe" to the opinion that *The Marriage-Hater* is the best of D'Urfey's comedies. Genest considers it a "very good comedy."166 The comedy was revived at Norris's benefit at Drury Lane, June 23, 1704, as not acted for three years.167

In spite of the superlative praise of Gildon168 and the more qualified approval of later critics, the writer con-

siders *The MarriageHater Match'd* to be among D'Urfey's poorest comedies. The plot is slight, and is padded out by a multiplicity of characters who have

M Pp. 51-52.
»in, 21-22.
i« *Stage,* II, 20. in *Ibid,* II, 301. 188 Gildon's appreciative and critical powers are best illustrated by his introduction to his butchery of Langbaine's *English Dramatic Poets.* but little to do with the action. The marrying of six couples at the masquerade, three of these weddings being due to mistakes of one kind or another, is the height of absurdity. D'Urfey's attempts at satire, here as elsewhere, are with the exception of his hits at the lap-dog lady, Madam La Pupsey, singularly futile.

However, the play has various interesting features about it f which result from its relationships with other plays. Two Elizabethan plays present themselves as possible sources (or at least parallels) for part of the plot of Sir Philip, Phœbe, and Lady Subtle. In Middleton's *More Dissemblers besides Women,* Lactantio promises marriage to a lady whom he then betrays. She serves him as a page. Refusing to carry out his promise to the lady, Lactantio courts Aurelia and the Duchess. With both of them he is unsuccessful. His perfidy to his former mistress being discovered by her bearing a child, he is forced to marry her. In Brome's *Northern Lass* (which had been revived in 1684 at the Theatre Royal), Sir Philip Luckless deserts Constance (who, he thinks, confusing her with another woman, has had a child by him). Sir Philip marries a rich widow, but does not consummate the marriage, which later is dissolved. Sir Philip finally marries Constance. A masque occurs in *The Northern Lass,* as does the marriage of a fool to a prostitute. A bogus marriage performed by a servant in disguise (that of Fitchow and Sir Philip) also takes place. The reader will remember also that in *The Virtuous Wife* Olivia in male disguise obtains a casket of jewels from Jenny Wheadle.

The title of D'Urfey's comedy recalls *The Woman Hater* of Fletcher. Callow's oaths are reminiscent of those of Master

Stephen, *Every Man in his Humor,* III, 1. Codshead in *The Triumphant Widow* is a similar character. In Darewell, the sea-captain, we have a figure like that of Captain Porpuss in *Sir Barnaby Whigg.* Solon and Bias with their foolish father, Sir Laurence, are reincarnations of Zechiel and Toby, and their father Captain Tilbury in *Madam Fickle.* Of the same sort are Old Winelove and Tim in *The Fool Turn'd Critic;* and Sir Carolus Codshead with his sons, Charles and Henry, in *The Bath.* Berenice is a repetition of Gratiana in *Sir Barnaby Whigg.* Her tilts with Darewell and his subsequent victory over her are suggestive of the plays of *The Scornful Lady* type. Margery, as a lisping girl, has but one prototype, so far as the writer is aware, that being Amoretta in Ford's *Lady's Trial.* As a hoyden, Margery is akin to Phillida in *A Fool's Preferment,* Molly and Jenny in *Love for Money,* Gatty in *The Bath.*

Doggett, the famous comedian, is said first to have displayed his 1 ability as an actor in the part of Solon.169 As Quickwit in *The Richmond Heiress,* I, 1 (p. 2), Doggett refers to his own success as Solon in the present comedy. Sir Quibble Quere, *ibid* (p. 5), mentions Doggett's having acted Solon "so purely." The play was revived, as J "not acted there for 5 years," at Drury Lane, March 8, 1708.170 Lord Lansdowne in *The She Gallants* has used the relations of Sir Philip, Phoebe, and Lady Subtle. There Bellamour deserts Angelica to whom he is engaged. He courts Lucinda, but Angelica in male disguise, exposes his perfidy and wins him back to her. In Holcroft's *Road to Ruin* is what may be a borrowing from *The Marriage-Hater Match'd.* Silky in Holcroft's play obtains Mr. Warren's will, which should have been sent to Sulky. He withholds the document from the legitimate heir until Sulky and Milford obtain it by a trick (V, 3). This resembles Sir Philip's receiving Sir Solomon's will from Van Grin, who believes Sir Philip to be Counsellor Splutter. Sir Philip keeps the will from Lady Subtle, until by a ruse Phoebe gets it from him.

In I, 1 (p. 9), Callow alludes to a contemporary occurrence (the defeat of the Dutch-English fleet off Beachy Head, June 30, 1690, and the French naval attack on Teignmouth in July, 1690) when he mentions to Darewell, "the fresh-water Captains, that was so purposely blind that you would not see the French Fleet, when they were out, for fear of fighting, but still laid excuse upon a great Fog." The following passage, which, according to Gildon's letter as quoted above, might have applied to the first night of *The Marriage-Hater,* may have had something to do with what ill reception it received: *"L. Subt.* 'Dslife, there's no avoiding him Lord Brainless, he will visit every body, nor is every House sufficient, but like a Fly he'll be buzing in every Corner on't.
Beren. Just as he uses the Play-house, from the Box, whip he's in the Pit, from the Pit, hop he's in the Gallery, from thence, hey pass between the Scenes in a moment, where I have seen him spoil many a Comedy, by baulking the Actors entrance, for when I have eagerly expected some Buffoon to divert, the first nauseous appearance has been my Lord. " 1W Gildon's Langbaine's *English Dramatic Poets,* pp. 51-52. Genest, *Stage,* II, 399.
The characters and actors are listed as follows:
L. Brainless.
Sir Pilip J
Freewit. 1
Sir Lawr. J
Limber. 1
Capt. Darewell.
Myn Heer
Van Grin.
Bias.
Solon.
Callow.
Mac Buffle.-
Thummum.-
"The Names and Characters.171 A Pert, Noisy, Impertinent Boy, always thrusting himself into the Ladies Company, and receiv'd for his Treats, and the Diversion his Folly gives;
a great Admirer of *La Pupsey,* and jealous of her
Lap-dog: Acted by Mr. *Bowman.*

A wild witty Gent, of the Town, who being Jilted by Lady *Subtle,* whom he once Loved, professes himself a *Marriage Hater:* Acted by Mr. *Monfort.*
A peevish old-fashion'd Courtier, ridiculously Indulgent and Fond of the two Fools his Sons: Acted by Mr. *Sanford.*
An honest blunt Sea Captain, true to his Country's
(Interest, and the Government: Acted by Mr. *Hodson.*
(A Clownish fat Flanderkin, always laughing at
what he says himself, and believing it a Jest, tho'
never such Nonsence: Acted by Mr. *Leigh.*
Eldest Son to Sir *Lawrence,* a blunt rude Booby,
sawcy with Women; and tho' despis'd by 'em, very opinionated of his own Merit: Acted by Mr. *Bright.*
Youngest Son to Sir *Lawrence,* a dull softly Fool, till vex'd, but then robustly stout and jealous of Danger:
Acted by Mr. *Doggett.*
A raskally Lieutenant, disaffected to the Government,
tho' he has taken a commission to serve it; a fellow of no Principles, and always ending every Paragraph of his Discourse with an Oath or a Curse: Acted by
Mr. *Bowen.*
-An ignorant Irishman, Servant to Sir *Philip:* Acted by Mr. *Trefuse.*
-A toping Parson, Brother to *Mac Buffle;* by Mr.
Smeaton.
Splutter. A Cunning Tricking Lawyer, a Creature of Lady Subtle's.—Acted by Mr. *Colly."2* WOMEN
A Proud, high spirited Widow, who thinking her self affronted by Sir *Philip* by his Intrigue with *Phoebe,* tho' she had ingag'd to Marry him, breaks off all, and takes another: Acted by Mrs. *Barry. m* Imperfect and incorrect. Lady Hockley and Miss Bandy are not given (they appear, III, 2). In the play Comode is Lady Subtle's woman, and Pimpwell (Primwell in the *dramatis persona*) is Berenice's. See V, 3.
Mr. Colley Cibber; see Genest, *Stage,*

II, 19.
Phcebe, *ali.*
Lovewell.
Berenice.
Margery.
'A Prating, Matchmaking, Eating, Impertinent
Creature visiting every one for the sake of a good
Dinner, and always teizing 'em with fulsome stories of the Intrigues about the Town: Acted by Mrs.
Cory.
A pretty Innocent well-natur'd Creature, who being in Love with Sir *Philip,* and debauch'd by him upon his promise of Marriage, puts her self into Boys Clothes, and manages his business against the
Widow, underhand: Acted by Mrs. *Bracegirdle.*
A witty Sister to Lady Subtle, a Brisk Humorous Freakish Creature, who tho' She is in Love with Captain *Darewell,* is always teizing and playing tricks with him to know his Temper: Acted by Mrs. *Lasselles.*
!An Impertinent Creature, always stuffing her Discourse with hard words, and perpetually kissing and taking to her Lapdog: Acted by Mrs. *Butler.*
1Daughter to Sir Lawrence, a Lisping, Raw, Ignorant, Skittish Creature, Modest before Company, but otherwise awkerdly Confident: Acted by Mrs. *Lawson.* Comode.—Woman to *Berenice* Pimpwell.—Woman to Lady Subtle.
Singers, Masques, Drawers, *Footmen, and Attendants.* Scene, *The Park near* Kensington. *The Space, Thirty Hours."*
The plot of *The Marriage-Hater Match'd* may thus be given: Sir Philip Freewit and his friend Sir Solomon Subtle are friendly rivals for a lady's hand. She chooses Sir Solomon. He dies in a short time, and, because of Sir Philip's generosity in their rivalry (Sir Philip had suggested that the lady choose between them after each had courted her), wills both his property and his wife to Sir Philip. Lady Subtle, however, will have nothing to do with Sir Philip, on account, of her discovery of his intrigue

with Phœbe. This had indeed been the reason for her choosing Sir Solomon rather than Sir Philip. Lady Subtle withholds from Sir Philip some part of Sir Solomon's estate which Sir Philip cannot prove had been bequeathed to him. To obtain the writings necessary to prove his right to this property (which is an estate left Sir Solomon by an uncle in Hamburg), Sir Philip enlists Phœbe, who, disguised as a man under the name of Lovewell, is admitted into Lady Subtle's family. Sir Lawrence Limber's foolish sons, Solon and Bias, come up to London from the country. Bias, the elder, is intended by his father as a husband for Lady Subtle, and Solon for her, sister Berenice.

Sir Philip disguises himself as Counsellor Splutter, Lady Subtle's lawyer, into whose possession Sir Solomon's will is to be given by her, so that the Counsellor may see if it is valid. In the meantime, the genuine Counsellor has been sent out of the way on a fool's errand. Van Grin, a Fleming and a suitor to Lady Subtle, who has brought the papers from Hamburg, is sent with them to» the lawyer. Van Grin gives them to Sir Philip disguised as Splutter.

Lady Subtle learns the cheat. As she rails on Van Grin'sstupidity in allowing himself to have been so deceived, Bias enters to court her. She attacks him and also sets on Solon (who has come to ask her intervention in his behalf with Berenice), on Sir Lawrence, who enters to see how his sons' suits are progressing, and on Van Grin himself. Lady Subtle finally drives them out with a pistol. Then Sir Philip enters and comes close to making love to her. Although really hating Sir Philip for his victory over her, Lady Subtle pretends to favor his suit; but finally she breaks out and rails at him and drives him from the room. Phoebe reminds Sir Philip of his promise to marry her, but he refuses, since he has contracted from Lady Subtle's dealings with him an aversion to marriage. Phoebe then resolves to trick Sir Philip into marriage with her.

Callow, a lieutenant, has been courting Margery, Sir Lawrence's ignorant, lisping daughter, who is modest before company, but forward in a *tete-a-tete*. Sir Lawrence eavesdrops and finds out hisdaughter's true character. At some scurrilous remarks of Callow concerning himself, Sir Lawrence breaks out and drives him from the house. Darewell, a sea-captain, courts Berenice, who flouts him. She sends for him to meet her, and then appears in company with Solon, whom she has sent for also, and whom, in order to anger Darewell, she pretends to favor. Phoebe, who has revealed her identity to Lady Subtle and has joined with her in an attempt to circumvent Sir Philip, obtains the papers and some jewels from Sir Philip by a ruse and makes her escape with them, while Splutter and Sir Philip are conferring over details connected with the inheritance. Sir Philip discovers the theft and its perpetrator. While he laments his loss, Lady Subtle and Phoebe mock him.

Phoebe is seized by pity at Sir Philip's plight and promises: him the papers and jewels if he will carry out his promise of marrying her. Sir Philip gives the required promise, intending to trick Phœbe by having Mac Buffle, his Irish valet, perform the ceremony in the course of a masquerade to be held that night at Lady Subtle's. Sir Lawrence, dressed as an old woman, appears with Bias also in disguise, the latter having been told by Lady Subtle that he should steal her away in disguise from the masquerade. Callow and Margery, who have eloped, appear in disguise, but are recognized by Sir Lawrence who follows them. Darewell, enraged at meeting Berenice with Solon again, forces Berenice to go with him and be married. Lord Brainless is married to Madam La Pupsey. Bias is married to Comode, Lady Subtle's woman, who is in disguise; while his brother Solon is discovered to have been married to Pimpwell, Berenice's woman, who is also disguised. Phœbe discovers her marriage to Sir Philip, then. He refuses to acknowledge her as his wife, and unmasks the supposed valet masquerading as clergyman, only to find that it is Thurnmum, Mac Buffle's brother, and a clergyman, who has performed the ceremony, which, therefore, is valid. Through a misapprehension of his master's purpose Mac Buffle has secured his brother to officiate, instead of doing so himself. Sir Philip's plot is thus frustrated. Finally Sir Philip is reconciled to his fate, after he has been jeered for having been trapped; and he promises to give back to Lady Subtle what of Sir Solomon's estate is rightfully hers.

The Richmond Heiress: or, a Woman Once in the Right, was printed173 with the following titlepage:

"the Richmond Heiress: Or, A *Woman Once in the Right.* A COMEDY, Acted At the THEATRE ROYAL, By Their Majesties Servants. Written by Mr. *D'URFEY. LONDON,* Printed for *Samuel Briscoe,* over-against *Will's* Coffee-House in *Covent-Garden.* 1693."

This comedy was probably first acted early in 1693 (Old Style).174 The dedication is dated May 6, 1693. In it D'Urfey refers to the length of the play being too great for the time of the year, indicating, it would seem, that the first performance had occurred in the spring when the days were lengthening and the weather becoming warm.

173 This play is exceptionally badly printed. The early part of IV, 1, seems to have suffered most. There the pagination leaps from p. 36 to p. 41. No material appears to have been omitted. In III, 3 (p. 29), occurs the stage direction, *"Exii Sir Quib. and* Dog.," meaning Doggett, who played Quickwit and who had just been on the stage; IV, 1 (p. 36), *"Exit* Dogget *and* Marm."; IV, 4 (p. 48), *"Enter Sin* Quibble, Fulvia, Doggett *and* Marmalett." Similar blunders occur in *The Injured Princess, A Fool's Preferment,* and other plays of D'Urfey. 174 See Genest, *Stage,* II, 46. *The Richmond Heiress* seems not to have been very favorably received.175 In his dedication to Sir Nicholas Garrard, D'Urfey says:

"Sir the Comedy I now present to you is in the best Judgment of my most judicious Friends one of the best of mine, and till I see more and better Matter and Humour in a scripture of this kind, I shall not be uneasie when I think on the little poor abuses and disturbances of a malecontent Party, that like the Devil have for some late Years ow'd me an ill turn, and I have reason to fear nor will never have done paying me.

"The entertainment of Songs and Dances in it, as they gave more diversion than is usually seen in Comedy's, so they were perform'd with-general Applause, and I think my Enemies have cause to say with greater than is ordinary; and though this had its Inconveniences by lenghtening the whole Piece a little beyond the common time of Action, which at this time 6' th' Year I am sensible is a very great Fault, yet the worst of malice has granted me this, that there appeared no defect of Genius, whatever there might of Judgment." In the prologue (spoken by Doggett), D'Urfey refers to a movement on foot, according to report, to damn the play. Gildon176 says the comedy pleased the town upon its being revived with alterations, *The Richmond Heiress* was played as "not acted 6 years" at Drury Lane, March 2, 1714, and was repeated for the author's benefit, June 7.177 It should be noticed that six years earlier (1708) *The Marriage-Hater Match'd* and *Love for Money* were both played at Drury Lane. Probably *The Richmond Heiress* was also then performed, no reference to the revival being now known. In 1777 at Richmond, an alteration by F. G. Waldron of the comedy was brought out, It would seem not unlikely that Vanbrugh in Lord Foppington's description of his day *(The Relapse, II, i)* drew on Sophronia's description to Hotspur of the day of a Man of the Town, II, 1 (p. 14). Possibly, too, Mrs. Centlivre founded Feignwell's disguise as Simon Pure, the Quaker, in *A Bold Stroke for a Wife* upon those of Quickwit and Cunnington.

Among the interesting features of the play are Rice ap Shinken, a comic Welshman, who differs from his predecessors in being a beau. In the name and general character of Hotspur, D'Urfey lre Gildon's Langbaine's *English Dramatic Poets*, p. 52. *TM Ibid.* 17T Genest, *Stage*, II, 525, 527. At his benefit D'Urfey spoke an "Oration" as a prologue, part of which was designed for

a new comedy called *A Wife Worth a Kingdom*. appears to have drawn upon *Henry IV, Part I*. In I, 1 (p. 7), speaking of Shinken, Hotspur says,

"A Fellow that makes Fritters of *English*, as

Falstaffe says?"

The allusion is to *The Merry Wives of Windsor*, V, 5, where Falstaff says of Sir Hugh Evans,

"Have I liv'd to stand at the taunt of one that makes fritters of English?" In IV, 4 (p. 49), Shinkin says,

".... The Prittaines have no such Pribbles and Prabbles." Sir Hugh Evans, *The Merry Wives of Windsor*, I, 1, says,

".... If we leave our pribbles and prabbles," and Fluellen, *Henry V*, IV, 8, "Keep you out of prawls and prabbles." Falstaff, perhaps, in *Henry IV, Part I*, II, 4,178 is drawn on in

"The Race of Men are all Deceivers. " *The Richmond Heiress*, V, 5, p. 64. Quickwit's description of himself as of the "De la Fool's of the South" is doubtless based upon Sir Amorous la Fool's pedigree, as given by himself in Jonson's *Epicoene* I, 1. The marriage of Fulvia, the heiress, to Quickwit, who has acted as Frederick's agent through the play, is suggestive of Millisent's marriage to Sir Martin's man, Warner, in *Sir Martin Mar-all*. Her choice of Quickwit tends toward the sentimental, however. The part of the play-which deals with Dick Stockjobb and his unfaithful wife was not unprobably suggested by Colonel and Mrs. Hackwell in Shadwell's posthumous comedy, *The Volunteers*, produced in 1692 with a prologue by D'Urfey. In I, 1 (p 2), Doggett as Quickwit refers to "Solon in the play." This is Solon in *The Marriage Hater Match'd*, a part created by Doggett, and performed successfully by him. I, 1 (p. 5), Sir Quibble Quere refers to Doggett's having acted Solon "so purely." Sir Quibble in the same scene (pp. 4-5) refers to many other actors and actresses: Betterton, Nokes, Sandford, Underhill, Mrs. Barry, Powel, Bowen, Mrs. Bracegirdle, Dogget, Bowman, Bright, Hudson, Hains, Kinaston. Of these he praises particularly Mrs. Barry as the Queen in *The Spanish* Friar; Pow-

el; Mrs. Bracegirdle as Statira in *The Rival Queens*, Dogget, as mentioned above; and Kinaston,179 "the last, not least in Love, the only remaining branch of the old Stock." 178 See *ante*, p. 39. ire The spelling of the text has been retained in this list.

In IV, 1 (p. 41), occurs "A piece of Wit like Hains." The same type of allusion occurs in other plays, as for example, Nokes playing Sir Credulous Easy, mentions himself by name in *Sir Patient Fancy*, IV. 1.

Genest's judgment180 upon *The Richmond Heiress* is that "it is a good bustling comedy but might be shortened to advantage." To the present writer the play seems rather feeble. Farce and high comedy are too injudiciously mixed; the same characters take part in both. As a result the play is neither serious nor comic, but rather a jumble of both. A surprise occurs in Fulvia's repudiation of Frederick in the last scene of the play. Fulvia's statement of her determination to fix her choice upon a worthy and noble man and her selection of Quickwit, the poor scholar, reveals D'Urfey again as a dabbler in sentimental comedy.181 Here the dramatist has displayed a certain recognition of moral values in making the fickle Frederick lose, the heiress because he had jilted Sophronia.

The characters and actors follow:

"The Actors Names and Characters.

Sir *Charles Romance*, A travell'd old Knight, grave and sententious, Guardian to the Heiress and Father-in Law, yet contriving her for his Son. Acted by Mr. *Freeman*.

Sir *Quibble Quere*, A soft, easie half-witted Knight, credulous to an extravagant degree, perpetually asking questions about the Play-House and Town-Intrigues, tho' always banter'd and kept in Ignorance. By Mr. *Bright. Tom Romance*, Son to Sir Charles; a young, vain, fluttering lying Fellow, always bragging of his Mistresses Favours, and shewing their Presents, perpetually intriguing, and never constant to any. By Mr. *Powel*.

Dr. *Guiacum*, An opinionated Chimical Doctor, a great pretender to cure Lunaticks and Claps. By *Mr. Sandford*.

Frederick, Half-Brother to Sir *Quibble;* a witty, young, TownSpark, who through the Vice and Inconstancy of his Humour, tho' he were contracted to *Sophronia,* breaks off with her upon a slight occasion, to pursue an Intrigue with the Heiress, who has much the greater Fortune. By Mr. *Williams.* . *Rice ap Shinken,* A young, whimsical, *Welsh* Fop, that imitates *Tom Romance* in intriguing, his Kinsman too and Companion. By Mr. *Bowman.*
Dick Stockjobb, An opionated impertinent Citizen, a great Stock-jobber, and always laying Wagers, and against the Government. By Mr. *Underhill.*
'» *Stage,* II, 47.
181 His previous essay in this field, and among the first, so far as the present writer knows, of sentimental comedies, is *Love for Money. Hotspur, A* rash, hot-headed, quarrelsom Fellow, Friend to *Frederick,* and intrigu'd with Mrs. *Stockjobb.* By Mr. *Hudson.*
Quickwit, A witty, but poor Scholar, that being hired by *Frederick* to steal the Heiress, feigns himself mad, and takes upon him the Name of the Lord *de la 'Fool.* By Mr. *Dogget.*
Cunningtotij Subtle and mischievous, and Antagonist to *Quick-wit* in his Design upon the Heiress. By Mr. *Bowen.*
Christopher, Servant to Dr. *Guiacum.*
Numps, A Country-Fellow, employ'd as Servant to my Lord *de la Fool.* WOMEN *Fulvia,* The Heiress, a witty, generous and virtuous young Lady, who being privately in love with *Frederick,* feigns herself lunatick to trick her Guardian, and avoid impertinent Suitors. Acted by Mrs. *Bracegirdle. Sophronia, A* Female plain-dealer, passionate and high-spirited, very satyrical upon the Town Humours, and particularly severe upon Frederick for deserting her. By Mrs. *Barry.*
Mrs. *Stockjobb,* alias *Pogry,* Stock-jobb's Wife, formerly a *French-man's* Widow in Picardy; but coming over as a Refugee, is married to *Stockjobb,* a trim,

gay Coquette, yet pretending to Religion and Good-breeding. By Mrs. *Bowman.*
Madam *Squeamish, A* young fantastical Creature of *Richmond,* horribly afraid of being Lampoon'd, and yet perpetually doing something or other to deserve it. By Mrs. *Knight.*
Marmalette, An old ridiculous Waiting-Woman of *Fulvia's,* very desirous of a Husband, and contriving all she can to get one. By Mrs. *Lee.*
Pomade. A Waiting-Maid.
Madmen, Clown, Musicians, Singers, Dancers, Constable and Watch, Footmen and Attendants. The Scene Richmond-//!//."
The plot of *The Richmond Heiress* is as follows:

To thwart the plans of her stepfather and guardian, Sir Charles Romance, who designs to marry her to his son Tom, Fulvia, an heiress, pretends to be insane. Frederick, her lover, who is in the secret of her feigned madness, gets Quickwit, a needy scholar, to aid him in eloping with Fulvia. Fulvia is attended by an ignorant quack, Dr. Guiacum.

Disguised as a madman under the name of Lord de la Fool, Quickwit is placed as a patient in Dr. Guiacum's care. Quickwit gives Fulvia a letter from Frederick in which are instructions as to her part in his device for accomplishing her escape from her stepfather's surveillance.

Cunnington, angered at Quickwit because he will not impart Frederick's project regarding Fulvia, resolves to frustrate the scheme. Disguised as a French fortuneteller and conjurer, Cunnington tricks Fulvia's waiting-woman, Marrhalette, into telling him the plans of Frederick and her mistress. Cunnington then promises Marmalette that she shall marry Quickwit who shortly will become a duke. Marmalette courts Quickwit who scorns her. She then calls in two other female servants with cudgels, as Cunnington has advised her to do in case of Quickwit's refusal of her, and all three beat Quickwit. Numps,

Quickwit's servant, and Fulvia enter now and announce that their plans have been betrayed to Sir Charles. They learn that the informer is Cunnington. Sir Charles and Dr. Guiacum enter with their servants. Guiacum orders that Numps-and Quickwit be beaten, ducked, and tossed in blankets. A stricter watch is then set upon Fulvia.

Quickwit makes love now to Marmalette, and so secures her cooperation in a further attempt at aiding Fulvia. Quickwit disguises himself as Zechiel, the Quaker steward of Fulvia's deceased father, in whose possession are the deeds to her estate. Cunnington, also in disguise as a Quaker, is sent as Sir Charles's agent to Dr. Guiacum to escort Fulvia to Sir Charles. Cunnington is also to carry with him the deeds. He resolves to abduct Fulvia. However, Marmalette has stolen Sir Charles's letter to Guiacum from Cunnington and has substituted for it one forged by Quickwit in which Cunnington is introduced to the Doctor as a new patient for his asylum. Cunnington is seized by Dr. Guiacum and treated as a lunatic, while Quickwit appears in his Quaker disguise with the genuine letter from Sir Charles and conducts Fulvia away. Sir Charles learns of Fulvia's flight. He and Guiacum are informed by Cunnington, who has escaped from the asylum, of the place of retreat of Frederick and Fulvia. As the young elopers are awaiting the parson, Sir Charles and a party come upon them and seize Fulvia.

Quickwit and Cunnington meet at a tavern to discuss their past rivalry. Cunnington tells Quickwit that a masque is to be held at Sir Charles's to celebrate the betrothal of Tom and Fulvia. Cunnington is to take the part of Pluto in the masque, but Quickwit arranges the seizure of Cunnington by some countrymen who take his costume from him. The masque is presented with Frederick as Orpheus and Quickwit as Pluto, but as Fulvia is being led off by them, she halts, and, unmasking them, reveals the perfidy of Frederick toward Sophronia, as previously related to her by that lady. Fulvia produces Frederick's contract of marriage with Sophronia, and breaks off her own clandestine engagement with him. She reveals that Tom Romance has paid his addresses to Sophronia, and so she refuses to have anything to do with him. Then, having secured from Sir Charles (who thinks that, after all, her choice will light upon Tom) permission to choose a husband to suit herself, she selects Quickwit, much to the discomfiture of Marmalette, whom Quickwit has courted for the advancing of his own and Frederick's plans.

An underplot is concerned with Tom Romance's intrigue with Mrs. Stockjobb, who has been Hotspur's mistress. Stockjobb, her husband, who is intent upon moneymaking, believes his wife to have none but business relations with Tom. Hotspur finally convinces Stockjobb of his wife's infidelity. She appears with Stockjobb's jewels which she is to give Tom. Instead, she gives them to her husband, who is muffled up in Tom's cloak and wears his hat. She is then disowned by Stockjobb.

Another thread of the play concerns the intrigue of Shinkin ap Rice with Squeamish, a lady who fears lampoons. *The Comical History of Don Quixote, Part I,* was first acted early in 1694.182 The titlepage of the play runs:

"the Comical History OF DON QUIXOTE, As it is Acted At The QUEEN"S THEATRE, In'Dorset-Garden. By their Majesties Servants, Part I *Written by* Mr. D'Urfey. LONDON, Printed for *Samuel Briscoe,* at the Corner of *Charlesstreet,* in *Russel-street, Covent-Garden,* 1694.188" Don Quixote, Part I, was well received on the stage it would seem. In his dedication of the comedy to the Duchess of Ormond, D'Urfey says:

"Don Quixote having not only been well Receiv'd upon the Stage, but also having clear'd himself with Reputation, from

"*Genest, Stage,* II, 55.
183 From there being printed within inverted commas passages in II, 1, 2, III, 1, were evidently omitted from the acting version of the play (see the preface to *Part II).* the Slander and Prejudice which malicious Criticks had resolv'd upon, to sully and blast him...." Gildon

speaks of the extraordinary applause accorded the play.184 It seems, however, not to have been as popular as *Part II. Part I* was revived at the Haymarket, February 1, 1710.185 The "two parts probably / and II made one by the author" was acted at the Haymarket, August 16, 1706.186 The performances at the same theatre on April 30, 1705, and at Drury Lane, June 9, 1712 (Thurmond's benefit), were probably of *Part I.*187 With the other two parts, *Part I* was reprinted in 1729. Whatever the popular opinion of the *Don Quixote* plays may have been, they were not approved of by one critic. This was the famous Jeremy Collier, who in his *Short View of the Immorality and Profaneness of the English Stage188* empties the vials of his wrath upon the head of D'Urfey. It seems best at this point to outline Collier's attack upon the dramatist.

Collier criticizes D'Urfey under three heads:

"I. *His Profaneness with respect to* Religion *and the* Holy Scriptures.

II. *His Abuse of the* Clergy. III. *His want of Modesty and Regard to the* Audience. " r Under the head of Profaneness189 Collier censures D'Urfey's songs in *Don Quixote, Part I,* II, 2 *(Song,* pp. 19-20; *Dirge,* p. 20);. Ill, 2 *(Song, pp.* 37-38); V, 2 *(Song,* p. 60); and the *Epilogue By l_Sancho Riding upon his Ass.* Collier objects to Gines's use of "dear Redeemer," as applied to Don Quixote *(Part I,* III, 2, p. 38) since the expression "among Christians is appropriated to our Blessed Saviour."190 The bringing of the Devil upon the stage, *Part II,* II, 2 (p. 17 ff.), is displeasing to Collier, as well as is the frequent "deep-mouth'd swearing."

As Abuse of the Clergy, Collier cites several passages in the plays.191 In *Part I,* II, 1 (p. 10 ff.), he fixes on Perez's assisting in the knighting of Don Quixote as an example. Another case is Sancho's saying, "A Bishop is no more than another Man without 184 Gildon's Langbaine's *English Dramatic Poets,* p. 50.
« Genest, *Stage,* II, 448.

'-*Ibid,* II, 352.
181 *Ibid,* II, 330, 499, respectively.
188 Chap. V, Sect. 2 (pp. 196-208).
188 *Short View,* pp. 196-99.
"'*Ibid,* p. 198.
181 *Ibid,* pp. 199-202.

Grace, and good Breeding," *Part I,* IV, 1 (p. 49). Collier stops a moment to poke fun at D'Urfey's characterization of Sancho in the *dramatis persons,* as "a dry shrewd Country Fellow." Collier terms this description misleading, judging from Sancho's conduct in the play.192 The critic then points out Sancho's "Irreverence and Profaneness" toward Perez, *Part I,* IV, 1 (p. 51). It is noted by the divine that the Country Wenches call Father Jodelet "a holy Cormorant" and remark on his unclerical appetite for breakfast and that they allude to him as a pimp *(Part II,* I, 1, p. 3).193 Collier comments upon the treatment of the Duke's Chaplain, Bernardo, in *Part II,* I, 2.194 Collier notes then the allusion to the"! clergy as "black cattle" in the Clown's Song. *(Part II,* IV, 3, p. 46). _j

Under the third head, Want of Modesty and Regard for the Audience,195 Collier takes up first the smutty talk of Sancho, Teresa, and Mary, and cites *Part I,* I, 2 (pp. 7-8); *Part II,* V, 1 (p. 57); the indecent closing couplet of the epilogue to *Part I;* and Marcella's ravings, *Part II,* V, 2 (p. 60). To show what he calls indecency mixed with profaneness, Collier instances *Part I,* III, 2 (p. 38), and *Part II,* II, 1 (p. 14). Filthy epithets, allusions and anecdotes are pointed out by the critic as occurring in *Part I,* I, 2 (pp. 7-8); *Part II,* V, 1 (p. 52), IV, 1 (p. 36), IV, 3 (p. 49), IV, 1 (p. 37), IV, 3 (p. 44). The preface to *Part III* is also objected to here. Again Collier casts a doubt upon the accuracy of the *dramatis persona* in describing persons in the play, this time as regards Manuel and Sancho as "pleasant sharp Fellows," on account of the dialogue, *Part II,* III, 2 (p. 31). Collier then characterizes the examination of the Taylor and the Gardner, *Part II, V, I* (p. 51 ff.), as lying "much in in the same Latitude of Understanding" as the conversation of Manuel and Sancho above-mentioned.

Part III gets its part of Collier's ridicule, both as to action and characters,196 but does not receive the attention accorded the other two parts. The dedications of *Parts I* and *///* to the Duchess of Ormond and to Charles Montague, respectively, come in for their share of Collier's attention.197

» *Ibid*, p. 200.

lmIbid, p. 201.

MIbid, pp. 201-02. Collier should have referred here to p. 12 of the play and not o p. 41.

"'Ibid, pp. 202-06.

MIbid, p. 206.

""Ibid, p. 207.

At length, Collier gives his final judgment on D'Urfey, summing him up in these words:

"Vox & praeterea nihil," Hetthen quotes a translation from Boileau's *Art of Poetry* which he applies to D'Urfey.

Collier's charges are undoubtedly well-founded. D'Urfey did introduce profanity into his plays; he undoubtedly abused the clergy; and he certainly shows a want of regard for the modest portion of his audience, supposing such to have existed. But unfortunately in many places Collier in dealing with D'Urfey's plays, as with those of the other authors he attacked, twists the meaning of expressions to suit his purpose, and in some places absolutely misinterprets the text. Too, had Collier gone to some of D'Urfey's early plays, he would have found much better examples of the objectionable elements which he attacks, than those he finds in *Don Quixote,19* In short, Collier's charges are well-founded in general, but the evidence brought forward is by no means the best.

As a sequel to Collier's criticism of *Don Quixote,* the following may be quoted:

"Narcissus Lutrel tells us that on May 12, 1698, 'The Justices of Middlesex did not only prosecute the play-houses, but also Mr. Congreve for writing The Double Dealer, D'Urfey, for Don Quixote, and Tonson and Brisco, booksellers for printing them.' "199

D'Urfey "answered" Collier's charges almost immediately in a long preface attached to *The Campaigners. 200* The strongest element in this is its abuse of Collier; the rest is exceedingly weak.

D'Urfey's *Don Quixote, Part I,* is based upon Cervantes's famous novel. The play is not unskilfully composed of bits picked out here and there from the novel and woven into a story. D'Urfey does not follow Cervantes in the order of events, nor does he scruple at the introduction of new material or the radical revision of the old. D'Urfey probably used Shelton's translation, and not the Spanish original, as he quotes Shelton in his preface to *The CamJ paigners. 201* 1M Certain of these the writer gives in connection with D'Urfey's answer to Collier, prefixed to *The Campaigners.* 199 Gosse, *Life of Congreve,* p. 119. 200 In connection with which the writer has considered it. 201 P. 23.

The relations of the play to the novel may be shown by the following table:

By

Mr. *Boen.*

Mr. *Powel.*

The characters and performers follow:

"Dramatis Personae.

Men *Don Quixote.* A frantick Gentleman of the *Mancha* in *Spain,* that fancies himself a Knight Errant.

Don *Fernando.* A young Nobleman.

Cardenio. A Gentleman, that being treach-Mr. *Bowman.* erously depriv'd of *Luscinda,* his Betroth'd Mistress, fell Mad.

Ambrosio. A young Student, and Mr. *Verbruggen.*

Stranger, a Friend to *Chrysostome.* and a great Woman-hater. *Perez.* A Curate. Mr. *Cibber. Nicholas.* A merry Drolling Barber. *Mr. Harris. Sancho Panca.* A dry shrewd Country Fel-Mr. *Doggett.* low, Squire to *Don Quixote,* a great speaker of Proverbs; which he blunders out upon all occasions, tho never so far from the purpose.

Gines de P'assamonte Mr. Haines.

Pallameque,

Lope Ruiz,

Quartrezzo, Gally-slaves.

Tenorio, Martinez,

Guarding the Slaves. Officers. 2d. Barber.

Vincent. A humorous Host or Inn-keeper. Mr. *Bright.*

Women. By

Marcella, A young beautiful Shepherd-Mrs. *Bracegirdle.* ess that hates Mankind, and by her scorn occasions the death of *Chrysostome. Dorothea* alias Princess *Micomicona,* a Mrs. *Knight.* young Virgin betroth'd to Don *Fernando* but deserted by him for Luscinda, but afterwards reconcil'd. *Teresa Panca,* Wife to *Sancho,* a silly Mrs. *Leigh.* credulous Country Creature. *Mary, the Buxom, Sancho's Daughter,* Mrs. *Verbruggen.* a Rude, laughing, clownish Hoyden, Incomparably Acted by

Hostess,

Maritornes, Her Daughter.

The Body of *Chrysostome.*

Knights of Several Orders.

Shepherds, Shepherdesses, Inchanters, Inchantresses,

Singers, Dancers, and Attendants.

The Scene, *Mancha* in *Spain.*

A Pleasant Champion with a Windmill in Prospect."

The plot of *Don Quixote, Part I,* may thus be outlined: Don Quixote, with Sancho Panca as his squire, sets out as a Tcnight-errant. As they are discussing Sancho's being made governor of an island by Don Quixote, the latter perceives a windmill, which, taking it for a giant, he attacks. He is cast into a fish-pond by the arms of the mill. Sancho is then beset by his wife Teresa and his daughter Mary who complain at his leaving them. He pacifies them by the promise of a share in his coming good-fortune.

Don Quixote who has stopped at an inn is knighted by the host, whom he takes for the lord of a castle. Thence he sets out in quest of adventures, and meets the funeral of Chrystome, a young shepherd who has died from love for the scornful Marcella. He rescues Marcella from rough usage at the hands of the companions of the deceased shepherd.

After leaving the funeral, Don Quixote captures a barber's basin which he uses as a helmet. He then sets free a band of prisoners who are on their way to the galleys.

Fearful of the consequences of this last exploit, Don Quixote and Sancho retire to the Sierra Morena. There they meet the mad Cardenio, with whom Don Quixote quarrels over knight-errantry. In the Sierra Dorothea has been living disguised as a boy. She has been betrothed to Fernando, who forsook her for Luscinda, the mistress of Cardenio. Cardenio as a result of his loss of Luscinda had run mad and fled to the Sierra Morena. Dorothea had been discovered by Perez, the curate, who is her uncle, after which she had met Fernando with Luscinda whom he had abducted. Dorothea had won Fernando back to her. They then all go to search Cardenio in the mountains. Perez and Nicholas, the barber, who are attempting to entice Don Quixote home, enlist the others in their project. Dorothea accordingly takes upon herself the part of Micomicona, an injured princess, and secures the aid of Don Quixote in righting her wrongs.

The party return to the inn. There Cardenio is cured of his madness, is reconciled with Fernando, and is reunited with Luscinda. Then by a stratagem, in the carrying out of which the host Vincente plays the part of Merlin, and other "enchanters" appear, Don Quixote is decoyed into a cage. Persuaded that the cage is an enchanted chariot, Don Quixote is carried away.in it to his home.

Don Quixote, Part II, appeared in the summer of 1694.202 The play was printed with this titlepage:203
"the Comical History of Don QUIXOTE, As it is Acted at the Queen's Theatre in *Dorset Gardens.* By Their Majesties 2K Genest, *Stage*, II, 55.
203 It is dedicated in verse to the Lord Chamberlain, Charles Earl of Dorset, long a patron of the poet.

Servants. Part the Second. Written by Mr. *D'urfey*, LONDON, Printed for 5". *Briscoe*, in *Russel-street, Covent-Garden*, and *H. Newman* at the *Grashopper* in the *Poultry*, 1694." The second part of *Don Quixote* seems to have been as

well received as the first.204 In the preface to *Part II*, D'Urfey mentions the success of both plays. Gildon says the comedy met with great applause.206 It is probably a revival of *Part II* which Genest records as having occurred at Drury Lane, June 17, 1713, as a benefit for Miss Willis.206 Another revival of the comedy took place at Covent Garden, May 17, 1739, as the benefit of Roberts, Yates, and Mrs. Mullart. It was advertised as "not acted 14 years."207

Genest considers *Part II* better than *Part I*, which he calls "a good play." He goes on to' say, "The scenes in which Sancho is Governour have great merit—D'Urfey has hit off the characters of Don Quixote and Sancho very well, and has introduced a great deal of humour of his own in Mary the Buxom, tho' of the lowest species."208 *f* In his preface, the author says Marcella in *Part II* is his own invention. He speaks highly of Mrs. Bracegirdle's acting of the *role* and of the great success of her last song (V, 2, p. 60).209 Mary the Buxom is "intirely my own," having been developed from a mere hint in the romance, says D'Urfey, "yet by making the character humorous, and the extraordinary well acting of Mrs. Verbruggen, it is by the best Judges allowed to be a Masterpiece of humour."210

"The rest of the Characters in both the Parts were likewise extremely well performed, in which I had as much Justice done me as I could expect, nor was the Musical Part less commendable, the Words every where being the best of mine in that kind, and if in the whole, they could draw such Audiences for so long time, in such violent hot Weather, I shall not despair, that when the Season is more temperate, to see at their next representation, a great deal of good Company.

"I have printed some scenes both in the first and second

» The *Dialogue between a Clown and his Wife,* IV, is said to have diverted Queen Mary highly *(Pills to Purge Melancholy,* I, 88).
805 Gildon's Langbaine's *English Dramatic Poets,* p. 50.
1M*Stage,* II, 517; see also I, xxxiii.

mIUd, III, 592.
»*Ibid,* II, 55..
"... A Song so incomparably well sung, and acted by Mrs. Bracegirdle, that the most envious do allow, as well as the most ingenious affirm, that 'tis the best of that kind ever done before" (preface).
"*A.* Song *upon* Mrs. Bracegirdle's *Acting Marcella,* in I*don Quixote. Set by Mr.* Fingar," occurs in *Pills to Purge Melancholy,* II, 304-05. 210 Sec the *dramatis persona* to *Part I.* part which were left out in the Acting—the Play and the Musick being too long; and I doubt not that but they will divert in the reading, because very proper for the Connexion."211 As in *Part I,* D'Urfey has used Cervantes rather freely, altering the order of incidents and changing and recombining to a more or less considerable degree the elements of the action taken over by him. Evidently he did not expect to write a third part, for *Part II* closes with D'Urfey's equivalent for the vanquishing of Don Quixote at Barcelona, an event which marks practically the end of the romance.
In the following table the dependence of *Part II* upon the original is shown:
Part II, Chap. 64
D'Urfey's invention.
Sancho's discovery of the imposture is D'Urfey's.
The departure of Teresa and Mary for "Barataria" is D'Urfey's.
The appearance of Sancho's wife and daughter at "Barataria" is D'Urfey's.
D'Urfey substitutes for Cervantes's incidents in Sancho's governorship, the trials of the Tailor and Gardener, and of the Canter.
2 D'Urfey substitutes a Page for Carrasco as Don Quixote's successful opponent. Marcella's entrance is D'Urfey's.
811 These omissions are indicated by inverted commas in *Part I.*

The alteration by D'Urfey of Cervantes's Samson Carrasco whodefeats Don Quixote and forces his return broken-hearted home212 is perhaps borrowed by the dramatist from Shirley's *Gamester,* IV, 1. There, the cowardly Young Barnacle is overawed by a Page with a false beard.213 The device of the talking-head and Sancho's discovery of the fraud, although the former is based upon *Don Quixote,* suggest in details the use of a similar imposture in *Dame Dobson* (Theatre Royal, 1684).

In the epilogue D'Urfey borrows his concluding couplet,
"Yet to conclude, I say this of the Play, I cod 'tis good, and if they like't they may,"
from the end of Jonson's epilogue to *Cynthia's Revels,*
"I'll only speak what I have heard him Jonson say, 'By 'tis good, and if you like't, you may'."

The *dramatis persona* of *Don Quixote, Part II* is thus printed: *"The Representee Names and Characters*

Duke *Ricardo.* A Grandee of *Spain,* Mr. *Cibber. Cardenio. A* witty young Gentleman, his Companion and friend, acted by Mr. *Bowman. Ambrosio.* A young Student of Salamanca, and Kinsman to the Duke, an inveterate enemy to women, ever since his dear Friend *Chrisostome* died for Love of *Marcella.* Acted by Mr. *Verbruggen.*

Don *Quixote.* A frantick Gentleman of the *Mancha,* who ran mad with reading Books of Chivalry, and supposes himself a Knight Errant. Acted by Mr. *Boen. Mannel.* Steward to the Duke, a pleasant witty Fellow, who with *Pedro* and the Page, manages all the designs used in the fooling Don *Quixote.* Acted by Mr. *Powel. Pedro Rezio.* A Doctor of Physick, and Assistant to *Mannel* in fooling Don *Quixote.* Acted by Mr. *Freeman. Bernardo.* Chaplain to the Duke—A positive testy, morose fellow. Acted by Mr. *Trefuse.*

Diego. A rough ill-natur'd vicious fellow, Master of the Dukes Game, and chief Shepherd, in Love with *Marcella.* Acted by Mr. *Harris.*

Page to the Another witty young Fellow, and agent in the Duke. fooling Don *Quixote.* Acted by Mr. *Lee.*

TM Part II, Chap. 64.
213 Similar incidents are not uncommon in the older drama. See Forsythe,

The Relations of Shirley's Plays to the Elizabethan Drama, p. 363. *Sancho Pan*-Squire to Don *Quixote,* a dull, heavy coun*cha.* try Booby in appearance, but in discourse, dry subtle and sharp, a great repeater of proverbs, which he blunders out upon all occasions, tho never so absurd, or far from the purpose. Acted by Mr. *Underhil.*

Taylor, Gardener, Painter, Grazier, Small Man and Woman, Petitioners to the Governor *Sancho.*

Dutchess. A merry facetious Lady, that perpetually diverts herself with the extravagant follies of Don *Quixote* and *Sancho.* Acted by Mrs. *Knight.*

Luscinda. Wife to *Cardenio,* her Companion. Acted by Mrs. *Bowman.*

Dulcinea del Page to the Duke, commanded by him to *Toboso.* personate Don *Quixote's* feigned *Mistress* Acted by Mr. *Lee..*

Marcella. A young beautiful Shepherdess of *Cordoua,* extremely coy, and Averse to men at first, but afterwards passionately in Love with *Ambrosio.* Acted by Mrs. *Bracegirdle,*

Dona i?o-Woman to the Dutchess, antiquated, opinionated *driguez.* and impertinent. Acted by Mrs. *Kent. Teresa Pan*-Wife to *Sancho*—a poor clownish Country-*cha.* woman. Acted by Mr. *Lee.*

Mary. Her Daughter, a ramping ill-bred Dowdy. Mrs. *Verbruggen.*

Ricotta, Flora. Two other Country Lasses.

Inchanters, Furies, Carver, Cryer, Constable, Watch, Musitians, Singers, Dancers and Attendants."

The plot of the comedy is as follows:

Don Quixote arrives near Duke Ricardo's castle. Sancho, who has been sent on a mission to Dulcinea, meets two country wenches. These he palms off on Don Quixote as Dulcinea and her waitingmaid, both enchanted. Duke Ricardo and his household meet Don Quixote and Sancho and invite them to the Duke's castle. A feast for Don

Quixote is given by the Duke and Duchess, at which Don Quixote and Bernardo, the Chaplain, quarrel.

Later, as the Duke and his guests are in the wood, various of the Duke's servants enter disguised, one as Merlin and another as Dulcinea, attended by various devils and enchanters. "Dulcinea" announces that by giving himself three thousand lashes Sancho can free "her" from enchantment. Sancho at first refuses, but reconsiders when the Duke promises him the government of an island.

Another prank is played upon Don Quixote. The "Princess Trifaldi," who is a servant of the Duke in disguise, enters with "her" retinue and enlists Don Quixote's aid in driving an enchanter from her country. Sancho who suspects a fraud discovers the cheat in a "talking-head" the Princess has, and exposes the whole plot, which is passed off by the Duke and Duchess as without their connivance or consent.

Sancho enters upon the governorship of his "island." His wife Teresa and daughter Mary join him, as a result of his report to them of his fortune. As governor Sancho decided various causes with much shrewdness.

However, when a feigned attack by "enemies" is made upon Barataria, his capital city, Sancho, in company with Teresa and Mary, runs away. They return to the Duke', castle to find that Don Quixote has been defeated in combat by a Page in the guise of a knight-errant. Sancho and his master depart for home to remain the year enjoined them by the disguised Page.

A portion of the play deals with the passion of the once coy Marcella for the cold Ambrosio, who has saved her from a rape by Diego, a wicked shepherd. Marcella confesses to Ambrosio her love for him, but he, whose best friend, Chrysostome, has died of love for Marcella, scorns her affection, and as a result she goes mad.

Don Quixote, Part III, seems to have appeared in 1696.214 The titlepage of the second edition215 runs thus:
"the Comical History Of *DON QUIXOTE,* With The MARRIAGE OE *MARY* the *BUX-*

OMB. Part Hi. *Non omnes Arbusta juvant humilesq; myricae.* Vir. *Written by Mr.* D'urfey LONDON, Printed for John Darby, Arthur Bettesworth, and Francis Clay, in Trust for Richard, James, and Bethel Wellington. M. DCC. XXIX." This comedy appears not to have been successful. In his 211 Genest, *Stage,* II, 69. r 216 The first edition was published in 1696. Its titlepage reads thus:

The Comical History of DON QUIXOTE. The Third Part. With The MARRIAGE Of Mary the Buxome. *Written by* Mr. D'Urfey. *Non omnes Arbusta juvant homilesg; myrica.* Vir. LONDON. Printed for *Samuel Briscoe,* at the Corner of *Charlesstreet,* in *Russelstreet, Covent-Garden.* 1696." f' The following advertisement occurs at the bottom of the titlepage: "Where is also to be had the Songs, set to Musick by the late famous Mr. *Purcel,* I Mr. *Courteville,* Mr. *Aykerod,* and other eminent Masters of the Age." dedication of it to the Chancellor of the Exchequer, Charles Montague, D'Urfey' mentions "its publick misfortune."

The failure of *Part III* D'Urfey in his preface attributes not so much to its defects as to the "Ill-nature of an inveterate Faction"; the actors, he says, thought it the best of the three parts. The author admits that the songs in the play had not been sufficiently rehearsed and the dancers not proficient enough. The indecency of Sancho and Mary, which had been censured, D'Urfey tries to condone by alleging that he makes them speak in their characters of a "Clownish Boor" and a "Romp." The author then says that in nineteen of his twenty plays he had striven to avoid indecency as much as he could. Another reason for the ill-success of the comedy, according to D'Urfey, lay in the fact that the puppet-show in IV was too far from the audience for them to follow it or the prolocutor. At the end of his preface D'Urfey with some variations repeats the couplet quoted in the dedication of *A Fool's Preferment.* Here he has it,

"Let but some few, whom I omit to name,
Approve my Work, I count their Censure Fame."

Genest considers *Part III* equal to the second part and very superior to the first. The puppet-show he thinks very good. The cast he believes inferior to those of the two earlier parts.216

The writer, however, cannot agree with Genest's judgment upon the comedy. There is not enough Cervantes and too much D'Urfey in it, for much of the play is rather suggested by Cervantes than based upon him. Humor is lacking, and its place is taken by dirt. The ending is unsatisfactory. Despite D'Urfey's own opinion of the songs as expressed in the preface ("not ill writ") they are certainly not among his best by any means.

The source of the play, or of part of it, is *Doth Quixote,* the romance. D'Urfey has dramatized certain incidents untreated in his earlier play, and has ended it with a curious perversion of the death-scene of the knight, as told in Cervantes. 217 More than in any of the other *Don Quixotes* D'Urfey has in *Part III* departed from the original. He has altered those incidents taken over, and has rearranged and recombined them. Much of the comedy is his own. 218 *Stage,* II, 69. 217 A will similar to Don Quixote's, made on his deathbed, is *A Young Man's Will,* in *Pills to Purge Melancholy,* V, 266 ff.

In the table following are shown the relationships of the respective scenes to the novel:

The characters and actors follow:

"Dramatis Persona?218 MEN.

Don Quixote.
Sancho.
Basilus, An accomplish'd Gentleman, but *I* poor, betrothed to *Quitteria.*)
Camacho, A jolly fat-headed Farmer, very rich, but very dull and ignorant, given by her Friends for a Husband to Quitteria
Jaques, A clownish Country Fellow, Hind to *Camacho,* and to be married to *Mary the Buxome.*
Carrasco, A Batchelor of *Salamanca,* Friend to *Basilius;* learned, drolling, brisk, and witty and perpetually bantring *Don Quixote* and *Sancho.*
Gines de Passamonte, alias Master of

the Puppet-shew. *Peter* 218 Incomplete, as not including Lopez, the servant and accomplice of Gines de Passamonte. *Charlemain.*
Marsilius.
Orlando.
Don Gayferos
Melisendra
Bishop *Turpin*
Guards and Retinue
Carter to the Lyon
Puppets, designed to be acted by Children.
Mr. *Smeaton.*
Mrs. *Finch.*
Mr. *Smeaton.* Mrs. *Powell.* Mrs. *Verbruggen.*
Mrs. *Cross.* WOMEN.
Quitteria, A young witty Virgin, Daughter to an old Gentleman of small Fortune, betrothed to *Basilius,* but forced by him to marry *Comacho Dulcinea del Toboso.*
Teresa, Sancho's Wife.
Mary the Buxome, His Daughter.
Altisidora, Woman and Confident to *Quit-)*
teria J
Clowns, Musicians, Dancers, and Attendants.
The Scene,
A Pleasant Meadow, near a Village."

The plot of *Don Quixote, Part HI,* may thus be summarized: Don Quixote, at the opening of the play, has met a carter who has in his cart a caged lion. The knight orders him to open the cage and let the beast out. Intimidated by Don Quixote's threats, the carter finally does so, but the lion pays no attention to Don Quixote and will not leave his cage. At the representations of Sancho and the carter, Don Quixote decides that the lion is afraid of him, and so they shut up the cage again, while Don Quixote rejoices over the power of his valor and takes the name of the "Knight of the Lion." Then, at the solicitation of Basilius and Carasco, Don Quixote sets out with them to the wedding of the rich Camacho and 'Quitteria, the former sweetheart of Basilius.

At the wedding-feast of Camacho, as great cheer prevails, Carasco enters and announces that Basilius has attempted to kill "himself on account of Quitteria's marriage and that he desires to-speak to the bride before he dies. Basilius is carried in with a sword apparently run through him. He asks that Camacho resign Quitteria to him until his death, which seems imminent, occurs. Fearing that Basilius's ghost will haunt him, Camacho agrees. Basilius then draws out the sword which is now seen to have been thrust through a tube of sheep's blood concealed under his arm. He claims Quitteria as his and bears her away, while Don Quixote covers his retreat.

Basilius and Quitteria are married. To have some sport with Don Quixote, their friend and guest Altisidora feigns to be in love with him. Just as the knight begins to soften towards Altisidora, her addresses to him are interrupted by the approach of Sancho's daughter Mary the Buxom who has just been married to Jaques. Some mirth is made by Mary, whose anti-nuptial coyness has changed to a bold domineering over her newly-acquired husband.

The guests at the wedding discover Gines de Passamonte, a convict formerly freed by Don Quixote *Part I*, III, 2, who now, as Master Peter, is proprietor of a puppet-show. They beseech him to give them an entertainment. He agrees to give a performance after supper. Gines and Lopez, his man, arrange that while the spectators are engrossed in the show Lopez shall pick their pockets. Don Quixote and Sancho now appear, both of them drunk, and Don Quixote resolved upon an adventure. While Don Quixote goes to get his horse Rosinante, Gines steals Sancho's ass Dapple. The loss of the ass is attributed by Don Quixote on his return to enchantment. The puppet-show is presented and Don Quixote becomes so interested that he joins in and attacks the puppets with his sword. Finally, he is calmed and convinced of his error, whereupon he has to pay Gines for the damage done to the puppets.

After his encounter with the puppets, Don Quixote goes to bed. He is visited by Altisidora who pretends still to be enamored of him. The knight is firm in his resistance to her advances, whereupon she leaves him. Merlin and Dulcinea, the latter being a disguised dairymaid, now appear to rise through the floor. Dulcinea complains that Sancho has not disenchanted her by the lashes which he had promised to administer to himself in *Part II*, II, 2. Then much to the chagrin of Don Quixote the two disappear. Sancho and his wife Teresa now appear and quarrel over the loss of the ass and of the purses given Mary and Jaques, all of which have been stolen by Gines and Lopez. After Teresa leaves, Don Quixote recalls his lashes to Sancho. They quarrel and Sancho beats Don Quixote until the knight is rescued by Basilius. Teresa, Mary, and Jaques then go to see a "Cunning Man" concerning the lost purses, which Mary believes Jaques to have stolen from her. Don Quixote is now reported to be dying as a result of Sancho's beating and the consequent mortification.' All go to the knight's bedside where he' is shown making his will, and bequeathing his various qualities, such as Conscience and Valor, to various classes of men. Afterwards he falls asleep. With a comic song the play ends.

D'Urfey's first opera, *Cinthia and Endimion: or, the Loves of the Deities*, was produced in 1697.219 The composition of the opera dates back to 1694, as it was intended for production at court before Queen Mary who died in that year. The titlepage of the opera as printed runs:

"a New OPERA, Called Clntbia an& En&tmton: Or,

The Loves of the Deities. As it was Designed to be Acted at Court, before the late QUEEN; and now Acted at the Theatre Royal, by His MAJESTY'S Servants. Written by Mr. *D'URFBY. LONDON:* Printed by *W. Onley* for *Sam. Briscoe,* in *Russel-street, Covent-Garden;* and *R. Wellington,* at the *Lute* in *St. Paul's* Church-yard, 1697."220 In his dedication of the opera to Henry Earl of Romney, D'Urfey says:

"It formerly had the Honour to be look'd upon with a gracious Regard by the best of Queens of late happy and glorious Memory, before whom it had been presented in her Court, if the ensuing National Fatality, had not, in. the interim, unfortunately happened;221 however, not to let it be intirely a Prey to ill Destiny, I have with great Care and Pains, at last made shift to strip it from its Mourning into a Dress proper to be seen by the Town, tho' it may want that Illustration which the CourtOrnament had adorn'd it with."

The opera would seem to have been successful, and to have been considered rather "above D'Urfey's usual genius, with the versification good and the expression often significant and poetical," as one writer puts it.222 With this judgment, Genest seems to agree, 219 So Genest, *Stage,* II, 110. The writer, however, is inclined to suspect that D'Urfey would not have allowed the opera to remain unperformed for three years. There is no available proof, nevertheless, that *Cinthia and Endimion* was acted before 1697.
220 The following interesting advertisement occurs on the titlepage:
"£3T *The Relapse: or, Virtue in Danger. Being the Second Part of,* The Fool in Fashion. *A Comedy, acted at the Theatre Royal. A new Opera, call'd* Brutus *of Alba: or* Augusta's *Triumph, Acted at the Theatre in* Dorset-Garden. *With Variety of new Songs. Both Printed for Sam Briscoe in* CoventGarden."
The first was by Vanbrugh; the other is anonymous.
821 Gildon in his edition of Langbaine's *English Dramatic Poets,* p. 49, does not approve of D'Urfey's referring both on the titlepage and in the dedication to Queen Mary's patronage of the opera. 222 Gildon, as cited in the note preceding. as he says *Cinthia and Endymion* "has considerable merit for that sort of thing."223
The source of the opera is given by the *Biographia Dramatica* as the *Metamorphoses* of Ovid and the *Golden Ass* of Apuleius (for the story of Cupid and Psyche).224 These were of course the ultimate basis of the plot, but the stories of Endymion and Cynthia, of Pan and Syrinx, of Daphne and Apollo, and of Cupid and Psyche were familiar to

every seventeenth century school-boy. There is no necessity therefore for comparing formally the plot of the opera with the ancient legends. D'Urfey's rather original treatment of the myths will come out in the synopsis of the plot.

D'Urfey has used in III, 1, in Collin's burlesque descriptions of the Gods and their exploits a comic device similar to that of Heywood in *Love's Mistress,* II, 1. There the Clown narrates the legend of the siege of Troy in burlesque fashion. Shakespeare's interpretation of Hero and Leander, *As You Like It,* IV, 1, and Shirley's of Arion and the dolphin, *The Duke's Mistress,* V, 1, are in a like comic vein. *The Power of Verse* (*Pills to Purge Melancholy,* VI, 142 ff.) is on the same order. In III, 2, Pan recounts to Syrinx the various forest delights which will be hers if she will love him, and enumerates various fruits and nuts for her food, with a chorus of birds to lull her to sleep. When these are ended, he asks, "Will you then love me?" Here D'Urfey shows the influence of that most popular of Elizabethan lyrics, which had been imitated for a century, *The Passionate Shepherd* of Marlowe.

The prologue to *Cinthia and Endymion* is sung by Saturnia, representing Night, the Pleiades, and Zephyrus. The epilogue which is comic was spoken by Doggett, who would seem to have played Collin. To deliver it, he rose "from under the Stage," appar-. ently from Hell. The epilogue thus refers to contemporary events:

"For Plotters, a huge Slaughter-house they the demons frame,

Where one expected was, of noted Fame;

Fer, fer,—fer, fer,—I' sure you know his Name:

I ask'd, If he, e'er yet, had seen his Room?

'Twas answer'd, No: But he was sure to come." Here the members of the plot in 1696 to assassinate William III are doubtless meant. He over whose name Doggett stumbles was prob m *Stage,* II, 111. 124 II, 149-50.

ably the Reverend Robert Fergusson, who had been implicated in conspiracies of one sort or another for years, and

who was arrested in connection with that above mentioned in March, 1696 (New Style).225

The *dramatis persona,22'* which unfortunately lacks the performers' names, runs thus: *"The Names and Characters of the Representers in the* Opera, *morally fashioning the Vertues and Vices of Human Nature.*

Jupiter,—

Cinthia, Representing Greatness and Honour, attack'd by natural Frailty and wavering Passion. *Apollo,* Representing Wit and Love, slighted by obstinate Pride.

Cupid, Representing Desire, wanton and unsatisfy'd.

Psyche, Representing innocent Vertue, o'ercome by insinuation, Opportunity and Love.

Daphne, Representing affected Pride and Ill-nature.

Pan, Representing Ignorance and Credulity.

Mercury, Representing Subtileness, Wantonness and Inconstancy.

Endimion, Representing Modesty, Integrity, and Goodnature.

Syrinx, Representing irregular Passion, Treachery and Envy.

Gods, Goddesses, *Neptune, Amphitrite, Pactolus, Ganges, Tyber, Thames, Saturnia, Pleiades, Zephirus,* Shepherds, Satyrs, Singers, Dancers, and Attendants.

The Scene *Ionia,* with Mount *Latmus."* The ingeniously complicated plot of *Cinthia and Endimion* may thus be given:

Cupid who is in love with Psyche obtains" from her the promise of her yielding to his suit, provided she sees the chaste Cinthia kiss a man. Cinthia, who, with other gods and goddesses, is made mortal for a month, is brought into love with Endimion by Cupid. Syrinx whom Pan loves is in love with Endimion. She becomes jealous of Cinthia, and obtains a sleeping-draught of great powers from Pan.

225 Macaulay, *History of England,* IV, 535.

1 Imperfect, as not including the follow-

ing:

Hobinell, a clown.

Clout, his son.

Collin,

Tarbox, -three clowns.

Lowbell, J

Flora, a country girl loved by Clout.

Endimion and Cinthia meet; he declares his love for her, but she suppresses his ardor and leaves him. As he is in despair, Syrinx enters with the potion. She gives it to him as a cordial sent to him by Cinthia. He drinks it and falls asleep. Cinthia enters, and, thinking Endimion dead, is in despair over his fate. An oracle is consulted, which announces that Endimion merely sleeps and that only at a kiss from Cinthia will he awaken. Remorseful over the fate of Endimion, Syrinx meets Cupid in search of Psyche. She speaks slightingly of Psyche's beauty, whereupon he promises to punish her. Syrinx takes refuge with Pan, who, at first indignant with her for the use made of the potion, is soon coaxed by her into another frame of mind. They are summoned then before Jupiter for trial on the charge of poisoning Endimion. Psyche learns from Cinthia of the oracle's reply, and then begs the goddess to awaken Endimion, her own desire being the accomplishment of her vow made concerning Cupid. Cinthia kisses the sleeper and awakens him. Cupid and Psyche then are united. Apollo appears redeified and adopts Endimion as his son. Apollo then recounts his discovery of the coy Daphne, whom he loves, in the act of courting a shepherd. She is transformed into a laurel by the angry god. Syrinx, who is tried also, accuses Pan of poisoning Endimion. The truth comes out, however, and Syrinx is turned into a reed.

Comic scenes full of indecent dialogue are furnished by a rebellion of countrymen against the deities. The revolt is headed by Collin. The rebels are defeated, of course, and Collin, deserted by his followers, is hurried off to hell.

For the first production of D'Urfey's next comedy two dates are given. According to Genest,227 *The Intrigues at Versailles: or, a Jilt in all Humours,* was produced in 1697. The author of *A Life of Thomas Betterton* dates the play in 1696.228 As a matter of fact, the two writers probably refer to the same year, Genest using the Old Style date and the anonymous biographer the, new. From the closing lines of the prologue the play would seem to have been produced before the signing of the Treaty of Ryswick, September 10-11, 1697. The verses are as follows:

"Wit has no Armour proof 'gainst being Thrash'd
Therefore in Terror of the Warriours Trade,
Suspends all Satyr until the Peace be made."

Stage, II, 119. Genest gives the second title incorrectly as *A Jilt in all her Humours*. a,P. 125.

The English characters too are said to be detained in France almost on the footing of prisoners.229 *The Intrigues at Versailles* was printed with the following titlepage:

"the INTRIGUES At VERSAILLES: Or, A Jilt in all Humours, A *COMEDY*, Acted ByimsflDajestp'sServants

At The Theatre in Lincolns-Inn-Fields. Written by Mr. *D'Urfey*. Wit will be wit tho' slighted by the Clown, As Roses sweet tho' Asses tread 'em down. LONDON, Printed for *F. Saunders* in the *New-Exchange, P. Buck* in *Fleetstreet, R. Parker* at the *Royal-Exchange*, and *H. Newman* in the *Poultry*. 1697."

The comedy was not successful, as is stated by D'Urfey in his dedication of it to Sir Charles Sedley the Elder and his son, also Sir Charles.230 D'Urfey says of the play:

"This new *Comedy* which I beg leave to Dedicate to ye, when it was first shewn to some Persons of Principal Quality and Judgment, and afterwards Read to Mr. *Congreve* and Mr. *Betterton*, had, from all, the good Fortune, to be esteem'd as one of the Best I have written.231

"It has been my Fortune, through the short Course of my *Poetry*, to run o'er the Rugged Ways of Publick Censure, with as much Indifference as any one; and as I have always Studied Variety to procure Diversion, so have I met with as

Various Success—yet have been easy by Teaching my Self the *Philosophy* of *Patience*, and the use of that Common Saying, *Many Men have many Minds, and those Many Minds possess'd with more Difficult Expectations then generally the best Undertaker could satisfy*. But to give Instance, that my Industrious Paines have not been wanting to please the Town, if they look into my former Peices, 'they may find, without much trouble, a Variety, which has not been every Bodies Tallent; they may find in the *Fond Husband*, Regular *Comedy* with a Good Plot; in the *Boarding-School, Satyrical Humour* and *Characters* with another; in the *Marriage Hater*, A Mixture of all digested with 228 Negotiations for peace between France and the Allies had begun early in the year and had dragged on until autumn. The Congress of Ryswick began its sittings in May, 1697.
230 See also Gildon's Langbaine's *English Dramatic Poets*, p. 50.
2,1 A line in the epilogue (spoken by Mrs. Barry) runs thus:
"The Play by Judges, has commended been."
Comical Turnes to the last Scene; Also in the *Don Quirros sic* Farsical Scenes of Mirth, mixt with Variety of Divertive Vocal Musick and Dancing, with many others, some from *Stories*, but most wholly my own Invention, and all of Different Kinds, which have had their several Lots; some have pleased more, some less, according as the Town Humour eb'd and flowed; but generally as 'tis the Fate of things of this kind, have met with Mistaken Judgment; the Meritorious having Indifferent Applause, the Indifferent Extraordinary.

"And 'tis in this manner that this last, the *Intrigues at Versailles*, has been us'd by the *Criticks*: Many less Labour'd, and Worthy, have had more Applause; the Model of it being Courtly, and wanting the Farsical *Scenes*, with which the Inconsiderate part of the *Audience* were formerly Entertain'd—and also the Turns requiring observation, and the whole Contriv'd Machine exacting more thought—then is Natural for heads that are Buzzing with other mat-

ters in the *Playhouse*, and sit on their Shoulders uneasy in a hot Summer season." The author then goes on to address the elder Sedley:

"... It has many years been my Advantage, as well as other *Poets*, to be Influenc'd by your Genius, and instructed by your Admirable Writings and Improving Conversation."232 D'Urfey then mentions the following in terms of praise: "The never-enough admir'd Soul and Genius of *Wit* and *Poetry* the Present Earl of *Dorset"*; and "the Earl of *Leicester*, the greatest Incourager and Patron of all the Muses, and their forlorn and desolate Sons."

Gildon points out what he considers defects in *The Intrigues at Versailles*. 2ZZ He thinks it unaccountable that Rambure should speak broken English when all the characters save Guillamour are French and the scene is Versailles. He cannot imagine how the critics could overlook Tonnere's absconding from the court in women's clothing when he had committed such an unpardonable fault as a duel there and have such a *confidante* as Vandosme, who could attack him with a better weapon than a pruning-knife (i. e., by giving him up to the authorities). Genest calls *The Intrigues at Versailles* "on the whole a good play," but adds, "the plot is too complicated."234 Indeed, if we may judge from D'Urfey's epistle 232 See also Shadwell's dedication to Sedley of *A True Widow*. 233 Gildon's Langbaine's *English Dramatic Poets*, pp. 50-51. 231 *Stage*, II, 119.
dedicatory, the difficulty of following the action was a reason for its failure. The inordinate use of disguise in the comedy probably contributed greatly to its obscurity of plot, for there are three cases of men as women (de Tonnere, Sanserre, and Grossiere) and one of a woman as a man (the Countess de Brissac).

According to Gildon, the play is a complication of plagiarisms. Tonnere's disguising himself as a woman and Count de Brissac, the husband of his mistress, falling in love with him are from *The Double Cuckold*, a novel. It will be remembered that a similar incident occurs in D'Urfey's *Sir Barnaby Whigg,* for which *The Double Cuckold* is said to be a source. The same writer thinks Vandosme a mixture of Wycherley's Olivia in *The Plain Dealer* and Mrs. Behn's Myrtilla in *The Amorous Jilt,* lacking the wit of the first and the gentility of the other.238 Summers agrees with Gildon and finds the original for Vandosme's infatuation with Sir Blunder Bosse in Myrtilla's marriage with Sir Morgan Blunder.236 We should remember, however, in connection with the last that D'Urfey has characters more or less similar to Vandosme in *Madam Fickle* and in *Love for Money.* Furthermore, the jilt was no novelty in either Restoration or Elizabethan drama. In regard to the likeness in name between Mrs. Behn's and D'Urfey's boorish knights, it should not be forgotten that Shadwell has a bully named Blunderbuss in his *Woman-Captain.* As to the characterization of Sir Blunder, we find like conceptions in such plays as, for example, Mrs. Behn's *Rover* (in Blunt), and Vanburgh's *Provoked Wife* (Sir John Brute). Gildon and Summers may be correct in their beliefs, but there is always some danger in attempting to trace a stock figure in the drama to any contemporary original.

Evidently D'Urfey changed the names of certain of his characters. In II, 2 (p. 16), the Duke de Sanserre is called "Marquess," and de Brissac is referred to as "Sessac." The catchword to p. 22 is *"Sess.* Where's." The first speech on p. 23 is Brissac's. Also in V, 1, Sessac is used for de Brissac. The title of the play probably was changed. In *Pills to Purge Melancholy231* is *A Prologue to my Play, the French Coquet.* This, pretty certainly, is *The Intrigues at Versailles.* The character called "Daubray" in the *dramatis persona* goes through the comedy as "Danbray"; this, however, may be merely a printer's error. What seems a personal allusion occurs in 235 Gildon's Langbaine's *English Dramatic Poets,* p. 51.
Works of Mrs. Behn, IV, 315.
354 ff.
II, 3 (p. 21), where Guillamour, mocking Sanserre in female costume, says:

"And the Night gown there so loose and Negligent, looks just like the tawdry Countess of Jersy in a morning without her stays."238

Sir Blunder Bosse's abusive love-letter (III, 1, pp. 26-27) is modeled upon that of Monsieur Thomas, *Trick for Trick,* II, 1, *Monsieur Thomas,* I, 3. A device similar to the disguised de Tonnere's embracing de Brissac (who thinks him a woman), while unobserved by her husband, Madam de Brissac slips out (III, 2, p. 35) had been employed by D'Urfey in *Sir Barnaby Whigg.* An interesting passage occurs in III, 2 (p. 35), in which the Duchess de Sanserre, the Countess de Brissac, and de Tonnere give a sort of summary of the play and suggest a title for it.

The characters and performers are thus listed: *"Drammatis Persona,239* and Characters.

Duke *de Sanserre.* Proud and Hot-Spirited; , T very Amorous, Jealous and Revengeful. Mn *betterton. Guillamour.* A Young English Lord, a great Intreaguer.

Count *de Brissac.* An Old Beau, Ridiculously Apish, and fond of young Company.

Count *de Fiesque.* Witty, Generous, and good Natur'd, but Amorous to a Fault.

Count *de Tonnere.* Young and Extravagant, Intreag'd with Lady *Brissac,* and

Disguis'd in Womens Clothes, upon the account of a Duel.

Sir *Blunder Bosses.* A dull sordid Brute 1 and Mongril whose Humour is, to call Mr. *Underbill.* every Body by Clownish Names. J *Rambure.* An Old Affected Fellow. Valett to *Fiesque.* WOMEN.

Dutch, *de Sanserre.* Poetical, High-Spirited, j *B irdg* and wanton.) *m* Why D'Urfey should thus publicly insult a woman of high rank is inexplicable. The Countess of Jersey, whom he-mentions was Barbara, daughter to William Chiffinch, closet-keeper to Charles II. She was married in December, 1681, to Edward Vllliers, created Earl of Jersey in 1697. She died in 1697 (Doyle Officio/ *Baronage of England,* II, 258-59;

Ebbsworth, *D. N. B.,* X, 228).

Incomplete; Roger, who appears, II, 3, and the Wench, who appears, II, 3, are L omitted.

Mr. *Verbruggen.*

Mr. *Boen.*

Mr. *Hodson.*

Mr. *Bowman.*

Countess *de Brissac,* Young, Wild, and Ex-). T travagant. J Mrs-*Bowman.*

Madam *de Vandosme.* A Fight Tilt in all),T

Humours. *Mrs. Barry. Daubray.* A Retainer, and Spy to the Duke / ,,, ,,,.. ,,, *de Sanserre. Mrs. WMts. La Busque.* Confident to the Dutchess. Mrs. *Lawson. Grossiere,* Page to AFinical Jilt, Confident).

Sanserre.) to *Vandosme. Mrs. Leigh.* Singers, Dancers, and Attendants.

The SCENE, *VERSAILLES."*

The plot of *The Intrigues at Versailles* runs as follows: Count de Tonnere, who has fought a duel at court, to escape the King's anger thereby incurred, disguises himself as a woman and takes refuge with his friend, the Count de Fiesque. De Tonnere has been seen in his woman's clothes by Count de Brissac, the aged husband of de Tonnere's mistress. De Brissac who has fallen in love with the supposed woman serenades de Tonnere at de Fiesque's house. De Fiesque is visited by Vandosme, his humorsome mistress, who purposes to quarrel with her lover. She meets de Tonnere and the two fall in love, but conceal their passion from de Fiesque.

The jealous Duke de Sanserre learns of an intrigue of his wife with Guillamour, a young Englishman, who lodges next the Duke's house. He gains his knowledge through Guillamour's clownish companion, Sir Blunder Bosse. Guillamour finds out the Duke's knowledge of his relations with the Duchess. Aided by the Duchess's woman, Guillamour devises that the Duke shall see a flirtation between two rustics in the place where the lovers have been reported as meeting. The Duke who has dressed himself in his wife's clothes to deceive Guillamour is surprised by the Duchess with Daubray, whom the Duke maintains as a spy upon his wife. The Duchess mocks him for his jealousy and his failure to prove her unfaithful. He is then jeered by a party who enter, until he leaves in a fit of shame and anger. After the Duke's departure, de Brissac grows jealous of the disguised de Tonnere whom Madam de Brissac, dressed as a man, courts before him. Meantime, Vandosme and Guillamour are attracted toward each other. Their flirtation is halted by a messenger who calls Guillamour away. As Vandosme follows her new conquest out, she meets de Tonnere with whom she quarrels.

De Tonnere and de Fiesque find Vandosme seemingly to have disappeared the next morning. In revenge for her treatment of them, they encourage the brutal Sir Blunder to send her a letter couched in his abusive style in which he appoints a meeting with her. As a matter of fact, Vandosme has merely been denied to the unwelcome visitors, and has been with Guillamour. Guillamour leaves when de Fiesque returns, but leaves a letter-case, which de Fiesque finds. De Sanserre enters and de Fiesque is about to give him a picture of the Duchess which is in the case, when Guillamour returns in search of his property and prevents the exposure of the lady. De Fiesque gives the portrait to Guillamour and refrains from telling the Duke of it; however, he keeps back a letter of the Duchess to Guillamour in which she arranges a meeting between them for that night. De Fiesque hopes to profit by his knowledge of the assignation, and to revenge himself upon Guillamour for that personage's successful rivalry with him. De Tonnere, still in disguise, goes with Madam de Brissac to the Duchess's apartments. Daubray sees them and, recognizing de Tonnere really to be a man, reports the visitors to the Duke. De Brissac enters now. To prevent his seeing his wife with de Tonnere, whom de Tonnere has been courting, the last named covers the old man's face, while Madame de Brissac escapes.

Vandosme who desires revenge upon Guillamour for his offensive treatment of her summons de Fiesque to visit her.

She obtains from him the letter of the Duchess to Guillamour and resolves to transmit it to the Duke. De Fiesque now goes to meet the Duchess. In the dark, he passes himself off as Guillamour. The true Guillamour enters and, thinking himself deceived by his mistress, attacks de Fiesque. The Duke enters and the rivals flee. The Duchess explains that she has been attacked by thieves, but she is unable totally to allay her husband's jealousy. His suspicions are aroused again by Daubray's news as to de Tonnere's disguise.

Desiring to learn who his rival is, Guillamour corrupts La Busque, the Duchess's maid, who tells him de Tonnere is the fortunate man. La Busque places Guillamour where he can observe a lady with de Tonnere. The Duke now enters with de Brissac and seizes de Tonnere. For some time de Brissac remains incredulous as to de Tonnere's true sex, but on the discovery that the lady with de Tonnere is not the Duchess, but her sister the Countess de Brissac, he is convinced of the disloyalty of his supposed mistress and of his wife as well. Finally de Tonnere reveals the reason for his disguise and Madame de Brissac recounts her pranks in masculine dress. The Duchess now enters and upbraids the Duke because she has discovered that he is to meet Vandosme. The Duchess brings in Vandosme who at first pretends shame and repentance, but soon turns on the Duchess and gives to the Duke the letter of the Duchess to Guillamour. In a jealous rage, the Duke leaves the stage to meditate upon revenge; Vandosme and her new lover, Sir Blunder, have a quarrel; and Madame de Brissac repents of her intimacy with de Tonnere. Thus, the play ends.

D'Urfey's next comedy, *The Campaigners: or, The Pleasant Adventures at Brussels,* was printed with this titlepage:

"The Campaigners: Or, The *Pleasant Adventures at Brussels.* A COMEDY. As it is Acted at the *Theatre-Royal,* With A Familiar Preface Upon *A Late Reformer of the* STAGE. Ending with a Satyrical Fable Of *The* DOG *and the* OTTOR.

Written by Mr. *D'Urfey.* LONDON, Printed for *A. Baldwin,* near the *Oxford Arms* Inn in *Warwick Lane.* MDCXCVIII." *The Campaigners* was produced probably early in 1698. Its composition and acting lie certainly between the conclusion of peace negotiations at Ryswick in September, 1697, and a date not long after the publication of Collier's *Short View of the Immorality and Profanity of the English Stage.*[2W] The present writer, indeed, inclines to the opinion that the comedy itself was intended by D'Urfey as a defiance to Collier.

The dramatist in a preface of some twenty-seven pages defends the cause of the stage, and incidentally himself, against Collier's attack. As men of much greater powers than D'Urfey failed in their attempts to confute Collier, the reader is justified in surmising that D'Urfey's defense did not rout the assailant. As a matter of fact, the preface is so weak[241] that the writer will content himself with giving but a few extracts from it.

D'Urfey begins his defense with an anxious effort to prove himself a good Christian. He spends pp. 1-3 in asserting his piety. He then attacks Collier for having accompanied to the scaffold the conspirators implicated in the assassination plot of 1696 (p. 4). D'Urfey quotes Randolph's *Muse's Looking-glass* against the divine This occurred in March, 1697-98. (Genest, *Stage,* II, 123).

241 Gosse says, "In *The Campaigners* of D'Urfey... Collier is rudely handled, but without wit or force" *Life of Congreve,* p. 113). (pp. 7-8). A great grievance is made of the fact that Collier had attacked D'Urfey and other living dramatists specifically by name (pp. 5, 16). After having devoted the first sixteen pages of his preface to an attack upon Collier, D'Urfey takes up and attempts to answer Collier's strictures upon *Don Quixote.*

D'Urfey's opinion of the character of his plays may be gathered from the following quotation from p. 3 of the preface:

"Amongst twenty of my Comedies Acted and Printed, he Collier never heard of the *Royalist,* the *Boarding School,* the *Marriage Hater Match'd,* the *Richmond Heiress,* the *Virtuous Wife,* and others, all whose whole Rots and designs I dare affirm, tend to that principal instance, which he proposes, and which we allow, *viz.* the depression of Vice and encouragement of Virtue."

The fable of the *Dog and the Ottor* (which is reminiscent of the apologue of the "Old Stanch Whigg" and the "knavish Daw" in the preface to *The Royalist)* occupies pp. 28-32. It consists of a dialogue between Tray, a setter, and an Otter, representing a nonjuring clergyman. D'Urfey may have intended Tray to stand for the writer himself. There is a certain faint resemblance in this poem to *The Hind and the Panther.* It is in the heroic couplet, and not the usual octosyllabic couplet of the fable.

In his dedication of *The Campaigners* to Thomas Lord Wharton D'Urfey mentions that Collier has had "a mighty Cry of his side." The dramatist refers to the bestowal upon him of "Particular Favour" by Lord Wharton. "The following sheets the play" he states had "been Encouraged by men of the first-rate understandings in *England."*

In his prologue (spoken by Pinkethman) D'Urfey returns to his attack on Collier, and accuses him of hypocrisy, rebellion, spite, and pride. The prologue is merely scurrilously abusive, not witty. A song in IV, 1 (pp. 40-41), called *The New Reformation,* is directed at Collier. Immediately after the song is concluded, the Prince de Landvile proposes a toast to King William, as "Great Umpire of Christendom, Genius of the War, and all our brave Confederate Princes; Saviour of our Lives, Honours, Liberties, and Estates; and eternally renown'd Procurer, Finisher, and Protector of our glorious Peace." Doubtless in this health D'Urfey hinted at Collier's noniuring tenets. D'Urfey mentions Collier in *The Occasional Ballad, Being a Supplement to the last, on the Occasional Bill; And upon the Bishops and Parsons preaching down the Playhouses.*242

To the person who has read those plays of D'Urfey which were acted up

to 1698, the reason for the resort of their author to ridicule and abuse of the writer assailing them on moral grounds is patent. In other words, the critic had a clear case. That Collier, although he adduces some rather doubtful instances in proof of his charges against D'Urfey's plays, was in general on very safe ground may be seen from the following, gleaned from other plays than those of the *Don Quixote* group, which seemingly were the only plays of D'Urfey's read by Collier.243

In *The Commonwealth of Women,* II, 1 (p. 13), occurs this passage: *"Hazard.* For my part, I have nothing of weight, but my Prayer-Book. And that I am resolv'd, shall not burden the Ship. There 'tis.— *Throws it Over-board. D. Pier.* Why, well said!"

In *Bussy D'Ambois,* V, 1 (p. 44), are the following lines:

"Montsurry—Since it is so, why will the Priests take pains

To tell us of Rewards for being Good;
Since Vice is Sickness Epidemical,
And curs'd Hypocrisie swayes Humane Nature;
Since no one can be Just, nor so rewarded,
There's no such thing as Justice or Reward." Montsurry in the same scene speaks thus of Teresia, his wife's governess:

"Why well Sanctity, I'm undeceiv'd
By this, in what I never had believ'd;
This Praying Saint, that talk'd of naught but God,
I' th' midst of strong Devotion was a Bawd;
They're all, they're all just so, the Weed Hypocrisie,
Spreads over all the Earth, and Buds and Blossoms;
'Tis Rank, 'tis Rank."

Du Pier, in speaking of the drowning of the Chaplain in *The Commonwealth of Women,* calls him "a poor Soul-Broker" (II, 2, p. 15). Chapman in his *Bussy D'Ambois,* III, 1, merely hints 242 *PUIS to Purge Melancholy,* I, 197 if.

!4S The order of Collier's three charges against D'Urfey, profanity, abuse of the clergy, and obscenity has been adhered to in the giving of quotations and ref-

erences. at the corruption of the clergy. With apparent great good will D'Urfey expands the passage and turns it into abuse *(Bussy D'Ambois,* III, 2, p. 22). Fulvia in *The Richmond Heiress,* II, 2 (p. 20), says in her pretended madness, "The Parson hates Lambswool, he loves the Bowl"; and in III, 2 (p. 31), of the same comedy Cunnington as a Frenchman says, "De People and de Priest make de grand difference; he can say ver little or noting dat dey believe, and dey, Begar, vill do noting vat he advise; so I never trouble de Shurch at all." In *The Intrigues at Versailles,* I (p. 5), Vandosme says, "I met a plaguy Black Coat at my first coming out this Morning—I am sure there is some ill coming towards me—would the Devil had them. I had rather a Raven should Cross my Way, than a Priest, a thousand times." In *The Bath,* V, 1 (p. 44), it is said," ".... Let us send for a Soul-broker, a Parson." Both blasphemy and abuse of the clergy are present in *The Rambling Rake,* a song in *Pills to Purge Melancholy.* In *A Song* in the same collection D'Urfey refers contemptuously to priests as "black-coats."244

Of D'Urfey's "Want of Modesty," the reader may judge from the opportunities for that fault which are displayed in the outlines of the plays so far considered.

According to the *Biographic Dramatica,* 246 part of the plot of *The Campaigners* is drawn from a novel called *Female Falsehood.* In regard to this, the writer cannot say, as the novel has been inaccessible to him. The seduction of Angellica by Dorange in his sister's clothes, as recounted in *The Campaigners,* brings to mind Monsieur Thomas's attempt upon Mary, *Monsieur Thomas,* IV, 6, V, 2. There is a possibility of D'Urfey's comedy being based upon Middleton's *Spanish Gipsy.* In that play Roderigo ravishes Clara (I, 3), each being unknown to the other. Roderigo marries Clara and is then informed of her identity (V, 1). The Angellica-Dorange plot of *The Campaigners* nearly certainly inspired the early relations of Farquhar's Standard and Lurewell, as revealed in *The Constant Couple,* V, 3. 24e

Bertram's taking from the Marquise the hundred pistoles which she has received from Dorange and his return to her of one piece as her perquisite while he gives the remainder back to Dorange, ".VI, 169 ff.; II, 120 ff., respectively. "II, 79.

Ms Farquhar's comedy appeared a year after D'Urfey's (1699). The reunion of Dorange and Angellica contains a greater deliberate appeal to the sympathy of the audience than does that of Farquhar's Colonel and his mistress. is based upon *Le Grand Parangon de Nouvelles Nouvelles,* Novel LV: "D'un jeune gallent de marchent qui donna cent escus pour coucher avec son hostesse, puis apres son mary par fortune en fut adverty et lui fit rendre les cent escus et a sa femme fit bailler ung petit blant *sic* comme a une paillarde." D'Urfey borrows from his own *Fool's Preferment,* I, 1, in the dialogue between Bertram and the Marquise, III, 1 (p. 24). Three passages are lifted from one play to the other with but minor changes. His repetition of an incident to be found in *The Virtuous Wife* (the Marquise's letter, I, 1, p. 5) has already been pointed out.247

Among other interesting points in the play is Min Heer Tomas's reference to Heywood's *Woman Killed with Kindness* in II, 1,."I have heard too much kindness once killed a woman."248 D'Urfey has introduced a novelty upon the stage in the person of the Nurse who speaks genuine "baby talk" to her charge,249 as in II, 2 (p. 19): ".... And pat a cake, pat a cake bakers man, so will I master as I can, and prick it, and prick it, and prick it, and prick it, and throw't into the Oven." D'Urfey has given the name of the hero of his *Royalist*—Kinglove. —to Dorange's friend in *The Campaigners.*

Genest calls *The Campaigners* a good play.250 There is, however, nothing notable about it. It is rather clever, but the subjectmatter is hackneyed. The comedy is strictly contemporaneous, the " scene being laid in Brussels shortly after the signing of the Treaty of Ryswick in 1697. Evidently D'Urfey was taking advantage of-the popularity of matters connected with the war which had just been ended. So far as we can judge at present, *The Campaigners* j was an ordinarily successful play. It seems never to have been revived.

The *dramatis persona* follows: *"Dramatis Persona.*

Prince *Landevile,* A Volunteer Campaigner.

A Noble *Italian.* Mr. *Evans.*

Don *Leon,* A Noble *Spaniard* Mr. *Sympson.* 7 p. 32.
248 There was a proverb to the same effect, however; see *The Taming of the Shrew,* IV, 1.
Delia in *The Bath* is in somewhat the same class. » II, 187.
The Sieur *Bondevelt,* An Affected Finical
Flanderkin, President of the Council of Trade
Collonel *Dorange,* A Campaigner, Collonel of Horse in the Kings Army during the War.
Kinglove, His Friend. A Volunteer Campaigner.
Min Heer Tomas, A fat Burgomaster. Mr. *Penkethman.*
Marqui *Bertran, A French* Gentleman.
A Volunteer Campaigner under Marshal *Boufilers.*
Van Scopen, Footman to Don *Leon,* when
Ambassador. Born in *Holland.*
Mascarillo, Footman to *Bertran.* Born in *France.* Mr. *Bullock.*
Mr. *Johnson.*
Mr. *Mills.* Mr. *Thomas.*
Mr. *Cibber.*
Mr. *Fairbank.* WOMEN.
Angellica, Sister to Don *Leon,* and Niece to *Min Heer Tomas* and *Anniky.*
Madam *la Marquise,* Wife to *Bertran*
Anniky, Wife to *Min Heer Tomas.*
Gusset, Woman to *Angellica.*
Fardell, An Affected Tattling Nurse.
Musicians, Dancers, Waiters and Servants.
The Scene *Bruxelles,* the Time 35 hours."
Mrs. *Knight.* Mrs. *Verbruggen.* Mrs. *Powel.* Mrs. *Kent.* Mrs. *Lynsey. The Campaigners* may be summarized thus:
Dorange, a colonel in the Royal army in Brussels, sees a lady in a coach and falls in love with her. He states in her hearing that he will give a large sum of money to enjoy her. She sends him a note fixing a time and place whereat she will expect him to "render himself to the justice of her Resentments."

On the night before his assignation with the lady, Dorange goes to spy out the land. He mistakes the house and goes'to that of Min Heer Tomas, the Burgomaster. Angellica, the Burgomaster's niece, has been kept a close prisoner by her aunt and brother to prevent her marrying and so alienating her fortune from them. Angellica plots to escape for a time from her uncle's house with the aid of the servant of her brother Don Leon, the Spanish Ambassador. Mistaking Dorange for Van Scopen, the servant, Angellica leaves with him. They go to the house of Fardell, who is nurse to Angellica's child by an unknown father. Dorange, who begins to suspect that Angellica is a young woman whom he had met and seduced in London, carries a letter for her to Bondevelt, President of the Council of Trade, who is a suitor for her hand.

The Marquis Bertran and his wife fall out because he will give hef no more money for basset-playing. She resolves to gain some by any means, preferably through the offer made by Dorange, as she is the lady with whom he has the assignation. Dorange visits Angellica again, but is surprised with her by her aunt and is forced to disguise himself as a tailor in order to avoid her notice. Min Heer Tomas enters with Bondevelt. To enable Bondevelt to avoid recognition by the aunt, he is hidden in a clothespress. Anniky, the termagant aunt, enters with firearms and forces her husband to give her a bond he has entered into with Bondevelt in which it is agreed that Angellica shall marry Bondevelt in return for the payment of three thousand pounds to her uncle. The Marquise enters and discovers Dorange's true identity. Angellica receives him as a gentleman, much to the amazement of Bondevelt, who has hitherto believed him to be a servant. Bondevelt assures Gusset, Angellica's woman, that Dorange is really a servant. Gusset informs her mistress of Bondevelt's assertion.

After a merry scene in which Min Heer Tomas is instigated to resist his wife, Bondevelt enters and, seeing Dorange, the supposed servant, in good company, is astounded. At Dorange's request, his companions carry out the jest and treat Dorange as a footman. Bondevelt takes Dorange with him to Angellica, meaning to expose her intimacy with the supposed servant and so shame her. After some confusion Dorange's friends, who have accompanied him, make known his true name to Angellica and her aunt and uncle. Dorange hands a ring to her which he had had from her on their earlier meeting in London. Angellica faints and is taken out. Dorange then leaves for his meeting with the Marquise. Min Heer Tomas with the aid of a monkey brings his wife Anniky to obedience and gets back from her Bondevelt's bond.

Angellica's brother, Don Leon, returns. He finds out from her of her discovery of Dorange. Don Leon resolves to force Dorange to marry Angellica. In the meantime, Dorange has spent the night with the Marquise. Enraged at his mistress's lack of generosity, Mascarillo, the Marquise's servant, betrays her to Bertran, her husband, who comes to her apartment. Dorange hides in the closet. Bertran starts to open the door of the room, but is threatened by Dorange. Dorange relates the facts in the case to Bertran. The Marquis takes the money which Dorange has given the Marquise and returns it to him, reserving one piece for the Marquise as her perquisites. Bertran then announces that he will put the Marquise in a convent. Don Leon now meets Dorange who admits having wronged Angellica in London. The two fight, but are reconciled when Don Leon is disarmed by Dorange who grants him his life'. Dorange and Angellica are then reunited and the play ends.

After having written practically nothing251 but comedies since his first play, *The Siege of Memphis,* D'Urfey turned to tragedy in the dramas immediately succeeding *The Campaigners.* His *Fa-*

mous History of the Rise and Fall of Massaniello would seem to have been acted (both, parts of it) in 1699, although Genest questions the performing of the tragedies at all.252 *Part I* was printed with the following titlepage:253

"The Famous HISTORY Of The RISE and FALL of MASSANIELLO. In Two Parts Written by Mr. *THO. D'URFEY, LONDON:* Printed for *John Nutt,* near *Stationers-Hall.* 1700."254

It has been stated that D'Urfey based his tragedies upon *The Rebellion of Naples, or The Tragedy of Massinello,* a play printed in 1651, as by T. B. who claims to have witnessed the insurrection. Genest who had compared the earlier play with those of D'Urfey denies the truth of this charge of plagiarism, and in support of his view outlines briefly *The Rebellion.*255 Judging from the synopsis, one is led to believe that D'Urfey had never seen the earlier play, much less have borrowed from it. He doubtless founded his plays upon some historical account of the rebellion.

The most complete narrative of Masaniello's256 career accessi 251 The exceptions are the alterations of *Cymbeline, The Sea Voyage,* and *Bussy D'Ambois,* ali of them alterations of earlier plays.
252 *Stage,* II, 158. Whincop in his *List,* p. 227, says the two parts were acted in Lincoln's Inn Fields in 1700. 253 The copy of *Part I* used in preparing this study, that in the Harvard University Library, bears the autograph of John Genest, and the date in that scholar's hand, "March 23, 1818." 254 *Part II* is dated 1699. A similar situation exists with regard to the publication of Crowne's *Henry VI. Part I* is dated 1681 and *Part II* 1680 (Genest, *Stage,* I, 307). Ebbsworth makes the mistake of dating *Massaniello, Part I* in 1699 and *Part II* in 1700 D. N. B., XVI, 253). 255 *Stage,* II, 161. 284 When dealing with the historical characters, the writer will employ the commonly accepted spellings of names; D'Urfey's spellings, or misspellings will be used only in connection with the figures as occurring in the tragedies. ble to the writer is de Reumont's, as given in his *Carafas of Mad-*

*daloni: Naples under Spanish Dominion.*TM A comparison of *Part I* of D'Urfey's *Massaniello* with de Reumont's history which may be of interest follows.

Masaniello's wife was really Berardina Pisa (p. 301).208 Genovino was Giulio Genuino, an aged priest who had been a slave in the galleys of the Barbary States (p. 302). Don Tiberio, Prince of Bissignano, promised the mob on its first gathering remission of the food taxes. He fled from them shortly, went to Rome, and there died insane (p. 305). Perone, the bandit, was an historical character (pp. 302 ff., 315). Mataloni's escape (II, 2) is based upon that of Naclerio (p. 307). The deaths of Perone and Peppo (IV, 1) are historical (p. 324 ff.). The plotting to blow up the marketplace (III, 2, etc.) is based upon the actual explosion of a mine beneath the Custom House (p. 303). Massaniello's order forbidding the wearing of long cloaks beneath which assassins might conceal their weapons (IV, 1, 2) is founded on fact (p. 328). The abuse of the severed heads of Perone and Peppo Caraffa (V, 1) actually occurred.

In the main, the tragedy follows fairly closely the historical. accounts, deviating generally in some minor details. However, the love of Massaniello for the Duchess of Mataloni, as related by D'Urfey is absolutely fictitious. The tragedy is in verse which is printed chiefly as prose. Songs, dances, and spectacles are scattered through it. D'Urfey in the course of the drama shows no sympathy whatever with the wrongs of the poor Neapolitans. He distinctly favors the side of the nobility. 259 *Part I* is dedicated to Thomas Lord Leigh, a patron of the author. Genest260 considers D'Urfey's two tragedies on Masaniello "far from bad ones," but condemns his having written them in two parts. Their merit, he thinks, lies chiefly in the comic passages. The great fault is that one who knew nothing of the historical facts would form an entirely wrong notion of Masaniello.

The two parts of *Massaniello* were combined into one play by Thomas Walker, the actor who created the part of Macheath in

Translation. Published London, 1854. Pp. 301-339. 258 The page numbers refer to de Reumont's book unless the contrary is stated. 288 In *The Moderator's Dream, Pills to Purge Melancholy*, II, 182 ff., "Massinello" is mentioned as an example of a rebel who rose against the nobles. 280 *Stage*, II, 163. Whibley is less complimentary. See *The Cambridge History of English Literature*, VIII, 199. *The Beggars' Opera*. This version was produced at Lincoln's Inn Fields, July 31, 1724.261 That Collier's attack upon D'Urfey and upon the stage in general had borne fruit is shown in the prologue to *Part I* (spoken by Pinkethman):

"Ah, Sirs, you are the cause of these our Streights,
You still have been our dire malignant Fates:
By your lewd Humours, first, which when'
we follow'd
Our Smutty Plays out of our Doors were Hollow'd,
And Zealous Spirits 'gainst our Function
Bellow'd."

The following lines in the prologue illustrate well D'Urfey's characteristic faith in his own ability:

"But since our Poet is resolv'd to day,
Once more to entertain you with a Play,
A famous Story, and known lately True,
Mixt with good Flumour, and good Musick too, Which there is in it, give the Devil his due." In the conversation of Massaniello with his friends in I, 1 (p. 4), there is a suggestion at least of Jack Cade and his followers in l *Henry VI, Part II*, IV.262 That the two parts of D'Urfey's tragedy were written virtually as one is shown by the following lines from the epilogue (spoken by Mrs. Rogers): "Suspend your Judgment, till the Truth be told.

A Rebel's Rise, we only now Present,
The Next Part shews his Fall and Punishment."

The *dramatis persona*,20 which lacks unfortunately the names of the cast,264 is as follows:

"Dramatis Persona;.
Don Tiberio, Prince of Bissignano, Duke of Matalono.265
Don Peppo di Caraifa, his Brother.266
Cardinal *Fillomerino*, Arch-Bishop of *Naples*.
» Genest, *Stage*, III, 148-49.
262 See Forsythe, *The Relations of Shirley's Plays to the Elizabethan Drama*, pp. 275-76. 263 Very imperfect and jumbled up. See the notes following. 264 Pinkethman was a performer or intended as such and Mrs. Rogers was cast for the part of the Duchess. 2W Sic. "Don Tiberio, Prince of Bissignano," and the "Duke of Mataloni" are two distinct and separate persons, "Bissignano" and "Don Tiberio" are interchangeably used in the text. 260 Mataloni's.
Principal of the Mob, belonging to *Massaniello*.
Massaniello, alias *Thomas Annello* of *Amalfi* (First a Fisherman, and after made
I Captain-General of the *Neapolitans*.
Pedro di Amalfi, his Brother—a Ruffian.
Julio Genovino, a Jesuit, his Counsellor.
IA famous Banditti; at first, accomplice with *Massaniello*, afterwards brib'd against him by *Mataloni's* Faction. *Rock Brasile*. (A Roguish Scrivener; afterwards made Secretary and Adjutant to *Massaniello*.
Bartallo—a Butcher.
Valasco—a Taylor.
Jacomo—a Miller.
Gaspar—a Smith.
Scipio—a Cobler.
Dona Aurelia—the Vice-Queen.
Belleraiza—her Sister.267
Dutchess of *Mataloni*.
Blowzabella—Wife to *Massaniello*.
Belvidore—a Tanner's Wife.
Ursula—Wife to *Pedro*.
A *Servant Wench*, with other Women, Wives, Sisters, &c.
belonging to the Mob; together with *Suitors, Priests*,
Choristers, Singers, Dancers, and *Attendants*. The *Scene, Naples;* the *Time*, Four days."

The plot of *Massaniello, Part I*, runs as follows:

Genovino, a Jesuit, fails election as cardinal through the opposition of the Neapolitan nobles. In revenge, Genovino allies himself with the fisherman Massaniello, the leader of the disaffected commoners, and engages in exciting Massaniello's followers against the nobility. Massaniello heads an uprising against the newly imposed taxes.

Genovino, whose idea is to rule Massaniello, suggests to the rebel chief that it is wasteful to destroy property that may be put to good use. Seeing Genovino's greed, Massaniello pretends to misunderstand the priest, and assents, saying that he himself will convert all loot to his own use and so raise a fortune for himself. Taking this seriously, Genovino resolves to ruin Massaniello. Certain of the nobles are proscribed by Massaniello and their houses are plundered and burnt. Blowzabella, Massaniello's wife, and other women riot in the street.

w Belleraiza is the Duchess of Matalcni. Perone, a bandit, who hates Massaniello, although serving under him, is persuaded by Genovino to join in working for Massaniello's destruction. As Massaniello is giving an audience to Don Tiberio, Prince of Bissignano, whom the insurgent chief desires to represent the people at the Viceroy's court, Blowzabella enters with the Duchess of Mataloni, with whose jewels Blowzabella has adorned herself. Massaniello falls in love with the Duchess, and appoints Rock, his secretary, to pay suit for him to her. In the meantime, Don Tiberio, hoping to secure better treatment from Blowzabella for the wife of his friend the Duke of Mataloni, responds to Blowzabella's advances to him. The Duke of Mataloni is told by Cardinal Fillomerino of Mataloni's brother's plan to explode a mine under the market-place and thereby slay Massaniello and his companions. The intention of Don Peppo (the Duke's brother) is to kill at the same time the traitor Perone who is to shoot Massaniello; simultaneously the Duchess and Duke will perish in the blast. Don Peppo wishes his brother out of the way, as he desires the Duke's position as tax-farmer. After the Cardinal leaves, the conspirators enter to Mataloni. He is assured of their plans by their language and takes his departure.

Disguised as a bandit, Mataloni goes to Massaniello and reveals the plot against him, in order to save himself and the Duchess from death. Massaniello takes steps to arrest the conspirators. Perone with his fellow bandits is seized in Massaniello's presence. Don Tiberio reports to Massaniello that the Viceroy has agreed to grant a charter to the Neapolitans. Massaniello goes to visit the Cardinal and enters just as an order of his own forbidding the wearing of long cloaks (on account of their convenience for the concealment of weapons under them) is being enforced by two officers who are stripping off the Cardinal's robe. The Cardinal and Massaniello converse. Won by the Cardinal's piety, Massaniello vows to return to his fishing as soon as the charter is ratified.

Massaniello sends Mataloni, who is still disguised as a bandit, with Rock and the Cardinal to visit the Duchess, so that he may report what she says to them. Mataloni hears the Duchess tell the Cardinal of Massaniello's advances to her. In his disguise the Duke tests his wife's fidelity to him, and finds her to be loyal to him. Rock and Genovino enter, and are seized by Mataloni who locks them up. Accompanied by the Cardinal, Mataloni aids his wife's escape from the prison. Rock and Genovino quarrel and then fight. Genovino then slips a purse into Rock's pocket. Massaniello comes in and finds the Duchess gone. Genovino alleges Rock to have been bribed to assist in the Duchess's flight. The purse which is found in Rock's pocket is taken as evidence of his guilt. Genovino, however, is betrayed as an accomplice of Don Peppo in his plot against Massaniello, and is hurried off to punishment. The play closes with the announcement of the ratification of the Neapolitan charter on the morrow. Massaniello's fury and raving at the escape of his prisoner lead Don Tiberio to prophesy that since-Massaniello's head has been turned by his success he will be ruined by his own ambition.

The titlepage of *Part II* of *Massaniello*TM runs thus:

"the Famous History and Fall Of MASSAINELLO: Or, A Fisherman A PRINCE. *The Second PART*, Written by Mr. *D'URFBY. LONDON:* Printed for *I. Nutt near Stationers Hall*, 1699." To judge from the prologue in which occurs the line, "Warm Weather and May-Fair are Martial Foes," *Part II* was produced in May, 1699.

The second part keeps in general close to history. For example, the meeting of the Viceroy and Massaniello in the Cathedral to ratify the terms given the rebels (II, 1) is historical (De Reumont, p. 333 ff.). Massaniello's conduct before the Cardinal (II, 1) is based on fact (De Reumont, p. 334). The entertainment of the Viceroy's wife by Blowzabella (II, 2, and also V. 4) are based upon an actual visit of Massaniello's wife and mother to the wife of the Viceroy (De Reumont, p. 335). Mataloni's second escape (IV, 1) is related to an earlier similar feat (De Reumont, pp. 31819). The plot for Massaniello's death is close to the historical conspiracy (De Reumont, pp. 336-37). The assassination of Massaniello (V, 3) differs from the true story of the incident. Really, Massaniello was set upon and killed in a Carmelite convent where he was resting (De Reumont, p. 337). The treatment of Massaniello's corpse (V, 4) is historical (De Reumont, p. 338). It seems not improbable that Massaniello's attempt upon Belleraiza was borrowed by D'Urfey from *King Edivard III*, a play by Bencroft (or Mountfort), produced at the Theatre Royal in 1691. 288 Through the play, titlepage, heading, *dramatis persona*, and elsewhere, occurs the curious misspelling, "Massainello."

The *dramatis persona* does not include the performers' names, but it would appear from the epilogue that Miss Campian played Fellicia269 and Mrs. Rogers Belleraiza. In V, 4, Pate appeared as Rebellion and sang a song.

The characters of the play are thus given:

"DRAMATIS PERSONA.270 *Don Rodrigo Pons de Leon*, Viceroy of *Naples*

and Duke of *Arcos. Don Tiberio* Prince of *Bissignano. Guiseppe* Duke *de Caivano. Cardinal Fillomarino*, Archbishop of *Naples.*

Duke *di Mataloni. Massainello*, General of the *Neapolitans. Pedro di Amalfi*, His Brother a Ruffian.

A Villain and Parasite, but Witty and Comical, Gentleman-Usher to *Blowzabella.* and I Two Young Lewd Fellows *Pie(ro* Companions to *Massainello.* WOMEN.

Dona Aurelia, The Vice-Queen. *Dona Beleraiza*, Dutchess of *Mataloni. Dona Fellicia, Daughter to the Duke di Caivano* and her Niece. *Blowzabella, Wife to Massainello. Ursula*, Her Woman.

Suitors, Musicians, Masques, Singers, Dancers, — and Attendants.

The Scene *Naples*, the Time Four Days."

The plot of *Massaniello, Part II*, is as follows:

The Duke of Mataloni, whose wife Belleraiza, has been imprisoned by Massaniello, has rescued her and they have joined the Viceroy of Naples, the Duke of Arcos. Massaniello writes to Aurelia, wife of the Viceroy, asking her to use her influence with her husband in inducing him to send back the Duchess of Mataloni whom Massaniello loves. In case of her failure to comply with this request Massaniello threatens her with his anger. They prepare to refuse 280 The ravishment of this character in V, 2, has various Elizabethan analogues; see Forsythe, *The Relations of Shirley's Plays to the Elizabethan Drama, pp.* 227-28. 270 Incomplete, as it lacks La Poop, a woman attendant upon Blowzabella.

Massaniello's demand. The Prince of Bissignano arrives as a messenger from Massaniello and reports him as being ashamed now of his previous demands, which he had made while drunk. It is then arranged that the Viceroy shall meet Massaniello in the Cathedral next day to ratify the charter given the city.

The Viceroy and Massaniello meet in the Cathedral. Massaniello prepares to retire to private life, since the object of his rebellion—the removal of the food-taxes—has been attained. Pedro and Cosmo, however, seek to prevent Massaniello's return to his trade of fishing.

Cosmo and Pietro warn Massaniello that he will be put to death by the Duke of Mataloni when he lays down his arms. They recall to Massaniello the charms of the Duchess of Mataloni. The rebel general now begins to waver in his resolution of giving up his power. Cosmo and Pietro surprise Aurelia, the Viceroy's wife, Belleraiza, and Fellicia, and carry them off as prisoners. The rebels capture Mataloni also, together with the Duke de Caivano. In a vision, St. Genaro promises the Viceroy that his wife will be unharmed. Cardinal Fillomarino, hitherto friendly to Massaniello, now turns against him on account of this outrage to the ladies, and supports the Viceroy. The prisoners are brought before Massaniello whom Pietro has made drunk. Aurelia defies Massaniello so courageously that in admiration of her fearlessness he releases her.

Belleraiza and the Duke are in prison together; the reason for their being confined in the same cell being that Massaniello thinks that the Duke in order to secure his release will bid his wife grant Massaniello's suit to her. Cosmo enters to conduct the Duchess to Massaniello. Mataloni stabs Cosmo and, assisted by a faithful servant, changes clothes with the dead man. The Duke and Duchess escape, but are pursued and the Duchess is recaptured. In a rage over the Duke's escape, Massaniello strikes Bissignano, and thus alienates him. Bissignano joins the Viceroy, the Cardinal, and the Duke. The Viceroy reports the rape of Fellicia by Pedro and the death of the Duke of Caivano, her father, of grief. A plot to assassinate Massaniello is formed. Bissignano is the leader.

Bissignano obtains the key to her husband's apartment from Massaniello's wife. Just as Massaniello, who is drunk, orders his companions to strip Belleraiza, Bissignano, Mataloni, and their Spanish guards enter and rescue her. Mataloni shoots Massaniello in the subsequent fight. In the meantime, Aurelia gives an entertainment to

Blowzabella and her companions. There a masque is presented, in which are depicted the fates of the guests. They are finally arrested. The play closes with an account of the turning of the populace against Massaniello, and the displaying of Massaniello's mangled body dragged by horses.

In his next play D'Urfey returned to comedy. *The Bath, orr The Western Lass,"*1 was acted first in 1701.272 The play was printed with the following titlepage:

"the BATH, Or, The Western Lass, A COMEDY, As It is Acted at the Theatre Royal in *Drury-lane,* By His Majesty's Servants. By Mr. *D'Urfey. LONDON,* Printed for *Peter Buck,* at the Sign of the *Temple,* at the *Middle Temple Gate* in *Fleetstreet.* 1701" *The Bath* seems to have been only moderately successful. In his dedication of the comedy to Archibald Duke of Argyll, D'Urfey says:

"And now to speak a word or two of the Comedy, which I most humbly present your Grace; tho' it was forc'd to push through the bryars of unreasonable Discourtesie, and critical Envy, yet it had generally the good fortune to please, only excepting here and there an Expression or two, which some of the over-curious might well have spar'd taking notice of, and done the Credit of their Wit no harm; and also the obnoxious Epilogue, which tho then so vilely exploded, has had-since as many, and as Judicious Friends, (of Quality, as well as Others) to commend it, as it had then Inveterate Enemies to cry it down. I confess, it being written as a thing of Humour for *Pinkiman* the Comedian, and the Theme as low as the Ropedancing in *May-Fair,* some grossness of Expression on such a subject might possible disgust the Ladies, who I could indeed have wish'd would have been so good natur'd to pass by a word or two in an Epilogue, after having been (as they seem'd) diverted with the Play: But that the Tavern-plyers and the Men of the Town should wrest the phrase of the *Best in Christendom,* only us'd there as a comparison in Professions, to the extreme of their fulsom Imagina-

tion, is a thing I could *m* The second title was obviously suggested by Brome's *Northern Lass.* 272 Genest, *Stage,* II, 235. Whincop probably incorrectly says 1697 *(List,* p. 227).

Vid. Epilogue note by D'Urfey. not pardon in 'em, if they only hiss'd at that; but I will do the Ring-leaders understanding now this Justice to declare, that 'twas the Salt of some Satyrical touches in the Lines, and not the Obscenity in 'em, which after being diverted so long, so suddenly provok'd their Indignation. "Comedy is at present so difficult to write, and new Humour so seldom found, and well manag'd, that, I think, I, that have furnish'd this with a pretty Plot and at least four new characters, particularly Mrs. *Verbruggen's* (whose incomparable performance answering my design, has rais'd it, if not to her Master-piece, yet at least second to any) may in some measure secure my reputation. The stopping of it from Acting by Superiour command, doing me no manner of Injury, (tho it might the Playhouse) but only for two or three days disappointing my friends; the Cause is so trivial that I am asham'd to mention it, nor can I accuse my self as yet of any disrespect to a Lady, whom I always honour'd, for taking the Poetical License of making the Mad man in my Scene Satyrically drink a Health, altering it into a modest phrase, (tho somewhat too familiar) which some of her seeming Admirers have made common and so often Toasted in another Phrase, abominably gross and fulsome.

"I am sorry to be the subject of any ones ill sentiments, much more of those of Quality; but I will satisfie my self that I have not so deserv'd their discourtesie; and descanting upon the Crowd, also be pleas'd that every one that carps cannot frame a piece of this nature right. Poets are as rare as right Politicians, and do but here and there shoot up capacitated to instruct and divert the rest of the people; of whom we may say with *Virgil, Apparent rari nantes in gurgite vasto."*

The writer is unable to throw any light upon the circumstances mentioned in the dedication, that is, the prohibition of the performance of the piay on account of some apparent application of a passage in it to a lady of high rank.

Here again in *The Bath* in Colonel's Philip's falsehood, told to protect his sister's honor, and in the general readjustment of the relations of Lovechace, Lydia, Sophronia and Transport, we have another instance of the sentimentalization of comedy.

Genest calls *The Bath* a "tolerable comedy,"273 and that is the most to be said for it. It was presented at Drury Lane as the author's benefit, December 8, 1702.274 There is no record of a later performance. Of Mrs. Verbruggen's performance of Gillian, so admired by D'Urfey, Cibber says:275

"In a play of D'Urfey's, now forgotten, called 'The Western Lass,' which part she Mrs. Verbruggen acted, she transformed her whole being, body, shape, voice, language, look, and features, into almost another animal; with a strong Devonshire dialect, a broad laughing voice, a poking head, round shoulders, an unconceiving eye, and the most bedizening, dowdy dress, that ever covered the untrained limbs of a Joan Trot. To have seen her here you would have thought it impossible the same creature could ever have been recovered to what was as easy to her—the gay, the lively, and the desirable." In Sir Sackfull Simile D'Urfey has imitated one of Congreve's characters—Witwoud in *The Way of the World*. The baby talk of Delia is a recollection of the language of the Nurse in *The Campaigners*. Sir Carolus Codshead, the lover of old times, is a recurrence of one of D'Urfey's stock figures.

As in *The Richmond Heiress*, I, 1, we find in *The Bath* (I, 1, p. 5) a reference to one of the actors by name, on this occasion "Pinkiman," or Penkethman, who acted the part of Charles. In II, 1 (p. 11), Gillian tells of having seen Lee's *Sophronisba* on one of her visits to London, and quotes five lines from the end of III, 3. fAn interesting commentary upon the taste of his old patron, King Charles, occurs, V, 3 (p. 56). Sir Carolus says,

".... Why they were just such Songs

as these now that promoted the pleasant hours of the Great King *Harry*, and King *Chorles sic* lov'd a humorous Song at his heart too." Possibly the allusion is to Charles I, however.276 A dialogue then is sung by Crab and Gillian in which the delights of the country are I expatiated upon.

" *Stage*, II, 236.

1*Ibi&*, II, 255.

275 *Apology*, p. 100 (edition, London, 1826). He had acted Crab in the play.

27a See the character of Sir Carolus in the *dramatis persona*.

The characters and actors are thus listed:

"Dramatis PersonaTM

MEN

Lord *Lovechase*, A blunt Country Lord, a Lover of Foxhunting and Country Sports, Intreagu'd with *Lydia*.

Acted by Mr. *Griffin Sir Oliver Oldgame*, A sneaking soft temper'd rich old

Knight, a Dissenter, and a great manager in City affairs and East-India Stock, but govern'd by his

Wife. Mr. *Norris*

Sir *Carolus Codshead*, A humorous haughty old fellow,

extremely fond of the liberty and methods of K.

Harry the 8th and K. *Charles*. Mr. *Johnson*

Collonel Philip, Son to Oldgame, a worthy honest Gentleman, and so very Loyal, that tho heir to a noble Estate, yet takes the King's Commissions and fights for him of a meer principle of honour. Mr. *Mills Transport*, A young handsome Gent, generous and witty, but extremely amorous, and betrothed to, and passionately in Love with *Sophronia. Charles*, Eldest Son to Sir *Carolus*, a peevish ill-natur'd fellow, brought sick to the *Bath*, but to his power very lewd and ungovernable. Mr. *Pinkiman Harry*, Youngest Son to Sir *Carolus*, a leud debauch'd

Rake. Mr. *Bullock*

Crab, Hind to Lord *Lovechace*, a sharp-witted fellow, a

Country Wit and Joker, and the mouth of the Boors of *Kent* and *Sussex*. . Mr. *Cibber*

Sir *Sackfull Simile*, A young fellow, that having spent an

Estate is fain to keep company with Sharpers. A

great Simile-maker, and vents very good ones on all occasions.

Plod and *Currycomb*, Groom and Footman

Serjeant of the *Bath*.

WOMEN.

Lydia, Wife to Sir *Oliver*, a Vicecountess, imperious and proud, very much affected with decorums in breeding, and to be noted to be of a great family. Intreagu'd with *Lovechace*. Mrs. *Knight 271* Imperfect, as not including Hairbrain, Mrs. Du Grand, Size Sink, Quater Trey,; Ams Ace, and Doublets. *Sophronia*, Witty and good-natur'd, a great lover of Poetry, which she often repeats in her common discourse, but very uneasie with her forc'd marriage to *Lovechace*, being betroth'd to *Transport*. Mrs. *Rogers Delia*, An old affected Creature, Wife to Sir *Carolus*, overfond of her booby Son *Charles*, and always using a whining Baby cant, the more to wheedle and impose upon her uxorious Husband. Mrs. *Kent. Gillian Homebred*, The Western Lass. A Country Gentlewoman of 6000 /. Fortune, but so awkard in her speech, behaviour and dress, that she affects to be Anti to all Fashions; she speaks the broad Somersetshire dialect, and is so very easie with herself that she is never out of humour. Mrs. *Verbruggen Combrush, Dearnwell, Sisse*, Three *Confidents*,

By Mrs. *Moor*, Mrs. *Stephens*, Mrs. *Baker* Chair-men, Musicians, Singers Dancers, and Attendants. Scene, The Bath." The plot of *The Bath* may thus be summarized:

Colonel Philip and his sister Sophronia are at Bath. Although she is in love with Transport, Sophronia has been forced by her brother into an engagement with Lord Lovechace. In spite of her protests she is to be married to him on her birthday. Lovechace is entangled in an intrigue with Lydia, stepmother to the Colonel and Sophronia.

Transport visits Sophronia secretly and arranges another meeting with her during the wedding ball. Lydia, who is jealous of her stepdaughter, makes Lovechace promise to come to her instead of to Sophronia on the wedding-night.

After the wedding Sophronia secures permission from her husband to be alone for the following two nights. She goes to meet Transport, but leaves him because of the violence of his passion. She surprises her stepmother and Lovechace making love in the dark. Sir Oliver Oldgame, Lydia's husband and the bride's father, who has designed to spy upon Lovechace and Sophronia, also finds the two together. They pretend to have known of his presence and to have enacted a love scene for his mystification. This explanation pacifies him.

Transport and Lovechace meet in a gambling-hell. Lovechace invites Transport to meet Sophronia. Transport then leaves for another meeting with Sophronia. He is to know her chamber door by a stand placed outside it. Lydia, however, stumbles over the stand in the dark, and, to get it out of the way, places it by her own door. Transport arrives, finds the stand, and enters Lydia's room, thinking it Sophronia's. Lydia discovers her visitor is not the expected Lovechace. To shield Sophronia, Transport pretends to be a housebreaker and to have just been turned from his evil life by the sight of Lydia's beauty. Much impressed, she tries to lead him to her closet to see his face, but he locks the door on her when she precedes him in, and then escapes. As Lydia cries out for help, Lovechace enters and releases her. As they talk, the Colonel, Lydia's stepson, who has been aroused by the noise, enters, and overhears their conversation. Lydia relates that the supposed thief had lost a picture in his flight. This Lovechace discovers to be one of herself given by Sophronia to Transport. In order to shield his sister from suspicion, the Colonel now reveals himself and claims to have been the "robber". He tells a story of having designed to ask Lydia's intervention in some business between Sir Oliver and him. Lovechace and Lydia accept the story as true. The lovers now independently determine to separate. Lovechace

resolves to be true to his wife.

Lydia tells Sophronia of her adventure. Sophronia knows of Transport's having lost her picture, but thinks that he has had an intrigue with Lydia, and has left the miniature in her chamber. Colonel Philip, who suspects Transport of being on equally good terms with both Sophronia and Lydia, intercepts a letter from Transport to Sophronia. The writer is shown therein to have had no relations with either lady yet. The Colonel then goes to meet Transport at a place where the latter has asked Sophronia to join him. He persuades Transport to leave Bath for the sake of Sophronia's peace. Lovechace, however, forces Transport to meet Sophronia, who regards him merely as a stranger, their mutual passion now being over.

The Bath has two underplots. Ont tells how Harry Codshead, in the endeavor to kill his invalid elder brother Charles by making him carouse, instead cures him of his illness. Harry then falls ill in his turn and is dosed with liquor by his now robust brother, who designs to remove him from any possible sharing in the family fortune. The other plot deals with the disguising of Crab, a shrewd countryman, as Captain Thumper, a Sussex militiaman, and his winning In that shape a rich rustic heiress, Gillian Homebred, the Western Lass. *The Old Mode and the New, or, Country Miss with her Furbeloe,* was first acted March 11, 1703.278 The comedy was printed, according to the *Biographic Dramatical* in 1709 ? with this titlepage:

"the Old Mode & the New, Or, *Country Miss with her Furbeloe.* A COMEDY. As it is Acted at the THEATREROYAL By her Majesty's Servants. *Written by Mr.* Tho. D'Urfey. LONDON: Printed for *Bernard Lintott,* and sold by Samuel Clark, at the Corner of Exchange Alley in Birchin Lane, Francis Faucet in the New Exchange, and Lucas Stowkey over against the Mews Gate in Charing Cross. Price Is. 6d."

In his dedication of the play to Charles Duke of Richmond and Lennox, a natural son of Charles II, D'Urfey says:

"It is not, my Lord, without considerable Satisfaction, that I know some of the Scenes of this Piece were so happy to cause your Diversion, and ingage your Liking, when it had the Honour of your Grace's Presence at the time of Action; your obliging Censure and Incouragement, not only at that time doing me a noble Favour and Benefit, but also brought fresh into my Mind the Idea of former Majesty of Glorious Memory, from whom you had your Illustrious Being, whose excellent Temper, join'd with admirable Judgment, would often, like another Apollo, graciously inspire the adventrous Muses, (amongst whose encourg'd Band, mine was not the least honour'd with his Favour and Indulgence) And who now, methinks, each happy Day, I behold anew in your Grace's Person and Character.

"I shall not inquire of any ill-natur'd Critick, whether this Comedy be good or no, neither wanting, nor caring for his Opinion, it being sufficient to fix my Credit, that it was read and put to the Test before some of the best Judges the Stage has, and receiv'd with general Liking by both Houses, before the Action; and tho' the faulty280 length, a Rock which sometimes (do what we can) we cannot save our selves from splitting on, and some ill Performance of under Parts, made that part of it n Genest, *Stage,* II, 269. Ebbsworth incorrectly says it was produced in *1709* CD. N. B., XVI, 253).

2TM III, 97. This date is probably incorrect. 1703 or 1704 is nearer the true date of publication, as no other acted play of D'Urfey's was kept six years from the printer after its performance. 280 On March 10, 1703, the comedy was acted as having been shortened an *hour* in, length; "a great improvement," as Genest says *(Stage,* II, 270). % tedious the first Day; yet I make no doubt in the reading, the Plot and Humours being observed and digested, your Grace will find the Honour you did it was not altogether lost.

"It is not every Poet's Talent, my Lord, in this Age, to invent a good Plot, or adorn his Play with that material Decoration so proper, and so applauded in former Times; yet that there is one in this, I dare affirm: And those that will but be pleas'd carefully to read the first Act, will find a Story not only intricate and difficult to be contriv'd, but divertive and full of Variety. And as for that part of the Audience, whose Heads full of volatile Chimera's, expecting other sort of flashing Entertainment, would not let 'em mind the opening of it, and so consequently lost the Connexion, and indeed the pleasuae *sic* of the following Acts, I am not mortified at all at their Censure, I know the Niceness of their Palates very well, and dare be' so bold to say, can please 'em at a much cheaper rate, than with a good Plot and Characters; but must beg leave to hint, as once a famous old Author did upon the same occasion,

I gave 'em Meat,

But they would Acorns eat:

Still undistinguish'd by their vicious Tast

The choice Pomgranat, &c. However, to countervail their illness of Appetite, another part of those that saw it were well enough satisfied with their Collation, and I as much pleas'd that it was not distasteful to 'em.

"And here I believe it a Duty incumbent on me to acknowledge also, that as I thought my self very happy in the Honour your Grace did me, so was I infinitely oblig'd by the uncommon Favour and Ornament some noble Ladies of the first Rank, as well as others, was pleas'd to confer; which extraordinary Condescention, as the Beauty of their Persons and Merit will be renown'd for ever, shall perpetually have place in my grateful Memory." . It is evident from the dedication that *The Old Mode and the New* was not very favorably received, although it was not positively damned. The play seems, however, to have been successful enough to have been acted as Mrs. Bicknell's benefit at Drury Lane, July 1, 1703.281 It is indeed an exceedingly complicated play with nothing to recommend it. Genest says of it, "The greater part of this comedy 281 Genest, *Stage,* II, 275. is dull—the last scene of the 4th act, and the greater part of the 5th are good.

"282 The *Biographia Dramatica* calls it a very indifferent play.283
The prologue spoken by "Pinkeman" (Pinkethman) is a satirical attack upon Italian opera and upon the demand for morality of word and action on. the stage.

Sir Fumbler Oldmode is another example of the old-fashioned men whom D'Urfey persisted in introducing into his comedies. Gatty is another hoyden like those of *Love for Money.* Will Queenlove's name is an interesting development of the Kinglove of *The Royalist* and *The Campaigners.* Problem's pride in her skill in making medicines and conserves would seem related to Farquhar's later Lady Bountiful in *The Beaux Stratagem.*

Several interesting points are to be found in the play. In I, 1 (p. 2), Queenlove says,

"...1 shall neither court ye in *Tom Sternhold's* grave

Sonnets, nor in *Tom Durfey's* airy ones, being equally unskill'd in both." Lucia says, I, 1 (p. 3),

"... There's Mrs. *Probleme* ...; and I'd no more hear the Stuff she talks every Minute, than I'd be condemn'd to hear a lewd Play that the virtuous, religious, and ingenious Grand

Jury have exploded at the Quarter Sessions." D'Urfey probably refers to his prosecution in 1698 on account of r*Don Quixote.* A dialogue between Queenlove and Maggot occurs, 1,1 (p. 12), in which the fable of the Belly and the Members *(CorioLJanus,* I, 1) is utilized as the Head and the Belly. In II, 1 (p. 23), Sir Fumbler Oldmode makes a patriotic speech upon the French war and upon Queen Anne. The Queen is praised and a health is drunk to her in II, 2 (p. 30). These two passages recall the health to King William, *The Campaigners,* IV, 1 (p. 41). *The Modern Prophets,* V, 1 (p. 72), should also be compared. In the relation of his amorous exploits, Tomazo, in III, 1 (p. 40), borrows from the *Decameron,* Day V, Novel 10, and Day VII, Novel 2. Tomazo's marriage to Smicket, the maid, thinking her to be her mistress Gatty is a repetition of the marriages of Bias and Solon in *The*

Marriage Hater Match'd.2Si '"*Ibid,* II, 270.

283 II, 97.

M See Forsythe, *The Relations of Shirley's Plays to the Elizabethan Drama,* p. 341.

The characters and actors thus are given:

"Dramatis Personae.

Men.

Sir *Fumbler Oldmode,* a rich old covetous Knight,

a Lover of former ancient Methods and Fashions of Queen *Elizabeth's* Days, very zealous for his Cause, and tho crippled with the

Gout and, and, and muffled Hand and Foot, yet perpetually busie in all things relating to worldly Affairs, and getting Riches.

Frederick, his Son, a young Gentleman, a great Lover of Court Modes, and the new Method I of living, somewhat extravagant, but witty, good-natur'd and a Man of Honour.

Will Queenlove, a well-bred honest County Gentleman and Scholar, Neighbour and Friend to *Frederick,* moderate in Opinion, and pleas'd with the present Reign and Posture of Affairs, —in Love with Lucia.

Monsieur *De Pistole,* a hot-headed French Merchant, who being of his Nation's Party and

Humour, decrys the War, and our Proceedings: He was correspondent with Sir *Fum-*

bler's Brother, Sir *Lyonel,* in *France,* who dy'd there; and by him being sent over and trusted with his Will, in which a vast Estate is given to *Gatty;* his Design is to wheedle

Sir *Fumbler,* and get her a Wife for his Son

Tomazo.

Tom. Pistole, al. Don *Tomazo, a.* young impudent

Fop, Son to *Pistole;* who being sent into Spain by his Father, and living 7 years at

Toledo, is infected with all the Spanish Formalities and Follies, a great Pretender to

Politiques, Business and Intrigue.

Misterious Maggothead, Mayor of

Coventry, a whimsical conceited Fellow, a rigid Fanatick and Commonwealth's Man, and a great Railer against high and low Churches, and Court Party; he was left Guardian to Miss *Gatty*
by Sir *Lyonel,* during his abode at Marseilles,
where he dy'd; and being let into the Secret of the Will, is uneasie at Sir *Tumbler's*
Hopes of an Heir, privately designing to over-reach all Pretenders, and have *Gatty* for himself.
Acted by Mr. *Johnson.*
By Mr. *Wilks.*
By Mr. *Mills.*
By Mr. *Bowen.*
By Mr. *Cibber.*
By
Mr. *Pinkeman.*
Major *Bombard,* an old surly Malcontent, who refus'd to serve all the last Reign, and now perpetually grumbling as uneasie in the present, not being offer'd a Commission answerable to his suppos'd Merit.
Captain Crimp, a *London* Sharper, pretending great Civility and Modesty, and comes into the Country with Design to bubble Country Gent, at Play.
By Mr. *Cross.*
By Mr. *Boyse. Collymor Hookem, Jack Jowler,*
Toby Touch-hole,
By Mrs. *Moor.*
A Lover of Fishing. 1 Companions A Lover of Hunting, to A Lover of Shooting. J *Fred. Abram,* a formal old fashion'd Fellow, Steward) to Sir *Fumbler.* By Mr. *Bullock. Combwig,* Valet to *Fred,* airy and new fashion'd. Mr. *Fairbank.*
Women. *Lady Oldmode,* a Coquet, first courted by *Fred* by afterwards by her Subtilty married to Sir *Fumbler;* yet through Fondness to him, carrying on *Fred's* Design upon his Father, counterfeits her self with Child, and humours her Husband in his antique Formalities, and covetous Methods.
Lucia, Daughter to Sir *Fumbler,* Town-bred and witty. By Mrs. *Oldfield.* Miss *Gatty,* Niece to Sir *Fumbler,* being Daughter' to Bernard, also deceas'd, his

youngest Brother, to whom Sir *Lyonel* in his Will gave his whole Estate of Fifty thousand Pounds at her Day of Marriage, provided Sir *Fumbler* had no Issue till the Age of sixty-three: Of I By a witty pleasant Humour, tho' childish and Mrs. *Moor.2* Country-bred, and banters her conceited Guardian with her Hatred of *London* Fashions, to gain more Liberty of Converse; but in private very eager to hear Town News, and very quick in making Remarks on 'em, in Love with *Fred. Smicket,* her Maid, a wanton Hoyden. *Problem,* a prating impertinent Nurse, Lady Old-") mode's Confident, valuing her self upon mak--
By *Mrs. Knight.*
ing Medicines and Conserves. J
Clowns, Singers, Fidlers, Dancers, and Attendants,
Men and Women.
The Scene, *COVENTRY."*
288 Obviously an error. Genest suggests that Mrs. Hook who had acted Hoyden in *The Relapse* played Gatty *(Stage,* II, 270).
The plot of *The Old Mode and the New* runs thus:
Fred Oldmode, the fashionable son of an old-fashioned father, and out of favor with him for his modern ideas, designs to trick his parent, Sir Fumbler Oldmode. As the fortune of Sir Fumbler's deceased brother Sir Lyonel has been willed to an unknown heir, if Sir Fumbler passes the age of sixty-three without a child being born to him between that time and his brother's death, Fred is concerned in finding this heir. 'He suspects his cousin Gatty of being the person in question. She is courted by her guardian, the Mayor of Coventry and later by a Frenchman, Tom Pistole, whom Sir Fumbler favors. Fred's stepmother Lady Oldmode with whom he was in love before her marriage to his father, to help Fred, simulates pregnancy, thereby intending to keep the suitors from Gatty and to afford a clear field for Fred's courtship of the girl.
Old Pistole and Tomazo, the latter of whom has been educated in Spain, arrive to make up the match with Gatty. Alleging his wife's condition, Sir Fumbler puts them off and will not agree

to the marriage of Gatty and Tomazo. Lady Oldmode carries on the deception by longing for several pieces of jewelry and plate which she secures from the unwilling Sir Fumbler.
Lady Oldmode pretends to be delivered of a child and, alleging fear of its being kidnapped by Pistole, removes from Sir Fumbler's house. Pistole and his son go to Sir Fumbler and claim that no child has been born, but he will not believe them. Sir Fumbler refuses to return to Pistole the money which the Frenchman has advanced to him. As they quarrel, the Mayor enters and announces that Gatty and Sir Fumbler's daughter Lucia have been kidnapped by soldiers (who are friends of Fred in disguise). The supposed soldiers then seize Sir Fumbler, Pistole, and Tomazo and carry them away. The captives are secured and the conspirators gain possession of Sir Fumbler's cabinet which contains Sir Lyonel's will and other papers. They try to get the key to it from Sir Fumbler who suspects some device of Fred's and resolves to trick them. He sends them to a place where he says falsely he keeps the key concealed. They go in search of it, leaving him in the room alone and unbound. Although Sir Fumbler has been suffering so with the gout as to be practically helpless, he now takes the cabinet and key and escapes through a trapdoor of which only he knows. The party return and wonder at Sir Fumbler's escape. The Mayor approaches with aid, whereupon they flee.
Fred and his companions go to Lady Oldmode's retreat. They are surprised there by Sir Fumbler who has recovered from his gout as a result of his exertions, fright, and a wonderful medicine. Lady Oldmode, who has no place to hide, on her husband's entrance pretends to be a cousin of Fred, and deceives her husband successfully. Sir Fumbler mocks the company concerning their failure to obtain the will, and offers to bet that they cannot get it from him even by magic. Lady Oldmode who had been given the document to read two days before, but who had not returned it now slips the paper to Fred who produces it. They read it. Sir Fumbler then an-

nounces the birth of a son to him, thus invalidating the legacy to Gatty. He invites all to the christening. Tomazo bribes the Mayor for a glimpse of Gatty. The Mayor designs to trick Tomazo, and to marry her himself. Disguised as a woman, Fred appears accompanied by Queenlove who pretends to be his brother, and by a parson. Queenlove claims Fred has given up Gatty and is to marry his sister—as whom Fred himself is disguised—while he is to marry Fred's sister Lucia. The Mayor falls into the trap and agrees to allow the counterfeit sister to stay with Gatty at his house, Queenlove having told a story of a disappointed lover with a design of carrying "her" off. Smicket, Gatty's maid, is introduced to Tomazo as Gatty, and he runs away with her, thinking her the heiress.

After having exposed their trick and the two marriages to the Mayor in the morning, the two newly-wed couples go to the christening at Sir Fumbler's. As Sir Fumbler awaits the company, his wife, who to please him has previously worn old-fashioned clothes, enters in a modern garb. She announces to him that she has deceived him in regard to her condition and confesses her love for Fred. Fred comes in accompanied by his bride. His repulse of his stepmother's advances so delights Sir Fumbler that the old man takes him back into favor. Finally, Tomazo with his bride.enters. On unmasking, she is discovered to his confusion, to be Gatty's former maid.

Wonders in the Sun, or, The Kingdom of the Birds, an opera, was first produced at the Haymarket, April 5, 1706. 286 The piece was performed five or six times and was then withdrawn, not having paid half the expense of its production. In the dedication to his comedy, *The Recruiting-Officer,* first performed at Drury Lane, 286 Whincop dates the opera erroneously in 1710 *(List,* p. 127). April 8, 1706, Farquhar amuses himself at the expense of D'Urfey and his opera. 287 Whincop says that the opera had "several Ballads in it that took very much with the Common People."288 The titlepage runs thus:
"Wonders in the Sun,289 Or, The King-

dom of the Birds; A Comick Opera. With great Variety of *Songs* in all kinds, set to Musick by several of the most Eminent Masters of the Age.290 Written by Mr. *DURFEY. LONDN; sic,* Printed for *Jacob Tonson,* within *Grays-Inn-Gate,* next *Grays-Inn Lane.* 1706."

The opera is virtually five acts in length.291 There are four acts given as such, and in the *Introduction to the Prologue* we are told that the prologue itself which was "all sung" is an act in length. Consequently, one is not surprised at the statement on the reverse of the titlepage that "several of the Songs will be omitted, the Performance being too long."

Only two composers besides Draghi, who contributed or were drawn upon for music can be identified. These are Eccles, who is mentioned as having composed the air of the *Ode* of Orpheus (prologue, p. 7), and "Seignour Baptist Lully," to a "Famous Sebel" of whom the *Dialogue between Ignorance and Housewifery* (III, 1, p. 53) is set. *The Dialogue between a Satyr and a Nymph* which occurs in the prologue to *Wonders in the Sun* apparently was a favorite of its author, for it is to be found also in *Cinthia and Endymion,* III, 2 (pp. 24-25), and in *Ariadne,* I, 2 (pp. 197-99). *The Wonders in the Sun* is doubtless based upon *The Man in the Moon* by "Domingo Gonsales" (Francis Godwin, Bishop-of Llandaff and later of Hereford). This book was published in 1638; a second edition was brought out in 1657. Domingo travelled to the moon in a chariot drawn by twenty-five geese. The tale is mentioned in Mrs. Behn's *Emperor of the Moon,* I, 1, II, 5, and in M7 Genest, *Stage,* II, 350.
Op. ciV±
286 The heading of the opera and the running titles are *Wonders of the Sun.* 2X1 The statement of the *Biographia Dramatica* (III, 421-22) that some of the most noted wits of the day lent assistance to D'Urfey in writing the songs is based_ upon a misunderstanding of this statement. It obviously means that the music for certain songs was composed by other artists than D'Urfey. Ebbsworth says *(J3. N. B.,* XVI, 252), that

the music for the opera was composed by Giovanni Battista Draghi, but gives no authority. Had Ebbsworth read the opera he would have seen that airs by various composers were used. 281 *Wonders in the Sun* was dedicated by D'Urfey to "The Right Noble, Honourable and Ingenious Patrons of *Poetry,* Musick, etc. The Celebrated Society of the Kit-Cat Club."

Summers's notes on the respective passages in his edition of Mrs. Behn's *Works.* The writer has not seen Godwin's book, and knows of it only through Summers. The "Daemon of Socrates" and his protection of the.two strangers seems to bear witness to D'Urfey's having followed Dante's progress through Hell and Purgatory with Virgil as his guide.

The jargon spoken by the Viceroy and his followers in I, 2, and elsewhere suggests strongly *All's Well that Ends Well,* IV, 2, 3, where the captors of Parolles pretend to converse among themselves. f In II, 1 (p. 30 ff.), the dialogue between Gonzales and Bellygorge on "affairs subsolary" in which the former discloses the pettinesses and rascalities of terrestrial life is a foreshadowing of certain passages in *Gulliver's Travels.292* Indeed the whole opera is in some , respects suggestive of the various voyages of Gulliver. The waiting upon Deviling of his father and the punishment of the latter for a fault seem to show, as Genest thinks,293 a knowledge of Brome's *Antipodes.* There, old men are sent to school by their sons (II, 9). Satire upon contemporary events is to be found through the opera as in II, 1 (pp. 41-42), where a *Song* is sung by Moderation directed against the "Humorous of two Parties in a certain Northern Kingdom known by the Name of the *High Flyers* and the *Low."* The allusion is to the trouble with Scotland regarding the Act of Security of 1704. In general, however, "High Flyer" and "Low Flyer" represent High Church and Low Church.

The performers' names are not attached to their parts in the *dramatis persona.* However, among the actors taking part were Pack,294 Mrs. Balwin,295

Mrs. Bradshaw, Mrs. Willis, and Mrs. Porter.296 The characters are thus listed:

"Dramatis Personam

Domingo Gonzalez. *A Spaniard and Phil-osopher, over Curious in Natural Productions and Secrets in Astronomy.*

Diego. *His Man, very Cowardly and Peev-ish, to find himself in such Distress, by serving his Master.*

Belonging to the World of the *Earth.* 2,3 As in *Part II, A Voyage to Brobding-nag* (chap. 6). m *Stage,* II, 351. Genest also suggests that the introduction of the birds on the stage was borrowed from *The Birds* of Aristophanes. 294 Pack took the *role* of Moderation in II, 1. 205 Mrs. Balwin took the part of the Nightingale.

""See respectively *Pills to Purge Melancholy,* I, 80; I, 83; I, 100; II, 214; the. epilogue.

to

High Flyers Painted figures belonging to the *Kingdom* of the *Birds.*

Daemon of Socrates.

Viceroy *Of a Province belonging*

Vicequeen) *the* Emperor *of the Sun.*

Deviling. *A Courtier and Principal Favourite to the Viceroy.* I Belonging

Bellygorge. *A Bramin or Mufti.* to the World

Coverfool. *Taylor or Dresser to the Court* of the *Sun.*

Solars, *also* Tamer *and* Keeper *of the Monsters,* Solar *Philosophers, and Guards.*

King Dove.

Plumply Lord Pheasant. *A prince of the Blood and nearly related to K.* Dove.

Croak Lord Raven. *Lord High Chancelor and President of the Court.* Strut Lord Cockerel. *High Steward and Constable.*

Magpy *Abbot of* Buzzardland, *and* Woodcocks *Sir* Robin Redbreast. *Secretary to the President.*

Sir Pratler Parrot. *Favourite and Historian to the King.* Low

Sir Owle Mouser. *Kings Attorney General,* j Flyers *Sir* Chatter Jay, *Sir* John Daw, *two eminent Lawyers. Sir* Crane Talbird. *Captain of the Guards.*

Screechowl *and* Ninnyhammer, *the King's Physitians.*

Thrush, Nightingal, Blackbird, *Musicians in Ordinary.*

Sir Epicaene Bat. *A Trimmer between both Parties.*

Turtles. *Two Choristers, and Genij of the Birds.*

Eagle *and* Vulture. *Two Serjeants or Pursuivants at Arms.*

Mr. Baron Wigeon, *and Mr.* Justice Gander, *two Judges. The Scene a Luminous Country, adorn'd with Gorgeous Rays of the Sun.*

Emblematical Figures, *performing* Odes, Dialogues, *and* Humerous Songs *in the* Prologue, *and several* Acts *of the* Comick Opera.

The plot of *Wonders in the Sun* is as follows:

Gonzalez, a philosopher, and Diego, his man, by means of a team of geese are enabled to fly to the sun. There they find trees bearing stones for apples, and tennis-balls for peaches, with other similar wonders. As Diego complains of his hunger, the Daemon of Socrates enters and greets Gonzalez, whom he promises to entertain and protect during his sojourn in the sun. The Viceroy of the sun now enters with his guards to seize the strangers. The companions of the Viceroy, such as Deviling, a beau, are in appearance directly opposite to their earthly prototypes. It is then made known that all things in the sun are contrary to what they are on earth. Diego beats Coverfool, the Viceregal tailor, for a misunderstood act of politeness on his part. The Daemon to divert the angered party provides an entertainment of singing by various abstractions, such as Honor, Courtship, and Modesty. The Solars are mollified by these songs, and, after placing bridles on the two visitors, lead them away.

The learned of the sun decide that Gonzalez belongs to a strange species of ostrich, and that Diego is a sort of baboon. The strangers are warned by Bel-lygorge, a Bramin, who knows their true nature, not to undeceive the Solars at their peril. At dinner Gonzalez, as an ostrich, is given a dish of old iron, while Diego, as a baboon of low quality, is given roasted fowls. The Daemon suggets, much to Diego's disgust, that in view of the miscellaneous diet of ostriches Gonzalez may partake of Diego's fowls. Another mischief is about to be devised against the visitors when the Daemon introduces again an entertainment of singing in which Industry, Profuseness, and other abstractions take part.

The entertainment does not allay the malice of the Solars. Bellygorge betrays to them that the captives are humans. This is a sufficient reason for their being put to death. They are also accused by an ambassador from the King of Birds of having slaint a brother of Plumply Lord Pheasant, a powerful nobleman. The strangers' transportation to the bird kingdom for trial is being prepared for, when Diego sings a comic song, at the suggestion of the Daemon. This is intended to soften the hearts of the Solars. The Daemon follows Diego's song with another emblematical entertainment in which Sport, Innocence, and other figures take part,

However, the entertainment does not prevent the taking of Gonzalez and Diego to the Kingdom of the Birds for trial. The Daemon accompanies them to advise and protect them. The trial takes place before King Dove. The prisoners are found guilty of murder' and are sentenced to be devoured by flies and gnats. However, their pardons are obtained from the King by Sir Pratler Parrot, the royal favorite, who had once been in the possession of Gonzalez's brother, and had then received kind treatment from the philosopher. The opera ends with various songs by certain birds, such as the Blackbird and the Nightingale. After these songs Gonzalez and Diego depart for the earth in the vehicle in which they had journeyed thence.

The last of D'Urfey's plays to be acted was *The Modem Prophets; or, New Wit for a Husband.* This comedy was first presented May 3, 1709.297 It had been composed probably in the preceding year but its presentation in the autumn of 1708 had been prevented by the closing of the theatres on account of the death of the Prince-Consort, October 28, 1708. Hence, on account of its strictly contemporary subject having passed from the public mind, the play, when finally produced, fell flat. It was printed with this titlepage:

"the Modern Prophets: Or, NEW WIT for a HUSBAND. A COMEDY. As it is Acted at the Theatre-royal In DRURY-LANE, By Her Majesty's Servants. Written by Mr. Tho' D'Urfey. LONDON: Printed for Bernard LinTott, at the Cross-Keys between the two Temple-Gates in Fleet-street. 1709."298

In his dedication of the comedy to Sir William Scawen DUrfey says:

".... I acquainted you with my Design as soon as I begun to write on the Subject, and had the Honour to receive from you, as well as from other Persons of Learning and Judgment, Incouragement to proceed.

"The Theme was altogether Novelty, and the ensuing Sheets morally intended, as I have hinted in the Prologue, to ridicule the Ridiculers of our establish'd Doctrine; and as it did not want your candid Approbation, neither did it the Encouragement of many considerable Persons, Clergy as well as others, who look'd with contempt upon the abominable Impostures of those craz'd Enthusiasts, and with Satisfaction approv'd of a Satyrical Endeavour to expose them as they deserv'd."

After a fulsome eulogy of Scawen D'Urfey proceeds:

".... Let for fear of an Author's general Vice, and that the plain Justice I have done you should, by my proceeding and others mistaken Judgment, be imagin'd Flattery, a thing 287 Thus Genest, Stage, II, 418 The Tatler, Number 11, for May 5, 1709, however, mentions the play as to be acted first on that day. The Tatler, Number 43, July 19, 1709, notes its withdrawal from the stage.

M8 This date has been added, apparently by a contemporary hand, to the titlepage of the Yale University Library copy of the play.

the Bluntness of my Nature does not care to be concern'd with, and which I also know you abominate. I will here withdraw my Pen...."

In his preface D'Urfey says of his play:

"The not timing its coming on the Stage, which was occasion'd by the late unhappy Mourning,299 and other Accidents, the Jest growing quite stale by the Dispersing and Absence of the Enthusiastick Impostors, was a great Hindrance to the Run of the Play;300 which otherwise had it been Acted when their Tryal was, or when the most impudent Affirmation of the Doctor's Resurrection was found to be so nauseous a Lye, might probably have lasted many Days longer.

"The Plot and Turns which you will find in the reading it are new, and entirely my own Invention: A thing of which nature in Playwritirtg, is not in every Author's Power to perform. The Characters are drawn as near as with Decency and good Manners they could be; and being extremely heightned by the sprightly and uncommon Humor and Action of Mrs. Bicknel, who did the Prophetess, gave extraordinary Satisfaction to the impartial Spectators in general.

"My Intention in writing this Comedy was very serious and moral, and grounded on a Resolution, encourag'd by some, both wise and learned Persons, which was to expose the ridiculous Attempt of some Impostors, to set up for true Prophets, undermine reveal'd Religion, and covertly allure the Mob to favour the late Invasion and the Protector's Interest: To which End the Plot is drawn in a graver Method than usual; no loose Intriguing, Cuckold-making, &c. which generally stuff other Plays, and that may succeed with the Audience, being here shewn at all; and if some few Words, or any accidental Indecency happen in the Action, it was only through want of heed and not Design.

"The Ladies I humbly thank 'em were very favourable to me (except one or two particular, whose great Niceness in finding" out what to perfect a re-

serv'd Character they should not understand too well made, judge unjustly) the rest came to encourage me.... The Plot was design'd modestly to divert them with a Novelty not seen before; for which reason I For the death of Prince George of Denmark, husband to Queen Anne. 800 Sir Walter Scott, as quoted by T. Scott, Swift's Works, I, 306, note, says that The Modern Prophets contributed not a little to disperse the French Prophets.

changed the lewd Character of Betty G y (who the Playhouse, and half the Town besides knew before her pretended Inspiration to be Scandalous and Abominable) into Betty Plotwell, the Name of the Prophetess in my Play; who tho' guilty of one Failure, thro' too much Love, yet repents and resolves against all Conversation in that kind agen, and then wittily insinuating her self amongst the Agitators, regains her Lover's Estate, and afterward him for her Husband; which Attention was wholly design'd and made, as fearing the original nauseous Character would shock the virtuous part of the Female Audience.

"A couple of bloody Male Cricks I have met with too; but yet for all their barbarous assassinating Attempts, am both Sound and Head-whole: The one stiles himself the Author of Tunbridge Walks,301 who dully forgetting the Plotless and trifling Quality of that, the worse management of another Piece of his, where he has conjuring brought Oxford upon Hampstead-heath;302 and his Abuse of the fair Sex, Call'd the Fine Ladies Airs, lately shewn and deservedly hist303—yet in a Prologue given to another304—tho' he never could write one tolerable for himself unprovok'd, has thought fit to shake his Dirt upon me; but I have contempt enough to answer his Injustice, and so shall leave him. The other is a profound Coffee-house Wit whom I shall pretend to undeceive, at some hour of Leisure; and in the mean time assure him, that if ever the Town has the Honour to peruse any of his Dramatick Productions, which I very much doubt, he will be in great danger of hanging down his Dogmatical

Head; and being pellited by some of his Brethren, blush for defect in writing as well as my self.305 The best Proof a Gentleman can give of his true judging a Play is by writing a Piece of that kind himself; but if 801 *Tunbridge Walks, or the Yeoman of Kent,* was brought out at Drury Lane, January 27, 1703. Its author was Thomas Baker (Genest, *Stage,* II, 268-69, and the annotator of the Yale University Library copy of *The Modern Prophets').* 802 Baker had printed his comedy, *An Act at Oxford,* in 1704, since its representation had been forbidden on account of a fancied insult to the University of Oxford. He rewrote it, changing the name and scene and it was performed at Drury Lane, October 30, 1705. This is the "conjuring" alluded to by D'Urfey (Genest, *Stage,* II, 335-36). 303 *The Fine Lady's Airs, or an Equipage of Lovers,* by Baker was brought out at Drury Lane, December 14, 1708 (Genest, *Stage,* II, 409). 304 Unidentified. 806 In the copy of *The Modern Prophets* in the Yale University Library the name of Farquhar is inserted in an old hand, as the object of D'Urfey's wrath. The annotator is obviously wrong for Farquhar died in April, 1707. Certainly too, nothing which D'Urfey says could have applied to Farquhar. Probably the annotator was thinking of Farquhar's preface to *The Recruiting Officer* in which he mentions D'Urfey's *Wonders in the Sun.* his Capacity fails to do Justice in point of Poetry (let his Confidence brave it out as he please) he shall never make me believe that it can do right in point of Criticism.

"The Kindness shown by Mr. *Rich* in letting me be the first to raise the Prizes for my Benefit, was not only advantagious to me, but a farther Encouragement to future Authors likewise; and since that Matter came off so well, I shall easily be induc'd to slight my too sharp-sighted Supervisors; and for a farewell only put them in mind of adapting to themselves Mr. *Dryden's Couplet:*

Criticks like Fleas, so little and so light,
You could not know they live, but

that they bite."306

D'Urfey's comedy is founded upon two pieces of contemporary"! history which he has skillfully combined. The first was the appearance of the French Prophets about 1706. They were a variety of Camisard307 who prophesied the speedy establishment of the Messianic kingdom. They were much given to trances and prophecies. Indeed, it is said that they had a regular school for prophets in which many young women were pupils. The Prophets made a great impression for the time being, but their fanaticism and wild claims destroyed their credit. One principal factor in this was the failure of the foretold resurrection of a deceased brother to occur— an incident introduced by D'Urfey into his play.808

These enthusiasts, or rank impostors, as D'Urfey makes them, are in the play concerned with the plot for an uprising in Scotland in 1708309 for the Old Pretender. They are, indeed, no more than French emissaries who foment rebellion under the guise of a new religion.

The Modern Prophets has been harshly dealt with by those dramatic historians who have noticed it. Whincop calls it a."wretched piece,"310 and the *Biographia Dramatica,* "an excessively 808 Misquoted from the prologue to *All for Love.* The lines run:
"Half-wits are Fleas, so little and so light,
We scarce cou'd know they live, but that they bite."
» *Religious Encyclopaedia* (Schaff's), II, 387; *Catholic Encyclopaedia,* III, 218. See."Swift's *Predictions for the Year 1708.* —. 808 The *dramatis persona* describes Father Marragn as a "Knavish French Camizar."! Genest, *Stage,* II, 418, places the expected resurrection on May 25, 1707. Unless this date is that connected with the historical prophecy there is nothing in the play to indicate the year exactly, save that in 1708 the Chevalier attempted to land in Scotland "but was prevented by storms and the vigilance of the English fleet (see the play, IV, 1, *V, 1). 1 TMList,* p. 227. bad play."311 Even Genest does not consider the comedy much better than tolera-

ble. The writer, however, cannot agree with these verdicts, if the standard of comparison be D'Urfey's other comedies. *The Modem Prophets* seems to him to be, on the whole, an amusing and rather cleverly written play.

The effects of the movement towards the reforming of stage manners are easily to be seen in this comedy. Not only do we have Jeremy Collier's old opponent writing for the approval of the clergy, as he states in the dedication, and to uphold the church, but we find in lesser points signs of the same change. For example, a note to the prologue says the following three lines were "Left out to please the Actress," who was in this case Mrs. Bradshaw:

"The Priests of old Times, we are taught to know,)
Would punish with Fox-tail's indulgent Blow,
And to a prostrate Sinner Favour shew. ")

The epilogue which Mrs. Bicknel and Mrs. Porter spoke is, however, rather free. Furthermore, in the position of Betty Plotwell and Ned Whimsey we find evidence of the transition from Restoration pure comedy to eighteenth century sentimental drama.

A novel figure in the play is Cub Deviling, Lord Noble's negro footman. His name is doubtless from Deviling in *Wonders in the Sun.* Guiacum, the name of the deceased doctor whose resurrection is promised by the Prophets, is found applied to a physician in *The Richmond Heiress.'* The relations of Ned Whimsey and Betty, it should be observed, are not unlike those of Sir Philip and Phoebe in *The Marriage Hater Match'd.*

The entrance of Lord Noble, I, 1 (p. 1), congratulating himself on having driven to Enfield in an hour and two seconds is a foreshadowing of the horsy character, such as is Goldfinch in Holcroft's *(Road to Ruin.* Cub Deviling's song (I, pp. 4-5) has a chorus strongly reminiscent of that of the *Song* in *The Bloody Brother,* (III, 2. In II, 1 (p. 24), is an interesting allusion to a contemporary character. The Squire says, "... I sent all up and down the Town for

Beau *F——ing* to stand for me, but no body can find him of late." Obviously, "Beau" Fielding is here meant.312 In III, 2 (41), Fidelia says, "This Scene is stole out of the *Rehearsal*—King *Phiz* and King *Usher* right—-." Lord Noble answers "Tis so, and therefore very fit to have Musick to 't." Perhaps D'Urfey at his 83. 812 Robert Fielding (1651-1712), a notorious broken-down rake, probably in prison at the time.

time was considering his sequel to *The Rehearsal.* In IV, 1 (p. 57), and V, 1 (p. 65), we have two quotations from Shakespeare, one from *Macbeth*, III, 1 (Davenant's revision),313 and the other from *Richard III*, 1, 2.314 A song by Deviling between III and IV on the third day celebrates British victories on the continent. At the end _j of the play (V, 1, p. 72), comes a speech by Lord Noble in which he lauds the Queen and defies the French. Similar patriotic passages occur in *The Campaigners,* IV, 1 (p. 41), and *The Bath,* II, 1 (p. 23), 2 (p. 30). The characters and actors in the comedy are listed as follows:

"Dramatis Persona;.315

Lord *Noble,* Witty and Generous in love with) *Fidelia.*

Sir *Charles Courtly,* Town-bred, and a polite)

Courtier, in Love with *Clora.*)

Squire *Whimsey,* A Whimsical Crooked Gen-)

tleman, who admires the Prophets.)

Ned Whimsey, An honest brave Captain, Friend to Lord *Noble.*)

Zekiel Magus, A grand Impostor and Sham j

Prophet.)

Father *Marrogn, A* Knavish French Camizar

and Priest.)

Scire Facias, A Lawyer, another Sham-Prophet.)

Limbeck, A Chymist, and Follower of-the Im-)

postors. *) Sal Magottile, A* humourous Doctor, very)

Talkative and Whimsical.)

Solid, Steward to Lord *Noble. Cub Deviling, A* Blackamoor Footman to Lord *Noble.*)

Dobbin and *Davy,* Two other Footmen.

Women.

Fidelia, Daughter to Magus.

Mr. *Powell.*

   Mr. *Mills.*

   Mr. *Norris.*

   Mr. *Booth.*

   Mr. *Johnson.*

   Mr. *Boen.*

Mr. *Cary.*

   Mr. *Bullock.*

   Mr. *Fairbank.*

Mr. *Birket.*

Mr. *Pack.*

Mrs. *Porter. Clora,* Her Companion, very freakish in Love) _,,

Matters. *Mrs. Bradshaw.*

sis "Things 111 begun strengthen themselves by 111." 814 "Was ever Woman in this Humour Woo'd? Was ever Woman in this Humour Won?" 00 "Squire Crump" (the name used at his entrance, II, 1, p. 22) is given in the *dramatis persona* as ''Squire Whimsey." He is called "Crump-Squire" in V, 1 (p. 59). Copyhold, who appears in IV, 1 (p. 50), is not given. —J *Betty Plotwell,* A witty goodnatur'd Girl, of' honest Inclinations tho' perverted by *Ned Whimsey,* whom she loves; she is let into the secret Roguery of the Sham Prophets by *Marrogn,* who designs to debauch her, Mrs. *Bicknel.* pretending Inspiration, at last by her

Cunning puts a Trick upon the Squire, gets *Ned's* Estate from him, and then her Lover for her Husband.

Kate Sponge, An Hostess at *Enfield.* Mrs. *Powell.*

Mrs. *Guiacum,* Widow to a late Physician, one) ,,.,.,.

of the Prophets. . Mrs-*mlhs* ! Prophetical Agitators Men and Women, Taylor, Carter, Smith, Cobler, Countryman, Servants, Singers, Dancers, and Attendants. -Scene *Enfield* and *Bunhil-fields.*

" The plot of *The Modern Prophets* may be thus summarized: Lord Noble drives down to Enfield from London to see Fidelia whom he loves. He learns from Kate Sponge, the hostess at his inn, of the strange doings of the French Prophets, a new and fantastic religious sect, who are concerned also with a plot for the restoration of the Stuarts. Magus, Fidelia's father, is a member of the Prophets. Ned Whimsey, Noble's

friend, meets Betty Plotwell, his mistress, who is also one of the Prophets and initiated into their rogueries. She promises to win back Ned's estate for him from Squire Whimsey, Ned's uncle, who has come into possession of it, on condition of Ned's marrying her. To this he agrees. Betty's tutor in the arts of the Prophets, one Father Marrogn, a rascally French priest, now enters and lays various schemes before Betty, while Ned listens in a closet where she has concealed him.

Lord Noble sends his steward Solid to Magus for a loan which is obtained by giving a mortgage. Noble and Ned follow. As they are discussing a letter which Ned is to deliver to Clora, Fidelia's companion, from Sir Charles Courtly, Clora's lover, Kate Sponge eavesdrops. She hears Ned reading Sir Charles's letter aloud to Noble and thinks that it is Clora whom Ned loves. She takes the letter promising to give it to Clora. Squire Whimsey see *dramatis persona* appears and is asked by Nted for one hundred pounds. The Squire refuses. The Squire, who is deformed, has been duped by the Prophets who have convinced him that they can remedy his physical defects. Mr.s. Guiacum, a widow, enters now and announces that it has been prophesied that her husband, who has been dead six months, will rise on the morrow. Betty Plotwell comes in apparently in an ecstasy and "prophesies." Noble and Ned simulate seriousness; and then leave to meet Fidelia in Enfield Chase.

Lord Noble and Fidelia meet at the appointed place. Fidelia rallies Noble on his expressions of love for her, and he pretends anger. They make a bargain that if Doctor Guiacum does not rise from the dead she will marry Noble—although secretly she expects no miracle. Ned Whimsey has met Clora, who has received Courtly's letter from Kate Sponge. Clora inclines more toward being courted by Ned than by Courtly. She simulates great indignation at his words in behalf of Courtly. Ned then resolves to have Courtly tame her. Betty Plotwell comes in with Squire Whimsey after the departure of the others. She tells him of a vision she has had concerning Ned, and engages busily in getting his nephew into the Squire's good graces. On meeting his uncle again, Ned pretends to have become a Prophet himself and so imposes on the Squire that the hundred pounds is given him straightway. Wishing for an opportunity for further planning with Ned, Betty attempts to get Kate Sponge to deliver to him a message for her. Kate, who mistrusts Betty, refuses, saying that Ned is in love with Clora and telling of her delivery of a letter to Clora for Ned. Betty is seized with jealousy and resolves revenge upon Ned.

The Prophets and the others collect on the next day for Doctor Guiacum's resurrection. Cub Deviling, Noble's negro footman, reports the rising of the doctor, but the story is false, having been concocted as a device for obtaining Cub a bottle of brandy to calm his perturbation of soul. After various quarrels among the disgruntled Prophets, Betty enters in a pretended frenzy, beats certain of those present and then thrashes Ned soundly. She becomes calm and announces that Ned has been inspired by a lying spirit. She exposes the plot against Squire Whimsey. Betty now receives from the Squire the papers of her marriage-settlement. She then gives Ned the verses sent to Clora by Courtly.

Ned upbraids Kate Sponge for her officiousness in misinforming Betty as to his relations with Clora. She is sent to undeceive Betty. News comes to Ned and Sir Charles Courtly, who has arrived, of the marriage of Lord Noble and Fidelia. Courtly arranges to be left alone with Clora, whom he pretends not to know. To her great amazement and indignation he treats her as coolly as a stranger. This has finally its effect on her. She is subdued and relents toward Sir Charles; and a match is made up between them. Father Marrogn resolves now to flee from England with his spoils, since the projected uprising in favor of the Old Pretender has been frustrated. He desires to take Betty with him. She leads him to expose his plans to her, and, incidentally, his villainy. Again, Ned is eavesdropping. Squire

Whimsey, who has been expecting his deformity to vanish and his stature to increase as the Prophets had foretold to him, enters. Betty tells him of how he has been tricked out of the writings to Ned's estate. The constable and his officers now appear. They arrest the Prophets for blasphemy amid the mirth of Lord Noble, Betty, and the others.

In 1721 D'Urfey published a volume with this titlepage:

"NEW OPERA'S WITH COMICAL STORIES, AND POEMS ON

Several Occasions, Never before Printed, Being the remaining Pieces *Written by Mr. D'urfey. Poets in tricking Times, Satyrick grown, Seldom excusing Faults their Plays have shewn, Oft with sharp Prologues lash the foolish Town. So* Bayes *his* Lyric Opera *brings to view, And what some Actors in blunt Satyr do, The* Prologue *and the* Epilogue *will shew. LONDON:* Printed for *William Chetwood, at Cato's Head in Russel-Street, Covent-Garden.* 1721."

The "operas" are three in number, *The Two Queens of Brentford, The Grecian Heroine,* and *Ariadne.* Each has a separate titlepage. The volume is dedicated to Philip Duke of Wharton, to whose father *The Campaigners* had been dedicated twenty-three years earlier.

The titlepage of *The Two Queens of Brentford: or, Bayes no Poetaster,* runs thus:

"the Two QUEENS Op BRENTFORD: Or, Bayes no Poetaster: A MUSICAL FARCE, Or Comical Opera; Being The Sequel of the Famous Rehearsal, written by the late Duke of Buckingham. With a Comical Prologue and EpiLogue. *LONDON:* Printed for William Chetwood, at *Cato's* Head in *Russel-Street, Covent-Garden.* 1721." In his preface to *New Operas,* D'Urfey says of *The Two Queens:*

"The Musical Farce, or Comical Opera, is a piece of Humour and Grotesque Wit, and is design'd as the second Part of the former Rehearsal, wrote by the late Duke of Buckingham, and others; but not design'd so Satyrical upon Poetry as that was against Mr. Dryden, but intended rather against the

Criticks, the Poet Bayes giving it all along a cast of Banter, and at last makes himself open in the Rank of a deserving Author. It was once very near being acted, as being Rehears'd upon the Stage, but afterwards was laid by, some Accidents happening in the Playhouse. The Reader will, I hope, find Diversion in the Humour and Plot of it, and particularly in the variety of Dialogues and Songs, which I have been told, by good Judges, are not indifferent. The Prologue and Epilogue belonging to it being somewhat Satyrical, the Town ought to relish as a Whim of Humour, and make no more of 'em than the Subject will give Occasion to bear; for if the Grandees or Great Wits of the Court, by hoping to be Giants in their Wealth and Power, are become Pigmies by a City Joke or Trick, they must bear with the Matter, and if they can, make a Jest of it as well as they are able."

When it was, that the farce came near presentation cannot be determined by any evidence now at hand, either internal or external. *The Two Queens,* as it stands, seems to the writer, to have been composed at odd times during perhaps fifteen years. Most of it doubtless was written after the Peace of Utrecht, which was ratified in April, 1713, for in III, 1 (p. 42), the "late War" is mentioned, and in II, 1 (p. 36), the Englishman is disaffected because "a sham Peace has lately stuck upon his Gizzard plaguily." Again, in II, 1 (p. 35), mention is made of the Muscovite (Peter I) having thrashed the Swede (Charles XII), who some time since depended on the Turk and was fed by him. The Swede has "set up for a King of Piracylends his Fleet and an Army to make a Descent upon those that aspire to new Kingdom." Allusion too is made to the Frenchman's "old Master Louis XIV... before the present Regency." The references to South Sea and Mississippi speculations, as in the epilogue, and elsewhere, bring the composition of the parts of the play in which they occur down to a date not far from that of publication. The accidents which D'Urfey says prevented the acting of the play cannot be identified, for the term is too vague. It may cover actual physical circumstances, the defection of necessary actors from the company, or a score of other matters.

The Two Queens of Brentford is a rather poor continuation of *The Rehearsal* from the point where the earlier farce ends. The object of D'Urfey's sequel is to turn the tables upon the critics by showing that Bayes's absurd play, or opera, in *The Two Queens* is indeed a "banter" upon them. Bayes in *The Two Queens* is, of course, D'Urfey, and the book, *Remarks upon Human Learning*, is not unlikely to be D'Urfey's collected songs.316 The songs scattered through *The Two Queens* are poor. The satire is very bad, and as a whole the farce drags lamentably. Genest says of it, "It contains some good hits, but on the whole it is rather dull than otherwise."317 It is not improbable that in the course of the farce there is a considerable amount of political satire.

In *The Rehearsal* Bayes's tragedy is halted at the end of the fourth act, yet D'Urfey proceeding from this point has, it would seem, more than one act in his rehearsed piece.318 The characters who appear in both *The Rehearsal* and *The Two Queens of Brentford* are Bayes, Johnson, Smith, the two usurping kings, Princes Prettyman and Volscius, Parthenope and Cloris (or Armorilis).

(In I, 2 (p. 19), is perhaps a hit at Langbaine's sweeping charges of plagiarism brought against D'Urfey in his *Dramatic Poets*. After a song, Johnson says, "A plague, this is none of his Bayes's, I'll . be damn'd if he wrote a line on't— No, no this must be stole." Later, in IV, 1 (p. 54), Johnson says, "The Conceit is stole—I have seen it before twenty times."

The *dramatis persona* follows: "Dramatis Persona. MEN.

Prince Prettyman, J and siding with the

Prince Volcius, 1 Phizgiggs against the KINGS. A Publisher of News, and a knavish IncedFirebrand Belrope I iary, inveterate for the *Ushers* against the. *Phizgiggs. nt* This may seem absurd, but D'Urfey was capable of any absurdity. m *Stage,* X, 156.

» See *The Two Queens,* I, 1 (p. 24). TOKAY, DISCIPLINE, (Secretary to a Nobleman. A Foreign Spy, who furnishes BELRope with News. Another News-monger, on the Party of the Phizgiggs, but secretly a Popish Priest. A Boy with Coffee and Chocolate. ARMORILIS,

PARTHENOPE,

THIMBLESSA, FLEABITTEN, WOMEN. TWO QUEENS Of BRENTFORD. (The two Princes

Mistresses.

An old Mistress of P.

Prettyman's, and formerly his Sempstress,

very violent and jealous.

Attendant and Favorite to the Queens.

Singers, Dancers, Guards and Attendants.

The inside of the Playhouse."

Scene.

The plot of the *Two Queens of Brentford* runs thus:

Smith, Chanter, and Johnson go to the playhouse to witness the last act or acts of the rehearsal. The prologue, read by Bayes, is a satire upon the South Seas speculation. Firebrand Belrope, a newsmonger, and Tokay, a spy, at the opening of the rehearsal proper, discuss the lack of news, but are quieted by Discipline, who hears them. A masque showing "some Humours in a Camp" follows with songs by a General, a Sutler, a Singer, a Tailor, and a Grazier.

The two Queens of Brentford fall in love with Prince Volcius and Prince Prettyman who are brought in to be judged before the Kings. The Queens secure the release of the Princes. A song in dialogue between an Irish Beau and a Lady follows. Other songs are then sung which in turn are succeeded by a catch sung by a Russian, a Swede, a Turk, a Dutchman, a German, a Frenchman, and an Englishman.

Princes Volcius and Prettyman enter with their respective mistresses Armorilis and Parthenope. Volcius and Armorilis go into the garden. Prettyman is about to follow them with Parthenope when his first love Thimblessa, a seamstress, halts him. Prettyman is on the point of sending Parthenope away,

when Fleabitten, the. Queen's favorite, invites her to drink tea with them, and so she leaves with Fleabitten, while Prettyman goes away with Thimblessa. Fleabitten and Discipline now have a dialogue concerning news. Discipline gives her false reports to spread. A masque "explaining the Humours of the City" follows, in which Discord, like a stock-jobber, Bigotry a.s a Jesuit, Faction as a fanatic, and Stubborness as a Quaker, each have songs. Envy and Jealousy appear then and sing.

Prince Prettyman and Thimblessa have a scene in which the latter shows her jealousy of Parthenope. Next, the Queens and the Princes are shown together. The Second Queen sends Volcius and Prettyman for a book and then rouses the rage of the First Queen who is jealous of her. The two race out after the Princes. Having been discovered by the Kings, the Queens are arrested and led in. Discipline, Belrope, Fleabitten, and Tokay are also arrested and undergo an examination by the Kings. The Kings postpone their sentences, and the act closes after songs by a Shepherd, Shepherdess, Milkmaid, and an Officer, Sergeant and Soldiers.

Thimblessa learns that the Queens are in love with Prettyman, and, jealous of them, she gives them, together with Parthenope and Armorilis, a draught of poison each, representing it as a cordial. The Princes enter, and see Parthenope's body, so they, too, poison themselves. The six apparent corpses are shown seated in a row. Thimblessa accuses Fleabitten of their murder. Fleabitten, however, announces that she has substituted an opiate for the poison in Thimblessa's flask. Thimblessa goes mad and the six corpses come to life. Bayes now announces to Chanter that the play, or opera, which has just been rehearsed has been a "bite" upon Smith and Johnson, the critics, who have displayed their want of acumen by their not penetrating the jest. The two critics, who have left the stage for a "dram," return, and are treated by Bayes to a further entertainment, consisting of various songs. Finally, Johnson and Smith give serious opinions against the "tragedy" they have seen rehearsed. Bayes then informs them of his jest upon them. Johnson admits that he and Smith have been "banter'd," and then praises a book called *Remarks upon Human Learning.* This is shown to be by Bayes. Thereupon Johnson and Smith recant their previous criticisms of Bayes, and admit him no poetaster. An epilogue concludes the farce. In it the Sun, Rain (Pluvia) and Wind (Boreas) take the parts of Mississippi, Directius, and Bubble, and satirize the Mississippi scheme.

The Grecian Heroine: or, the Fate of Tyranny, has this titlepage:

"THE GRECIAN HEROINE; OR, THE FATE of TYRANNY. A TRAGEDY, Written 1718, Vignette. *LONDON:* Printed for William Chetwood, at *Cato's* Head in *Russel-Street Covent-Garden.* 1721."

In the preface to *New Operas,* D'Urfey says of *The Grecian Heroine:*

"A Tragedy, written some Years ago, the Distress of the Plot that is in it, the Characters of Timoleon and Belizaria being done for Mr. Betterton and Mrs. Barry; and the Management of the whole, I hope, will speak for it self, without any other Assistance." Since Betterton died in April, 1710, and Mrs. Barry in November, 1713, it is clear that D'Urfey could not have written his tragedy for them in 1718. Moreover, at the end of the play is a blessing on "the happy Revolution." This would throw the date of the tragedy back to 1690 or '91. The second title of the play would perhaps point to this date, since it may allude to the dethroning of James II.

The Grecian Heroine is written in bad blank verse. It is a bloody, sensational sort of drama, but with the merit of a lack of dullness. In fact, there is in it, as in some of D'Urfey's comedies, perhaps too much action. There is a considerable amount of straining after the pathetic, as in the scenes in which the little Clindor and his fate figure (IV, 1, V, 1). Belizaria's heroism is extraordinary. She is copied by D'Urfey in the person of Aurelia, the Vicequeen of Naples, in his *Massaniello, Part II.* In the unsuccessful attempt at suicide (V, 3) and in Timoleon's revival *(ibid)* are shown the

author's tendency toward a happy ending for the principals in his tragedy and his general habit of shirking the ending of a play in a definite and positive manner. The tragedy is unhistorical. There was a Timoleon of Corinth, whose life was written by Plutarch, but he was not the original of D'Urfey's character in this play. D'Urfey's incurable propensity toward the introduction of songs and dances regardless of their appropriateness is illustrated in *The Grecian Heroine,* as in III, 2, and V, 1. The names which have been given certain of the Greeks are remarkable, to say the least. We have, for example, Grimoald, Gomond, Zizimo, Bilboe, and Gilmunda. Genest calls it "on the whole.... a strange play," although some parts are "not badly written."319 su *Stage, X,* 156.

A few of the events in the tragedy ought to be noted. In I, 1 (pp. 95-96), Damocles and Belizaria have a scolding scene which resembles that between Gloucester and Queen Margaret, *Richard III,* I, 3.320 "A Song and Dance,...., expressing the Reward of Tyranny," occurs in V, 1 (p. 140). Here is a use of the old device of revenge executed or foreshadowed in a masque,321 allegorical or otherwise.322 Aristander says, *ibid* (p. 143): "There is Divinity about a King Which is perpetual Guard," a plain restatement of Claudius's lines, "There's such divinity doth hedge a king,
That treason can but peep to what it would,
Acts little of his will,"
in *Hamlet,* IV, 5.

The characters are thus listed:
Dramatis Persona
MEN.

Tyrant of Corinth.

A Noble Lord, late Governor of *Mtolia,* and General under King Demetrius, chief of the Ellien Faction opposing Aristander.
Captain of the Guards, and Favourite to Aristander—A Villain.
'A Prince of the Blood Royal of Co-Rinth, sav'd in his Infancy by the Queen, from the Tyrant's Cruelty of the Ellien Faction, and often consulting with 'em in Disguise,

under the Name of Grimoald, in Love with Clorona.
t An honest Lord, Favourer of the EL-
l Lien Party.
f A Noble Collonel, formerly under Timoleon, and Friend to Deme-Trius.
(An honest Captain and Friend also to (
DEMETRIUS.
Cilon, A Fop, Courtier, and Parasite.
also, Forsythe, *The Relations of Shirley's Plays to the Elizabethan Drama,* ARISTANDER, TIMOLEON, DAMO-CLES, DEMETRIUS, POLLIDAMUS, GOMOND, no See 81-82. 321 The same incident occurs in *Massaniello, Part II,* V. *Ibid,* p. 188.
J Son to Timoleon, and Belizaria, Clindor, a Child of seven Years old.
LONGIN, J Sergeant and Corporal in the Ellien
Bilboe, *I* Faction against the Tyrant.
WOMEN.
J Eldest Daughter to Aristander,
GILMUNDA, j proud an(j Vidous j Her Sister, Pious, Mild, and Virtuous, AMIDEA, I both in Iove with DEMETRIUS
I Wife to Timoleon, the Grecian BE-LIZARIA, I HEROINE.
f Mute—Daughter to Timoleon
CLORONA, I by a former Wife
Helmige, Wife to POLIDAMUS.
Several other Ladies, Priestesses of Bacchus, Soldiers,
Masquers and Attendants.
The SCENE, CORINTH." i

The plot of *The Grecian Heroine* may be summarized thus: Damocles, favorite to Aristander, Tyrant of Corinth, slays Clorona, wife to Demetrius, rightful heir to the Corinthian throne. Damocles announces to Belizaria, the Grecian Heroine, who is wife to Timoleon and step-mother to Clorona, that Aristander is in love with her. She defies Aristander and is imprisoned. The fate of Clorona causes an abortive revolt by the followers of Timoleon, but Aristander subdues the rebellion and orders Clorona's body seized as that of a traitress, and then banishes Timoleon with his friends to jEtolia.

Demetrius, who, disguised and passing under the name of Grimoald, has been conspiring against Aristander, hides in the apartments of Amidea, Aristander's younger daughter, when he is pursued on account of an attack made on Damocles at the time of Clorona's death. Amidea, who is kind and virtuous, loves Demetrius, as does also her elder sister, the proud and wicked Gilmunda. Accompanied by Damocles and others, Aristander searches Amidea's apartment for the supposed Grimoald. They find Demetrius there with Amidea and Gilmunda. Aristander orders Demetrius to find Grimoald within three days on pain of death, but does not suspect the identity of Grimoald and Demetrius. The banished Timoleon and his companions send to Aristander to ask that their families be allowed to join them. Aristander pretends to accede to the request, but intends to attack and rob the women and children on their way to vEtolia.

As a result of the robbery of the families of the exiles, the Etolians in anger rise in arms against Aristander. Timoleon is placed at their head. Demetrius receives an invitation to join the Etolians with his friends. As he is in the Temple of Bacchus the ghost of Clorona appears to him and encourages him, prophesying Aristander's fall. He drops the letter from the.zEtolians in his ecstasy at the vision. Amidea entering, finds the letter and bears it away. Gilmunda now appears with masquers and profanes the temple, for which the Chief Priestess reproves her. Aristander enters and learns that the Etolians are about to begin a siege. He then seizes Belizaria and her companions, who had escaped from him previously, and had taken sanctuary in the temple. Upon the Chief Priestess's expostulating with him, he beats her. Gilmunda now takes from Amidea the letter which she has found. Amidea begs her sister not to use the letter for the destruction of Demetrius and reveals her love for him. Enraged and jealous, Gilmunda sets out to bear the letter to her father Aristander.

Aristander commands Belizaria to write to Timoleon, informing him that unless the siege is raised, the captive ladies will be killed. She refuses firmly, though her little son Clindor is slain before her eyes. As Aristander is about to kill Belizaria who is upbraiding him, Demetrius halts him. Demetrius says that Grimoald has been taken and further that aid for the besieged is at hand. Pleased with this news, Aristander leaves, giving to Demetrius as he goes a letter he has lately received from Gilmunda. On opening the letter, Demetrius discovers it to contain the,-Etolians' message to him desiring his co-operation against Aristander. Left with Belizaria, Demetrius consoles her with thoughts of revenge for Clindor's death.

The.zEtolians are admitted to Corinth by Demetrius and his friends. Disguised as Grimoald, Demetrius is brought as a prisoner before Aristander. Demetrius and his companions, among whom is Timoleon, discover themselves to Aristander. After a long and stormy dialogue, Timoleon and Aristander fight a duel in which Aristander is slain, but not before he has very seriously wounded Timoleon. In the meantime, the soldiers free Belizaria and capture the daughters of Aristander, whom they prepare to outrage. At the girls' outcries Belizaria relents toward them and ransoms them from the soldiers. She then gives them a dagger. Gilmunda first stabs Amidea and then herself. Timoleon apparently dies in the midst of the victory, after the story of the sisters' death has been told. Belizaria then unsuccessfully attempts suicide. It is then discovered that Timoleon has but swooned. Demetrius now assumes the regal dignity.

Ariadne: or, the Triumph of Bacchus, has the following titlepage: "*ARIADNE: Or, The Triumph Of BACCHUS,* An OPERA Vignette. *LONDON:* Printed for Wiluam ChetWood, at *Cato's* Head in *Russel-street, Covent-Garden.* 1721." . D'Urfey thus writes of *Ariadne* in his preface to *New Operas:* "j "An entire Opera, exactly done to Recitative and Air, with Verses proper for the Occasion. I hope our English Judges will give it a Judgment equal with the buzzing and squeaking Trilladoes of the Italian; or else I shall condemn my own, and my skill in Musick as long as I live.

" In a few places earlier D'Urfey had ridiculed or attacked Italian opera, as in the prologue to *The Old Mode and the New,* or in *Wonders in the Sun,* I, 2 (p. 25).

Ward describes *Ariadne* as a "trashy opera";328 while on the other hand, Genest says, "D'Urfey has managed the original story very well."324 To the writer it seems that while some of the songs are not bad, still, altogether, *Ariadne* is a poor performance. It is a three act opera on a familiar subject. The comic element which Genest notices is concerned with the love of Bombey for Doppa325 which is in relief to the passion of Bacchus for Ariadne. Too, the love of Berontus for Cellania is more or less comic. _J

The characters are as follows: *"Dramatis Persona.* MEN.
BACCHUS.
Theseus, Prince of Athens.

Pirithous, Prince of the Lapithes, his Friend.

An Indian King, whom Bacchus conquer'd there, and afterwards, for Wit and good Humour, made his Favourite.
323 *History of English Dramatic Literature,* III, 454, note.
320 The duet between Bombey and Doppa, I, 2 (pp. 96-97), has already been men-") tioned as occurring in *Cinthia and Endimion* and in *Wonders in the Sun.* " *Stage,* X, 156. ABDALLA,
A Scythian Prince, of a Saturnine Humour; an Enemy to Love, and a Berontus,- Disliker of Bacchus, but Friends to Theseus, at last in Love with CELANIA.
BOMBEY, A foolish SATYR. *CHORUS* of BACCHANALS, MNADES, INDIANS and Satyrs. WOMEN.
Ariadne, Daughter of King Minos of CRETE.
(Her Favourite, very Satyrical on Cellania, Mankind. A brisk humorous Girl, waiting
DOPPA' on ARIADNE.

Shepherds, Shepherdesses, Clowns, Singers,
and Dancers.

The Scene *NAXOS,* an Island in the ARCHIPELAGO."

The author thus gives the argument of

his opera:326

"Theseus, *Prince of* Athens, *having conquered the* Minotaur, *and by the means of* Ariadne, *Daughter to King* Minos, *who fell in love with him, escap'd out of the Labyrinth, brings her along with him to* Naxos, *she hoping he would marry her, as he had promis'd, before his coming away; tho' at that instant he design'd otherwise, having resolifd an Expedition to* CEbalia *to steal away* Helena, *Daughter to King* Tindarus, *whom he was in Love with; they arrive at* Naxos, *where* Bacchus *is newly come from the Conquest of the* Indians, *bringing with him* Abdalla, *and other* Indian *Kings, Captive; and where he also meets his dear Friend* Theseus, *accompany'd by* Pirithous *and* Berontus, *a Prince of* Scythia. Bacchus *at sight of* Ariadne *falls in Love with her, which* Theseus *favours, gaining thereby a Pretext of leaving her so well to her Advantage, and furthering his own Pursuit of* Helen. *This is plotted and done at the Triumph of Bacchus, where* Ariadne *and her Favourite* Cellania, *coming to see it,* Theseus *is miss'd being gone with* Pirithous, Berontus *remaining, who is newly fal'n in Love with* Cellania; Ariadne *rages, weeps, and is in great Distress for some time; but* Bacchus *appearing with his Glory and Courtship, especially* ,2fl P. 190. The original italicization has been preserved.

presenting her a Crown, to be made a Constellation, and a promise of deifying her, her Tears are afterwards turn'd to Joy, and the Marriage with great Solemnity being perform'd, finishes the Opera."

In 1727 there appeared a curious piece with this titlepage:

"the *ENGLISH* Stage ITALIANIZ'D, In a New Dramatic Entertainment, Called *DIDO,*and *2ENEAS:* Or *HARLEQUIN,* A Butler, a Pimp, a Minister of State, Generalissimo, and Lord High Admiral; dead and alive again, and at last crown'd King of *Carthage,* by *Dido.* A Tragi-Comedy, after the *Italian* Manner; by way of Essay, or first Step towards the farther Improvement of the *English* Stage. Written by Thomas D'urfey, Poet Laureat *de Jure. LONDON: Printed for* A. Moore *near St. Paul's.* 1727. Price *6d."* The introduction to this satire announces that the object of the production is to drive from the stage Shakespeare, Jonson, Dryden, Otway, Wycherley, Congreve, Rowe, Addison, "and all those formal

Fellows," and their "abettors" the actors and actresses W ks

Wilks, B th Booth, C r Cibber, O d Mrs. Oldfield, P r Mrs. Porter. For these playwrights and their interpreters Italian opera is to be substituted. *The English Stage Italianiz'd* is an attempt at introducing this form of entertainment into England. The introduction is signed *"Your Old, Tho' much injured Bard,* THOMAS D'URFEY, *Poor Knight of Windsor,*

Where I may be seen alive and well at any Time of the Day, notwithstanding the malicious Authors of the Town, have long since reported me to be dead. But if Occasion be, I will swear my self alive before any Magistrate in England."

At the end of the book is the following *"Affidavit concerning the Publication of* Dido *and* iEneas, *by Mr.* D'Urfey; *printed for*

A. Moore *near* St. Paul'j:"

"To invalidate the notorious and scandalous falsehoods contained in the publick Papers, which have reported the ingenious Mr. *Thomas D'Urfey* to be dead; *B. Moore* maketh Oath, that a Book by him herewith produced, intituled the *English* Stage *Italianiz'd,* &c. is published by the aforesaid Mr. *D'Urfey,* and printed from an original Manuscript, by him given to this Deponent.

"This Deponent farther saith, that Mr. *D'Urfey* was alive when he gave him the Copy, and that when the abovementioned Book was printed, he returned the original Manuscript to Mr. *D'Urfey,* who was likewise alive at that time at his Chambers in *Windsor* Castle.

Jurat 14 Die Nov! 1726
Coram me
C. Richardson.

B. MOORE."

The question arises now as to whether *The English Stage Italianiz'd* really is D'Urfey's or not. Judging from the farce itself, the writer would answer in the negative. The piece is written in a style utterly unlike D'Urfey's. Its prose is clearcut, vigorous, and concise. From the frequent quotations from D'Urfey's prefaces and dedications given in the preceding places it can be seen that his style has anything but these qualities. In other words, D'Urfey belongs to the seventeenth century, to the age of Dryden, when modern prose style was in its infancy. The author of *The English Stage Italianiz'd,* on the other hand, is of the school of the eighteenth century, the age of Scriblerus.

Then, too, the handling of the material of the satire seems not to be D'Urfey's. *The English Stage Italianiz'd* is broadly—even Rabelaisianly—comic. D'Urfey in his attempts at such humor is merely disgusting, never amusing. The piece is a ridicule of two popular varieties of entertainment of the day—the Italian opera and the pantomime. D'Urfey nowhere shows any particular malice against either. He has his jests upon Italian opera in certain pieces but none is in the slightest other than goodhumored. Similarly, D'Urfey refers to pantomime without the slightest degree of illfeeling. In the prologue to *The Modem Prophets,* for example, he says:

"And if you bring good Humour to the Play, Not *Scaramouch* himself could please you better, Nor famous *Harlequin* of comick Nature, Shew more Fools Tricks, than our Arch Agitator." Again, it is hard to believe that even a man so vain and so fond of telling his injuries to the world as D'Urfey would have allowed his name to appear on a titlepage accompanied by the legend, "Poet Laureat *de Jure."* It is true that D'Urfey was mentioned for the laureateship in 1718 at the death of Rowe,327 but nowhere in his prefaces to works published after that time does there appear any bitterness over his failure to obtain the appointment. As a final point against D'Urfey's authorship of the satire, it should be remembered that all of the dramatist's biographers agree that his death occurred no later than 1724,328 and that on his monument in St. James's Churchyard he is specifically said to have died February 26, 1723. His will, moreover, was probated March 15, 1723.829

The only reason for believing *The English Stage Italianiz'd* to be by D'Urfey is the joint evidence of the titlepage, preface, and "B. Moore's" affidavit. These to the writer do not seem convincing. The offer in the preface, to which D'Urfey's name is attached, to "swear himself alive before any Magistrate in England" and "B. Moore's" deposing that "Mr. *D'Urfey* was alive when he gave him the Copy" have more an air of conscious absurdity than of veracity about them. Again, why should an affidavit by B. Moore be appended to a book published by A. Moore?

A third solution of the problem remains. It is possible that the bookseller received the manuscript from D'Urfey and kept it in hand for several years, not publishing it until 1727. However, this view of the matter does not explain the difference in style between the farce and D'Urfey's unquestionable work or the statements in the affidavit as to D'Urfey's being alive.

What to the writer seems the actual state of affairs is this: some wit of the day desiring to attack Italian opera and pantomime, not wishing to use his own name took that of D'Urfey—he having been a dramatist and opera-writer who competed against these obnoxious forms of amusement with little success. The case of Swift and Partridge, the astrologer, regarding the "death" of the latter in 1708,330 and Steele's assistance in the jest through the *Tatler331* perhaps furnished the idea for the protestations of D'Urfey's being alive.

m Letter of Dr. Arbuthnot to Swift, December 11, 1718, Swift's *Correspondence,* edited by Ball, III, 22. See also the Duke, of Buckinghamshire's *Election of a Poet Laureat in M. DCC. XIX.* 828 *The Biographia Dramatica* says the farce was posthumously published (II, 198).

» Aikin, *Life of Steele,* II, 290.
" Swift's *Works,* edited by T. Scott, I, 299 ff.
881 Numbers 1, 59, 96, 99, 118, 216. For the original *Predictions* of Swift see Swift's *Works,* as cited in note 330.
As to who the author really was, if he was not D'Urfey, conjecture would be well-nigh fruitless. It may have been a wit of the time, or perhaps some one connected with the legitimate stage. It should be mentioned here that on January 12, 1734 (New Style), a "dramatic masque," *Dido and AZneas,* by Barton Booth, the actor, was presented at the Haymarket. With this was "Intermixed (by particular desire)... a Grotesque Pantomime, called The BurgoMaster Trick'd."332 Such combinations of classical legend and pantomime are said not to have been common in the early eighteenth century.333 There is a possibility that Booth, perturbed and angered at the inroads of pantomime and foreign opera tried his hand secretly at a satire on them in a form not unlike that of his later and posthumous piece.

In 1677 appeared a farce by Ravenscroft, called *Scaramouch a Philosopher, Harlequin a Schoolboy, Bravo, Merchant, and Magician.TM* The title, at least, is not unlike that of *The English Stage Italianiz'd. The English Stage Italianiz'd* is in five acts, each of which has twelve scenes. There is no dialogue, merely the scenario being given. It is a curious and amusing jumble of the pantomime and the classical legend of JEneas and Dido. The entertainment is written with such vivacity and comic spirit that its frank indecency is not revolting.

At the conclusion of the piece is the following "Advertisement": *"For the Benefit of the* English *Quality, and others who have forgot their Mother-Tongue, This Play is translating into* Italian *by an able Hand; and will be sold by the Orange-Women and Door-Keepers, at Sir Pence each, during the Time of its Performance."*

A quotation from *The English Stage Italianiz'd* may be of interest: "act I, SCENE I.
A Hall in Queen Dido's *Palace.*

Enter Pantalon.
Followed by several Waiters bringing in covered Dishes.
She *sic* gives Directions for placing them, and kicks the
Waiters off one after another.
""Genest, *Stage,* III, 419. Perhaps the "intermixture" is not Booth's; if that is the case, the conjecture based upon it falls to the ground.
843 So the writer has been informed by his friend Mr. Richard F. Jones of Western Reserve University. ssl Summers's Mrs. Behn's *Works,* III, *97.*
SCENE II.
Enter *Harlequin.* Followed by several Waiters with Goblets, which they set down, and are kick'd off by *Harlequin.*
SCENE III.
Enter *Dido.* Attended by *Colombine* and other Attendants, and places herself at Table.
Scene IV.
Enter the *Doctor.* He makes a Reverence, approaches the Table, tastes of every Dish, shews his Approbation, and goes off.
SCENE V.
Enter *Scaramouch.* He comes in and goes out at the Heels of his Master.
SCENE VI.
Enter *Mneas.* He comes in nobly attended, seats himself at Table, and makes a Reverence to the Queen, which she returns.
SCENE VII.
Enter *Anchises.* He comes in led between two; places himself near *Mneas,* and makes his Reverence to the Queen, which she returns.
SCENE VIII.
Enter several *Nobles* and *Courtiers.* They place themselves at Table with much Ceremony.
SCENE IX.
Enter *Guards, Waiters,* and *Attendants,* Insomuch that the Hall is quite full.
SCENE X.
Enter the *Candle-Snuffer.* He snuffs the Candles with a Theatrical Air, and goes off.
SCENE XI.
The Queen desires *Mneas,* to give an Account of his Misfortunes, he tells her no such thing can be done, and yet he'll

do it, and accordingly does it; mean while *Harlequin* steals all the Meat from off his Plate.

Scene XII.

The Queen perceiving *Harlequin's* Villainy, orders him to he hang'd. *Mneas* is pleased at the Frolick, and begs his Life; and withal, that he may be his *Valet de Chambre,* which the Queen grants. Many amorous Glances pass from the Queen to *Apneas,* from *AZneas* to *Colombine,* from *Harlequin* to the Queen, which conclude the first *Act."*

The characters are thus listed: *"Dramatis persona.* MEN. » *Apneas,* Prince of Troy, in Love with *Colombine. Anchises,* his Father, in Love with no Body.

Harlequin, chief Butler to *Dido,* in Love with the Queen. *Pantalon,* chief Cook, in Love with his Belly.

The *Doctor,* in Love with ready Money. *Scaramouch,* in Love with himself. WOMEN. *Dido,* Queen of *Troy,* in Love with *Atneas.*

Colombine, a Coquet, in Love with every Body.

Guards and Attendants, &c.

SCENE *The Court of* Carthage."

The following "Argument" is printed with the piece:

"tineas, the wandring Prince of Troy, is entertained at the Court of Carthage, by Queen Dido, where by a graceful Narration of his Lamentable Adventures, he makes a Conquest of the Queen's Heart. Harlequin being then Butler to the Queen, commits a Fault, for which he is doom'd to die, but is reprieved at the earnest intercession of. ZEneas, who begs Harlequin of her Majesty for his Valet de Chambre, but in fact makes a Pimp of him. for.#£neas being deeply smitten with Colombine, Harelquin's Mistress, buys her of Harlequin who at the same time is half mad for Love of the Queen. Eneas runs away by Night with Colombine; and Harlequin, pretending to be the Queen's Friend in this Affair, is made chief Minister of State. The Queen runs mad for the Love and Loss of JEneas. Harlequin dies for Love of the Queen. The Doctor brings the Queen to life by a transmigrative Secret, and Scaramouch runs mad

in her Stead. Harlequin is restored to Life by the Doctor. The Queen falls in Love with him, and he is crowned King by Dido. The Doctor is loaden with Riches and Honours, and the whole Audience highly satisfied." WESTERN RESERVE UNIVERSITY BULLETINS

New Series VOL. XX. M AY. 1 8 1 7 LITERARY SECTION SUPPLEMENT

Western Reserve Studies, Vol. 1, No. 3.

A STUDY OF THE PLAYS OF

Thomas D'urfey WITH A REPRINT OF

A FOOL'S PREFERMENT

Part II BY ROBERT STANLEY FORSYTHE, Ph. D. *Instructor in English.* Western Reserve University Press Cleveland, Ohio

PREFACE.

The following reprint of *A Fool's Preferment* concludes my *Study of the Plays of Thomas D'Urfey, Part I* of which appeared in May, 1916, as Volume I, Number 2, of the *Literary Section* of *The Western Reserve University Bulletin.* The comedy is here republished for the first time since 1688, and is the only play of D'Urfey to be reprinted since 1729.

I have based my reprint upon the 1688 quarto of *A Fool's Preferment,* a copy of which is in the Cleveland Public Library. My intention has been to reproduce D'Urfey's text as nearly as possible, with the exception of the long "s's" and of certain minor typographical irregularities, such as the accidental use by the old printer of type of different sizes in the same word. I have preserved all of the eccentricities of the old edition in regard to punctuation and spelling, noting (ibut'not correcting) only the important errors. In a few passages I have supplied missing words or letters in the text; these insertions I have enclosed in brackets. The stage directions, additions to the *dramatis personae,* scene headings and scene divisions inserted by me have been set in Roman type and bracketed, each being preceded by an asterisk. Where it has seemed advisable I have called attention in the notes to my insertions. I have made no alteration in the text or addition of any kind which is

not plainly indicated. I have attempted, in other words, to reproduce D'Urfey's exact text, with the exceptions noted, and at the same time to offer it in a condition easily readable for the modern. Hence, I may say, one of my endeavors has been to reduce the number of footnotes to a minimum. The numbers in brackets at the outer margins of the pages of the reprint represent the pagination of the original quarto of the play. A list of Corrigenda for *Part I* is included in the present volume.

I desire to express my appreciation of the kindness of Librarian W. H. Brett of the Cleveland Public Library who has permitted the use of the Library's copy of *A Fool's Preferment* as a basis for this reprint. To Vice-Librarian C. P. P. Vitz I am indebted for many favors, and to Miss Nellie M. Luehrs of the Cleveland Public Library for her cordial assistance in my work. To Librarian George F. Strong of Adelbert College and his assistants I am grateful for frequent aid. For assistance in preparing the footnotes I am indebted to Mrs. R. S. Forsythe; and I owe Professor O. F. Emerson of Western Reserve University, who has read the proofs, for valuable criticism. To the General Editor of the literary division of the *Western Reserve University Bulletin,* Professor W. H. Hukne, who has been constantly ready with helpful suggestions and criticism and who has read the proofs, I am deeply grateful.

R. S. Forsythe.

Cleveland, Ohio, May, 1917.

INTRODUCTION. *A Fool's Preferment, or the Three Dukes of Dunstable,* a reprint of which is given in this volume, seems to have been first performed at Dorset Gardens in the spring of 1688.1 That the play was not well received may be seen from D'Urfey's dedicatory epistle. A letter of Sir George Etherege to the second Duke of Buckingham (?) is thus quoted in the *Biographia Dramatical* "By my last packet from England among a heap of nauseous trash, I received *The Three Dukes of Dunstable;* which is really so monstrous and insipid, that I am sorry Lapland or Livonia had not the honour of producing it;

but if I did penance in reading it, I rejoiced to hear that it was so solemnly interred to the tune of catcalls." As D'Urfey admits,[3] *A Fool's Preferment* is founded upon a Fletcherian play; but the indebtedness, in fact, is much greater than for a mere "hint," as he calls it. D'Urfey has rewritten and altered to a certain extent *The Noble Gentleman* of Fletcher, but enough of the original in language and plot remains to enable the most careless reader of the two comedies to see their relationship.

The following table shows the respective dependence of D'Urfey's scenes upon those of Fletcher: *The Noble Gentleman A Fool's Pre/ermett*

I, 1	I, 2
II, 2	
II, 3	I, 1, 3 II, 4 I, 3 II, 1 II, 1 III, 1 III, 1
III, 2	III, 2 III, 3 III, 3 III, 4 III, 2, 4 IV, 1
IV, 1	
IV, 2	
IV, 3	IV, 2 IV, 4 IV, 3, 4
IV, 5	
V, 1	V, 1

From the table above it appears that every scene in *A Fool's*

'Genest, *Stage,* I, 464.

'II, 244. How Etherege could have written to Buckingham, who died April 16, 1687, of a play printed in 1688, the *Biographia* does not deign, and the writer will not attempt, to explain. Obviously, the letter, if there were one, was not to the Duke.

In the prologue.

Preferment is based upon one in *The Noble Gentleman,* insofar as the action is concerned. Of a total of fifteen scenes in Fletcher's play D'Urfey has drawn on twelve.

Thus, it may be seen that, in all, D'Urfey used 633 lines and fractional lines which occur in *The Noble Gentleman.*

For purposes of further comparison the following outline of Fletcher's play would seem useful:

Mount-Marine has come to Paris with the intention of seeking court preferment. His wife who rules him keeps him in Paris seven years, holding him there with promises of honors, while they spend their fortune. His cousin Clerimont tries to persuade Marine to return to the country, but Marine refuses, being still deluded by his dreams of advancement. Marine's wife enters and asks her husband for money. As he has none on hand, she persuades him to sell some land. He sends Jaques, his servant, to dispose of the property. Jaques goes to Clerimont to endeavor to enlist him in another effort to induce Marine to return to the country. After some debate Clerimont agrees to attempt to reason with his cousin.

After having considered the delights of rural life, Marine, with the aid of some urging from Jaques, resolves to return to the country. He orders his wife to make ready for the journey. She is averse to leaving Paris, and so she sends a message to her lover, announcing the projected departure of herself and her husband, and laying down a course of action which the lover and his friends are to pursue in order to prevent Marine's removal. The Gentleman to whom Marine's Lady is mistress in accordance with her desires appears with a pretended message from the king, who, he says, is much disturbed over Marine's departure, as he fears Marine may draw around him in the country other disaffected persons. Marine is not to be persuaded to remain, and so Longueville, a friend of the Gentleman, enters and pretends at the king's command to create Marine a knight. Still Marine proposes to depart. Then Beaufort, a third plotter, enters with the news that the king has made Marine a baron. Marine, who now believes that, if he will but hold to his professed intention of leaving Paris, he will obtain the highest possible honors, continues to refuse to comply with the supposed desire of the king that he stay in the city. Longueville reenters with the announcement that an earldom has been conferred upon Marine. As Marine still is obdurate, Beaufort returns with the news of his elevation to1a dukedom. Marine now yields and agrees to remain in Paris. He chooses the title of Duke of Burgundy and assumes great state. To his wife he yields dominion over him because he deems her instrumental in securing his preferment.

Jaques, Marine's servant, now goes out, and, on meeting Clerimont, informs him of Marine's good fortune. Clerimont, who, like his cousin, is a dolt, is greatly impressed with the news, and resolves to try for preferment also. He sends for his wife and dispatches his congratulations to Marine. Marine's wife and her accomplices arrange to keep Marine in Paris and at the same time to maintain his ignorance of their imposture. They station persons in the streets to cheer him and commend his greatness. On going abroad, Marine is so pleased with these manifestations of his popularity that he starts to make a speech to the populace, but is cut short in it by Longueville. On Marine's return home, he is met by Shattillion, a gentleman who has gone mad from disappointed love. The lady, Shatillion's Love, has returned to him and, though unrecognized by him, strives through the play to bring him to his senses. Marine and Shattillion now dispute over the genealogy of the king, and the madman attacks Marine who is rescued by his followers.

As he is seeking the post-house, Jaques, who has been sent to the country with a message to Marine's tenants concerning their lord's preferment, meets Shattillion in the street. Shattillion persuades Jaques that by stopping to talk he has endangered his life, since Shattillion is suspected of treason. Believing this, Jaques is easily brought by Shattillion into the idea of assuming a female dress, which Shattillion is to provide, and then escaping in it by ship to Calcutta. While Jaques is dressing, Shattillion's Love comes to the door of his house and knocks for admission. Shattillion takes her for a guard sent to arrest him, and sallies out with his sword. She flees. Jaques then comes out in his disguise. He meets Shattillion who has forgotten him and who now thinks him a spy. Consequently, he refuses further aid to Jaques. Thus deserted, Jaques is discovered by Beaufort, who is one of the conspirators against

Marine and a profligate. Beaufort thinks Jaques really a woman and so insists on Jaques accompanying him home. There they fall into a trap set by Longueville and the Gentleman. Beaufort has boasted of his secrecy in lovematters and of his not knowing with whom he has been owing to his conducting his amours in darkness. They set Maria, the maid of Marine's Lady, upon him. She enters after Beaufort and the disguised Jaques and calls the former out. Maria explains that she has been one of the women whom he has been intimate with, and that she is now pregnant by him. Longueville, who now enters, mocks Beaufort for his having been so easily caught by Maria in spite of his boasted precautions. Beaufort asserts that he is married to Maria.

Jaques now enters and makes himself known. In the meantime, Clerimont and his wife come to wait upon Marine. The Wife pleases Longueville who courts her before her husband, while the Gentleman calms Clerimont by assuring him that if he allows his wife to do as she pleases, his preferment is sure. Finally, the Wife and Longueville leave together and her husband departs without her.

Jaques returns home and tells his master of his adventure of the night before and the failure of his trip to the country.

Marine then determines to go down to his old home himself. His wife reminds him of his "promise" to the king, but he is firm in his resolution. She then gives her accomplices their instructions. Longueville accordingly enters as Marine and his household are about to set out. He pretends that the king has sent him to degrade the disobedient "duke," which he proceeds to do, much to the chagrin of Marine and the disgust of Clerimont. Marine refuses to be degraded and has Jaques appear as a champion to defend his master's right to his dukedom. The mad Shattillion enters and assumes the rôle of a challenger. Jaques will not fight, so Shattillion attacks Marine and gets him down. Shattillion's Love enters and is at last recognized by him. Having regained his

senses Shattillion falls into a slumber. Beaufort's marriage is now revealed together with the trick put upon him. Seeing Shattillion soundly asleep, Marine again raises his ducal pretensions, but withdraws them at his Lady's suggestion that he test his ennoblement by entering a lion's den, since lions will not harm a prince. The Gentleman settles the matter by announcing that the king has ruled that Marine may be a duke, but that he must let no one know it. To this Marine agrees. Shattillion now awakes sane, and is led away by his faithful Love.

It will be seen from the preceding outline that D'Urfey has made certain changes in the plot. Of these one of the most important is the introduction of the game of basset as the motive for the desire of Cocklebrain's wife to stay in London. The gaming scene in D'Urfey's play, it should be stated, is said by Gildon to have come from a novel called *The Humors of Basset*. The part of *The Noble Gentleman* which deals with the duping of Beaufort by Maria and his friends has been omitted very wisely by D'Urfey. At the close of the play, as is his custom in alterations of old dramas, D'Urfey departs from his source. He successively has the plotters make Grub and Toby dukes.

Certain changes in the characters also occur. In Darley's edition of *The Noble Gentleman* (to which all references, unless otherwise indicated, are made) is the following list of *dramatis personae.*

"monsieur Mount-marine, *the* Noble Gentleman, *but none of the wisest.*
JAQUES, *an Old Servant to* MARINE'S *Family.*
Clerimont, *a Gull, Cousin to* Marine.
Gentleman, *Servant to* MARINE'S *Wife.*
"Edition of Langbaine's *English Dramatic Poets,* p. 50. The writer has not had access to this novel.
Two Courtiers that plot to abuse MA-RINE.
Longueville,
Beaufort,
SHATTILLION, *a Lord, Mad for Love.*
Doctor,
Page.

Gentlemen.
Anthony, Clerimont's *Servant.*
Servants.
Lady, *Wife to* MARINE, *a witty Wanton.*
Wife *to* CLERIMONT, *a simple Country Gentlewoman.*
SHATTILLION'S Mistress, *a virtuous Virgin.*
MARIA, *Servant to* MARINE'S *Wife."*

In the first place, D'Urfey has added certain characters. These Jare Sir Jasper Lost-all and Lady Lost-alPJTleaflint, Sharpe, and the Usher of the Black Rod. Other characters are renamed. Mount Marine in *The Noble Gentleman* = Cocklebrain in *A Fool's Preferment;* Jaques=Toby; Clerimont=Grub; the Gentleman=Clerimont; Shattillion = Lyonel; the Page=a Footman; Anthony = Roger; the Lady=Aurelia; the Wife to Clerimont = Phillida; Shattillion's Mistress=Celia. The only persons who correspond in name and character through the two plays are Longueville (Longoville), Beaufort (Bewford), the Doctor, and Maria. In most cases D'Urfey's changes in the characters have consisted of changing their names or of naming them definitely. Three of them, Phillida, Toby, and Roger have more to do in *A Fool's Preferment* than had their originals in the Fletcherian comedy. The name of Clerimont, one of Fletcher's gulls, is transferred by D'Urfey to Aurelia's lover as Clermont. The corresponding character is unnamed in *The Noble Gentleman.*

D'Urfey has to some degree recharacterized Fletcher's Clerimont in his Justice Grub. He seems to have based the latter upon Shadwell's Justice Clodpate in *Epsom Wells,* who, in the *dramatis persona* to that comedy, is thus described:

"A Country Justice; a publick-spirited, politick discontented Fop, and immoderate Hater of *London,* and a Lover of the Country above Measure; a hearty, *true English* Coxcomb."

The hatred of London of Shadwell's character is well shown in *Epsom Wells,* I, 1, II, 1. Grub's solicitude over his wall-eyed mare, as shown in *A Fool's Preferment,* I, 1, is plainly borrowed

'Omitted from the *dramatis persons* of *A Fool's Preferment,* as are also Phillida and Winnall.

from Clod pate's affection for his dapple mare, *Epsom Wells,* I, 1, III, 1, and elsewhere. Sir Credulous Easy in *Sir Patient Fancy,* 1,1, displays the same sort of solicitude for his horse. Toby, as the name of Cocklebrain's servant, may be borrowed from Toby, Clodpate's man in Shadwell's comedy.

With the exception of only a few passages Fletcher's blank verse has been turned into prose, or at least, printed as such. Various songs also have been added.

All things considered, *A Fool's Preferment* cannot be deemed an improvement upon *The Noble Gentleman.* While certain omissions of irrelevant parts have been made, other material as unconnected with the plot has been added. Too, D'Urfey has heightened the farcicality of the play to the utmost degree of absurdity. His creation of three dukes of Dunstable has made the plot too improbable to be really amusing. On the other hand, by the introduction of the satire upon basset playing, he has brought in an element of seriousness much less suited to his play than to Fletcher's.

Etherege's criticism of *A Fool's Preferment* has already been quoted. Genest says of the play, "It is very far from being a good comedy," and again, "D'Urfey is more to be blamed for selecting one of Fletcher's worst plays for alteration, than for the alteration itself." He states, too, that he does not approve of Etherege's harsh judgement.6

Langbaine's strictures upon the play7 are confined to D'Urfey's presumption in addressing Lord Morpeth as "My Dear Lord," and in subscribing himself "like a Person of Quality, only with his Sir-name." Further, Langbaine comments upon D'Urfey's giving credit to Fletcher only for a "hint", whereas practically the whole comedy is founded upon that writer's work. He.concludes his notice with a comparison of D'Urfey to the Celsus of Horace *(Epistles,* Bk. I, Epist. 3).

A Fool's Preferment was revived at

Drury Lane, July 16, 1703, as not having been acted for sixteen years.8 After this time, the comedy appears never to have been revived. There has been only one edition of it, that of 1688, upon which the accompanying reprint is based. '*Stage,* I, 463-64. '*English Dramatic Poets* (Ed. 1691), pp. 180-81. Genest, *Stage,* II, 275.

The Noble Gentleman was revised by J. Sheridan Knowles as *The Duke of London,* but this alteration was, it seems, never acted, and was printed in 1874. Holberg's comedy, *Den Politiske Kandestbber,* produced in Copenhagen in 1722, has a general resemblance in theme to Fletcher's and D'Urfey's comedies, but there probably was no borrowing.

A

Fool's Preferment, OR, THE

Three DUKES of Dunstable.

A COMEDY.

As it was Acted at the Queens Theatre in *Dorset-Garden,* by Their MAJESTIES Servants.

Together, with all the SONGS and NOTES to 'em, Excellently Compos'd by Mr. Henry Purcell. 1688.

Licensed,

May 21. 1688. *R. P.*

Eupolis atq; Cratinus, A ristophanesque Poetce, A tq; alii, quorum Comaedia prisca virorum est; Si quis erat dignus describi, quod Malns, aut Fur, Quod Meechus foret, aut Sicarius, aut alioqui Famosus; multa cum libertate not abunt. Hinc Omnis pendet Lucillius. Horat Styr. 4.

Printed for *Jos. Knight,* and *Fra. Saunders* at the *Blue Anchor* in the *Lower Walk* of the *New Exchange* in the *Strand,* 1688.

TO THE HONOURABLE CHARLES Lord MORPETH.' *My Dear LORD,*

I am in Debt so many ways, for Obligations to your Self, and Noble Family, that, with all the Gratitude I have, I am puzzled in findmg occasions to express my Thanks; be pleased therefore to receive in a Dedication of this slight Piece, my Hearts true Acknowledgments, and as true an Endeavour to dievrt you, by Reading a Comedy, which was only design'd to please such

as look on this sort of Dramatick Poesie, as you do, with Judgment and good Humour. I have studied these things long enough to know the Humor of the Town, and what is proper for Diversion; but I cannot always bring my Inclinations to flatter the *(Would be WITS,)* nor spare the exposing a notorious Vice, th6 the price of a Third Day10 were the fatal consequence of such an Indiscretion: It is, and shall be, enough for me at any time, if some few of the many Noble and Worthy Persons, that did me the Honour to appear for me, in spite of the Party that was malitiously made by some eminent Gamesters of both Sexes, who thought themselves touch'd: If such as your Lordship, and those others of my unbyass'd Friends,

'"Charles Lord Morpeth"; Charles Howard Viscount Morpeth, later third Earl of Carlisle at that creation. He was born in 1669. From 1690 to 1692 he was Member of Parliament for Morpeth, succeeding to the earldom of Carlisle in the latter year. He was Governor of Carlisle in 1693; Lord Lieutenant of Cumberland and Westmoreland, 1692-1712, 1714-38; Gentleman of the Bedchamber, 1701-02; Deputy Earl Marshal, 1701-06; Privy Councillor, 1701; First Lord of the Treasury, 1701-02, 1715; Commissioner for the Union, 1706; a Lord Justice of the Realm, 1714 Constable of Windsor Castle, 1723-30; Master of the Foxhounds, 1730. Lord Carlisle died at Bath, May 1, 1738. He is said to have been "a Writer and Poet" *(Complete Peerage,* etc. Ed. by G. E. C. II, 153). To his predecessor as Earl of Carlisle (his father) D'Urfey dedicated *hisBussy D'Ambois.* 10"Third Day"; the author received the proceeds from the third day of performance of his play; hence should a drama fail on its first presentation the writer would lose his benefit.

will please to think it worth their liking, and alluding to a late Honourable, and Renowned Author; I Declare, // *You, and Others, I omit to Name, Approve my Lines, I count your Censure, Fame.11* As to the Play, I will only say this of it, the first hint was taken from an old Comedy of *Fletcher's;* and as it was improv'd, and several new Humours added, it was generally lik'd before the Acting. I knew *Basset12* was a Game, only proper for Persons of great Fortunes; and therefore I thought, that a wholsome Satyr of this kind might have oblig'd some Country-Gentlemen, or Citizens of small Estates, whose Wives ne're heeding the approaching Ruin, took only care, they might have the Honour, to be seen at Play with Quality. But some certain, very nice, Persons, especially one, took it so to Heart, that dear *Basset* should be expos'd, that my honest Intentions were quite frustrated, and that the Piece might be sure to be ruin'd, their Majesties were told, it was so obscene, that it was not fit to be Acted; when, I can prove, there has not, these seven years, been any Comedy so free from it; and some good Judges were pleas'd to Declare, they thought that, the only Reason some people had to find fault. Obscenity is a thing of that abomincble Nature, that unless it be detected so thoroughly, that it may be punished, it were better not heeded at all, (especially, by a *Lady*) who, in my Opinion, being too Witty in such a Discovery, will only give People to understand, how well skill'd She is in the Matter.

My LORD, I most Humbly beg your Lordships Pardon for this Digression, th6 I could not well Publish the Play, without some Defence in this kind; but I have done with 'em now, and the hottest Censurer shall at leisure cool of himself: I will only rally my own ill Fortune, and say, with that admirable *French* Moralist; *Fortune, Je me repends de t'voir suivie, & cognoissant que tu ne peux chos. du monde advouc que la vertu est la seul port oil les hommes peuvent trouver leur veritable tranquillite,13*

A Sentence, which, I'm sure, your Lordship throughly under

"This couplet, which is also quoted in the dedication of *Don Quixote, Part III,* concludes the Earl of Rochester's *Allusion to the Tenth Satire of the First Book of Horace.* li"Basset"; a game at cards much like the modern faro, which was popular in the seventeenth and early eighteenth centuries. In I, 2, Aurelia

uses a number of the technical terms of the game.

"According to Langbaine, *English Dramatic Poets,* p. 181, this passage is garbled from Montaigne. A careful search of Montaigne's works by the editor, however, has not revealed any passage more than very faintly resembling it.

stands, having been with choicest Care Bred, and Learned in the nicest Rudiments of Morality, Wit, and Religion, and therefore skill'd in what concerns all Mankind in general, as well as Poets, who are Condemn'd to Traffick with all sort of Humours, and to be oblig'd to such as will *own* themselves pleas'd, with what they like. A Fatigue, which I can the better bear, because it offends me little *r* which way soever it happens, always believing, that, next diverting my Friends, to please my Self, is the best method; but as my Friends satisfaction takes Place first, I hope this Comedy will not appear distastful to 'em, especially to you, being Corrected, And My Lord, thus Humbly Dedicated, By *Your Lordships Most Obliged, And .a Humble Servant, D'URFEY.*
Dramatis Personae *Cocklebrain.* A halfwitted Country-Gentleman, whom his Wife rules, and keeps in Town spending his Estate at) Mr. *Nokes.14 Basset;* yet still bubbles him in hopes of Preferment. Justice) An old Peevish Country Justice, an) *Grub.* hater of the Town, and its Fashions. *Mr. Leigh.15 LyoneL* A Well Bred Ingenious Gentleman:") who, being hindred of his Mistress, Mr. *Montfort1* by the King, fell distracted.) *Clermont.* .Basses-Players and Agents with") *Mr.Kinaston.11 Longevile Aurelia,* in the Bubling her Hus-Mr. *Powell Bewford.*) band.) Mr. *Bowman.19* l"Nokes;" James Nokes began acting immediately after the reopening of the theatres as a member of Rhoades's company in 1659-60. He at first played female parts. In his later career Nokes returned on several occasions to the representation of women, taking coarse and unrefined roles, in which he won much applause. Because of his success as the Nurse in Payne's *Fatal Jealousy,* he was

knownas "Nurse" Nokes. As a representer of stupid characters Nokes excelled. He retired from the stage some time before his death (which occured in 1692), with enough wealth to purchase an estate of four hundred pounds per annum. The parts in D'Urfey's plays which Nokes sustained were: Bubble in *The Fond Husband;* Toby in *Madam Fickle;* Squire Oldsapp in *Squire Oldsapp;* Lady Beardly in *A Virtuous Wife;* and Megaera in *The Banditti.*

""Leigh;" Anthony Leigh was of a good Northamptonshire family. He joined the Duke of York's company about 1672. Leigh was successful as a comedian, having been cast usually for the parts of comically foolish old men. He was a favorite with Charles II who called him "his" actor. Leigh died in December, 1692. He acted the following characters in D'Urfey's plays: Fumble in *The Fond Husband;* Zechiel in *Madam Fickle;* Sir Frederick Banter, in *Squire Oldsapp;* Sir Lubberly Widgeon in *A Virtuous Wife;* Sir Oliver Oldcut in *The Royalist;* Frugal in *A Commonwealth of Women;* Don Ariell in *Thg Banditti;* Lady Addleplot in *Love for Money;* and Myn Heer Van Grin in *The Marriage Hater Match'd.*

'"Montfort"; William Mountfort was born in Staffordshire in 1664 (D. *N. B.*) In 1678 he began acting, playing juvenile roles at Dorset Gardens. He was married in 1686 to the actress Susanna Percival, who was later noted as a performer in low comedy parts as Mrs. Verbruggen. Mountfort is said to been the author of six plays. His greatest success was in polite comedy, but he was excellent in tragedy as well. His skill, combined with his fine presence and voice, adapted him especially for lovers' parts. As Alexander in *The Rival Queens* Mountfort was particularly admired. He was a favorite of Chief Justice Jeffreys with whom he lived on terms of great intimacy. Mountfort was murdered by one Hill, dying December 10, 1692. He had acted in D'Urfey's plays the parts of Bussy D'Ambois in *Bussy D'Ambois;* Jack Amorous in *Love for Money;* and Sir Philip Freewit in *The Marriage Hater Match'd. An El-*

egy on Mountfort is printed in *Pills to Purge Melancholy,* V, 244-45. It is probably not D'Urfey's.

""Kinaston;" Edward Kynaston was born about 1640. He was an under-apprentice with Betterton in Rhodes's bookshop, when Rhodes organized his company of players in 1659-60. Kynaston entered this troupe as a performer of female parts, being well fitted therefor by his remarkable beauty. He is noted as a vigorous and skilful actor, especially good as Morat in *Aurengzebe,* Muley Moloch in *Don Sebastian,* and Henry IV in *Henry IV, Part I.* His chief defect is said to have been a shrill voice. Kynaston retired as a well-to-do man from the stage about 1699, and died in 1706. He had played only Don Antonio in *The Banditti,* and the Duke of Guise in *Bussy D'Ambois,* in the plays of D'Urfey other than *A Fool's Preferment.* 18"Powel;" George Powell was born about 1658, the son of an actor ("Powel, Sen."). He began acting about 1687, hence Longovile is among his earliest parts. Powel showed great promise as an actor, but ruined his health and lost his popularity because of his intemperance and indolence. Powel was the author (or adapter) of three plays. He acted the following parts in D'Urfey's plays: Montsurry in *Bussy D'Ambois;* Nedd Bragg in *Love for Money;* Tom Romance in *The Richmond Heiress;* Don Fernando in *Don Quixote, Part I;* Mannel in *Don Quixote, Part II;* Don Quixote in *Don Quixote, Part III;* and Lord Noble in *The Modern Prophets.*

""Bowman;" This actor was born in 1651, and long outlived any contemporary (Cibber being twenty years younger than he). He died March 23, 1739, aged 88. On the preceding October 31, he had played Priuli in *Venice Preserved.* The parts acted by Bowman in D'Urfey's plays were Crochett in *A Virtuous Wife;* Broom in *The Royalist;* Nicusa in *A Commonwealth of Women;* the Dancing Master in *Love for Money;* Lord Brainless in *The Marriage Hater Match'd;* Rice ap Shinken in *The Richmond Heiress;* Cardenio in *Don Quixote, Parts I,* and *II;* and Count de

Tonnere in *The Intrigues at Versailles.*
Servant to *Cocklebrain,* a sly Drolling "
Fellow that hates the Town, and Mr. *Jevon.*20 his Master's living there.) vMr.
Estate at *Basset.*) A foolish Knight, that has lost all his) '.
j Estate at *Basset.* J
Two Rooks at *Basset.*
A Gamester.
Usher of the Black Rod.
Servant to Grub.
WOMEN. *Aurelia,* Wife to *Cocklebrain,* a Town-bred) Mrs. *Bowtel*P Jilt, a great *Basset-player.*) *Celia,* A maid of Honour. Mrs. *Jordain*P
Phillida, Wife to Grub.
Lady Lost-all. Wife to Sir Jasper.
Maria, Woman to *Aurelia.*
Gamesters, male and female.
Doctor, Citizens, Barber, Dancers, and Attendants.
SCENE, The COURT, in the Reign of *Henry* the Fourth.

""Jevon;" Thomas Jevon was born in 1652; and after starting as a dancing-master went upon the stage in 1673. He was a brother-in-law of Shadwell. Jevon was popular in his day as a comedian. He was the author of the popular farce, *The Devil of a Wife.* Toby was his last part, as he died December 20. 1688. Other r&ies taken in D'Urfey's plays by Jevon are: Sneak in *The Fond Husband;* Harry Jollyman in *Madam Fickle;* Sir Frolick Whimsey in *A Virtuous Wife;* Sir Paul Eitherside in *The Royalist;* Franvil in *A Commonwealth of Women;* and Signior Frisco in *The Banditti.* 2,"Powel, Sen."; This actor, the father of George Powell, was originally a member of the King's Company but joined the Duke's at the union of the companies in 1682. He died about 1698. In D'Urfey's dramas the elder Powell had played only Sir Peregreen in *Trick for Trick;* and Sir Barnaby Whigg in *Sir Barnaby Whigg,* besides his acting of the Usher in *A Fool's Preferment.*

""Bowtel;" Mrs. Boutel was a veteran actress who was among the first women to appear on the stage, her first recorded part being in 1663 as Estifania in *Rule a Wife and have a Wife.* Her specialty was

the representation of innocent young ladies. Mrs. Boutel retired from the stage in 1696. An interesting story is told of a fight between her and Mrs. Barry over a veil appropriately enough to be used in *The Rival Queens.* Mrs. Boutel played Cellida in D'Urfey's *Trick for Trick.*

""Jourdain;" Mrs. Jourdain was perhaps related to Thomas Jourdain (1612-85), a pre-Res-' toration actor in the King's Revels Company, who played some parts after the opening of the theatres and who succeeded Tatham as City Poet.

PROLOGUE
Spoken by Mr. JEVON.
A Poets Trade, like Hazard, does entice;
He's the unlucky Caster, you the Dice.
Constant ill Luck attends at every Throw
You Criticks are like Fullhams,24 *high and low, Yet 'tis his Fate, he can't give over so.)*
Like a young Wife, just ready to Lie in,
That whines and cries, I'le ne're come to 't agen; Altering his
When th' danger's past, and pains forgotten all, J Voice.
Her Heart's not broke, She'l venture 'tother squawl.
To all new Plays, like Towns besieg'd, you come,
And each pert huffing Whipster throws a Bomb,
Whilst th' trembling Author all the Shot retains
Of several Nations, and their several Brains;
'Tis strange, you Beaux *at home should do such harm,*
Pray find another Buda, *if you'l Storm;*
One good sound Battel would some Thought provoke;
For Brains are never seen, till Heads are broke;
From Famous Fletcher's *Hint, this piece was made,*
All Mirth and Droll, not one reflection said,26
For now-a-days poor Satyr hides his Head.
No wholsome Jerk dares lash fantastick Youth,
You wits grow angry, if you hear the

Truth,
Old Fumble now, may at Doll Com-
mons *strip,*
Without being flagn'd27 by a Poetick
Whip.
The Noble Peer may to the Play repair.
""Fullhams"; dice so loaded as to fall
consistently either high or low; cf. *The*
Merry Wives of Windsor, I, 3, 1. 94.

""The late memorable Siege of *Buda*"
is mentioned by Young *Brags. Love for*
Money, II, 2 (p. 27), and is referred to
elsewhere in the play. Buda was unsuccessfully besieged by the Germans in
1684. After a second protracted siege
the city, defended by Abdurrahman
Pasha, was captured by storm by the
Germans under Duke Charles of Lor-
raine on September 2, 1686, and a
frightful massacre of the Turkish inhab-
itants ensued.

""All Mirth and Droll, not one reflection said"; this contradicts D'Urfey's
assertion of an intention to satirize gaming, as expressed in the dedication.

""Flagn'd"; a misprint for "flaug'd,"
meaning "flog." See *The Injured*
Princess, I, 1 (p. 6); *The Royalist,* IV,
1 (p. 39); *DonQuixote, Part II,* II, 2 (p.
20); *Part III,* V, 1 (p. 287).
Court the pert Damsel with her China
Ware.2S Nay, Marry her, if he please,
no one will care?3 The Whore too may
with Quality be Box'd, 1 *And set up for*
a Virtue, though She's Pox'd. The Fop
in Love may his dull Genius try; 1 *The*
Soldier Drink, so Quarrel, and so Dye.
The Alderman may Cheat, the Lawyer
Lye. And Satyr now not dare to ques-
tion, why; You shall scape too, at th'
Trading end o' th' Town, Your Wit sticks
fast, although your Charter's gone;30
Therefore brave Knights o' th' Apron,
and the Yard, All fear of a Satyrick Jest
discard; Let not this Play, through your
shrewd censure, fall, j *And then cheat*
on, and prosper great and small, You
shall have Liberty of Conscience, *All.)*
""China Ware"; not porcelain, but China oranges. The reference is to an or-
angergirl. "For the three preceding
lines, cf. *Don Quixote, Part I,* prologue:
"The Orange-Miss, that here Cajoles the
Duke, May sell her Rotten Ware without Rebuke." The prologues of *A Fool's*

Preferment and *Don Quixote, Part 1,* it
may be said, bear a general resemblance
to each other.

""Although your Charter's gone"; the
charters of the city of London were de-
clared forfeited to the crown in 1683.
THE
Fool's Preferment; OR, THE THREE
DUKES
O F DUNSTABLE.
ACT I. SCENE I. 1 *A Garden, discovering*
Lyonel *crown'd with Flowers, and*
Antickly drest, sitting on a Green Bank.
Enter Celia. *Celia.* Yonder he is: Oh
that Heart-breaking Object,
The Darling of the Times, his Country's
honor,
Our Sexes Joy, and Glory of his own,
That was all Bravery, All Wit, All Mer-
it,
Wild as the Winds;31 lies there bereft of
Sense;
Whilst here I mourn, that am the Fatal
Cause.
Fall, Fall, ye Tears! and throbb, unhap-
py Heart!
That in a luckless Hour, refus'd such
Love;
Threatened by Friends, and forc'd by
Royal Power.
I threw a Dearer, Brighter Jewel from
me, 2
Than e'er deckt Woman's Beauty.
Oh wou'd to Heaven,
That I had known the Curse of stubborn
Will,
Or I had dy'd e'er I had done such 111.
"The preceding passage which
D'Urfey adapted from *The Noble*
Gentleman, I, 3, seems to ihave been
based upon Ophelia's comments upon
Hamlet, *Hamlet,* III, 1, 1. 158 *If, Lyonel*
sings.
I sigh'd, and I pin'd,
Was Constant and Kind
To a Jilt that laugh'd at my Pains:
Though my Passion ne'r cool'd,
I found I was fool'd,
For all my Abundance of Brains.
But now I'm a Thing
As great as a King:
So blest is the Head that is addle!
The dull, empty Pate
Soonest comes to be great:
Fate doats on a Fool in the Cradle.

Lyon. Madam!
Celia. Ay, Sir.
Lyon. How goes the World? From
thence the Zodiack, the 1 Sun, the Moon
and Planets; In what Meridian are we?
Celia. Do but hear me, Sir! *Lyon.* With
all my Heart. I know your Cleft Sex are
in great Trust with *Lucifer:* and can do
at man a Favour; a handsome Woman is
the Devil's Soul-Broker, a Place worth
ten of his Gentleman-Usher; you shall
find I have Court Breeding. Come, pro-
nounce. *Celia.* Sir, I am come. *Lyon.*
From the Dread Soveraign King; I know
it well: I am all Duty, all Courtier, all
Cringe; as supple as my Ladies Page;
he is a Gracious Prince, Long may he
live. Belong you to his Chamber? *Celia.*
Not I indeed, Sir, that Place is not for
Women! *Lyon.* Not for Women!—What
Place more fit for Women than 3 a
Chamber? They were begot in Chambers! Born in Chambers! Dress'd in
Chambers! And if you take a Woman
out of her Chamber, you'll find her
good for nothing *Celia.* For nothing,
Sir! Can you say so of me? D'you know
who I am? *Lyon.* Most exquisitely.
Celia. What is my Name? *Lyon.* Dam-
nation! *Celia.* How, Sir? *Lyon.* The
Gossips call'd you first *Phillissida,* be-
cause of your little Mouth, and narrow
Gaskins: but you are puft out like a
Pumpkin since, Hell Gate's not wider
than a Woman's Conscience. *Celia.*
Fye, Sir, All this to her that loves you!
Lyon. Love me, nay, that's a Lye! I had
but one Love, and her the good King
Henry has taken from me, to bribe his
Favorite for his Legs and Cringes.32
But hush——mo more of that; I must
be wary, Pitchers have Ears. Some one
may call this Treason. *Celia.* That
Favourite, Sir, is now in great Disgrace;
And the King pitying you, has sent me
hither. *Lyon.* To soak me like a Spunge:
Drain all my Secrets, and then hang me
up. Ha, I find it out: This Woman here
is sent to undermine me; to buz33 Love
into me: to try my Spirits, and make me
open and betray my self: Hah, Is not this
true? *Celia.* No indeed, Sir
Heaven knows I love you too well to
betray you! *Weeps. Lyon.* Such was the
Heavenly Musick of her Voice, (*sadly*

Soft as the Flute-like Sounds that charm'd my Ear, *I raving.* When my dear *Celia* lov'd me, but she's gone: The Fiend Ambition bears her on his Wings: She mounts, she soars, and leaves her Vows behind her.

Celia. Oh my Curst Fortune! *Lyon.* Do you weep, let me see? Pray, let me taste your Tears. Ha, ha, ha, ha, Rose-Water by this Light: Nine pence a Pint, sold at the Pothecaries: Oh thou Dissembler! that is, Thou very Woman: All thy Sex carry perpetual Fountains in their Heads, and make their Eyes spout Mischiefs when they please. SINGS. 4

There's nothing so fatal as Woman,
To hurry a Man to his Grave;
You may think, you may plot, You may
sigh like a Sot:
She uses you more like a Slave.
But a Bottle, altho' it be common,
The Cheats of the Fair will undo,
It will drive from your Head The De-
lights of the Bed;
He that's drunk is not able to wooe. Ex *Lyon.*

""Legs and Cringes"; scrapes and bows.
    M"Buz"; buzz, meaning to suggest to, to incite by suggestion.

Celia. Method in Madness, Grace even in Distraction.

I'll never leave him, 'till, by Art or Prayer,
I have restor'd his Senses to their Office.
Oh most unnatural Vice in silly Women!
We oft refuse what best deserves our Love,
J_ And often chuse the contrary!
    Thus Shadow-like, we make the Sentence true,
Follow'd we fly: but if they fly, pursue.34
I that this Sun of Vertue could not see,
    When long his Beams were hourly cast on me:
Like blushing Flowers wanton'd when I shone,
But ne'er his Value knew till he was gone:
Unhappy Sex! Thy Fortune never drew
So great a Blessing as a Love that's

true,
    But to be sold by Friends, by Coxcombs griev'd;
    Match'd for thy Plague: and born to be deceiv'd. *Ex.* Celia.

SCENE II.

A Room in Cocklebrain's house.

Enter Cockle-brain *and* Toby.

Cockl. Sirra, Sirra! I say once more, The Court's a Glorious Place, and I am much honour'd with the Society of my Wives Noble Friends there. Therefore leave off your grumbling, and let me have no more of your mouldy Advice, or as I am a true Courtier, and consequently a Wit *Tob.* A Wit! No, no, Sir, you are *John Cockle-brain,* of 5 *Plowden-Hicket,Sb* in the County of *Staffordshire,* Esquire. *Cockl.* A Squire, which is as much as to say a Fool; is it? Very well, Sirra. *Tob.* Why the Devil will you be a Wit, Sir, you had as good own your self a Bastard: For there has not been Wit in your Family since the Conquest. *Cockl.* Sirra, if I am a Wit, I will be a Wit, and let my Family rise and deny it if they dare; But whatsoever I am, Sirra, I am sure you are an Impudent Rascal; and don't you think, Sirra, because you found me with a Whore t'other Day at *Green-Goose-Fair,*36 ,4The preceding couplet is based upon *The Merry Wives of Windsor,* II. 2, 11. 215-16: "Love like a shadow flies when substance love pursues; Pursuing that that flies, and flying what pursues." "The hero of *Twanzdillo. A New Ballad* in *Pills to Purge Melancholy,* I, 19, is "Jolly *Roger Twangdillo* of *Plouden* Hill." ""Green-Goose-Fair"; perhaps the same as "Gooseberry Fair," mentioned by Besant, *London in the Eighteenth Century,* p. 471. -when I was drunk, and I desir'd you not to tell my Wife; that I 'll bear every Flirt from you. The World would be finely govern'd indeed, if every Man's Servant, because he is a Pimp, must pretend to be sawcy. *Tob.* And shall we never go into the Country agen then, Sir? Will you run out all your Estate here, for this confounded Name of a Courtier? *Cockl.* Sirra, You sawcy Rascal, 'tis a Name that draws Wonder and Duty from all Eyes and Knees. *Tob.* Ay, 'Twill draw

your Worship's Land within the walls too, where you may have it, all inclos'd and sure:37 Oh, here comes your Country Uncle, Old Justice *Grub,* he'll *grub* you now i' faith; he'll firk you for your Feathers and your Fooleries. He has had no Drink but Juice of Crabs and Vinegar this week, to fit him for you. He'll make you a Courtier. *Enter* Grub. *Cockl.* Good morrow, good morrow, Uncle. *Grub.* Good morrow, Cod'shead: *Cockle-brain* and Cod'shead are much at one. Own'z! dost wear that damn'd Cap upon thy Head with a Summer-fly Flap, like the Fore-Horse of a Waggon? And dost thou bid me good morrow? Why, you Ninny, you Nicompoop, you Noun Adjective, for thou canst not stand by thy self, I am sure; must my Family be disgrac'd and ruin'd by a flanting38 Fopdoodle, that is too finical to" learn any Sense. A Pox on thee, I am asham'd on thee. *Tob.* Ay there, there, Sir, there's a Courtier for you. *Cockl.* Why, good Uncle, what's the matter? *Grub.* Gadzooks. What's the matter? why, you Scatterbrain! you Son of a Whore; and yet I think my Sister was honest: 6 What's the matter? Why thou 'rt undone. Thou art lost. I would not lend thee Two pence on thy Land: Thou art a meer Bankrupt. *Tob.* Very well! Very fine indeed: this is but the first Course. I'll leave you together and go and laugh. *Exit. Cockl.* Not too fast, not too fast, Uncle: Pray consider a little. *Grub.* Not a Jot, Faith! What dost thou do at Court but to be ruin'd? Hast reckon'd up thy Income? Dost thou know the value of thy Tenants Sweat and Labour, and thy Expences here? *Cockl.* I think I do.

""Draw all your Worship's Land within the walls, "; the land will be turned into money and brought so within the walls of London. See Dyce, *Beaumont and Fletcher,* X, 113, note. ""Flanting"; flaunting.

Grub. Think, nay, that's a Lye: thou hast not thought these seven Years, to my knowledge. Thou hast a Wife, a handsome Wife, Men say: Canst thou pretend to have a Grain of Thought, And yet bring her to Court? Ah *grins. Cockl.* Pray, Sir, what ill can she get there? *Grub.* A Bastard, Sir, it may be, to inherit your Estate. Ownz! I shall ne'er have Patience! *Cockl.* Oh Sir, you are Splenetick!39 *Grub.* You are a Jack-pudding, A Pragmatick40 Spend-thrift, A Fellow that I would beat into a Powder, if I had the Law on my side. Can there come any thing of Essences, Pulvilio's,41 and Perfumes, more than the Head-Ach? Take your Wife to task, ye Blockhead, and Thrum her Jacquet42 well, she'll ne'er be good else; She's of the right Strain, I know her to a hair; and if thou wouldst be Famous, beat thy self, for thou deserv'st it richly. *Cockl.* What your froward Gall can vent on me I bear, but if you rail against my Wife *Grub.* What then? *Cockl.* Why you shall know that I am a Fighter. *Grub.* A Fool: That fair 1200*i,* a Year will shrink into a Tester,43 by next Summer, and all to be a Courtier, in the Devil's Name. *Cockl.* Well, Sir: And is not that enough? *Grub.* You Dogbolt,44' Enough! Will that Frothy Title keep firm your Credit, Sir? Will your Spindle Shanks there e'er carry you to win the Goal of Honour? They look already as they could7 scarce drag thee over the Kennel, with a Pox to you, good Mr. Courtier.., *Cockl.* Yes, Sir, I am a Courtier, and intend to be a Cherubin. Courtiers are all Cherubins and Seraphims; and I think I have some Reason. *Grub.* How, Reason! I have seen a Dapper thing more like a Courtier, set up to scare the Crows out of the Corn. *Cockl.* Ha, ha, ha, Much good may 't do your Heart, Uncle, you are merry, and I could entertain you with a Joke against your

""Splenetick"; ill-humored, irascible.

""Pragmatick"; conceited, opinionated, dogmatic.

""Pulvilio's"; a perfumed powder, used often for powdering the periwigs of the seventeenth century. See *The Injured Princess,* II, 2 (p. 19); *Massaniello, Part II,* III, 3 (p. 28); *Wonders in the Sun,* II, 1 (p. 38); *Bury-Fair,* II, 2, III, 1; *The Woman-Captain,* I, 1.

""Thrum her Jacquet"; beat her jacket, equivalent to the modern "dust her jacket".

""Tester"; a shilling of Henry VIII's reign.

""Dogbolt";a term of reproach or contempt, perhaps suggested originally by an arrow or bolt worthy only of being shot at dogs.

Countrey Life, were I so dispos'd; your Ditches and your Dunghils. I could nettle you i' faith.

Grub. Ye Jackanapes, Gadzooks! Speak a word more against the Countrey and I'll beat thee, I'll swinge thee, before thy Wife and all thy Family: I will i' faith, therefore don't provoke me! *Cockl.* Nay, Why so angry, Uncle? I pass by your Lowing of Cows, Bleating of Sheep, and your damn'd Noise of chattering Rooks in the Morning, that would not let one sleep. You see I am patient. *Grub.* Rooks! There's ne'er a Fop at Court has half their Sense, to my knowledge, No, nor their Harmony: The finest Vocal Musick in the World, this Fool calls Chattering. Ah, thou art a Dunce. I had rather hear a Rook sing than *Si Fachi.4i Cockl.* Nor do I rally on your fine Discourse, which is commonly about your Dogs and Horses; and for your part, Uncle, you have a Passion for your Wall-Ey'd Mare, exceeds the Love of Women. *Grub.* Here's an impudent Rascal, here's a Rogue, to debauch my Darling-Mare before my Face. And the Dog knows too I love her as well as I do my Wife. Why, you slanderous Villain! Now could I even weep for Madness: Sirra, leave your Prating, or provide your self a Second. Gad I'll fight for the Honour of my

Mare, sooner than for any Lady at Court by th' half.

Cockl. Nay, nay, I have done, good Uncle. *Grub.* 'Tis well you have, Sir: Wall-Ey'd Mare, you Puppy! 'Tis true she's queer of an Ogle or so: But what then? Look you into the Park, or into your Damn'd Play-house, and see what Crowds of Female Sins come thither, and then let's hear you prate. *Cockl.* But, Uncle, why are you so inveterate against the8 Court? Were you ever there? *Grub.* Not I, thank Heaven: I got down t'other day as far as 'Charing-Cross, and had like to have been choak'd at that distance. *Cockl.* Come, come, Uncle! Leave off your snarling, and ridiculous Anger, and bring your

Wife to Court. I hear she's handsome: let her not live there to be a Farmer's blowing; and be confin'd to Serge with Silver Edging; and Petticoats far coarser than my Horse-Cloath: But give her Velvets, Tissues, Pearls, and Jewels. *Grub.* Oh Lord! Oh Lord! *Cockl.* A Coach and Usher, and two running Footmen, and I will send my Wife to give her Rules. i »"Si Fachi"; Signior Fachi; perhaps an Italian singer of the time. "Fachi" may be a corruption of Faggio (1649-?) composer of *Bethsabea.* No positive identification has been made. *Grub,* 's Heart! I had rather send her to *Virginia,* and make her plant Tabaco. This Fellow's mad. *Enter* Servant. *Cockl.* Sirra, How slept your Mistress? and what Visitants are come this Morning? *Serv.* Sir, as I came out, two Lords were newly entred. *Cockl.* This is great now, do any Lords, Uncle, come to see your new Wife? *Grub.* No, Lord have Mercy upon her if they did: Heaven keep my Wife, and all my Issue Female still from their Lordships. *Cockl.* Oh, you are dull and pall'd! You have no Pallat. *Grub.* This Fellow's a Cuckold too, a rank Cuckold! I smell him: Well, God b'w'y':46 thou art a rare coxcomb, and I'll not see thy Folly any longer. When you want Money, Friend, for a new Fund of Prodigality, I suppose, I shall hear of you; but not a penny: let thy own Folly feed thee. Ownz! To be a Cuckold too, that plagues me most of all Ah you senceless Ass! Gad! I have a great mind to take the Dog cross the Face; a Cuckoldly Rogue. Gadzooks! If I stay I shall murder him. *Ex. in anger. Cockl.* A strange dull angry old Fellow this: But just such another Piece to Dirt47 was I, before my Eyes were open'd by my Wife. *Enter* Aurelia. 9

Oh, here she comes: Good morrow, Dearest.

Aur. Good morrow, my Jewel. Thou look'st well this Morning. *Cockl.* Thank thee, Sweet Heart: I have no other reason. *Aur.* I am glad on't: Now, then to my present business, which is Money. *Cockl.* Faith, I have none left. *Aur.* I hope you will not say so: nor imagine so base and low a Thought: I have none

left! Are these words fitting for a Man of Honour, and Dignity that shall be. *Cockl.* The Lord knows when: Thou hast been seven Years about it, and yet I am where I was, Child. But I know thou hast daily and nightly labour'd with thy Friends for my Advancement. 8"God b'w'y' "; good-bye. See also "Good b'we", IV, 4; and "God b'w'y," *Pills lo Purge Melancholy,* I, 313; "god-buy", *Love for Money,* I (p. 10); *The Marriage Hater Match'd,V,* 2 (p. 46); "Good buy". *Love for Money,* III, 1 (p. 28); "Good b'uye". *Pills to Purge Melancholy,* I, 5, 6; ''God b'w'e", *The Bath,* V, 3 (p. 55), *The Amorous Bigol.IV,* 1;"Godbu'y", *Henry VI, Part 1,III,*2.
T"Such another Piece to Dirt"; such another piece of dirt or clod.
Aur. Very well, Sir: And do you pop me off with this slight Answer, i' faith I have none left? i' faith you must have! *Cockl.* I must have! *Aur.* You must have. Nay, stare not, Sir; 'tis true, I must have Money: for be perswaded, if we fall now, or be but seen to shrink under our fair Beginnings, 'tis our Ruine, and then good night to all, but our Disgraces. *Cockl.* Why, where's the Hundred Pound I gave you yesterday. *Aur.* Oh that! I lost it at *Basset,* last night." *Cockl.* Then you may win it at *Basset* this morning: Why, can you think, Wife, I'll endure such Doings? Why, how the Devil could you lose all that? *Aur.* I had horrid luck, Child: Come, I'll tell thee how. Dost understand the Game, Hony? *Cockl.* Not I: I understand none of the Game: A Pox o' the Game, if this be the Fruits on't. *Aur.* Not understand it! Well, I am resolv'd I'll teach it thee. 'Tis the most Courtly, the most Grand, the most Graceful Game. And has the finest Terms in't that e'er were heard: As thus now! First, there's the *Fasse,* then the *Alpieu,* or *Paroli,* the *Sept* 6s *le10 va, Quinze. & le va, Trent. & le va, Sonica,* nay sometimes the *Soisant le va. Cockl. Soisant,* and the Devil and all: Why this is Conjuring, Confound it What a damn'd Game's here to lose a 100 *I.* at! *Aur.* I tell thee, Child, I had the worst Luck in the Whole World: I lost a *Sept & le va* upon an Eight King. *Cockl.* Gadzooks! And

wilt lose a King's Revenue at this rate. This is a Game that's fit for none but Kings and Queens, to play at, for ought that I see. *Aur.* Ay. 'Tis a Royal Game, indeed; but prithee do but observe my ill Fortune! I was *Fass'd* every Card, I set, or when I drew a lucky one it did not go. I had lost seven Kings before, and made a *Sept & le va* upon an Eight: When to see the Prodigy of ill Luck, A Citt, a strange Punt,48 that sat next me, a pert forward pushing Fellow follow'd the winning Knaves, and won a *Quinze &f le va* before ever I could make an *Alpieu:* But what vext me most intolerably was to see my Fat Lady Thump Cushion make *Paroli,* and then a *Sept & le va* upon the same Card, and when I lost my King four times in one Deal, she, upon a filthy Knave, every time won *Sonicd.*
""Punt"; one who punts, or lays a stake against the bank.
Cockl. The Devil take my Lady's *Sonica,* and My Lord's too; What a Noise is here with 'em? *Aur.* I think never poor Punt was so Embarrass'd: but I have done: Come, now what say'st thou to this Money? I'll soon fetch up my Losses, Sweet Heart: I must have, let me see 500 *I.* by to morrow night: Nay, ne'er flinch at it; 'Tis for thy Preferment, thou know'st. *Cockl* Nay, faith, I know not what to say to 't: 'tis such a Devillish hard World, that my Tennants write me word they are all running away. The last 50 *I.* I laid down for your tall Cousin's Horse and Equipage: He that's going to be an Officer; And I han't a ragg more left as I am a true Courtier. *Aur.* Hark you, Sir, have you no Land in the Country? *Cockl.* Why yes, but I had forgot that. *Aur.* It must be remembred: some of it must fetch this Money: Thou shalt not lose Preferment, my Dear, for the sake of a few dirty Acres; Especially when, by my means, the Sun of Honour is just going to break out upon thee. Dost hear, Child?11 This Land must be in *London* by to morrow Night. *Cockl.* Well, well, if it must, it must: What, 300 Acres will serve the Turn? Hum! *Aur.* 'Twill do very well: And now you speak like a Man, and like a Courtier that shall be great, and

suddenly; I have said it: Well, adieu! You'll dispatch; I must go get the *Basset-Cards* ready; for I expect my Lord. 's Company, and all the Punts here after Dinner: Mr. *Winnall* Taillies, and I am to be his Croupier: If I want Money I'll make shift to borrow out of my Lord's Fobb. *Cockl.* Well, well, prithee borrow what thou wilt out of my Lord's Fobb. Go, leave me a little. *Aur.* Adieu, Child, Adieu, my Pretious. *Claps his Cheek, & ex. Cockl.* 'Tis a good natur'd ingenious Devil; and does so bustle about the Courtiers to make me great, and is so caress'd by this Lord, and by t'other Knight, that 'twould do ones Heart good to see her: that's the truth on't, she must have this Money; but how to make this Sale handsomely now, let me see! Gad, I am almost afraid to tell my Man *Toby* on 't, 'twill break the poor Fellow's Heart, to hear that I am going to sell: but hang't, it must be done, and there's no more to be said. Who's within there? *Toby. Enter* Toby. *Tob.* Did you call, Sir? *Cockl.* Ay, honest Toby, I would have you run presently to the *Exchange,* and there to Sir *John Cutchinele,* the Merchant, offer 300 Acres of my Land: Why dost thou stare so? *Tob.* Why faith, Sir, see how strangely things will happen, I dream't last night that you were in *Bedlam,* and now my Dream is out. *Cockl.* Oh spare your Wit, good *Toby,* for your Business, Tell him, d'ye hear? 'Tis choice and fertil, and ask upon 't 500 /. *Tob.* Sir, do not do this; pray take my Cap and consider a little: This honest Land, that you are parting with, hath been true to you, and done you loyal Service. *Cockl.* As'twas in Duty bound: But whatever happens, my 12 Wife must not want Money: for if she do, either she or her Friends, I may whistle for Preferment. Go, go, begone, I say, and when you come back look for me in the Presence. *Exit* Cockl. *Tob.* ,'Tis this damn'd Wife that is the Cause of all, and this, Oh this is the dear Marriage Blessing; Man is the Shuttle, and his Wife the Loom; and so they weave themselves into a Knot, that when 'tis done, they'd hang themselves to unty: I'll to his Uncle presently, and tell him all, perhaps, 'twill stop his Journey, and make him come and rail, and beat my Mistress: I'd give my Wages to see't done handsomely: I'll whet him I am resolved. *Exit.* SCENE III. *Grub's* House. *Enter* Grub.

Grub. There's no good to be done upon this Fool, my Kinsman, so I'll into the Country, presently, and leave him to the Fool's

Whip, Misery. Let me see I may recover 20 Miles to night.

Ho! Within there Some body call a *Barber;* I'll be shav'd first, however: I shall ride so much the lighter. Call a *Barber,* there.

Enter Lyonel.

How now! Who have we here?

Lyon. Sir, I have follow'd you in here. *Grub.* So methinks, Sir. *Lyon.* 'Pray what may I call your Name? *Grub.* My Name? Why my Name is *Grub,* Sir.

Lyon. Grub! right: you are a *Mohometan.*

Grub. The Devil I am.

Lyon. I know it; but am secret: Of what Faction are you? What Party join you with? *Grub.* Prithee, I know no Factions, nor Parties, not I: I am a plain Countrey Gentleman, and am just going out of Town.13J What, a Devil, does the Man mean? *Lyon.* Then wear this Cross of White, and where you see the like, they are my Friends: observe 'em well, the Time is dangerous. *Grub.* I'll wear none of your Cross, not I: I know not what you mean. *Lyon.* Not know my meaning! you may spare your Cunning, Sir, you can pick nothing out of this: this Cross is nothing but a Cross, a very Cross: plain, without Spell or Witch craft; search it; you may suspect Poison, Powder, or Wild-fire; but you are mistaken. *Grub.* Well, Sir, I see 'tis a plain Cross, what then? What a Plague, is this Fellow? *Lyon.* Then do your worst: I care not. Tell the King, as I am sure you will, of all my Actions: and so God save His Majesty. This is no Treason.-*Exit.* *Grub.* Tell the King! What a strange, odd, whimsical Rogue is this! But this Town is full of nothing else: Nothing but Fools and Madmen throng the streets. I'll get out on't as soon as I can. Come, where's the Barber? *Enter* Barber. *Barber.* Here, here, Ready, Sir.

Grub. Come, come, away with't quickly: but d'ye hear, Sirra?" Ha'n't you got the Itch now, which your Town-Breeding would complement upon my Face? Let's see your Fingers.

Barber *lathers him. Barb.* Oh clear, clear, as a Sucking Infant, Sir. *Grub.* A smooth-fac'd Rogue: Sirra, you are a Whore-Master. *Barb.* A little given that way, Sir; but I want Money. *Grub.* Alas, poor Fellow! 'tis great pity, faith. *Claps his CheekBarb.* If I were a great Man, Sir.

Grub. You would keep a Whore, and starve your Wife, as they do. *Barb.* Yes, Sir. *Grub.* Very well: Ha, ha, ha. I have not met with a more14J honest Fellow: a good handsome, sleek Rascal too! How many Bastards have you, Friend? *Claps his Cheek. Barb.* Not very many, Sir. I have only two at Nurse, and another a coming Will your Worship be pleased to give me an old Shirt? *Grub.* No, you Dog; I have a Kid of my own in the Countrey, that must be serv'd first. But, my bonny Shaver, you get your Living honestly, I hope? You are not given to Thieving? *Barb.* To no Burglaries, Sir, they are troublesome; But for the neat Conveyance of a Hand into a Pocket, or so. *Grub.* Hum! 'Tis as I said. Thieves, Fools and Madmen overrun this plaguy Town Would I were well a Horse-back. *Enter* Toby. *Tob.* Oh Sir, undone, undone, all lost, ruin'd! *Grub.* How now? What's the Matter? What is there a Fire? ha! Who's there, *Toby? Tob.* Ay, Ay, Sir, poor *Toby,* undone, utterly undone. *Grub.* Be undone, and be hang'd! what, a Devil, dost fright me about it?—.—— Pox I thought the Town had been a Fire. *Tob.* Sir, If ever you had any Respect for the Antient Family of the *Cockle-brains,* to which that of the *Grubs* is Worshipfully join'd, turn back to our House, and beat my Mistress. *Grub.* Prithee, beat her self, and be hang'd, if thou hast a mind to't. *Tob.* 's Bud.49 wTould I might, I'd strap her with a Vengeance— Besides my Master is undone, unless you go, Sir. *Grub.* I'll not come near him, an extravagant Rascal, he has not a peny of Money; and I warrant his Land will be going e'er long. *Tob.* 'Tis going, Sir, 'tis

going now. *Grub.* What's that? Is he going to Mortgage? *Tob.* To sell, Sir, to sell 300 Acres are doom'd this night,15 unless you stop it, Sir. *Grub.* Give me my Hat and Gloves. *Starts off his Chair. Barb.* What is't you mean, Sir? *Grub.* 300 Acres! Oh intolerable Rogue! I'll be with him: Gadzooks! *Barb.* Why, Sir, your Beard is not half off. *Grub.* Pox o' my Beard. I'll go with half a Nose to save 300

's Bud"; the same as "'s bodikins," or "God's bodikins." "Bodikin" is an obsolete diminutive of "body." For "'s bud," see *MadamFickle,* 1,1. (N.E.D.) Cf. *A Fool's Preferment.* IV. 2 J (p. 65); V, 1 (p. 87), and elsewhere.

Acres. Come along, *Toby* Gad I'll thrash him into Stubble, but I'll change him, I am resolv'd on't. *Exit. Tob.* Good Luck be with thee, I ne'er had till now Half so much cause to bid God speed the Plough. *Exit.* ACT II. SCENE I.

A Room in Cocklebrain's House.

Discovers the Basset-Table;60*Aurelia, Clermont, Longoville, Bewford, and other Gentlemen and Ladies sitting round at Play,* Winnall *is dealing; several are standing by, and others walking about; Acting the several Humours of Winners and Losers. Enter* Sharpe and Flea-flint. *Sharpe.* Well! What Times, *Flea-flint?* What purchace to night? What Rate bears Money? Hah! *Flea.* Pox, not worth a Man's trouble: I have lent but Three Eight and forties61 yet.. *Sharp.* But you'll draw so many Fifties, I hope! *Flea.* Yes, certainly, I should hardly wait here else: there's no Pawn stirring neither; Not so much as a Table-Diamond,52 nor my Lady's Locket, the Devil's in't! I think, this Trade will hardly find a Man Salt to his Radishes; Prithee, what News about Town, *Ned? Sharp.* Why young *Lyonel,* they say, is mad.

Flea. Mad! Prithee for what?

Sharp. It seems the King once parted him and his Mistress,16 who was a rich Orphan, intending to bestow her on his Favourite; Grief for which Chance and her Inconstancy has since that time much distracted him, and now in his mad Fit, he conceits the King designs to hang him, and trap him speaking Treason. *Flea.* Alas, poor *Lyonel!* Mad! and mad for Love too! Thou art a Miracle indeed. *Enter Lady* Lost-all. *Sharp.* What Lady's that? *Flea.* Sir *Jasper Lost-all* 's Lady, one that's so much in Love "*Discovers the* Basset-Table"; cf. *The Bath,* IV, 1, Shirley's *Gamester,* III, 4; and see Forsythe, *The Relations of Shirley's Plays to the Elizabethan Drama,* p. 363.

'l"Eight and forties"; a loan of eight and forty pounds, fifty to be repaid (?).

""Table-Diamond"; a diamond cut with a table or large flat surface surrounded by small facets; especially a thin diamond so cut having a flat under surface *(N. E. D.).* See *Sir Martin Marall,* IV, 2.

with her Coach63 that she's hardly ever out on't: prithee let's observe 'em; I find, by his fidgetting about, the Bank has script him. *Lady.* Well, Sir *Jasper,* I have told you of this a hundred times, pray come away now, I find your Money's all gone, by that sheepish Look of yours. D'ye hear? Pray let some body order my Coach to come to the Door. You'll never leave this *Basset, Sir Jasper.* till you have ruin'd me. My Coach and Horses there, quickly. Come, I protest, I'm quite tir'd with coming up Stairs. *To a Footman.*

Sir *Jasp.* Gad, Madam, to tell you the truth, I have lost your Coach and Horses since you went.

Lady. Lost my Coach and Horses!

Sir *Jasp.* Yes, faith, you must e'en beat home upon the Hoof, there's no Remedy? *Lady.* Why, Thou Monster! thou darest not, sure, put such an

Affront upon a Woman of my Quality; one that

Sir *Jasp.* One that shall scold with any Woman of Quality in Town, I'll say that for her, but I'll not stay to hear more on't. *Exit. Lady.* Oh intolerable! Was there ever such a Brute seen! that whilst I was paying an innocent Visit to my Cousin *Doll Feetly* here in the House, could have the Barbarity to lose my dear Coach and Horses, without which, alas! what is a Lady? How can a Lady subsist without her Coach and Horses? A Husband! A Clown; A Beast: one I married and got Knighted to have

Comfort of him, and now the Brute, to reward me, has lost my dear Coach and17 Horses at filthy *Basset,* the Devil take him, how does the Monster think, a Lady dress'd in a Gown, as I am, shall foot it Home now? j *Takes up her Train, & discovers her Stock*

I ings down, Shoes tatter'd, 6s Exit.

Ha, ha, ha, ha, this was pleasant enough.

Win. Tre winns, *Six* loses, *Knave* winns, *Ten* loses, *Eight* winns

Madam, you lose the *King. to* Aurelia.

Aurelia and Clermont *rise. Aur.* A Curse on all ill Luck; *Fass'd* so many times, a *Paroli, Sept,* and *Quinze & le va* lost in a Moment. *Tearing the Cards. Cler.* Plgue on't, I am stript too, and this is all the Treasure I have left in this World. *Kissing her Hand. Aur.* Well, Sir, do not you complain till you lose that Treasure, I shall wheedle my Husband and get Flush again within few hours, and then, Sir, perhaps you may hear from me; in the mean time

""Coach"; an anachronism, as coaches were not known in England in the time of Henry IV. Cf. Ill, 4.

Flea.

Sharp.

Good Morrow, 'tis almost Sun-rising, I'le to Bed now. *Ex. smiling. Cler.* She gives me the *Ouglebi* to follow her. Oh this damn'd Itch of Play, yet cannot I give over, if I were to be hang'd. *Fleaflint,* Prithee come hither.

Flea. What's your Pleasure, Sir? *Cler.* Thou know'st, I have always been thy Friend, and given thee *BarrattoSi* freely, Prithee lend me another Eight and forty upon Honour. *Flea.* Not without a Pawn, Sir, I have sworn the contrary.

Cler. As I am a Man of Honour.

Flea. As I am a Man of Honour, Sir, I must not break my_Oath. *Cler.* Thou wilt not do me this Courtesie then. *Flea.* I cannot, Sir, what, would you have me damn my self for a

Trifle: if you have e're a Pawn?

Cler. I'le give thee Bond and Judgment. *Flea.* Pish, Paper, Paper, I'le do nothing without a Pawn, I tell ye. *Cler.* Well, come hither, thou shalt have a Pawn. *Flea.* Where, what is't?

Cler. And such a Pawn, as never was propos'd to Man before. thou saw'st that Lady that went out? *Flea.* Well, Sir, and what of her? 18 *Cler.* She is my Mistress, and the dearest Jewel that e're unlucky

Gamester pawn'd before: One, that I value equal with my Life; yet such a Witchery there is in Play, that for this Money, I'le contrive it so, that thou shalt be Caress'd instead of me, till I return what's lent.

Flea. This I confess is the strangest Pawn I ever heard of, but I lend no Money upon Faces, Sir, I must beg your Pardon: However I shall make bold to tell the Lady, what a Faithful Spark she has. *Aside. Clerm.* Dog, Rook, Rascal! What a Slave was I to offer such an inestimable Treasure! Sirra, get you gone, or I'll cut your Pate. *Flea.* Ay, Ay; Rail, rail! Ha, ha, ha. *Ex.* Flea-flint.

Longoville *and* Bewford *rise. Long.* Clear'd stript: by this Light, not a Rag left.) *tears the Bew.* Ha, ha, ha, I won two Hundred Guineas: f *Cards.* What's the matter, *Jack?*

""Ogle"; ogle (not listed in *N.E. D.*) K"Barrato" from the Italian "baratto,"kbarter'exchange. Itperhaps means interest here.

Cler. Nothing, nothing, a Pox on him, come, Prithee let's go, and beat up the Rogues at *theBlue-Posts,M* for a quart of burnt Sherry. *Long.* With all my heart, a Plague of this damn'd Basset-Table. *Exeunt. Enter* Cocklebrain, Grub, *and* Toby. *Tob.* Do but see, Sir, they're at it still, at this time o' th' Morning. *Grub.* Oons speak to 'em, souse in upon 'em, Nephew. *Cockl.* No, pray, Uncle, do you, for my part I'm asham'd. *Grub.* Gad, and so I will, what's here to do, what a Pox de'e make an Ordinary of my Nephew's House? A Bawdy-House were a better Name by the half, nothing but Cheating, and Gaming, and Roaring, and Tearing, Gad-sookers, 'tis past Suffering, and as I am his Friend, and Uncle *Sharp.* How now, who have we here, Sir, will you venture Fifty Pieces, here's a Stool. *Grub.* And there 'tis at your Head, Dogbolt. Draw, Nephew, draw, *Toby,* draw, draw, we'le *Basset* the Rogues. *Enter*

Lyonel, *with a Helmet on, and Sword drawn.* 19 *Lyon.* What's here, Treason going forward, I'le make one against ye, Faith. *(First attacks* Grub, *and has him down, then 1 throws the Cards about, and falls upon the Gamesters, till* Grub *rises, and they then beat* Lyonel *and all out.* Grub. So, so, now lock the Door upon 'm *Toby*

Toby *locks the Door.* Cockl. Bravely fought, i'faith, why, Uncle, you beat the Madman too, you fought like *Scanderbegf* you are not hurt, I hope *Grub.* No, hang 'em, they are all *Polltroons*, Rogues that have no more Souls in 'em than so many Fleas, therefore hear me once more, and mark me well: If thou dost not instantly break this damn'd Custom, and make thy Wife know her self, 111 desert thee for ever, never see thy Face, but leave thee to ensuing Rags and Poverty, a thing not worthy for the Dogs to piss upon *Tob.* Ne're think to see honest *Toby* again neither, I'me too proud of my Parts, to serve a Beggar, I thank ye.

Cockle. Do you really think my Wife deceives me then? *Grub.* 'sbud, think it, 'tis past thinking, for I know it. ""Blue-Posts"; a tavern in Spring Gardens, later notorious as the rendezvous of the conspirators in the assassination plot of February, 1696, asainst William III. See *Love's Last Shift,* I, 1. ""Scanderbeg"; Iskender Bey, national hero of the Albanians; born 1403, died 1467. See *Madam Fickle. Ill,* 1 (p. 27); *The Campaigners, 111,* 1 (p. 29); *Massaniello, Part I,* II, 1 (p. 18), *The Woman-Captain,* II, 2; *Sir Martin Mar-all,* IV, 1. V, 1, 3; and Forsythe, *The Relations of Shirley's Plays to the Elizabethan Drama,* p. 235. *Tob.* Sir, she came Home at three a Clock yesterday Morning, and was led up Stairs between two Thundring Whoremasters, one had a great Patch on 's Nose, you may guess by what, and there they were two Hours in her Chamber: What they did there, the Lord knows. *Cockle.* Tis likely, they were plotting my Preferment. *Grub.* Plotting to make thee a Cuckold, that's your Preferment. *Tob.* And a Beggar most certainly. *Grub.* For she knows no end in Lavishing. *Tob.* And for Eating

and Drinking, she's the very Devil, her Belly is ameer Parson's Barn, all your Tenants pay Tyth to 't,and yet 'tis never satisfyed. *Cockl.* The Truth is, she has been given to take a Cup, of late. *Grub.* A Cup, 'ds heart I have seen her as Maudlin as a Midwife at a Crying out. *Tob.* And when she's in her Beer, she's wondrous Chast; No20 doubt. *Grub.* Come, come, once more I say send for her, for my Part, I shall have no Patience if I see her: send for her I say, and pack her into the Country, instantly, or never see my Face more. *Cockl.* Well, Sir, your Hearty Love, and Reasons have prevail'd, it shall be so. *Grub.* It shall? *Cockl.* Yes, Sir, it shall be so. *Grub.* Why, that's well said, Gad, Fle slap thee down another Hundred Pounds in my Will for this, and let Wives know their Duty. *Cockl.* She has lost a Plaguey deal of Mony lately, at this damn'd *Basset,* that's the Truth on 't. *Grub.* A Mint, a Mint, the Devil and all, I know it, for 'tis a greater Cheat, than the *Lottery*; 'tis just like giving a man twenty Pounds, to let you lose 100. *Cockl.* But she shall have no more, Uncle. *Grub.* Thou 'rt in the right, Boy, it makes 'em Wild and Wanton. I make my young Jade at home leap at a Crook'd Nine-pence: give a Wife Money, give her a Pudding. *Cockl.* Mine has had the *Indies. Grub.* Ay, *Jacky,* thou hadst better have sent her thither by Half, take heed for the future, now hold fast, and prosper, I'll presently take Horse, and tell thy Tenants such a Story; this will be joyful News at *Plowden,* farewel, good *Jacky,* be but resolute, and then the Devil, I mean, thy Wife will have no Power over thee. *Tob.* Blessings go along with ye, Sir, you have made me a New-Man too. *Grub.* Farewel, Honest *To.* I shall see thee in the Country shortly, now little *To.* where we'le crack a Flagon, and roast Apples, ye Rogue. Farewell. Nephew, God-b'w'y.' To, your most humble Servant, good Nephew Come, my Horse, my

Horse there. *Exit* Grub.

Cockl. Good Journey to'e, Sir, I'll be with ye to Morrow. *Tob.* Oons I could leap for Joy, this is the happiest Day.

Cockl. Go, *Toby,* and call your Mistress. 21 *Tob.* But shall she not prevail, Sir, and out-talk ye as she us'd to do? For you know she has a plaguy Tongue. *Cockl.* I'll not hear her, but rail at her till I am ten Miles off. *Tob.* If you are forty, so much the better, Sir, for she's so shrill, that, if the Wind sit right, she'll sound from hence to *Barnet. Cockl.* 'Go, go, call her hither. *Tob.* I could leap out of my Skin, my Heart's so light, a Plague o' this stinking Town! now we shall get a little Air, and go a Hunting, and a Fishing agen. *Exit. Cockl.* Why, what a thing was I, that such a Creature as a Wife could rule me? Do not I know that Woman first was made for

Man's Diversion: she shall know now, a thing that few do,

She has a Husband that can govern her.

Enter Toby *hastily.* Tob. She's coming, Sir, and in a Plaguy Fret. Stand upon your Guard, Sir. *Enter* Aurelia. *Aur.* What Planet reigns? or what mad Whimsey have you now i' th' Head, that makes you call me from my Rest, that know I have not been in Bed all Night? *Cockl.* Oh, you shall go to Bed betimes hereafter, and shall be rais'd again at thrifty Hours. *Aur.* What does he mean! *Cockl.* I'll have no more of your Court Tricks, your Honours, your Offices, and all your large Preferments I'll be content to lose: for, to be plain w'ye,

I now at last begin to small a Rat,

And understand too late what you'd be at.

Aur. The Man is mad sure! *Cockl.* The Woman would have him so; but it shall be a Country Madness then, for I'll be gone this Morning. *Aur.* Very fine; and who's Advice is this, Sir, I beseech ye,22 your Swabber *Toby's? Tob.* I shall have my Head broke, I see by her Looks. *Cockl.* No one's Advice, good Wife, but my own Reason; therefore make ready. *Aur.* Sir, I hope you'll stay till the next Ball be past however. *Cockl.* Not I: I have been Balling on't too long, you have kept me here these seven Years a Balling, treatng your Friends, and wasting all my Substance in Riot and Fine Cloaths, which was the way you told me to be preferr'd: but I find no such matter, therefore make ready, and in that Gown which you came first to Town in, your Grogram-Safe-guard and Hood suitable. Thus on a double Gelding shall you amble, and my Man *Toby* shall be set before ye. *Tob.* Hem, hem, well said, Old Stiff Rump, i' faith, I begin to take Heart a little. *Aur.* And will you go then in earnest? *Cockl.* Yes faith will I, and how dare you oppose my Will and Pleasure? Was not the Man ordain'd to rule his Wife? *Aur.* True, Sir, but where the Man does miss his way, it is the Woman's part to set him right; so Fathers have a right to guide their Sons in all their Courses, yet you oft have seen poor little children that have both their Eyes lead their blind Fathers. *Cockl.* She has a Plaguy Wit. *Tob.* A devillish one, Sir, therefore take care of her, she'll talk ye mad else. *Cockl.* Come, come, you're but a little piece of Man. *Aur.* But such a Piece as being taken away, what would Man do? The fairest, tallest Ship that ever sail'd, is by a little Piece of the same Wood steer'd right and turn'd about. *Cockl.* Ay, that's all one, you shall steer me no longer; I'll keep my Rudder in my own hand now. *Tob.* Well said agen i'gad, a Plague, how the Jade lears now! *Aside. Aur.* 'Tis your Clownish Uncle, I know, that hath put this into your Head, who is an Enemy to your Preferment, because I should not take place of his Wife; Come, by this Kiss, Sweet Heart, thou shalt not go. *Cockl.* By this other Kiss, Sweet-heart, I will, and therefore 23 on with your Trinkets; I know your Tricks. And if Preferment falls e're you are ready, 'tis welcome, else farewel to Court, i' Faith. *Aur.* Well, Sir, since you are resolv'd, I must obey. *Cockl.* You must, therefore about it. *Tob.* Ay, ay, you must, you must, there's no more to be said. *Cockl.* Go, go, get ready. Women are pleasant things when once a Man begins to know himself. *Aur.* But, hark ye, Sir, because you use me, thus, though I did look for present Honour this Morning for ye and at such an Hour, yet if it does not come e're I am ready, which I will be the sooner, lest it should,

when I am once set on a Countrey Life, not all the Power of Earth shall alter me, not all your Prayers, or Threats shall make me speak the least Word to my Honourable Friends, to do you any Grace. *Cockl.* With all my Heart. *Aur.* And never more hope to be Honourable *Cockl.* Not I, I have been tyr'd with hoping, if that be Court Preferment, I have enough on't. *Aur.* Nor to live greatly, you shall be so far from the Name of Honour, that you shall never see a Lord again. *Cockl.* Why, what care I, if you had never seen one, I think your Honour had been ne're the worse for't. *Aur.* But amongst Sheep and Oxen you shall live at home bespotted with your own lov'd Dirt, in nasty Cloaths, as you were us'd to do, and, to oblige you, I will live so too. *Cockl.* And 'twill become ye well, come, the Day wears, therefore make hast, it shall be my Care to see your Stuff pack'd up *Toby* come. *Exit* Cockle. *Tob.* Ay, ay, Sir, here am I, Lord, how she looks now! *Ex. Aur.* It shall be my Care to gull you, my wise Husband. You shall stay, and more than that intreat me too, you shall have Honours presently. Who's there? *Mar.* Madam. *Aur.* Prithee, bring hither Pen, Ink, and Paper, quickly. *Mar.* 'Tis ready, Madam what's the Matter? *Aur.* Your Master will not stay in Town, he says, unless Pre ferment fall within an Hour. *Sits down, and writes. Mar.* Let him command one of the City Gates, the *Mobile?* are mutinying, or get him made a Constable, and walk the Rounds at Midnight, to catch Drunkards, any thing that has Hurry in't will please him. *Aur.* No, no, I have it for him, I have been prepar'd a good while for this Occasion: and when the World shall see what I have done, Let it not move the Spleen of any Wife, to see me make an Asse of my dear Husband. If they are Just, and know well how to use a Woman, then it were a Sin to wrong 'em, but when they grow conceited of themselves, and 111 performers, then shew 'em no Mercy. Here, Carry this Letter to young *Clermont,* and bid him and his Friends come hither instantly, and do as I have order'd there. *Mar.* It shall be done, Madam. A Duce take him, I warrant he intends to

pack us into the Country, to weed his Barley, or churn his Butter; but we'll churn him, and make Butter of his Brains first, here's that will fit him. *Exit. Aur.* In the mean time, I'le go and dress my self, In all the Country Cloaths, I us'd before, Not to be gone, but make the Mirth the more. *Ex.* Aurelia.

Re-enter Cockle-brain, *and* Toby, *laden with*

Riding Equipage.

Cockl. Is all pack'd up, *Toby? Tob.* All, all, Sir, there is no Tumbler runs through his Hoop, with more dexterity, than I about this Business, 'tis a Day, that I have long'd to see. *Cockl.* Come, where's my Boots? *Sits down. Tob.* Here, here, Sir, and now y' are a made man. *Cockl.* Ay, *Toby,* now thou shalt know, I can command my25 Wife. *Tob.* I am glad to see it, Sir. *Cockle.* I do not love always to be made a Puppy, *Toby. Tob.* No, Sir, but yet methinks your Worship does not look right like a Country Gentleman. *Cockl.* I will presently; give me my tother Hat *Tob.* Here, Sir. *Cockl.* So, now my Jerkin. ""Mobile"; a shortened form of *Mobile Valgus*—the excitable crowd.—later contracted into the modern "mob." See *The Roundheads,* V, 5; *The City Heiress,* III, 1; *The Younger Brother.* Ill, 3; *Bury-Fair,* II, 2; *The Woman-Captain,* II, 1. "Mob" occurs in the *dramatis persona;* of both *Love for Money* and *Massaniello, Part 1,* by D'Urfey.

Tob. Yes, Sir. *Cockl.* On with it, *Toby,* thou and I will live so finely in the Countrey, *Toby,* and have such pleasant Walks into the Woods, and then bring home Riding-Rods and Walking Staves. *Tob.* And I will carry 'em, Sir, and sturdy Sticks for the Children. *Cockl.* So thou shalt, and thou shalt do all, oversee my Workfolks, and at the Weeks End pay 'em all their Wages. *Tob.* Yes, Sir, if your Worship gives me Money. *Cockl.* Thou shalt eat Money, Man. *Tob.* Beef, Beef, and 't like your Worship: as for eating of Money, let that alone. *Cockl.* Give me my Trowzes, and I will make my Wife, thy Mistress, look to her Dairy well, and to her Landrey, that we may have our Linnen clean on *Sundays.*

Tob. And *Holydays,* Sir. *Cockl.* Ay, and e'er we walk about the Grounds provide our Breakfast, or she shall smoak; I'll make her a good Houswife; she now shall make no Journey to her Sisters, but live at home and feed her Poultrey fat, and see her Maids in Bed before her, and lock all the Doors. *Tob.* Rare, rare, Sir, Why, this will be a Life for King and Queens. *Cockl.* Come, give me my Buff-Belt, and Hanger.

Tob. 'Tis done, Sir.

Cockl. So, this is as it should be; now, my Gloves. *Tob.* Here they are, Sir. *Cockl.* A Riding-Rod, now, Come. *Tob.* There's nothing wanting, Sir. *Cockl.* So, so, How dost thou like me now, hah? 26 *Tob.* Exceeding well, Sir; Now your Worship looks just like-your self; A Man of Means and Credit; so did your wise and famous Ancestors ride up and down to Fairs to cheapen Cattle. *Cockl.* Go, hasten your Mistress, and make ready, I long to be on Horse-back. *Tob.* I'll be ready in a Twinkling, Sir; never was Man so jocund; 'ds heart, I could dance all the way. *Ex. Toby. Ent.* Clermont *and* Foot-man. *Cler.* Who's that? Who's that, Friend? *Foot.* I know not, Sir, I think it is my Master. *Cler.* Who, he that walks in Gray, Whisking his Riding-Rod? *Foot.* Yes, Sir, 'tis he. *Cler.* 'Tis he indeed, and at all Points prepar'd for his new Journey: Sirrah, when I wink upon ye, run out and tell the Gent, below, 'tis time. *Foot.* I will, Sir. *Cler.* Mr. *Cockle-brain,* Good Morrow t'ye. *Cockl.* The same to you, Sir, this is one of my Wife's Court Friends; how simply he looks now, to see me in this Dress,: My Wife's within, Sir, but she's busie. *Cler.* As she pleases, Sir; My Business is now with you. *Cockl.* With me, Sir! Your Pleasure? *Cler.* 'Tis reported, Sir, I know not whether by some Enemy, malitiously,-that envies your great Merit, and wou'd be ready to sow Discontents between his Majesty and you; or truly, which on my Faith I would be sorry for, that you intend in haste to leave the Court. *Cockl.* Faith, Sir, within this half Hour. *Toby. Tob. within.* Sir. *Cockl.* Is my Wife ready? *Tob. within.* Presently, Sir. *Cler.* But, Sir, I must needs tell you, as a Friend,

you should have taken your Journey privater; for 'tis already blaz'd about the Court. *Cockl.* Why, Sir, I hope 'tis no Treason, is't? *Cler.* 'Tis true, Sir; but 'tis grown the common Talk: there's27 no News else, in Town; and in the Presence, all the Nobility and Gentry have nothing in their Mouths, but only this, That Mr. *Cockle-brain,* that Noble Courtier, is now departing hence: Every man's Face looks ghastly on his Fellows; such a Sadness, before this day, I ne'er beheld at Court; Mens Hearts begin to fail 'em, when they hear it. *Cockl.* Sir, I had rather all their Hearts should fail 'em, than I stay here until my Purse fail me. *Cler.* But yet you are a Subject; and beware, I charge you, by the Love I bear to you, how you do venture rashly on a Course to make your Soveraign jealous of your Deeds.

For Princes Jealousies, where they love most,

 Are quickly found, butthey are hardly lost.

Cockl. Sir, I know not what you mean by this! All the Love that I have found at Court, is.They have let me spend my Money there. *Cler.* Have I not still profess'd my self your Friend? *Cockl.* Yes, yes. You have all profess'd, but you ne'er prov'd so yet. *Cler.* Now, Sir, I will then; because I see you are wise, and give you thus much light into a Business, that came to me just now. Be resolute, stand stiffly to it, that you will be gone, and presently. *Cockl.* Troth, Tis what I intend. *Cler.* And, by this Light, you may be what you will. Will you be secret, Sir? *Cockl.* Ay. What's the matter?

Cler. The King does fear you.

Cockl. Sir!.

Cler. And is now in Council about you.

Cockl. About me!

Cler. About you, Sir, I tell you; you will find he is in Council about you: his Councellours have told him all the Truth. *Cockl.* What Truth have they told him? *Cler.* Why, Sir, that which now he knows too well. *Cockl.* Too well! Prithee what is't? If any Rogue has sworn Treason against me now, I am in a fine Condition! *Aside. Cler.* That you have follow'd him these seven Years,

with a28 great Train, and though he has not grac'd ye, yet you have div'd into the Hearts of thousands with Liberality and Noble Carriage: And if you should depart hence unpreferr'd, all discontented and seditious Spirits would flock to you, and thrust you into Action; with whose Help and your Tenants, if you were so dispos'd, who does know, how great a Part of this yet Peaceful Realm, you might make desolate: But when the King heard this! *Cockl.* What said he? *Cler.* He sneez'd, and shook, as never Monarch shook'd before,-and to be short, you may be what you will: but be not Ambitious, Sir, sit down with moderate Honours, lest you make your self more fear'd. *Cockl.* I know not what to think of this: his Looks cire very serious. *Cler.* The Gudgeon69 bites. Oh, here comes *Longoville. Enter* Longoville. *Long.* Where's Mr. *Cockle-brain?*

""Gudgeon"; a kind of small fish, the name of which was often applied to credulous and easily deceived persons.

Cler. There, Sir, he stands: would you ought with him?

Long. I should hardly sweat thus else. Good Morrow, Sir.

Cockl. With all my heart, Sir.

Long. His Majesty does recommend himself most kindly to you, Sir. *Cockle.* His Majesty? *Long.* Yes, Sir, and has, by me, sent you this Favour, kneel down, and rise a Knight. *Cockl.* A Knight, Sir? *Long.* A Knight, Sir, and he does farther request you, not to leave the Court so soon; for though your former Merits were neglected, after this time, there shall no Office fall, but you shall stand fair for 't as any Man. *Cler.* What think you now, Sir? Hark you, a Word in your Ear: if you yield yet you are a Novice. *Cockl.* Do you think so? *Softly aside. Cler.* Most certainly, therefore be resolute. *Cockl.* I understand you; a Knight, let me see; a Knight.29 Sir *John Cockle-brain!* No: it won't do. Besides, I have known a Cheese-monger a Knight; a hundred Sniveling, addle-headed Citizens for Cheating, knighted: and Pimps and Cuckolds innumerable: No, no; I must go, I must desire his Majesty to excuse me. *Long.* I'll bear your Knightly

Words straight to the King, and send his Princely Answer back again. 'Ex. Longo. Cler. Very well done, Sir, stand out stiffly, a while, 'twill be the better: I know there is a Tide of Honours coming. Cockle. But with my stiff Standing, if I should lose my Knighthood, I should wish I had been more limber. Cler. Oh, never fear, Sir, 'tis impossible: Hark, there's a Noise below: 's Death, here's my Lord what de'e call him: pull down your Hat over your Eyes, look Grave and Sullen. So; so. Enter Bewford. Bew. Where is this new made Knight?

Cockl. Hem, hem; who's that? here I am.

Bew. Let me embrace you first within my Arms: then call you Lord. The King will have it so: who does intreat your Lordship, to remember his Message, sent to you by Longoville. Cler. If you are sneaking, and dare mount no higher, you may yield now. I know what I wou'd do. Cockl. Peace, he observes us. A Lord, Hum, to be Lord Cocklebrain! Pox, I know a Crook-back'd Fidler call'd a Lord: No, no, this is too light too. Besides I have been sick of a Lord, ever since I met my Lord Mayor t'other Day, ty'd to his Horse, and with a great Brass Chain about his Neck, weighing of Butter. Bew. You'll return the King some Answer, my Lord. Cockl. Yes, my Lord, you may thank his Majesty, but the Lordship is too light. I must begone, were he Ten Thousand Kings and Emperours. Bew. I'll tell him what you say, Sir, but I know he'll be extreamly concern'd. Long.60 Oh damnably! the Rogue does it to a Hair. Away,30 away. Bew. I must, or I shall laugh in 's Face. Ex. Bew. Cler. Why, this was like your self, my Lord. Cockl. I think so; The Devil's in't, if that was not stiff enough. But if I should lose this Lordship by Fooling, my Wife would be plaguy angry. A Ladyship, you know is a pretty Bawble, enough for her to play with. Cler. Oh, you'll have a bigger Bawble, I warrant you for her to play with. See, see, here comes t'other again. Enter Longoville. Long. Give me your honour'd Hand, right Courteous Peer, and from hence forth be a Noble Marquess,

the King so wills, and Subjects must obey. Only he still desires you to consider his late Request. Cler. Faith! You are well now, my Lord. I'd consent. Cockl. 's Bud. I'll be one Step higher, since I am so far. Cler. Ha, ha, ha, 'Tis the finest Lord: I am afraid anon, he'll stand upon't to share the Kingdom with him. Long. Pox on you. Speak lower. Cockl. Troth, I must own the King is very gracious: but that scandalous Ballad of that abominable Marquess, and that damnable Patient Grizel,61 has made that Title so nauseous to me If his Majesty would but please to change that. Long. Faith, my Lord, I believe you may be what you please. Here's another Messenger.

"This speech is wrongly given to Longoville. It should be Clermont's, as Longoville has already left the stage.

tl"Patient Grizel"; many versions of the Griselda story in ballad form are extant. Theoldestof these is reprinted in The Roxburghe Ballads, II, 269. Enter Bewford, and Footman carrying a Robe. Bewf. Make Room here. Where's this Noble Marquess? The King, my Lord, once more has sent me to you, and finding no Dignity above your Merit, so you will freely grant to his Proposal, he bids you be a Duke, and chuse of whence. Cler. 'sHeart, if you yield not now, you are undone: What can you wish to have more than the Kingdom? Cockl. Why then, so please his Majesty, I would be Duke of31 Dunstable?2 Because I like the Sound. Bewf. 'Tis very apt, Sir: I know the King is pleased. There's your Patent with a Blank. Cockl. Pray give his Majesty Thanks, Sir; and you may tell him now that I will stay. Bewf. He'll be a glad man when he hears it, Sir. Cler. I must have vent to laugh, or I shall burst. Aside. Bewf. Keep your Countenance, and be hang'd. Long. But how shall we keep it from the Worlds Ear, that none undeceive him? Cler. We'll think of that anon: Why, Gentlemen, is this a gracious Habit for a Duke? For Heaven's sake each one employ his Hand to pluck the Clouds off from this Radiant Sun, that must shine on us all I'll pluck one Boot and Spur off. Long. And I another. Bewf. This

scurvey Hat, and plaguy Peruke,63 do not become his Grace's sprouting Forehead: For Shame let's off with 'em. Long. Now set your Duke-like Foot to this of mine,' one pluck will do it. Cockl. Hold! Hold! thou 'It pluck my Leg off; prithee go more gingerly to work, my Grace is yet but tender. Long. My Lord, I beg your Pardon. Cockl. Well you have it, Friend. Cler. So, now off with this Jerkin, and throw away that RidingRod. Bewf. Here, here: on with the new Robe the King has sent. Cockl. Robe 'Tis but an odd sort of a Robe, methinks:

Prithee, what's the Name on't?

Bewf. My Lord, 'Tis call'd a Solyman:M 'Tis made in Imitation

""Dunstable"; a town in the southern part of Bedfordshire.

""Peruke"; probably an anachronism. The first use of the word recorded in the TV. E. D. la in 1548, when it referred to one's natural hair. Littre' finds perruque in fifteenth century hrenclk with the same meaning. The word is D'Urfey's addition.

""Solyman"; Suleiman II (1641-1691) who succeeded his brother Mahommed IV in 1687. of the new Sultana's; this Mode is for the great Lords, as t'other for the great Ladies. Cockl. Oh ho! Is it so? They put it on. Long. So, So, Where are his Grace's Slippers? Enter Toby, booted and dress'd for a Journey. 32 Tob. Come, come, Sir, all's ready: The Horses are brought out; The Pillion on, and my Mistress stays in the Hall. Ownz! what's here to do? What a Devil do you mean, Sir. Cockl. My Slippers, Toby, my Slippers. Gravely. Tob. Slippers! 'sbud, will you ride a Journey in your Slippers? Long. Oh thou mighty Duke! Pardon this Man, that thus has trespass'd in his Ignorance. Here are your Grace's Slippers. Cockl. The poor Fellow is honest I pardon him. Tob. Why, what's the matter? Cler. Fellow, he's a Duke. The King has rais'd him above all the Land. Toby starts, and then kneels. Tob. A Duke! Oh, that ever I was born! Do you hear, Sir, Do you know what I am, pray? Cler. Chief Gentleman o' th' Chamber; Secretary, any thing, what you please: you may be a Lord in time, if things go right. *To Long. Tob.* D'ye hear, Friend? Prithee pull off my Boots too. *Cockl.* No, let them alone, and get thee into the Countrey presently, and tell my Uncle what has happen'd. *Tob.* 'sHeart, here's Luck for you. I'll post thither instantly, and tell his Uncle this amazing News. Oh what dull Dunghill Countrey Rogues are we! A Duke! 'sheart, we shall be all Lords at least. *Exit. Enter* Aurelia, *dress'd Awkwardly for a Journey. Aur.* Thus to your Will, as every good Wife ought, I have bent all my Thoughts, and now am ready. *Cockl.* Oh Madam!, I am not worthy to kiss the least of all your Grace's Toes,66 much less your Thumb, which yet I would be bold with. All your Council has been to me as prudent as an Angel's, but mine to thee as dirty as my Boots. Dear Dutchess, there's no going now, we must both stay. *Aurel.* Pray, Sir, don't mock me, nor make me dress and33 undress like a Fool, because you find me easy: said I not, the whole

""The least of all your Grace's Toes";note Grub, IV, 4,and Zechiel, *MadamFickle,!* (p. 8), "I kiss your Lordship's great Toe."

World should not alter me, if once I were resolv'd; therefore let's away.
Cockl. Behold, a Knight does kneel. *Kneels.*
Aur. A Knight!
Cockl. A Lord.
Aur. A Fool!
Cockl. I say a Lord does kneel, nay a Duke.
Cler. In Trowses, Madam.
Bewf. Without Shoes.
Aur. Are you all mad?
Long. No,gracious Lady,if you dare credit your faithful Servant's
Word, Your Husband's made a Duke.
Aur. What think you now, Sir?
Cockl. Ah dear, dear Dutchess! I am made by thee for ever, and here in Token, that all strife shall end, 'twixt Thee and Me, I let my Trowses fall, and to thy Hands I do deliver 'em, To signifie, that in all Acts and Speeches, From this time forth my Wife shall wear the Breeches. *Exeunt Omnes.* ACT III. SCENE I. 34 A Room in Grub's House in the

Country. *Enter* Grub, *and* Phillida. *Phil.* Well avads! You are welcome home a thousand times, dear *Hubby;* and will my Cousin be here so soon do you say? *Grub.* Ay, I have laid it home to him, i' faith! I have made a new Man of him! we shall have no more Court Fooleries now! *Phil.* Why, *Hubby,* is not the Court a fine Place then? *Grub.* Not half so fine a Place as my Barn is in Harvest-time. *Phil.* What, and so many tall, young, handsome *Scotch, French* and *Irish* Wits there, that come for Preferment? Why, *Hubby,* I heard here that my Cousin *Cockle-brain* was to have been made a Lord. *Grub.* A Lord! A Loggerhead he would have been made, had I not clear'd his Eye-sight, what with his Wife's Tattling, and her Bullies Bantring him with Honours and Titles, he was almost mad amongst 'em: but I rouz'd him i'faith! I got the better of him at last, and made him forswear ever coming near that damn'd Town again. I expect him here to morrow; He's upon his Journey by this time. *Phil.* What has he forsworn sweet *London,* to come and live sneaking here in the Country, *Hubby?* *Grub.* Sweet *London!* 'sbud I warrant this Fool thinks it pav'd with Nutmegs and Ginger; ha, ha: besides, why sneaking, you
Baggage? why sneaking?
Phil. Why is not our Countrey Life a sneaking Life, *Hubby? Grub.* No, *Hubby,* and let me hear you call it so agen, if you dare: I shall have her get an Itch of seeing this sweet *London,* and run away from me there, if I han't a Care. *Aside. Phil.* Nay, Dear, pray don't be angry! what Preferment can35 my Cousin expect here? *Grub,* 'sBud, is he not Lord of a Mannor? which he may thank me for too, for that was just degrading, had not I been in the way, and exercis'd upon him: besides, if he wants more Preferment, he may be a *Justice of Peace,* as I am: Lash the Whores out of the Countrey; live godlily, and take Bribes, ye silly Jade. *Enter* Toby. *Phil.* He's coming, *Hubby,* for look here comes his Man, Mr. *Toby. Grub.* 'Tis he, i'faith! What, *Toby*—my Friend, *Toby!* welcome, faith: Spouse, go lay down the Pheasant *Roger* shot this

Morning: I suppose my Cousin's alighted at the Gate, and we must get something to entertain him; go, go; why don't you move? now I see, *Toby,* he's a Man of his Word. Ownds run, lay down the Pheasant, I say. *Pushes her. Tob.* Your Pheasant must fly into St. *James's Park* if you intend to treat him, I can tell you that. *Grub.* Why, is not he come? *Tob.* No, nor like to come, that's more, Old Fellow. *Grub.* How, Sauce-box! What's that you say? Will he break his Word with me? does the Rascal dare to affront me? *Tob.* Rascal! Have a Care what you say, Friend, I have sworn Homage to my Prince, and hold my Place by my Fidelity, therefore, Friend, keep good Words in your Mouth. You are but a *Justice of Peace. Grub.* But a *Justice of Peace!* Why, you sawcy Rascal, what would you have me be, a *Cherubin?* Here's an insolent Rogue! He makes nothing of a *Justice of Peace.* « *Tob.* Not in Comparison of his Grace, or my self, I thank ye. *Grub.* His Grace! whose Grace, Dog? 'sbud, speak quickly, and don't plague me with these Riddles, or old Crab shall fly about your Ears? Why does that Scab, your Master, use me thus? and where is he? *Tob.* His Mighty Grace is at his House, I suppose. 36 *Grub.* Mighty Grace! *Phil.* Nay, nay, *Hubby,* prithee do not call my Court-Nephew such Names. *Tob.* Ay, ay, Old Mole-hill! things are alter'd since thou and I met *atLondon:* to be short, the King has made your Nephew Duke of *Dunstable:* now repent of what is past, and extend your Manners to me, as my Place deserves, or look to't. I shall stick upon your Skirts: I shall *grub* ye! *Grub.* The Duke of *Dunstable,* Oons! *Tob.* Even so, Sir, and greatest Favourite at Court, no better, nor no worse, Sir. *Grub.* But, *Toby,* dost not thou dream? Art sure? *Tob.* Sir, I'll hold no Discourse without my Title. If you want Court-Breeding I'll teach you some. I am stil'd now Mr. *Secretary. Grub.* Mr. *Secretary! Tob.* A little Step to future Dignity. About two Years hence I expect to be a Duke my self. *Grub.* The Devil you do! This must be down-right Madness. *Tob.* Believe so, and be wretched! *Grub.* Nay, nay, I beseech you, good Mr. *Secretary,* be not angry! 'Tis such high News it almost gravels me: I desire only to be satisfy'd, and if you are sure my Nephew is a Duke. *Tob.* As sure as you are Justice *Grub,* Sir. *Grub.* And that's pretty sure indeed. Gadzooks, if this be true I have undone my self, I call'd him Son of a Whore! But, Mr. *Secretary,* I have great Confidence in your Worship's Patience and Mercy. *Changing his Tone. Tob.* Well, Mr. *Justice,* I can wink at Faults. *Grub.* But if the Sun should dazle now! *Tob.* Yet more Doubts! Have you a Nose on your Face? *Grub.* A Nose! Yes, yes; I am sure I have a Nose. *Tob.* Why then I am sure he is a Duke. *Phil.* O Gemini! If our Nephew be a Duke, I wonder what I am, *Hubby! Grub.* A Fool, *Hubby.* Pox, prithee hold thy peace; I'll tell37 thee more anon: this is the rarest News! We are all made for ever. *Tob.* I saw the Courtiers bow, and heard 'em cry, Good Health and Fortune to my Lord the Duke; God bless him, cries another; and to his Grace's right Hand, the Worshipful Mr. *Secretary,* says a third: And when I came away to bring this News, his Chamber was hung with Nobles like the Presence. *Grub.* I heartily thank you, Sir, I am satisfy'd. Why, Great as he is, he is my Kinsman, Mr. *Secretary;* I am his poor unworthy Uncle. *Tob.* That's true, Sir; but I could wish his Greatness could make him lose his M,emory; yu have been formerly a little sawcy with him, you know, Justice. *Grub.* I have so indeed, a great Failing in troth: I am asham'd on't heartily; and will repent and mend. What, I warrant his ingenious Lady was the Means of all this! *Tob.* Even so, Sir; You know I was for having you swinge her, Gadzooks, I would not have her know it for a 1000 /. *Grub.* Nor I have done it for Ten Thousand. *Tob.* For she has ferk'd out all our Preferments upon her own Anvil, as cleverly as a Smith would do a Ten penny Nail. *Grub.* Ah, I always thought her an ingenious Person. But now to see what Fortune some Men have! I might have been a Duke too, if I had had but luck. I had an Estate and a Wife as fair as his, that could have brook'd the Court as well as his, and

laid about her for her Husband's Honour. Ah, *Toby,* had I ever dreamt of this! *Tob.* Yet again, Sir? *Grub.* I cry your Mercy, good Mr. *Secretary. Tob.* Why faith, Sir, it came above our Expectation: we were wise only in seeking to undo this Honour: which show'd our Dunghill Breeding, and our Dirt. *Grub.* 'Tis very true, we were both arrant Puppies, Mr. *Secretary.* 'Tis as his Noble Grace hath often said, we understood just nothing. *Tob.* 'Tis Time then that we now improve our selves, that38 rising, as we may, with our great Master, we may attain some Wisdom with our Places, and not be Fools in Office, Mr. Justice. *Grub.* Right; and Troth this Grandeur of the Duke's, my Nephew, I cry thy Mercy that I am familiar, methinks should make for us. Hum! *Tob.* How the Fates may order in this poor Thread of Life, as yet I know not; but I think I was not born to hold a Trencher: Let Time rowl on, I shall see what 'twill come to! *Grub.* Well, The first thing I'll do, I'll fit my Wife for the Court; Buy her new Cloaths, and Trinckets. *Tob.* That's the Way, Sir. *Grub.* I was a dull Countrey Clod, to let my Nephew rise and get the start before me. But I'll dispatch and put my self in Money. *Phil.* To buy me fine Cloaths, *Hubby!* O Gemini! And must I go to Court then; And see the fine Houses, and the fine Horses, and the fine Gentlemen that I have dreamt of a thousand times, when you have been talking the Night before, ivads I have, *Hubby. Grub.* Thou shalt see all: It shall go hard but I'll have Preferment too. I'll about this Money instantly. *Phil.* Oh Gemini! I could leap out of my Skin for Joy methinksf *Tob.* You do well, Sir, and now you talk of Money, the former Business, for taking up the five hundred Pounds, must be dispatch'd; This little Plat in the Countrey lies most fit to do his Grace such serviceable Uses. *Grub.* By no means, Mr. *Secretary;* his Grace shall have it of me, 'twill be a Courtly Complement, to introduce my self. *Tob.* Why, Troth, I thought so, but would not be too forward. *Grub.* Oh, by all means, Sir, come, come! pray walk in, Wife, conduct Mr. *Secretary* into the Buttery; and

desire him to take a Glass of what we have: And d'ye hear, recommend your self handsomely to the great Duke, our Kinsman, and his Dutchess; and write them word you shall attend 'em suddenly. I'll go and dispatch these Bills, and follow you. Zooks! I hardly know where I am. *Tob.* Sir, I shall wait on you. 39J *Grub.* By no means, Sir, 'tis much below your Place. *Phil.* Come, sweet Mr. Secrecy, please to walk in, I know not what to get that's good enough for you, for ivads you have made me a joyful Creature! *Tob.* Keep your Joy till you come to Court, pretty Mistress! *Exeunt. Grub.* And that shall be quickly, i'faith, since there are Dukedoms, and Don-ships, and the Devil and all to be gotten so easily: I'll trouble my self no more with Sowing and Reaping; but laugh and lye at Ease, let the Weather change as it will: I know I shall be a Devil of a Courtier the first Year; but what then, my Wife shall shine for us both.

And toy and treat, whilst I wink at the Matter,

But for the rest, odzooks, I'll watch her Water. *Exit.* SCENE II. *Cocklebrain's* House.

Enter Aurelia, Longoville, Bewford *and* Clermont.

Aur. It must be carried closely with a Care, that no Man speak to him, or come near him without our private Knowledge, and then my good dull, honest, drowsie Husband you shall not hinder me from the Pleasure of *Basset:* And I will go into the Countrey when I please, and not when you think fit. *Long.* Let him be kept in's Chamber under Show of State, and Dignity, and no one suffer'd to see his Noble Face, or have Access, but we that are Conspirators. *Bewf.* Or else down with him into the Countrey, amongst his Tenants, where he may live much safer in his Greatness, and play the Fool in Pomp amongst his Fellows. *Aur.* No,-he shall play the Fool in the City first: I will not lose the Honour of the Jest, that shall be given my Wit, for all his Land i' th' Country. *Cler.* Alas, poor Duke! I do but think how he will sweat40 when he finds at last he is made an Ass on. *Omn.*

Ha, ha, ha, ha. *Cler.* In the mean time we'll keep a Guard about his Person, that no Man come too near him, and our selves always in Company have him into the City to see his Face swell, whilst in divers Corners some of our own appointing shall be ready to cry, Heaven bless your Grace, Long live your Grace. *Aur.* 'Twill be rare Sport, and shall be as rarely follow'd: I'll teach him to rail at me for losing *Sonicci.* To think Beauty, such as mine, was only fit to wither in the Countrey. *Bewf* Poor sordid Earthworm! *Aur.* I can scarce hold from open Laughter, when I hear him cry, come hither, my sweet Dutchess; let me kiss thy gracious Lips; for this is still his Phrase. I shall fear nothing but his Legs will break under the mighty Weight of so much Greatness. *Cler.* Hark, hark! He's coming: set your Faces right, and bow like Countrey Prologues. Here he comes. Room, Room, before there: The Duke is entring. *Enter* Cockle-brain, *with Attendants.*
The choicest Blessings wait upon the Duke.
Long. And give him all Content and Happiness.
Bewf. Let his great Name live to the end of Time.
Cockl. I thank you all; and am pleas'd to give you Notice, at a fit Time, I shall consider of you: till when be near me: My dear Dutchess, prithee let thy Grace lend me thy Keys; there is a Book of Heraldry in thy Closet, I must peruse. ""
Aur. Here they are, my Lord.
Long. He does it to a Hair. *Cler.* Is he not a Duke indeed? He's alter'd so, he's now scarce knowable. *Cockl.* Get Candles there. *Bewf.* Lights, Lights there for the Duke. *Ex.* Cockl. *Aur.* His very Stile and Air alter'd: Why, here's the Effect of Grandeur, Gentlemen. *Lyon.* The Duke! What Duke is this, ha? Do you know him? *Aur.* 'Tis the poor mad Gentleman I told you of; he runs thus over all the Town, and where he finds a Door open, he enters. *Lyon.* Or is the lucky Favourite made a Duke, He that has married *Celia? Cler.* What *Celia,* Sir? *Lyon.* I know not what I say, Sir: You shall not snap me: this is no Treason: I said only *Celia,* she was my Love,

Sir, *in Diebus illis,* But now alas! *Cler.* Where is she, Sir? *Lyon.* Dead! Dead! Alas, poor Soul! she dy'd of the Heartburning, in spight of the Benefit of *Crabs Eyes* or *Spaw-water,* Sir: you are an *Apothecary. Long.* Alas, poor Wretch!
Lyon. You have a strange odd kind of an Apocryphal Phiz; methinks a Face that's full of hard Words: Zowns, Sir, d'ye come to pose me? I am a Scholar. *Aur.* He knows it, Sir, and knows *Cdia* too, who greets you kindly, and would not have you be so melancholly. *Lyon.* Thank her; but 'tis too late, tell her! *SINGS. I'll Jay me down and dy , within some hollow Tree, _ / TKe Raven and Cat, the Owl and Bat shall warble out my Elegy.*
How d'ye like that Dirge now, was it not quaint?
Enter Cockle-brain, *with a Book. Cockl.* I have found the Book of *Heraldry.*
Lyon. A Book of *Heraldry!* Have you so, Sir?
Cockl. How now! Who's this? Yes, Sir, that I have: what then?
Cler. Here's like to be rare Sport!
Aur. We can't miss it, now the Fool and Madman are met. *Lyon.* What then? Why then, Sir, I suppose you were sent to dispute with me about King *Henry's* Title: Come on, Sir: I'll be cunning enough, I warrant you, Begin, state your Point. *Cockl.* A strange sort of Fellow this! does any here know him? *Cler.* I believe your Grace will find him a Male-content, sent by some Enemies that envy your new Greatness, to pump your Loyalty with a fallacious Argument about the King's Title. *Cockl.* Oh, is that the Business? Well; I'll be prepar'd for him, I'll warrant ye: Come, Sir, sit down; I'll clear this Business: *Henry* of *Hereford,* Son of *John* of *Gaunt. Lyon.* Sir, I shall answer nothing, till these Witnesses depart the Room; you must not think to trap me. *Cockl.* Pray leave us together: I'll have no Man stay; no not my Dutchess. *Bewf.* Come, let's go, and behind the Hangings hear this fine Argument. *Exeunt. They sit. Cockl.* Henry of *Hereford,* Son of *John* a *Gaunt,* Impeach'd of Treason by *Thomas* Duke of *Norfolk,* demanded

Combat. » *Lyon.* Well, Sir, and what then? *Cockl.* Pray give me leave, Sir: But King *Richard* the second loving and fearing his great Uncle *Lancaster,* deferr'd the Fight, and banish'd both the Kingdom. *Lyon.* Sir, give me better Reasons for his Banishment, or yield your self confuted. *Cockl.* What, before we have half done. Pray give me leave, Sir. *Lyon.* Pray, Sir, give me leave: I'll give you better Reasons, They swell within me, and must have vent. *Cockl.* Will you but hear me, Sir? 43 *Lyons.* I'll hear nothing, Sir, till I have fill'd your Belly full of Reasons: I say, King *Richard,* Sir, forbid the Combat, doubting the Justice of his Kinsman's Cause; and therefore, Sir. *Cockl.* I know what you infer, Sir. *Lyon.* Sir, you know nothing: for then comes *Vortigern* the *Saxon* Monarch, and cuts off the Entail. *Cockl.* Ownds, what Entail? The Devil's in this Fellow; He's running back to the beginning of the World, if I don't contradict him: why what has *Vortigern* to do with *Richard* the second? *Lyon.* How, Sir, not to do with him? Did they not combat on the Bank of *Humber* and thump each other soundly for the Kingdom, with Batts and Sandbags? *Cockl.* No, Sir, that ever I could read. *Lyon.* Why then you are a Traytor, and I arrest you of High Treason, for not knowing History better, and seize you on the behalf of *Vortigern. Cockl.* Pox on *Vortigern* and you too. Seize me? alas, poor Fellow! know'st thou who I am? *Lyon.* I care not what you are: Come along to Prison, and willingly, or I'll plume thee as a Hawk does a Partridge. *Cockl.* The Devil is certainly in this Fellow: within there? who waits? *Lyon.* Do you rebel? Thus I claim the Combate. *beats* Cock. *Cockl.* Help, Help, here. *Enter Footmen. Enter* Aurelia, Clermont, Longoville, *and* Bewford. *Aur.* How now? Alas, what's the matter here? *Cockl.* Help, help thy Duke here! *Cler.* Take him off; forbear his Grace's Person. *Lyon.* A Horse; a Horse; my Kingdom for a Horse:66 What's here, a Woman, charging at their Army's Head? then we are betray'd. *I'll mount to yon, blue* Ccelum, *To shun these Female Gypsies;*

I'll play at Bowles with Sun and Moon,
And scare ye with Eclipses.
"A Horse"; from *Richard III, V,* 4. The
quotation is D'Urfey's.
Long. Away, away with him. 44 *Lyon.*
How, seiz'd! then here's my Ransom:
This was my Father's Sword, I'll call
it *Vortigern:* It lightens when I draw it,
and when I strike it thunders! *Bewf.*
Away with him, the Man's mad.67 How
does your Grace? *Cockl.* Indifferent
well; but I believe he has broke my
Head with the Hilt of *Vortigern. Cler.*
How did you find his Title, my Lord?
Cockl. The Devil take his Title and him
too. Dear Dutchess, prithee go get me
a.Plaister. *Long.* It needs not, my Lord;
'tis nothing but a Contusion, upon my
Honour, and nothing so good for it as
Air. Will your Grace be pleas'd to see
the City? *Cockl.* It shall be so: prepare
there. A Plague o' this *Vortigern! Aside.*
Cler. Your Grace determines not to see
the King. *Cockl.* Not yet: about some
ten Days hence I shall be ready. *Long.*
Clear the way there: Room for the
Duke! *Ex.* Cockl. Cler. Away, before,
Bewford, and raise a Guard sufficient
to keep him from the reach of Peoples
Tongues, and remember how the Streets
must be dispos'd with Cries and Salu-
tations: in the mean time, Madam, you
keep your State at home. *Exeunt. Aur.*
Ha, ha, ha; thus far'tis acted rarely:
what hereafter I do intend, lies not within your level, my sweet Friends; nor
shall not, till 'tis ripe for a Discovery.
Enter Page with a Letter.
As I live, from my new Countrey Aunt,
I know the Hand: To the great Lady,
High and Mighty Dutchess of *Dunstable,* be these delivered: Ha, ha, ha, Oh
for a stronger Lace to keep my Breath
in, that I my laugh the nine Days, till the
Wonder fall to an Ebb! What high and
mighty Blockheads live in the Countrey!
Reads the Letter.
My good angry Uncle, I find by the
Contents, you want Preferment too, and
you shall have it, or my Wit shall fail
me.
Enter Celia. *Cel.* Madam, I hope you'll
pardon this Intrusion: 'twas told me that
a poor distracted Gentleman, that owes

his great Misfortue to my Folly, was
seen to enter here; Pray is it so? 45 *Aur.*
Such a one, Madam, has been here, indeed, but he is gone: Was he your Husband, Madam?
"Probably at this point should be inserted the stage direction, *"Exit* Lyonel."
Cel. That he was not my Husband, was
the Cause that he is nothing now: curst
lawless Force, and impious Cruelty,
ravish'd the Blessing from his longing
Heart, and cast a Mist before my feeble
Eyes, blinded by Wealth and treacher-
ous Dignity, I could not see his Merit,
till too late.
Aur. I hope he's not past Cure, Madam?
Cel. There's a Physician learn'd in these
Extreams, that gives me mighty hopes,
if he were taken! *Aur.* I believe, Madam,
my Servants can give you some Account of him: if you please I'll examine
them. *Cel.* The Courtesie will be both
generous and charitable. *Aur.* Madam,
You should command far greater Services than these, if they were in my
Power. *Exeunt.* SCENE III. *The Street.*
Enter Bewford, *and six Gentlemen.*
Bewf. Every Man take his Corner, here
am I, you, and you in that place, and
as he comes by, be sure you salute him
with loud Voices, and Faces full of de-
jected Fear and Humbleness. Away,
he's coming. *Enter* Toby. *Tob.* Fy! How
these streets are throng'd here with
these same rascally People. I am just
come to Town, and, as I am a Gentleman, am almost choak'd already, with
the very Steam of 'em: They have
crowded his Grace almost to Death yonder, they follow him like a Baboon to
the Bear-Garden. There is in the World
no true Gaper like your Citizen: the
Bears shall not pass by his Door in
Peace, but that he, and all his Family
shall be ready to ride upon the Backs of
'em. Room, before there. *Enter* Cockle-
brain, Clermont, Longoville, *and Servants.* 46 A Pox on you, keep your
Places, and then you may see him till
your Hearts ake. *1 Gent.* Bless your
Grace. *Cockl.* And you, with all my
Heart. *2 Gent.* Heaven grant your Grace
long Life, and happy Days. *Cockl.*
Thank thee, good Friend. *2 Gent.* Perpetual Blessings crown you. *Cockl.* I

thank you all. *Longoville. Long.* My
Lord! *Cockl. '* I'll make a Speech to 'em.
Hem, hem! *Long.* Silence there, his
Grace will make a Speech. *Cockl.* Good
People! I shall divide my Speech into
three Branches; First, it has pleas'd the
King, my Master, for sundry, Virtues in
me, not unknown to Him, and the wise
State, to lend his Hand, and raise me
to this Eminence: My second Branch is
to examine how this may seem to other
Men, or stir the Minds of such as are my
Fellow-Peers against me; since I desire,
and will deserve their Loves, as I do
yours, good People. My third and last
Branch is upon Amity, for as the Tree
Cler. Your Grace had best take care,
'twill be inform'd the King, your Greatness with the People. *Cockl.* A Pox on
him! he has hindred me from branching
into the finest Metaphor, and I am the
worst in the World to get in again when
I am once out: My last Branch, I say,
dear Friends, is, Hem, hem! a Plague of
this *Clermont!* is, I say, Faith,
I know not what it is at present But if
ever you catch me branching it again,
in this Fellow's Company I'll give you
leave to hang me upon the Tree I was
speaking of, And so I share my Bowels
amongst you all.
1 Gent. A Noble Duke! a very Noble
Duke! *Exeunt.* SCENE IV. Cockle-brain's
Hall.
Enter Aurelia, *and* Maria.
Aur. Is my Uncle coming, art sure?
Mar. As sure as he expects to be made
a Duke too, Madam. Lord, methinks, I
long to see his new Countrey Wife, I47
wonder how the Creature looks. *Aur.*
Very prettily, as I have heard: 'Twill be
Diversion to see how our Court Sparks
will ogle her Countrey Dress. *Mar.* Yes,
Madam, and paddle in the Palm of her
Hand. *Aur.* Hold your tongue, you Gip-
sie, and go and see what time the Coach
comes in: I must set another Springe
ready to catch the Buzzard, my Uncle;
I'll teach him to preach against the
Court and my Town Pleasures. Hark!
His Grace, the Duke is coming. Away,
away to your Business. *Re-enter Duke
and Train.*
Your Grace is welcome home.
Cockl. Why, thank your Grace. How

fine these Titles sound, Sweet-Heart, I am well and merry, never more able to be thy Bedfellow, my Dearest. *Bewf.* Bless us, what a hot Meat this Greatness is! *Long.* It may well be, for he has not got a snap these two Months ,, to my Knowledge, or is she damn'd for swearing it. *Cockl.* I thank you, Gentlemen, for your Attendance, and your great Pains, pray know my Lodgings better and oftner: do so Gentlemen: now by my Honour, as I am a Prince, I will consider your Deservings. *Toby. Bew.* Where's Mr. *Secretary* there? Some body call him. *Enter* Toby. *Cler.* Mr. *Secretary!*
Tob. Who calls?
Long. His Grace wants you, Mr. *Secretary.*
Cockl. Toby.
Tob. My Lord.
Cockl. Be ready for the Countrey once more, *Toby:* And let my Tenants know the King's great Love; say I would see 'em; But the weight of State lies heavy on my Shoulders, and therefore tell 'em, I expect their Attendance. Go, take up Post-Horses, and make haste. *Tob.* I begin to find this under-hand Dignity a little48 troublesome, and care not much for jumbling my Honour thus a Horseback. Well, for this once I'll be a Servant; but when I come back, I'll try if I can set up for a Duke, as well as others. *Exit* Toby. *Aur.* My gracious Husband, you must now prepare in all your Pomp, to entertain your Uncle, who is a Convert now. And with his Wife intends to be here to night. *Cockl.* Alas, poor Countrey things, how they will blush to see my Grandeur! But I will be pitiful, Gentlemen, pray be ready, I do intend to morrow early,
To shew before my Uncle's wondring Face,
The Greatness of my Pomp, and of my Place.
Cler. We'll all be ready. Away, Boys, till to morrow. *Bewf.* This Countrey Uncle must needs prove a rare new Scene of Diversion. *Long.* Most certainly, in the mean, let's to *Pontack's*TM to Supper. *Exeunt Omnes. u" Pontack's";* this tavern, very popular in the early eighteenth century, was situated in the City

in Christ Church Passage between Newgate Street and Christ Church, near Bagnio Court (Sydney, *England in the Eighteenth Century,* I, 193). Among its patrons were Swift and Evelyn. Its proprietor was a M. Pontaq of Bordeaux. The statements of Besant and others that Pontack's was first opened in the reign of William III seem from the mention of the place in this play to be erroneous. D'Urfey's reference to Pontack's is of course a rank anachronism. ACT IV. SCENE I. 49
SCENE, *St. James's Park.*
. *Enter* Grub. Phillida *and* Roger. *Grub.* Are all things carried to the Taylor! *Roger? Rog.* All, All, an't shall please you: che were with 'en69 by break of Day, along while avore yow were out of your Neast, an't shall please you. *Grub.* That's well; we must know of the Duke my Cosin,70 Wife, what Fashion his Grace will please to have us in? For my own part, I have an old fashion'd Velvet pair of Breeches, that when I have made a new Suit and Cloak of 'em, will steal into the Presence well enough. *Rog.* And does your Worship intend to leave *Plowden-Hicket,* and your House in the Country for good and all, an't shall please you? *Grub.* As his Mighty Grace, my Nephew thinks fit: 'Tis as preferment comes, *Roger! Rog.* Gads-bread; and thick vine Gown71 will make Mistress look like a Countess too, an't shall please you. *Grub.* Ay, ay, before the Duke and the Court have done with her, I hope to see her look like a Dutchess, *Roger.* Come, Wife; What are you staring at? *Phill.* Oh *Jemmini!* Hubby I never saw so curious a place in my life: The Trumpets and the Drums make so pure72 a noise, methinks I am almost substracted with it: And look, look, *Hubby* what are these Birds that fly over our Heads? *Grub.* Ducks, Ducks, Fool. *Phil.* Good me! and why do they fly about so? And, pray *Hubby,* tell me who's that naked Black Man, that holds a thing in his hand so. *Grub.* O Lord! a naked Black Man with a thing in his hand, was there ever such a Fool? Why, that is a Statue! a Gladiator, a thing set up for Ornament; or to scare the Rooks73 here about the

Court A Pox I can't tell what it's for? Come prithee,50
Come along.
""Che were with'en"; I was with him.
""My Cosin"; by the Elizabethan and more rustic persons of Restoration times cousin and nephew were interchangeably applied to the same person. Cocklebrain is really Grub's nephew. Tl"Thick vine Gown"; this fine gown.
""Pure"; fine, excellent, pleasing. In *The Richmond Heiress,* I, 1 (p. 5), Doggett is mentioned as having acted Solon in *The Marriage Hater Match'd,* "so purely." See also *The Scowrers,* IV, 1.
'"Rooks"; a pun on "rook," a sort of bird, and "rook," a sharper, especially at cards or other games of chance or skill. *Phill.* Nay, pray *Hubby;* let me know all the fine things. And what are those that lye there by the Water side, *Hubby. Grub.* Geese, Geese, you Fool! odszooks! those! no, those are Gentlemen of the Guard that lye a Sunning: s'bud She'll tire me with questions! if I stay longer Come, come prithee, come away *Roger!* a word. *Enter Footman Singing. Foot.* Lol-throl-lol How now! What pretty Country thing is this, that stares at me? I'le speak to her: Your Servant, pretty Mistress, whither are you a going? *Phill.* Oh *Gemini!* what a pure sweet fine young Gentleman is here! Indeed Sir, I don't know! but I think I am going home with my *Hubby! Foot.* Her *Hubby* What a pox is that, her Hobby-horse? *Grub.* You're mistaken here, Friend, She's meat for your Master hum hum (Grub, *pulls her away. Foot.* Why then, Friend, I would my Master had her; and so your Servant *(Exit. Phill.* Oh law! Do you know him then! prithee dear *Hubby,* who is it? *Grub.* Odzooks! a lowzy Footman, that I would not have had! his Grace seen you talk with for 1000 l. *Rog.* What, a Footman, with thick vine Silver lac'd Coat on's back, as sure as cham here, I should have taken him to be a Knight of the Shire at least, if chad seen him come riding through *Plowden. Grub.* Oh thou art come to a new World, *Roger,* the Lords and the Lacquies are all brave alike here! *Rog.* Would I were at home

agen for my part, and sitting by the fire with old *Joan* I'de ne're come here to seek for parferment, not I; odsooks! the Cries of the Street, and the ratling of the Coaches have almost maz'd me: besides chant74 slep a wink since che come to Town. *Grub.* Hold your Tongue, ye Clod pole: Don't you see what preferment your Country-man *Toby* is come to? And if I can51J. get to be a Duke, as if my Wife manages well, I intend to be, who knows, but thou mayst come to be Secretary as well as he, Buffle?76 *Rog.* Should not a Secretary Write and Read, an't shall please you?

""Chant"; "Ich ha'n't";.,"I_haveInot."

""Buffle"; fool.

Grub. 'Tis all one; some do, and some do not, if he has but a Clark that can, 'tis no matter whether he can Write and Read, or no? But come, by this time his Grace is rising: lets go and give our attendance. Nay prithee come away; What-a-devil art thou staring at? *Exeunt.* SCENE II.

A Street before Lyonel's House.

Enter Lyonel *meeting* Toby.

Tob. Save you, Sir.

Lyon. Save the King, Sir.

Tob. Pray Sir, which is the nearest way?

Lyon. Save the King, I say, Sir, this is the nearest way.

Tob. The nearest way, I mean to the Post-house, Sir.

Lyon. Gad save the King and his Post-horse, Sir.

Tob. Pray, Sir, direct me to the House.

Lyon. Here must be no directions; you cannot catch me, Sir.

Tob. I don't understand you, Sir.

Lyon. Read *Hugo Grotius*TM then. I say you can't catch me, Sir. *Tob.* Not catch you, Sir?

Lyon. No Sir, nor can the King with all his cunning Stratagems and Plots, although he put his Nobles in disguise, never so oft, to sift into my words by course of Law lay hold upon my life. *Tob.* This must be some business, that the Duke my Master is by the King employ'd in, and he thinks that I, as being Secretary, am acquainted with it-hum hum. *Lyon.* I shall not need to rip the Cause up to you, nor need you tell me the place you hold i' th' State I know

your Name is *Phizgigg.77 Tob. Phisgigg,* Sir! *Lyon.* Ay the Mothers side you come from the Right Honourable the *Bominellies;n* you give for your Coat Argent, a Polcat Mountant Azure, a Bar direct between Culters pendant Sables: You are, Sir, sprung of a great Family.

Tob. An ingenuous Fellow, this, I warrant him: s'bud, he52 knows more of me than I ever knew of myself. ""Hugo Grotius"; Hugo Grotius (1583-1645) was the founder of the science of international law, as it exists to-day. His most important work was *De Jure Belli ac Pads* (1625). In 1609 he published *Mare Liberum.* The reference to Grotius is D'Urfey's. The anachronism in making this jurist at least contemporary with Henry IV is patent. -""Phizgigg"; Phizgigg is the name applied to the partisans of King Phiz of Brentford in D'Urfey's *Two Queens of Brentford.* ""Bominellies"; perhaps an allusion to Beaumavielle, the French baritone, who died in 1688.

Lyon. Besides, you have a scar upon the top of your Nose, which denotes Dignity, a Semicircle upon your Crown, and a double fold upon your right Ear: your Great Unkle was a Bassaw. *Tweaks him by the Nose, and Cuffs him.* *Tob.* A Bassaw, s'heart, this fellow will make a Great Turk of me presently—— I have lately come to some preferment indeed, Sir. *Lyon.* 'Tis nothing, you shall have more, and greater: Let me see You shall be before Christmas next *Tob.* A Duke, Sir.

Lyon. A Duke at least.

Tob. Odsheart! I thought so always! I know I was not born to hold a Trencher: this is a most admirable Man! *Lyon.* But there is one ill Planet that hangs o're you. *Tob.* An ill one! a lack-a-day What is it. Sir? *Lyon. Saturn! Saturn!* you will within this hour be taken up for High Treason! *Tob.* Bless me! for high Treason! *Lyon.* Has no one seen you talk with me, think you? *Tob.* Yes, a great many, Sir. *Lyon.* There 'tis, there's your undoing: I am pursu'd by the whole State! Continual Treasons laid to my Charge, and all that talk with me fall into the same predicament. I cannot help

weeping, to think you should fall into such danger for my sake! *Tob.* S'heart! would you had been hanged e're I had fallen into the predicament, as you call it. *(weeps. Lyon.* You will be apprehended within this half hour, you are beset already oh *(weeps. Tob.* I'le whip out of Town. *Lyon.* Oh then your Head's whipt off the next minute, if you but offer at that. Oh———. *Tob.* Why the Devil did you stop me, could you not be contented to be hang'd by your self like a good Christian. But on my Conscience, this comes of my Ambition, my plotting to be a Duke before my time.79 *Lyon.* Oh, oh, oh! *(Both howl out. Tob.* But, good Sir, is there no remedy? 53 *Lyon.* Yes, yes Fate does allow a remedy; but then you

""My plotting to be a Duke before my time." See Sir *Barnaby Whigg,* V. 1 (p. 51), "My Astrologer's a damn'd Dog for telling me I shou'd be a Duke" though." Sir Barnaby who utters the above line, has just been arrested for treason after successive changes from Whig to Tory, Catholic and Mahometan.

must take a Manly resolution, and suffer your self to be hang'd a little, to appease the Fates. *Tob.* Oh a little! pray how little will serve, Sir! for you know there's no jesting with those things. *Lyon.* Why, two or three hours hanging will do it, I am sure; and if you can endure that bravely, you will certainly live to be a Great Man. *Tob.* Oh Lord; 'Tis impossible: I know my Constitution so well, Sir, that I shall be choak'd in half the time: But if punishment for a High Misdemeanor, instead of High Treason would serve the turn, I would be burnt in the Hand with all my heart: if that would appease the Fates. *Lyon.* 'Twas generously said; and 'tis pity such Honor e're should be a prey to Fortune: Take Courage, Friend, I will preserve thy life with hazard of my own. *Tob.* A Blessing on your Heart. *Lyon.* This night thou shalt be lock'd within my Doors, and in the Morning FIe so provide, that in disguise you shall have free access to the Sea-side, and then, e're any know it, be Shipp'd away for *Bantam.0 Tob.* For *Bantam!* Gadsooks!

that's a devilish way: What shall I do when I am there? Oh Fortune, Fortune! but come, any thing's better than hanging by the Neck two or three hours, in hopes to be a Great Man after it. *Lyon.* Follow me softly then, and no more Thoughts of Honor, d'ye hear: lest the Fates frown, and contradict our purposes. *Tob.* Ah no, no, Sir, my Pride is fallen low enough by this time.

This comes of my Ambition, Rogue, Pimp, Scoundril as I was

I must be a Duke in the Devils name— Oh, I deserve to be hang'd, that's the Truth on't. *Exeunt.*

Lyonel, Toby *go above. Enter* Celia *and* Doctor. 54 *Cel.* This is his House, and here I saw him enter; his better

Angel has directed him to leave the wandring streets poor

Gentleman, would I were able, with as free a Heart, to set his Soul right, as I am to grieve the ruine of his Sense, which Heaven forgive me!

" *Bantam*"; the western portion of the island of Java, from which the British factory had been expelled by the Dutch in 1682. The city of Bantam soon after became one of the chief ports of the East Indies, *la Love for Money,* I (p. 8), Jiltall says, "When am I to act the *Indian Heiress* and take my Voyage from *Bantam?*" See also *Sir Patient Fancy,* I, 1, and *Pills to Purge Melan choly,* V, 244. *Doct.* If you could win him but to take my Medicine, and get some Rest, my Life upon the Operation. *Cel.* I'le call to him: Sir, if you are within, pray speak to me. , (Toby *above,* Lyon *above.*) 81Yes Sir, I am within, and will be. *Tob.* Oh, oh Who is't, Good Sir, Who is't? *Lyon.* The Captain of the Guards: take heed you are not seen: there the Disguise lies; on with it immediately, 'twas what I had provided for myself but you shall be serv'd first now, Friend. *Doct.* Sir here's a friend of yours would speak with you. *Lyon. A* Friend! no Sir, you must pardon me——. I am acquainted with no such I see you are a *Switzer'1* by your Habit.

Doct. Alas! poor Gentleman! *Tob.* A *Switzer!* Oh Lord, what will become of me? *Cel.* Sir, I am a Messenger from

her you love: nay, and from her that loves you more than Life, more than fresh springing Flowers the indulgent Sun; or pretty Birds ensnar'd their liberty: and can you be so cruel not to hear me? *Lyon.* Let it suffice that you hear me, and hear me loudly, once more, God Save the King. Come Friend, are you ready the

Troops are all drawn off, the Coast is clear now, only the Captain and the *Switzer. Tob.* And what's to be done with 'em, Good Sir?

Lyon. We'l scow'r 'em, Boy, we'l scow'r 'em: you shall bring up the rear. I'le Charge i'th' Van! nay, prithee, why dost thou shake so? *Tob.* Alas! Sir— — 'Tis impossible for me to Charge, I am turn'd Woman now! (Toby *comes down. Lyon.* Why then I'le do 't myself: This bloody Sword55 through millions of our Foes shall be thy Guard, and set thee safe aboard. *Doct.* Come, Madam, let us be gone: This is no time to stay to tempt his Fury: we'l take a fitter season. *Cel.* Heaven send it.

Exeunt, followed by Lyonel from his house.

"This line is Lyonel's, *ls" Switzer";* Swiss mercenaries, who are often referred to by the old dramatists, were frequentlyemployed by sovereigns as guards; hence Toby's alarm. See *TheLaw against Lovers,* V, 1, and, for similar references in Elizabethan drama, Forsythe, *The Relations of Shirley's Plays to the Elizabethan Drama,* p. 302. *Enter* Toby *in Womans Apparrel. Tob.* They are gone sure! I can see no body. Oh how I shake! would I were safe under hatches once, that I might be out of my fears Farewel the Court now; Instead of being a Duke, or at least a Baron, I am going the Devil knows where, to *Bantam?*

And farewell, my dear Lord too I shall never see thy Glorious

Face agen Oh, oh *Enter* Lyonel.

Lyon. How now! Who's here, another Undertaker?83 Another Plot upon me? *Tob.* 'Tis I, Sir,'tis I.

Lyon. I. Why who are you?

Tob. Your Friend, Sir whom you are sending to *Bantam? Lyon. Bantam;* and my Friend: here's a sly trick now, they

know I have no Woman Friend but one, who is too closely kept from me, to be here: pray, come hither and let me look on you. *Tob.* Why Sir, 'Tis I. *Lyon.* You should not be a Woman by your Stature! *Tob.* I am none, Sir I am none. *Lyon.* I know it then, keep off:

Strange Men and Times! How am I still preserv'd?

Here they have sent a Yeoman of the Guard,

Disguis'd in Womans Cloaths, to work upon me,

To make love to me, to trap my Words, And to ensnare my Life, keep off, I say. *Tob.* Oh do not leave me, I beseech you, Sir, for I shall ne'r be able to find the way to *Bantam,* without you. *Lyon.* Ha— are not these my Cloaths? *Tob.* Yes, Sir, you lent 'em me to make escape in. 56 *Lyon.* Here's an impudent Rogue: First rob me, and then talks of making his escape—— Come, strip, sirra I'le make an example of you. *Tob.* Oh Lord, strip, Sir? *Lyon.* Ay, ay, all off Rogue, and presently, or I will pound thee into Mortar. (*Strips* Toby. *Tob.* Oh dear *Toby.* What will become of thee? *Lyon.* The Drawers too, Rogue; the Drawers. *Tob.* The Drawers Why Sir, I shall be naked, for I've but a half Shirt on.

""Another Undertaker"; another person intending to undertake the arrest of Lyonel.

Lyon. Sirra If you have but a half Breech on, I'le see what you have! *Tob.* Oh the Devil's in this Fellow. I must run for't, he'l flea84 me else. (*Starts from him, and runs out. Lyon.* Hah, fled—— Why then, like conquering *Tamberlain,* I carry off the spoils *Victoria, Victoria.* SCENE III.

An antechamber in Cocklebrain's House.

Enter Grub, Phillida, *and* Roger, *in tawdry (Call* Longo, *new Cloaths.* Bewford.8S *Grub.* Wife be sure you hold up your Head now; and primm it as you did one Sunday at Church in the Country, when you put the Parson out of his Sermon, with staring at you and let the

Courtiers see you understand yourself! do you hear?

Phill. I warrant you, *Hubby,* let me alone for primming out. *Rog.* This is a woundy86 gallant place, an't like your Worship. There's ne're a Chamber che ha gone through, but is as big as our *Town-Hall* at *Plowden,* an't shall please you. *Grub.* Peace! peace, the Door opens, and two Gentlemen are coming this way: Wife, look to your *(Enter* Longovil *and* self. *Roger,* be mannerly. I'le speak to 'em. Bewford. Save you, Gentlemen! belong you, I beseech you, to his Mighty Grace the Duke? *Longo.* We do, Sir, and are your Servants. S'life! What pretty Country Creature's that? *Bewf.* If there be any thing that we can serve you in, to his6587 Grace, Sir, be please'd to Command us. *Grub.* Gentlemen both I thank you, *Roger,* your Hat, under your Arm Sirra! when did you hear such words before. Wife hush Answer nothing: let me alone with 'em. Pray

Gentlemen, is it fit so mean a person as myself should desire the

""Flea"; flay.

""Call Longo, Bewford"; evidently the prompter's memorandum on the MS. through the-. _ i,,,TMQDO hQg w,nt *intr,* thp tpvt Thpse characters enter several lines further on. A Tamira, Chariot"; and in *Bussy,* IV, 3 (p. *M).* "Call Mount burry, Monsieur, *ana* ymse; *una* (d 39) we find "Call Chariot *Letter."* In *The Richmond Hetress.* IV, 1 (p. 41), occurs Call Quick witt." Evidently D'Urfey gave little time and trouble to the correction of proofs. See *Part I,* p. 91, note 173, of this study.

""Woundy"; exceedingly, extremely.

«"65"-at this point the pagination leaps nine, so that p. 56 is followed by p. 65, and continues with this incorrect numbering to the end of the play. There is no break in the text. A similar error in pagination occurs in *The Richmond Heiress,* IV. (see this study, *Part I,* p. 91, note 173).

favour, as that you would be pleas'd to help me to the Speech of the Great Duke your Master *Longo.* Sir, we shall be proud to serve you. Pox on him, what a Tone the Rogue has? *Bewf.* Be pleas'd, Sir, to discuss your Business, and your Name, And we will presently

inform him of ye. *Phill.* O *Jemini, Roger!* I never heard such fine talk in my life; why our Minister at home is nothing to 'em. *Rog.* Ah, thick Gentlemen would make a fool of him, quick alack, they are too vine to have much Religion in 'em. *Phill.* Well, well, *Roger,* I hope to be too fine myself too shortly. *Grub.* Leave your chattering, and be hang'd, and don't discover your Country breeding, ye silly Baggage *(aside.*

Gentlemen both my Name is *Grub. Longo. Grub.* I cry you mercy, Sir, you are his Graces Kinsman, if I mistake not.

Grub. Troth Gentlemen, I think there may be a quart or two of his Graces Blood in me if I may be so bold. *Bewf.* Sir, no doubt, but you have a gallon of it in you, and we must all be yours, his Graces Kinsman.

And we so much forgetful, 'twas a rudeness, we must beg pardon for, and beg the favour to welcome you to Town. *(kiss* Grub.

Grub. Your servant, Sir, they slabber confoundedly, th6. *Rog.* Oh Lord, what do thick Men mean by Bussing my Master? *Bewf.* Next Madam, to you we humbly address our selves! A Cherubim, by this Light. *(aside. (They kiss* Phillida. *Grub.* This kissing is the worst Fashion in the Court; would they would leave it off Come hither, Wife *(whisper. Longo.* 'Tis He! this is the Unkle; I find it now; dost hear66 *Bewf.* He must be preferr'd too? *Bewf.* And so he shall, if all the Art we have can make him noble. I'l dubb him with a Cuckoldom if his Wife will but join issue. *Longo.* Soft and fair, Sir, we must draw lots about that business. *Grub.* Throw away that Pole, and be hang'd! What a devil dost think we are come to play a Hit at Quarter-staff! we stand upon our preferment; therefore take care of your Behaviour, Booby. *Longo.* Wilt please you, Sir, to walk a turn or two here in th' Antichamber, whilst to his Grace we make your coming known. *Grub.* I thank you, Sir, 1 shall attend his pleasure. Now, *Roger,* what think'st thou: Is not this rare ha! *(Ex.* Long, *and* Bewf. *Rog.* The Gentlevolkes are huge loving, an't like

your Worship, Godsdiggers, I was afraid they would have Buss'd me too. *Phill.* Oh dear *Hubby*—lets never go into the Country agen; Foh methinks *Plowden* is such a stinking dunghil to this sweet place! *Grub.* Odsooks the door opens now, now hold up your Head, and Primm, be sure.

SCENE IV.

An Inner Room in Cocklebrain's House.

SCENE, *Discovers* Cockle-brain *seated with* Aurelia, Maria, Longovile, Clerimont, Bewford, Servants. *They* place Grub *and his Wife in a Chair.*

Phill. Oh *Jemmini!* Is that he, *Hubbi? Grub.* Ay Godsooks is it: make a low Curtsy, quickly ye Jade. Most Gracious Duke—my—poor *(Bowing.* Spowse, and my Self, do kiss your mighty Foot, and next to that, the great Hand of your Dutchess; ever wishing your Fame and Honor springing as your years.

Cockle. Unkle, you are welcome! *Clerm.* Pithy and short. *Longo.* And stately too, I'le assure you. *Bewf.* Look, look the old Gib-Cat is got down on's Knees. *Grub.* Oh! High and Mighty Duke. Your Graces Vassal, far Unworthy the nearness of your Blood Wife! down on your67 Mari-bones. *(She kneels. Clerm.* I swear, the prettiest Wench that e're I saw.

Bewf. Oh! is she so, Sir? Come, come, here are the Lots! *Longo.* Now, Fortune *(They Draw. Bewf.* Mine by Heav'n! and you are to assist me! *Clerm.* We are so! a pox take you. *Cockl.* Unkle, you must rise: so must your Lady the charge of whom I give to my own dearest here. *Aur.* Oh! how yon Coxcombs shrugg, and Ogle this new Face already Tis well my fine Fops, I shall have an hour for you too! *(Aside. Grub.* Now *Phill.* now *Phill.* now or never little *Phill. Cock.* Well Unkle are you convinc'd yet of your old Error? *Grub.* Oh Gracious Duke I was a very Rascal a Country Rogue! I do beseech your Grace, out of your mighty Bounty, to liftup your Noble Foot and give me half a'score good kicks!

Kick me! my good Lord, I beseech you, do it.

Cockle. No Unkle, not so neither: I remember you a little Familiar with me indeed! *Grub.* Ah! Zoons I was bewitcht, my Lord, merely bewitcht, I call'd your Mighty Grace Son of a Whore: for which, besides my begging pardon on my knees, I was the Son of a Whore myself for my pains, my Lord. *Cockl.* Well, well, 'Tis all forgotten, I know it was your zeal, and therefore blot it from my memory; have you, according to my Orders, resolved your self for Court, and utterly renounced the slavish Country, with all its Dirt and Care. *Grub.* I have, so please you. *Cockl.* Have you dismist too your Garlick Eating-houshold, your Hobnail'd Lubbers, with their crook'd horn'd Noses, and dry chopt Hands. *Grub.* All, all, my Lord: All but my Man *Roger* there! *Cockl.* You mean that Booby yonder foh how he looks! put him in Livery, or let me see him no more; away with him: I hate a fellow in Grey, like a Badger! *Rog* Oh Lord! What am I to be hang'd now? *(They hurry him out. Cockl.* And have you sold your hangings of *Nebuchadnezzar,*68 and the Prodigal, with the antient History of *Baalam's Ass,* piec'd out with the *Wisdom of Solomon,* and the *Two Harlots.8 Grub.* All taken down, my Lord, and ready for a Chapman.89 *Cockl.* 'Tis well, for now your Mind must quite be alter'd as your Condition shall be: One word more in private I must impart to you your Ear a little. *Grub.* In troth, my Lord, I am unworthy. *Cockl.* No more words: Come hither when I bid you: *(whisper. Aur.* As I was telling you first, your Husband must learn *Basset,* and must be no more your Master. *Phill.* No forsooth: I warrant you I'le order him. *Aurel.* Change that forsooth for Madam, when you talk. 90 *Phill.* Yes Madam. Oh *Jemini!* this is rare, I vow.

"In the earlier drama there are many allusions to hangings with scenes from the Scriptures painted upon them. For some of those to representations of the Prodigal, see Forsythe, *The Rela Hons of Shirley's Plays to the Elizabethan*

Drama, p. 341.

'"Chapman"; a hawker or peddler— here, a ragman.

""Cffange that forsooth for Madam"; see *Henry IV. Part I,* III, 1,1. 251 ff. *Aur.* Nor must you Eat with him, nor keep him company! If you would make him great; you see this Duke here, *Phill.* Yes forsooth, Madam I mean *Aur.* He was an Ass when he came first to Town, an arrant Ass: Nay, I may truly call him just such another Coxcomb as your Husband Till I push'd on his Fortune. No more words now:

Come to me to Morrow I'le put you in a way *Phill.* Yes, Madam, well, Iv'ads91 I'm sure I shall be a Dutchess too, methinks I'm too proud for a Country Gentlewoman already *(aside. Cockl.* Think on my words, and so farewel for this time: Gentlemen, conduct my Unkle to his Lodging. *Exit* Cockl. *and* Aur. *Grub.* I am your Graces Slave, your Vassal! My Lord Ah Gadsooks I am made for ever. *Clerm.* Oh! for a private place to ease my Lungs I am ready to burst! such a pair of Jades were never ridden sure. *aside to* Bewf. *Bewf.* Take him aside Good Ned, whilst I break in upon the body of his strength, his Wife. *Clerm.* Advance then, and be hang'd, why don't you board her? *Longo.* Ply her to windward, ye Rogue! she rides fairly. *Clerm.* Faith, Sir, you have taken the most compendious way,69 to raise your self; if his Grace stand your friend, you must be a great man! *(to* Grub. *Grub.* Why, troth he puts me in great hopes, Gentlemen! *Longo.* What do you think now, Sir, as first step to your preferment, if you could get to be Dew-beater.92 *Grub.* A Dew-beater; what a Devil's that? *Longo.* Why, your Office is to walk before the King a Mornings, and beat the Dew off: I see you have a good large flat Foot for the business. *Grub.* Yes, yes, my Foot would do well enough, you need no doubt: But what's that Gentleman doing with my Wife yonder! *Clerm.* Oh, what's matter what they are doing, or Sir, if you love your ease suppose you should put in for Gentleman of the Charcole.

'"Iv'ads"; in faith. This expression is

to be found very often in D'Urfey's plays, being particularly affected by persons of more or less rusticityor lack of refinement. See *Love for Money,* V. 1, (pp. 45, 46), 3 (p. 55); *The Marriage Hater Match'd,* III, 2 (p. 30); *Cinthia and Endymion,* III, 1 (p. 14); *The Bath,* II, 2 (p. 16), III, I (p. 18, etc.), IV, 2 (p. 33, etc.); *The Old Mode and the Nev1,* II, 3 (p. 35, etc.). Ill, 2 (p. 43, etc.), IV, 2 (p. 58), V. 1 (p. 61).

""Dew-beater"; regularly a pioneer; here used as a term of contempt. Sir Lawrence Limber in *The Marriage Hater Match'd,* V, 3 (p. 52), is called a dew-beater. Sir Lawrence often speaks of himself, it should be noted, as "an old Courtier." *Grub.* Gentleman of the Charcoal.

Longo. Ay ay To see good Fires made in all the Rooms about the Court, and disperse News to all the Courtiers that come to warm 'em. This place brings in a mint of Mony, if you can persuade 'em but to pay well. *Grub.* Ods-heart! I persuade a Courtier to pay well! that were a work indeed—— But pray Gentlemen, by your leave, A little I don't like to see my Wife hugg'd thus! *Clerm.* .Not love to see your Wife hugg'd? have a care what you say, Sir, I would not have the Gentleman hear you for a thousand pound. *Grub.* What a Devil care I what he hears: pray, let me go Gentlemen! *Clerm.* Not for the World, Sir, s'life do you know what you do? *Grub.* Why, what's the matter? *Long.* The matter! He's one of the greatest Favourites at Court, And one that can do any thing with the King; I swear you are a lost Man if you stir. *Clerm.* If you have a mind to Rise, Sir, never mind 'em. *Grub.* Zoons, Sir, They are kissing! *Clerm.* Let 'em kiss, and much good do their hearts, if your Wife can but niggle93 him right, Sir you are a made Man, I can tell you that. *Grub.* But Sir, to kiss her, and in that rumpant manner! 70 *Longo.* Ay, ay, any manner, Sir: they must kiss, and double kiss, and kiss agen: or you may kiss the Post for your preferment. *Grub.* I know not but look, look: he's at it again! *Longo.* Agen and agen too: and the more happy Man you: would he would kiss me as much, or my Sister, or any of our Family. *Phil.* Good b'we, *Hubby,* good b'we, *Hubby Ex.* Bewf. & Phill. *Grub.* Zooks, Sir, but this is unconscionable, do but see, he has taken her into a private room. *Clerm.* Has he! why then your business will be done, Sir? *Grub.* Her business will be done, you mean, Sir. *Clerm.* You'l be the happiest Man by this days work, except the Duke your Cosin, of any in the Court; For my part I envy you, and will Marry certainly, and not let every Man out-run me thus; 'tis ""Niggle"; to cheat or trick *(N.E.D.)*— here probably to obtain by bargaining. time to be my own Friend now: I live in Court here, and teach the readiest way to prefer others, and be a slave myself. *Grub.* Nay, good Sir be not mov'd I thank you heartily for your Instructions, but *Clerm.* But, no more but but come away. *Grub.* I should be glad, methinks, to have my Wife with me. *Longo.* Yet agen, your Wife! will you ruine all? Go, go! begone! and take no notice where you left her: let her return at leisure. If She stay a Month 'twill be the better I tell you once more, that Gentleman can make ye *Grub.* A Cuckold it may be. *Long.* What he pleases, Sir! *Grub.* Well I will go! and dost hear *Phill,* don't forget *Hubby* a Duke, *Phill.* a Duke! be sure to remember *Hubby!* Gentlemen, your most Humble Servant I'le leave 'em together for a time; since 'tis the Court-way Gentlemen—your most Humble. *(Exit* Grub. *Longo.* Ha ha ha. To me the gulling of this Fool is Venery.

Clerm. *Thus Country-Fops, that of Court-Grandeur heard,*
Post up to Town; and thus they are preferr'd. Exeunt.
The End of the Fourth Act. 71 ACT V. SCENE I.
A Room in Cocklebrain's House.
Enter Cocklebrain. Tis somwhat strange; that I have had no Letters, nor no Accompt of my Affairs in the Country, since I sent *Toby* down among my Tenants: I did expect the very Bells of *Dunstable,* giving the sound to the near neighb'ring Steeples, would lead the joyful Tidings, like a Train of Gunpowder, from thence to *London;* But I hear

nothing: Fame has lost her Trumpet, and the loud voice of my young flourishing Glory is as mute as a hoarse Clerk setting a Psalm. *(A noise within. Enter* Servant.
Ser. Sirrah, keep back here's no place, for such Vermin: This is no Barn for Beggars. *Enter* Toby *in a Blanket? forcing the Servant forward. Tob.* Beggars! here's a Rogue now! to rank a Great Dukes 9,"Enter Toby in a Blanket;" see *A Virtuous Wife,* IV, 1; *Every Man in his Humor,* V, 4; *The Devil is an Ass,* V, 1 (related); *The Nightwalker.* V, 1; *The Constant Maid,* IV, 1.
Secretary, because he appears a little in disguise, amongst Beggars.
Serv. Ye sawcy Rascal, you will come on! nay then, I'le try my strength *(Goes to force him. Cock.* How now, what's the matter there? *Tob.* My Lord, my Lord, the Duke! do you know me: Tis I my
Lord 'tis I.
Cock. What! *Toby! Tob.* Ay! ay! Faith old *Toby* of the World, that has such things to discover! such a Catastrophe to tell you:
Hark you, Squire of the Curry-comb *(To the Servant.*
    You may go to your Stable, and make Love to your Coach-Mares! What a pox, because a Gentleman returns home a little in Disabillum!96 you cannot know him agen, you Rascal, can you; go rub rub; avant Oat-stealer. Turn out.
Serv. What, Mr. *Toby?* this is wonderful. *Cock.* Sure thou hast design'd some Farce to entertain me?72 What is the meaning of all this! What Catastrophe hast thou to tell me? *Tob.* Oh! a damn'd Catastrophe: as I was saying, a Devilish Plot Will your Grace be pleas'd to call for a clean Shirt: Gad!
it will make you sweat through your Cloaths in a moment. *Cock.* What are all my Tenants run away in the Country? What a Devil can this be? *Tob.* Nay, that the Fates can tell, not I: I have been no nearer the Country than I am now: Ah, your Grace little thinks, how dang'rous 'tis to be an Officer in Trust! why, since I saw you, I have been! *Cock* In a Bawdy-house; I believe: Ay, ay; it must be so: And there stript: this sly Rogue

has been in a Bawdy-house. *Tob.* A Bawdy-house at *Bantam,* my Lord Too hot a Country for Whoring, I thank you. *Cock. Bantam! Tob.* E'en so: I was within a stones throw of it, for above two hours, I am sure: Does not your Grace begin to sweat yet? *Cock.* To hear you lye, Rascal. *Tob.* Nay if you doubt this What will you do when you hear that I have been hang'd, drawn, and quarter'd for High Treason, since I saw ye. *Cock.* Away Coxcomb Thou art drunk sure.
'"Dishabillum"; *dtshabilli. Tob.* Drunk, it is with the Cup of Sorrow then, nothing but my tears have moisten'd me. Since I saw you last, I am as dry as a Bakers Bavin,96 and fit for nothing but to be thrown in with them to heat an Oven: for since I left your Graces House.
Cockl. My House what House is that, hah? *Tob.* Why, this House, your Graces House here! *Cockl.* This House Why you Son of a Hedg-Hog: has it no name, has my House no name! no Title, Sirra *Duns tableHouse,* ye Ass. Must a Man be always telling you these things? *Tob.* I beg your Graces pardon And as I was saying, my
Lord. just as I had left *Dunstable-House,* there comes up to me a Devil of a Fellow, Friend, says he—.— and stares me in the Face
    You are the Man beset Come instantly with me, and73 be shipt away for *Bantam,* or you'l be instantly apprehended, and hang'd for High Treason. ' *Cock.* A Devil of a Fellow indeed: it must be some mad Man, sure.
Tob. Mad-man! no he was a Politician I am sure, for he was mightily given to Musick, and Sung one profound Ballad, that to my knowledge, was made of on old Proclamation. *Cockl.* This must be some Spy from some foreign Enemy; coud'st not thou have train'd him to *Dunstable-House,* that I might have examin'd him. *Tob.* No more than I could carry *Dunstable-House* upon my
Back to *Dunginess97* Oh he had a plaguy pate of his own, and was, I am sure, a great Courtier, for he was in 20 several Minds in the space of a minute. First, he was for cloathing me in a dis-

guise to escape, within a minute after Wheigh with a *Powder le pimp,TM* He fleas me, as a Cook does an Eel; after which I ran away, and not being able to get into *Dunstable-House by* mere chance my shoul Joy, ish borrow'd thish *Irish* Cloak here of an honest *Clanbriggian"* of my acquaintance; and lay all night perdue in thy little worshipful place, call'd *Dunstable Privy-house* indeed.

Cock. There must be more in this, than at present I see, which

"Bakers Bavin"; bundles of brushwood used by bakers for producing a quick hot fire. See *The Two Queens of Brentford.* IV, 1 (p. 54); *Pills to Purge Melancholy,* 111,18. Dunginess"; a promontory on the Kentish coast opposite Boulogne.

nPowder4c-Pimp"; perhaps gibberish uttered by a juggler or conjurer, or an allusion possibly to such an entertainer. *"Pimper-le-pim0"* is mentioned as a " *High German* Juggler" in *Bury-Fair,* II. 2; and as an attraction at Bartholomew Fair in *Pills to Purge Melancholy,* II, 297. The date of *Bury-Fair* (1689) is so close to that of *A Fool's Preferment,* as to make it probable both Shadwell and D'Urfey allude to the same person or whatever it may be. ""Clanbriggian"; the editor has no clue as to the meaning of this word. at better leisure I will sift into: In the mean time, get ye in and uncase; You are a fine Secretary indeed. *Tob.* The Truth on't is at present, I look more like a Sow-gelder than a Secretary; the Learned observe, Men of Merits often taste the greatest misfortunes Well Sir, I'll go and uncase, as your Grace Commands little does he think that the Man in the

Rugg here has his Fortune told to be as great as himself shortly.

But Mum, *Toby* There's some comfort still, however. *(Aside. (Exit* Toby.

Cockl. Now I have consider'd o'nt, Since *Toby's* intended Journy is so crost, My State and Grandeur will much more be shewn

Appearing in my person in the Country; My Tenants needs must be much better satisfy'd, with seeing me, than hearing of my Greatness:

It shall be so; I'le down to 'em this Morning. 74 Who waits there?

Enter Maria. *Mar.* My Lord! *Cock.* Go tell your Ladies Grace; that She must rise, I have instant business with her. *Mar.* Would your Grace have her rise to do your Business? *Cock.* Yes that I would, Minx! here's a young Pert Quean100 already. *Mar.* My Lord, 'tis cold, and she may catch an Ague! *Cockl.* Why then I'le Trot her till she catch a Feaver to 't, How now, dare you dispute? *Mar.* I am gone, my Lord on my life he's mad agen. *(Exit* Mar. *Cockl.* There is no way to grow popular like Courtesie, A gracious Nod, a wink, or such a trifle will gain the Peoples Love and Approbation, more than a thousand Messages, or How-de'es. *Enter* Aurelia.

Oh! are you come, Wife?

Aur. What, is the House on Fire, or has your Grace A fit of the Vertigo that I am rowz'd thus? *Cockl.* Oh neither! neither! *Aur.* What then, in the name of Wonder? *Cockl.* Why, I am resolv'd, on good Consideration

""Quean;" jade, hussy, harlot.

This day to see the Country, and 'tis proper

That we set forward early.

Aur. The Country for Heavens sake, my Lord, What is't you mean? Have you forgot the King's Request?

Cockl. Prithee! I'le but shew myself: I'le only air my Titlesthere amongst 'em; and so return, which, by your leave, good Wife, will be for the King's Honor. *Aur.* Well, you may leave me here, you know I am breeding. *Cockl.* Oh! Air will do you good. *Aur.* Besides, I dare not forfeit my Allegiance. Your Grace75J may do your pleasure. *Cockl.* Your Allegiance!

That is, your Duty to obey your Husband:

Go, go, I say: and bid your Maids pack up your things.

Aur. Nay, pray my Lord be rul'd: you know the Coronet that now adorns your Head, descended by my management. *Cockl.* Yes, yes: and the other Ornaments that branch there, were all of your contriving: what then? go and dispatch, I say. *Aur.* The King will surely hear

on't; and Heaven knows what the result may be? *Cockl.* Well, well; I'le venture that: pray spare your Politicks, and do as you're Commanded. *Aur.* Pray hear me, Sir! *Cockl.* Yet agen, Impertinence! where got you this presumption? Am I the Duke, or you? *Aur.* Well, Sir, th6 you are Duke, 'twas I that Dubb'd you. *Cockl.* Dubb'd me; nay, the truth is, you did Dubb me I believe; but no more of that now: obey my Will, or *(Call* Maria. 101 *Aur.* Will no Reason take place? *Cockl. A* Womans Reason! that's good i'faith prithee away, go, go, good crooked Rib, and do not provoke me. I know what thou would'st say; the King will take it ill: Alas! thou dost not know, my main design is for his Glory, by this Expedition, which I'le recount to him at my return, and what I've done for his security, by diving into the Humors of the People: But these are Riddles to thee, Child Begone, I say, and within an hour let your duty wait i'th' Hall, with your Riding-dress on, do you hear? *Aur.* Sir, you'l be undone! *Cockl. A* Dunce, shall I not be? *Aur.* Yes by my Faith. *'"See ante,* p. 70, note 85. *Cockl.* Oh! nay, if you grow Malepert! I must take other measures: Hear me once more; if all things are not ready in that time, I'le have thee carry'd like an *Essex* Calf, ty'd Neck and Heels, stuffed in a pair of Panniers:102 and I my self will drive thee on before me You shall know who I am? *(Ex.* Cockl. *Aur.* I do too well, for a dull stubborn blockhead, and know76 not how to mend thee; s'life, if this Humor hold, I am half undone, for I am engag'd this Afternoon to meet the Widow Tireman, pretty Mrs. *Primm,* and three or four of the *Beaux Esprits,* at my Lady *Wagbums* this Afternoon, with design to play Crimp,103 and break the Bank, the *Pareli,* and *Sept-et-leva,* being made by those we have the design upon, for we have agreed what Cards shall win, and Mr. *Shufflewell* is so adroit in managing, that 'tis impossible we should miscarry, and now in the instant, is this Beast for hurrying me into the Country, but I'le have another trick to divert that Instantly He shall stay in spite of him. *Maria! Enter* Maria. *Mar.* Madam! *A ur.* Quick, quick; thou dost not dream, what

Eggs are hatching; this Beast is for the Country agen; and all my dear Delights and Joys o' th' Town destroy'd in th' Instant. *Mar.* The Devil shall have him first.

I'le bring him one shall swear there's a great Flood,

And there's no likelyhood to pass these ten days.

Or that a party of 2000 Robbers have sworn to pillage for a week that Road; you know he loves his Money.

t Aur. No, no, his Grace must be degraded; there's no way like it: *Clermont* and his Friends are all prepar'd for this last Plot; Therefore be swift as Thought, to find em out, we have but an hour of Trial. *Mar.* Swift as the Mischief, Madam, never doubt me. *(Exeunt. Msince Marriage is a yoke two Fools must wear,*

The ablest Fool the heaviest part should bear.

Thus let it then my Husbands Neck weigh down,

I'le try to make it easy for my own. (Ex. Aur.

10i"Panniers"; a pair of baskets slung over the back of a beast of burden, one on either side. Sbadwell mentions "an *Essex* Calf" in *The Scowrers,* IV, 1. 1""To play *Crimp";* to bet on one side and by foul means to allow the other to win, the bettor sharing in the winnings. See *Pills to Purge Melancholy,* II, S3, 54 *(N. E. D.). '"The* four lines following are spoken by Aurelia. The preceding *"Exeunt"* should be *"Exit,"* as only Maria leaves the stage at this time. *Enter* Grub, Phillida, *and* Roger. 77 *Grub.* What! lye out two whole nights, and no preferment come, yet;

How hast thou spent thy time?

Phill. Oh! very well indeed *Hubby!* for the Gentleman told me you should be a great huge Man; very suddenly. And for joy of it you can't Imagine *Hubby,* how I briskt up to him! *Grub.* Briskt up to him, a pox, th6 you briskt up to him so mightily! nothing comes on't, that I see. *Phill.* Oh! all in good time, *Hubby,* for he told me the King had knowledge of you already: And how you were resolv'd to be a Courtier. *Grub.* Hush, here comes Mr. Secretary!

Enter Toby in haste, with a Servant.

Tob. Run you, and see the Sumpter105 got ready; and let my Lords Cloaths be brush'd, and laid in order; tht Trunks and Boxes see nail'd fast, and corded, d'e hear? *(To a Serv. Grub.* What's the matter, good Mr. Secretary? *Tob.* Oownz! Sir, my Lord's going Post into the Country o'th' sudden I am almost out of my wits here. *Grub.* The Country: *Tob.* Ay ay, Sir, nay prithee Mr. Justice, you see I've a world of

Business upon my hands and d'ye hear, put the Womens things in the New Panniers, the Linen, and the Box of Cordial Waters: Bid Nurse take care of My Ladies Eagle Stone too:1061 hear she's breeding. « *Serv.* I will, Sir! *(Ex. Serv. Tob.* The rest I'le do myself: Oh! how I sweat *(Exit. Grub. Roger:* this suits well for me, for when he's gone, my Wife alone can do my business better: Odzooks, I strangely long to be preferr'd, that I may twit my Neighbors in the Country, and contradict our Parson, that's a main matter. *Rog.* Zo'tis! an't shall please you: and that will make him contradict all the Parish. *Phill.* And never fear me *Hubby* I'le push it forward. ""Sumpter"; a pack-horse.

i«"Eagle Stone"; "a hollow nodule or pebble of argillaceous oxide of iron, having a loose nucleus, which derives its name from being fabled to be found in the eagle's nest, and to which medicinal and magical qualities were assigned" *(N. E. D,,* art. "Aetites"). The eagle was supposed not to be able to hatch its eggs when there was no eaglestone in its nest. The stone seems to have been thought efficacious in cases of pregnancy. *Grub.* Do, do, *Phill.* do: Why, well said, *Phill:* methinks I am o'rejoyd at the conceit on't: But see, here comes his Grace. *Enter* Cocklebrain *and* Aurelia. 78 *Cockl.* Why, this is well now: though you can talk, I see you understand Obedience! *Aur.* Very well, Sir.

Alas! 'tis all poor Women were design'd for.

Cock. Very Good. Very Good! Oh Unkle. I did not see you. Why, I must court your Patience, some few days to live without me: We Great Men Dive sometimes: 'Tis a State trick that you are yet

unskill'd in: But have patience, we shall appear agen to your satisfaction. *Grub.* Health to your Graces both. *Cockl.* Set forward then: Sure *Toby* has by this time pack't up the things, and seen the Coach got ready? *Enter* Clermont *and* Longovile. *Clerm.* Stand, thou proud Man, once more I bid thee stand. *Cockl.* Thieves, Thieves! where are my People all? who waits there? *Clerm.* Let'em stir if they dare. And thus I am to say: Thou haughty Man, Thou art a Monster; for thou art ungrateful, and like a fellow of a Rebel nature; hast flung from his embraces; therefore he bids thee stand, thou Insolent Man, whilst thus with whisking of my Sword about I take thy Honor off;

This first sad Whisk takes off thy Dukedom,

Thou art but a Marquess.

Cockl. What mean you, Sir.

Cler. This second Whisk divides thy Marquisate; Thou art yet a Baron. *Grub.* Oh Lord! Oh Lord! *Cock.* Prithee be quiet, I'le have no more of thy Whisks: what a Devil dost think I am an Ass. *Cler.* You must have patience. *Grub.* Oh! that ever I was born. *Rog.* Oh! Oh! Oh! *(Howls out. Clerm.* Two Whisks are past: and two are yet behind: yet all must come: then not to linger time, with these two dismal79 Whisks I quite degrade thee now; Goodman *Cocklebrain:* for that sums all your Titles: Thank the King for punishing no further. *Aur.* Oh! Undone, undone! I thought what his stubborness would bring him too? *(Feigns to weep. Grub.* I am amaz'd. *Cockl.* This cannot be in earnest, sure. *Cler.* You'll find it so, Sir.

Grub. I am confounded, shot to the Brain, I know not where I am! *Cler.* Nay for your part, my Gracious Lord, the Fates have a far different doom *(To* Grub. *Grub.* How's that, Sir? *Clerm.* Glory attends you, what Honors flow upon you. This Patent will inform your Grace *(Gives a Patent. Grub.* My Grace! s'heart if this should be a Dream now

And yet I feel the Parchment in my hand: Good Sir, explain your meaning you have transform'd me.

Rog. Hum, hum! *Clerm.* Thus then in

short, my Lord: The King who still so much preserves the memory of that unhappy Man to let the Honors remain in's Blood, has in his stead, made you the Duke of *Dunstable;* And as such, he bids you wear this Robe of State. *(Puts a Antick Robe and Turbant on his Head. Grub.* Godzooks! Why *Phill.* Am I awake, Art sure I am awake *Phill? Rog.* Ods-diggers! I must be a Secretary too I see, there's no remedy! *Phill.* Ay, ay, *Hubby!* and did I not make the most of a thing, think you, to get to be a Dutchess so soon? *Grub.* Zooks, Thou hast made more of a thing, Girl, than ever

Dutchess did107—— I am all Air: Gad I can fly, methinks

A Duke already; why this is prodigious.

Clerm. Your Grace, I hope, will remember your poor Servant. *Grub.* O Lord, dear Sir you shall have any thing. *Longo.* I must beg leave to make my Court to her Grace, that way I am sure preferment lies. *Grub.* Oh! by all means, Sir. Do'st hear, dear Wife: wemust80 be civil to these Gentlemen. *Phill.* Well, well the Gentlemen know I han't been behind hand with 'em. *Aur.* False Villain: 'Tis as I suspected now, th6 late, I see his

"'Perhaps a reference to the Duchesses of Cleveland and Portsmouth, notorious in the preceding reign.

Treachery, and will revenge myself, tho I undo 'em all. *(Aside. (Exit* Aurel. *Grub. John Cocklebrain,* th6 the Kings Kings Royal Judgment has at last found where he should place his Honors: it is not fit thou shouldst be quite forgot *John,* come to my House, and

Eat somtimes, dost hear! I'le get thee into the Guards, or somewhere, because thou art my Kinsman.

Cockl. The Guards ods-heart I'de as leive 'twere the Gallows. Oh! Oh I shall run mad. *Grub.* Mad! you Jackanapes! han't I told you of your fantastical Humors a thousand times: Thou fit to be a Duke! Alas poor Fellow! *Enter* Toby. *Toby.* My Lord! The Coachman stays: and all your Equipage, rank'd by my Care and Order, wait your Motion; I have had the Devil and all to do

amongst 'em yonder; but they are ready at last. *Cockl.* Oh! Oh! Oh! *(Looking discontentedly on* Grub. *(xvho looks scornfully on him. Tob.* Hey-day! What Farce is now to be acted? What is Mr. Justice going a Morice-dancing?108 *Grub.* Make him cease his babling, Friends: and then let the poor Rascal know who I am. *Tob.* Who you are, why you are a Cuckold, and a Justice of Peace I know who you are well enough. *Rog.* How's that? Have you a mind to be hang'd, Sirra? *Tob.* Why, what's the matter, are you all mad? *Clerm.* Sirra! he's newly made a Duke, down o' your knees, or *Tob.* A Duke! yes; and so am I as much? What d'e think I do not know old Justice *Grub? Grub.* Nay if the Fellow grows saucy, let him be whipt, d'e81 hear, and then toss'd in a Blanket: 'Tis fit I begin a little severely. T'will make me the more terrible. *Clerm.* Away, away with him: you are a saucy Knave indeed. *Long.) Tob.* Why, my Lord the Duke help, help. *Cock.* Oh! Oh!

Jos' 'Morice-dancing"; properly, the morice-dance was performed by persons in fancy costume representing Robin Hood and his companions. However, the name was often applied to any mumming performance of which fantastic dancing was an important part.

Tob. What a Devil is the meaning of this, S'heart, you will, not let me be toss'd in a Blanket, will you? *Enter* Bewford, *and a Boy with a Robe and Cap. # Bewf.* Not for the World, unbind him, Gentlemen, upon your perils. *Clerm.* Why how now, *Bewford,* whence comes this Insolence, that you dare contradict his Graces Order. *Bewf.* His Grace! You'l find he has no such Title! *Grub.* Oonz—— but I have, Sir, and will maintain it. Dare you fight, Sir? ha. *(Offers to draw. Bewf.* Oh! Rage will do no good, Sir. To explain all, Gentlemen, thus it is, All you have acted hitherto, is by mistake, a Courtier, that his Lady made her friend, made shift to steal his name into a Patent, but now 'tis raz'd out; and instead of him the King has chosen this Noble Gentleman109; and this is now the Duke. *(Claps* Toby *on the Back, and Looks big. Tob.* Hem.

Hem. *Bewf.* His Majesty has heard of your wise Conduct, and with this Robe invests you. *(Puts on an Antick Robe. Tob.* Air, air, good friends! by my troth this news warms mightily. *Bewf.* And if for this good news, I may deserve to kiss your Graces Hand, my Lord. *Tob.* My Hand: Faith Friend I'le have it wash'd first

Dost hear, old Fellow: prithee fetch me a Bason of Water. *(To* Grub.

Grub. Fetch a Halter, Come, draw, draw: I'le fight for't: I'le not be chows'd110 out of a Dukedom so, not I: since you have these tricks, I'le take the right way to secure my Title, and settle it by the Sword. Draw, Draw, I say. *Rog.* Ay, ay Draw, as my Lord Duke says: Zowns! I'le82 thrash some of you! *Omnes.* Oh! there must be no Bloodshed. *Tob.* The old Fool has often these Fits: some of you that wou'd deserve my Favour, take the old Dotard away, and toss him in a Blanket a little: there's nothing like it to cure his Fits.

""This Noble Gentleman"; an introduction of the name of the comedy from which D'Urfey borrowed.

""Chows'd"; cheated. See *The Fond Husband,* IV (p. 32); *Lote for Money,* V, 3 (p. 52); *The Modern Prophets,* III, 1 (p. 28), V, 1 (p. 60); *The Old Mode and the New,* III, 1 (p. 41), *Pills to Purge Melancholy,* I, 5, 165, II, 53, 243. As a noun, meaning a deceit or one deceived, "chouse" or "chowse" occurs in *The Old Mode and the New,* IV, 2 (p. 55, etc.); in *The Athenian Jilt,* p. 176; and in *Hudibras, Part IV,* Canto I, p. 54.

Grub. How, Sirra! a Blanket: s'bud can I bear all this? *Cockl.* Have but patience, Unkle, and I'le speak to his Grace, to take you as under Butler, or somthing: I know you come to Town for preferment. *Grub.* Fool. Cuckold. *Cock.* Ay, look at home, Unkle! my Aunt has stirr'd her stumps, you know! *Grub.* A pox stirr her: *Phill.* Nay, pray *Hubby* be not so angry: you know I did all for the best. *Grub.* Hold your Tongue, Whore but do you hear Gentlemen! Have I dreamt all this while of Dignity, and am I really no Duke? *Tob.* No, no: Friend! a Duke! I prithee call thy Wits agen. *Grub.* What tho I formerly rail'd against the Court, when I was not preferr'd I have more Honesty and Conscience now. for if I am a Duke *Tob.* Yet agen a Duke! Why, thou art no more a Duke, than thou art a Dromedary; but as poor a Clumsie, Clod-pated old Justice as ever was drunk with *March* Beer at a Sheriffs Feast. *Enter Usher of the Black Rod, Aurelia, and a Guard. Grub.* Ownz! How I could swinge these Rogues, if I had my

Will What, my Wife lye with a topping Courtier two whole nights, and I no Duke! 'tis impossible?

Tob. I tell thee once more, thou art no Duke: I think the old Fellow is be-witch'd. *Ush.* No, no: nor you neither, good Yeoman of the Poppets111 I shall Un-Duke you. *Tob.* What's the matter now? *Longo.* Ha! The Usher of the Black Rod! Would I were safe at my Lodging. *Clem.* And I. 83 *Bewf.* f And I. *Ush.* Guard—.—-Seize those Duke-makers, disarm 'em: nay, if you strug-gle, we shall hamper you: Here's a War-rant to bring you before the King and Council. You are for disposing the King's Honors, and granting Dignities; let's see now how you'l dispose your Estates to pay 20000 l. a piece Fine be-sides 7 years imprisonment.

""'Yeoman of the Poppets"; an atten-dant in a puppet-show.

Aur. This I have help'd ye to, my lewd Court-swaggerers! You are for every Face you see, you are for flying at all Games: You! but I'le teach you to af-front your Friends. *Bewf.* Ah! malitious Devil, we shall get off some time or other. *Longo.* And then the World shall know you. *Clerm.* What a fine Jilt you are. *Aur.* Do, rail, rail; poor fools. *Tob.* I begin to shake: what is the meaning of all this! *Ush.* As for your part, my Lord of *Lubberland.112 Tob.* Lubber-land; prithee Friend thou mistak'st my Title: I am Duke of *Dunstable. Ush.* A Duke, a Dog-whipper you are! such a knot of Fools, that the King, instead of punishing, pities you But I shall make bold to turn you out of your Dignitie, my Lord Duke. *Tob.* Hey-day, the World's turning upon wheels,113 sure, What-adevil d'e take me for. *Ush.* For a Fool I take you, I confess, *Tob.* A Fool,

you might as well have taken me for an Alderman, But prithee don't trouble thy Head, man. *Ush.* Sirra, leave your fooling, and have a care of the Porters Lodge; there are Whips with Bells: and so I take my leave of all your Graces: you *Cocklebrain,* you shall escape for your Wives sake, because she is my Kinswoman But for the rest, away with' em. *(Exeunt Guards, with the Gentle-men. Grub.* Your Humble Servant, my Lord Duke. *Cockl.* Ah! the Devil take this confounded Town: wou'd it were burnt agen Will your Grace have a little more Air. *(To* Toby. *Tob.* Thank your Grace; I am very cool o' th' sudden: Be-sides, I am reflecting upon the strange mutability of human Affairs—84

But however the world goes, Brethren let's make some shew of our Dignity, before we part: What think you of Dancing the Hey?114 *Cockl.* Agreed. *Grub.* To be thus fool'd, and in my old age well.

'""Lubberland"; an imaginary land of plenty without labor. See *Bartholomew Fair, III,* 2; *The Gamester, 111,* 4.

""The World's turning upon wheels"; the same as the proverb. "The World runs on wheels"; that is, time causes many sudden changes in its rapid pas-sage. See *Sir Patient Fancy,* II, 2.

'""Dancing the Hey"; the hey, or hay, was a country dance with a winding or serpentine motion; a sort of reel.

Here they Dance the Hey, and whilst they are Dancing; Enter Lyonel *in a mad posture, with* Celia, Doctor, Singers and Dancers. *Lyon.* Hah! here they are! and in the height of Revelling *Pluto Minos, Radamanthus,* the King of the Infernals, and the Judges. *Grub.* Oh the Devil: here's the Mad-man agen Come, come away. Come, Dutchess, Troop.

I'le not stay an hour in this cursed Town.

D'e hear, Sir, that 500 l. must be paid back again.

Cockl. Not a penny, Unkle, your Grace shall take it out in Offices *Grub.* Plague take you all: Zowns! You Whore, Come away. *Phill.* Oh! dear *Hubby.* Shall I never see a Play, nor lye abroad agen? *(Weeps. Grub.* What! You have a mind

to be a Dutchest agen: have you? Come away, and be hang'd, I'le Dutchess you. *Exit* Grub, *and Wife. Rog.* A Plague of this cursed Town, if this be all one gets! *Lyon.* Great *Pluto* know that I am *Or-pheus,* and through the dismal shades of direful night, am come to seek my long lov'd *Proserpine,* I'le charm thee God, with Musick, my soft Aires shall lull the Pow'rs of thy barb'rous Empire, and set my Love at liberty. '*(Sings. Doct.* Pray, sooth his Humor. Till we can lay hold on him, then never doubt his Cure. *Aur.* Madam, I thought he had been seiz'd before. *Celia.* He was, but by main strength he broke away; his Madness still increasing: These are People plac'd by the Doctors Order, to humor the dis-temper. *(They seize him, and carry him out. Doct.* So, now Madam, never give belief to Art, if you to Morrow, find him not recover'd. *Celia.* Heaven grant he may, he shall not want my wishes. *Tob.* Nay, Gentlemen: a little of your help will be convenient. Brothers by Ti-tle, what think you to divert our selves, if we should Act a Farce, and that we call it *The three Dukes of* Dunstable. *Cockl.* Not I; I have been in a Farce late-ly enough: but I am resolv'd to go into the Country Eat nothing but Turnips 7 years, to recover the Estate I have spent in waiting for preferment, and never so much as look towards old *Sodom* here agen. *Aur.* And thus, Sir, on my knees, I promise ye henceforth to be Conform-ing to your pleasure with all the Care; and Diligence, and Duty of a most Pen-itent, Obedient Wife, to atone for my past Follies: and no more to heed the senseless Fopperies of the Town, nor the more senseless Fops remaining in it. *Cockl.* Well I am forc'd to believe thee: We that are

Married, have but small variety of rem-edy.

Tob. I have been fool'd my share too. But for my part, since it is so I'le off with my Mantle *de la Guerr* here, and into the

Barn, and Thresh agen: there's no Revolution of State there, if the Harvest be but good; And if ever I ex-pect to be exalted agen, may I be hang'd upon a Beam there, in one of our own Cart-ropes.

And may no Fool for better Fortune look;

That just from Digging, thinks to be a Duke:

Ex. Omnes. EPILOGUE:

Spoken by Mr. Montfort.

Of which (because it was particularly carp'd at) I desire every one that has more Wit than Malice, to Judge.

Fond of his Art; the Poet has to day
Mistook, and made me mad the silliest way;
Pride, Wealth, or Wine, may Frenzy often move:
But that's a Strang Brute that runs mad for Love,
few now, Thank Heaven, such lewd examples find,
Tis forfeiting the Charter of our Kind;
Shall Men have all, and Women no remorse?
Then let the Cart hereafter drag the Horse.
Let each Eve *wrest the Scripture false, and swear;*
She was not made for Man, but Man for Her;
No, this had been a most unpardon'd Crime;
Did not the Lady here repent in time.
Besides, the Notion's false, for sure no Man
Can Love so well, and faith no Woman can:
'Tis true, degrees of Madness all may fit, l
Some with too much, some with too little Wit,
I have been Mad, or I should ne'r have Writ.)
'Tis a Disease that Reigns in every station, i
First, amongst Gamesters I have found occasion,
Somtimes to make a pretty Observation;)
At Hazard I have seen a Witty Lad
Eat up a Candle, if his luck were bad;115
What think ye, Sirs, Was not that Fellow mad? J
A Lady too, in Tears has left off Play
(Alas poor Punt,) *for losing* Sonica,)
But above all, Wine does worst Frenzy raise,

""*Eat up a Candle, if his luck were bad;*" cf. Wilding coming from an unsuccessful session at play "gnawing a box (dice-box)". The Gamester, III, 4.

For then Fop comes, and Whistles at our Plays,
Calls some one Whore, that to some Spark belongs,
Who calls him out, and whips him through his Lungs.
Thus, on our Nation, a vile blot remains "

None but the Dutch *and* English *take such pains*
To fill the Paunch, and empty all the Brains.
The last, worst sort too, does your Heads invade,
That's Whoring, that Vice makes ye all stark mad:
Not Poverty has power to stop its force,
Poor Rogues, that ne'r could pay their Alehouse Scores
.Shall brag they've at Command a Leash of Whores.
To th' Camp those Militant Doxies116 yearly stray)
Where each mad flitt'ring Fool that's given that way
To purchase Pox, melts down a whole Months-Pay.)
Many more Theams of Madness I could name,
And quote, indeed too many to our shame.
But, Sirs, to prove that you have all your Wits,
Let every Critick, that in Judgment sits,
Our Poet to an easie Penance doom,
Wink at small faults, for all of you have some.

""Doxies"; a doxy was a beggar's wench; a low prostitute.

NEW SONGS SUNG IN

The Fool's Preferment OR, THE

Three DUKES of Dunstable, *In the* SAVOY:

Printed by *E. Jones*, for *Jos. Knight* and *Fran. Saunders*, at the *Blue Anchor* in the Lower-Walk of the *New Exchange* in the *Strand*, 1688.

INTRODUCTORY NOTE.

Both the words and music of the songs in *A Fool's Preferment* are printed with

a separate titlepage immediately following the text of the play itself. They take up fifteen pages of the old edition. Among them are five songs which do not appear in the play as printed. These are reprinted here. Only one of the additional songs, as they may be called, can be accurately and exactly located as to the place of its insertion in the comedy. This is the last of those reprinted, *A Song Sung in the Fifth Act, by Mr. Monfort*. It should follow Lyonel's last speech in the play.117

According to the titlepage of the play the "Notes" to the songs were composed by Henry Purcell the famous composer. 118 The music of six of the lyrics is signed by Purcell.

"'See p. 89 of reprint.

mHenry Purcell (1658P-1695) was England's greatest native composer. He was author of airs for many songs, sacred and profane, operas, and of some purely instrumental music. He furnished the music for various of D'Urfey's lyrics, includinc those in *The Virtudus Wife, Sir Barnaby Whigg, A Fool's Preferment, The Marriage Hater Match'd, The Richmond Heiress, Don Quixote, Parts I, II, III.* v *A Song sung in the Third Act, by Mr.* Monfort. 6

Fled is my Love, for ever, for ever, ever gone!

Oh, mighty Loss! Eternal Sorrow, Eternal Sorrow!

Yet prethee *Strephon*, why should'st mourn?

For if thy *Celia* wont return,

To her thou shalt go, to her thou shalt go to morrow;

To her thou shalt go, to her thou shalt go to morrow.

A Song sung in the Third Act. 8

Tis Death alone, 'tis Death alone, can give me Ease,

For all the mighty Pain, for all the mighty Pain, I've felt;

In his cold Tomb my Heart shall ever freeze,

Since hers could never, never melt;

Since hers could never, never melt, could never melt.

A Song sung in the Fourth Act. 10

I'le sail upon the Dog-Star, I'le sail upon the Dog-Star,

And then persue the Morning, and then persue, and then persue the Morning: I'le chase the Moon 'till it be Noon, I'le chase the Moon 'till it be Noon, But I'le make, I'le make her leave her Horning. I'le climb the frosty Mountain, I'le climb the frosty Mountain, And there I'le coyn the Weather; I'le tear the Rainbow from the Sky, I'le tear the Rainbow from the Sky, And tye, and tye both ends together.

The Stars pluck from their Orbs too, the Stars pluck from their Orbs too, And crowd them in my Budget; And whether I'm a roaring Boy, A roaring Boy, Let all, let all the Nation judge it. *A Scotch Song sung in the Fourth Act.* *A Dialogue by* Jockey *and* Jenny. *Jockey.* Jenny, gin you can love, And have resolv'd you will try me; Silly scruples remove, And do no longer deny me: By thy bonny Black Eye, I swear nean other can move me; Then if still you deny, You never, never did love me. *Jenny.* Jockey, how can you mistake, That know full well when you woo me; My poor Heart does so ake, It throbs as it would come through me! How can you be my Friend, That thus are bent to my Ruine? All the Love you pretend, Is only for my Undoing. II. *Jockey.* Who can tell by what Art This Chiming Nothing, called *Honour,* Charms my *Jenny's* soft Heart, When Love and *Jockey* has won her? *Jenny.* 'Tis a Toy in the Head, And Muckle Woe there's about it; Yet I'd rather be dead, Than live in Scandal without it. But if you'l love me, and Wed; And guard my Honour from Harms too *Jockey,* I'le take to my Bed, And fold him close in my Arms too. *Jockey.* Talk not of Wedding, dear Sweet, For I must have chains that are softer; I'm of a Northernly Breed, And never shall love thee well after. CHORUS: Bass *and* Treble. *Then since ill Fortune intends, Our Amity shall be no dearer;*

Still let us kiss and be friends, And sigh we shall never come nearer. A Song sung in the Fifth Act, by Mr. Monfort. If thou wilt give me back my Love, For ever I'le Adore thee; And for the favour, mighty *Jove,* With Souls from Heaven shall store thee: To the Queen of *Shades,* she shall advance, And all shall wait upon her; Kings shall Adore her Countenance, And I'le be her Page of Honour.

ERRATA ET ADDENDA.

Part I, p. 15, l. 29. Read "III, 1", for "III, I".
p. 33, l. 27. Read "Sir" for "sir",
p. 53, l. 7. Read "summarized" for "sumarized".
p. 63, l. 31. Insert comma after "Shirley",
p. 70, l. 37. Read "Bragg's" for "Brag's",
p. 89, l. 22. Read "Primwell" for "Pimpwell".
p. 92, l. 31. Read "II, 1", for *"II, I".*
p. 93, l. 20. Insert comma after *"Epiccene".*
p. 97, note 183, l. 2. Read "their" for "there",
p. 98, l. 6. Read "77" for "II",
p. 99, ll. 24, 29. Read "Mannel" for "Manuel",
p. 114, l. 13. Read "gods" for "Gods",
p. 118, l. 34. Read "having" for "have",
p. 120, note 238, l. 4. Insert comma after "Doyle",
p. 126, l. 34. Read "Bertran" for "Bertram",
p. 127, l. 7. Read "Bertran" for "Bertram",
p. 130, l. 29. Read "had" for "have",
p. 140, l. 26. Read "D'Urfey's" for "his",
p. 144, note 280, l. 1. Read "March 13" for "March 10",
Part II, Introduction, p. 2, l. 3. Add as footnote 8a, "'In 1874'; Hasberg, *James Sheridan Knowles' Leben,* pp. 25-26."
p. 24, l. 1. Add as footnote 33a, "'Method in Madness'; cf. *Hamlet,* II, 2, ll. 207-08. The passage is D'Urfey's addition."

You Like Your Laundry?
TELL US AND YOU
ARE CERTAIN TO
HAVE YOUR WAY
The Cleveland Laundry Co.
2820-2840 Carnegie Ave., S. E.

Prospect 2SOO

The Crooks Whigam Co. PURE MILK
AND CREAM-WHOLESALE AND RETAIL
Our goods are as good as the Best. Pure
pasteurized Milk and Cream heated to
140 held 30 minutes. Let there be a trial
and CREST 140 the servjce wj &0 the
rest.
BELL, EDDY 266 110.112.114
L0CKW00D AVE. EAST CLEVELAND
CITY ICE DELIVERY CO. PURE CRYSTAL
ICE
DISTILL AT A
THE PURE TABLE WATER
Principal Offices:
1935 Euclid Ave., Cadillac Building
Prospect 3100 Cleveland, O. Erie 217

Save Your Money and Lend it to
Your Country

We will be glad to receive your sub-
scription to the new United States War
Loan and transmit it to the proper au-
thorities without charge to you or to the
Government.
THE TILLOTSON & WOLCOTT COMPANY
INVESTMENT BANKERS

Cleveland Detroit Cincinnati

Guardian Building Penobscot Building Mercantile Library Building GEO.
H. FOOTE

Does business with the College dor-
mitories in milk, cream and other dairy
products.

He welcomes an examination of his
dairies and of all that he does in' supplying first-rate milk and cream.

Garfield 6093 W. 2288 East 97th St.

Questman & (get?
jflotoer
5923 Cuclfo &be., Clebelanb, 0. Our
Corsages have a distinct "Air" $ $

Why College Bred Men
Prefer Davis Clothes
UAnc. 111 They ate subject to no "tai-
lors' delays" gHOPS to them are stan-
dardized-and carry witll them t & of re-
fine_ like reference books-or they are
ment and good sense which is of such
unworthy of attention. distmct vajue in
clothes

Davis "Good Clothes" have long
been *AM* for the coum club and for
known to Western Reserve undergradu-
ormal dre85 tne appropriate ares and
alumni as being high in quality appare)
is at hand_ and unequivocally correct—
"correct" in the sense of good taste, as
well as Coats $20 to $50.
smartness. Suits $20 to $65.

The W B Davis Co 301-305 Euclid
Avenue "Proverbial Quality"

"A Good Book and
Stationery Store"
BOOKS

Whenever you need a book on any
subject remember that at BURROWS you
receive prompt and courteous attention.

In our Rare and Old Book Depart-
ment, on the second floor, there are
many out-of-the-ordinary interesting
books with autographs and other dis-
tinctive features—well worth inspec-
tion.
THE BURROWS BROS. COMPANY JOHN J.
WOOD, President
Guardian Building Cleveland, O.

N. O. STONE & CO., 312-18 EUCLID
AVENUE, CLEVELAND.

Bell Phone, Main 3560 Cuy. Phone,
Central 3560

The Schafer-Suhr Coal Co.
WHOLESALE AND RETAIL COAL and
COKE *Sole Agents for the Celebrated
Dixie Gem Soft Coal*
General Office
Room 410 Cuyahoga Building Cleve-
land, Ohio

Wm. Ramsdell, Son & Co.
GROCERS 10551 Euclid Avenue
E. B. BROWN PRESCRIPTION AND MAN-
UFACTURING OPTICIAN 314-315
SCHOFIELD BUILDING
CLEVELAND
JOHN C. MILLARD MEATS SHERIFF
STREET MARKET

No stronger testimony of the worth
of our goods, or of our service, is need-
ed than that we furnish every day of
every month of the college year a large
amount of provisions to one of the great
departments of Western Reserve
University.
ROBERT A. KUMMER TAILOR

Lightning Source UK Ltd.
Milton Keynes UK
UKOW05f0923021115

261902UK00007B/72/P